Multicul†
Education of Children
and Adolescents

Multicultural Education of Children and Adolescents explores the foundations of diversity through cultural portraits of young people from a variety of backgrounds, and provides practical strategies for shaping and implementing a multicultural curriculum.

Content and features new to the seventh edition include the following:

- Every chapter opens with a real-life story that introduces the subject matter by showing the ideas in action.
- Points to Ponder boxes urge readers to reflect more deeply on information they have just read.
- Case Studies with accompanying Questions for Discussion in all chapters enable nuanced consideration of the crucial differences between culturally specific learning styles.
- Chapter 13 now includes a section on teaching and understanding LGBTQIA+ youth, with updated teacher resources to support learning.
- The book addresses newly emerging issues in multicultural education throughout, including discussions around Critical Race Theory, culturally relevant pedagogy (CRP), the impact of the #BlackLivesMatter movement, the impact of xenophobia and hate towards Asian communities during the COVID-19 pandemic, as well as migration and refugee issues.

Through a series of applied chapters, teacher candidates will learn to use the most effective instructional practices with diverse learners, and to work successfully with families, school personnel, and administrators to implement a multicultural program.

G. Lea Lee is Professor and Director of the Tidewater Writing Project in the Department of Teaching and Learning at Old Dominion University, USA.

Multicultural Education of Children and Adolescents

Seventh Edition

G. Lea Lee

Routledge
Taylor & Francis Group

NEW YORK AND LONDON

Designed cover image: melitas / Getty Images

Seventh edition published 2025
by Routledge
605 Third Avenue, New York, NY 10158

and by Routledge
4 Park Square, Milton Park, Abingdon, Oxon, OX14 4RN

Routledge is an imprint of the Taylor & Francis Group, an informa business

© 2025 Taylor & Francis

First edition published by Allyn and Bacon 1992
Sixth edition published by Routledge 2017

Library of Congress Cataloging-in-Publication Data
Names: Lee, G. Lea, author.
Title: Multicultural education of children and adolescents / G. Lea Lee.
Description: Seventh edition. | New York, NY : Routledge, 2025. |
Includes bibliographical references and index.
Identifiers: LCCN 2024049090 (print) | LCCN 2024049091 (ebook) |
ISBN 9781032552118 (hardback) | ISBN 9781032552101 (paperback) |
ISBN 9781003429531 (ebook)
Subjects: LCSH: Multicultural education—United States. | Indians of North
America--Education. | African American children—Education. | Asian
American children—Education. | Hispanic American children—Education.
Classification: LCC LC1099.3 .B37 2025 (print) | LCC LC1099.3 (ebook) |
DDC 370.117—dc23/eng/20241031
LC record available at https://lccn.loc.gov/2024049090
LC ebook record available at https://lccn.loc.gov/2024049091

ISBN: 9781032552118 (hbk)
ISBN: 9781032552101 (pbk)
ISBN: 9781003429531 (ebk)

DOI: 10.4324/9781003429531

Typeset in Palatino
by codeMantra

To my dearest husband, Frank, who remains my devoted companion and best friend, and to my cherished family and friends from Korea and the United States of America

Contents

About the Author

G. Lea Lee is Professor and Director of the Tidewater Writing Project in the Department of Teaching and Learning, Darden College of Education & Professional Studies at Old Dominion University. She immigrated from the Republic of Korea to the United States four decades ago, and earned a Master's degree from Chicago State University and a Ph.D. degree in Curriculum and Instruction from the University of Minnesota. Her areas of expertise include culture and family literacy, culturally sustaining instruction, bilingual education, and educational issues of underrepresented students globally. She has authored and edited numerous articles and book chapters, illustrating her expertise and contributions to the field. Her research articles have been published in *Childhood Education, Multicultural Education, Kappa Delta Pi Record, Journal of Research in Childhood Education, Teacher Learning and Professional Development, Journal of Early Childhood Teacher Education, International Journal of Early Childhood Education, Teacher Learning and Professional Development,* and *Journal of Information Technology Education Research.* In addition, she has delivered countless national and international presentations at conferences encompassing AERA, WERA, CIES, ILA, ACEI, NAEYC, NAECTE, OMEP, LRA, NCTE, WCES, Global Literacy Summit, World Congress on Reading, Pan African Reading for All, and more. Dr. Lee has not only led as president of various community organizations but has also been instrumental in enriching cultural heritage, championing the social justice of marginalized groups, and demonstrating her strong leadership and commitment to diversity, equity, and inclusion.

Preface

The United States' Increasing Cultural Diversity

Multicultural Education of Children and Adolescents is based on the premise that people from culturally different backgrounds enrich the United States and that a better understanding of people and their differences leads to higher levels of acceptance and respect for all people. This seventh edition is being published at a time when all demographic projections indicate that the number of people of differing cultures in the United States will increase.

The Hispanic American population outnumbers the African American population, and people of European ancestry will soon be in the minority. At this time, the Asian American population is increasing dramatically. Without a doubt, the high birthrates among some cultural groups, increasing numbers of Spanish-speaking people, and the recent influx of immigrants from Southeast Asia will increase the cultural diversity of the United States, and challenge its citizens to accept and respect all people whatever their cultural background, ethnicity, race, sexual orientation, socioeconomic status, gender, or religion.

At one time during the nation's history, the "melting-pot" theory proposed to erase differences and to acculturate, or "melt," cultural differences. In essence, the person of a different cultural background was supposed to forsake cherished and traditional cultural values and adopt "American values," probably those of the middle-class European American population. This concept viewed differences as wrong or inferior and promoted wholesale abandonment of cultural heritage.

Realistically, the melting pot is not an accurate model—people have difficulty giving up cultural characteristics or they live in enclaves in which assimilation with the mainstream society is unnecessary. Likewise, some people have chosen to maintain their culture as well as to adopt American values. Regardless of the reasons, the melting pot has not accounted for all the citizenry as some proposed; the nation is a heterogeneous mixture of different peoples.

Serious questions continue to plague educators and other concerned people: Why is there an increase in racism? More than 50 years after the landmark *Brown* decision, why are schools still segregated? Why do elementary and secondary schools address primarily the needs of some learners and allow others to fall behind? Why do people fear diversity? Why are victims often blamed for their problems? These questions defy easy answers and evince many people's belief that differences are negative manifestations in need of eradication.

Rather than provoke anger or cause fear, differences in values, customs, and traditions should be celebrated and considered a means of enriching the United States. The author does not claim that the people who perceive differences as enriching will eliminate racism and acts of violence. Celebrating differences, though, is a first step, especially if efforts focus on today's children and adolescents, who will lead the nation during the twenty-first century. Considering differences to be positive and enriching, however, is only a beginning. Significant change will require more comprehensive and deliberate efforts.

Elementary and secondary schools can play a major role in teaching acceptance and respect for all forms of diversity. The schools, in fact, are logical places to begin instilling feelings of acceptance for all people. Schools, however, must do more than pay lip-service; effective curriculum reflects diversity, and appropriate learning materials represent all people in positive and meaningful roles. The author believes wholeheartedly that multicultural education should be a total-school approach, rather than simply a unit or Multicultural Education Week approach. Although teaching about multiculturalism is an admirable concept, schools should also model acceptance and respect for cultural diversity. Schools that teach about cultural differences and celebrate diversity but whose actions indicate racism or a lack of respect fail in their multicultural efforts.

Reasons for Writing This Book

The seventh edition of *Multicultural Education of Children and Adolescents* provides pre-service and in-service educators with a knowledge of the six prevalent cultural groups and shows the components of responsive multicultural education programs. The text staunchly maintains that multicultural education programs require a total-school effort—that is, administrators, teachers, librarians/media specialists, special-education teachers, counselors, and communications disorders specialists have vital roles in the multicultural education program. Similarly, the author believes that multicultural efforts should be comprehensive. The curriculum, instructional strategies, materials, environment, and school practices should reflect multiculturalism and should show a genuine respect for all forms of diversity.

Selection of Cultural Groups

After careful consideration of and reflection on the increasing cultural diversity of the United States, the author decided to focus on six broad groups of people (listed alphabetically): African American, American Indian, Arab American, Asian American, European American, and Hispanic American. These groups are, and in all likelihood will continue to be, the most populous groups in elementary and secondary schools. Choosing only these groups does not negate the importance of other cultures. The author hopes and expects that learning about diversity in these cultures will motivate readers to explore the values, customs, and traditions of other cultures.

A Word of Caution

In today's global society, cultural diversity has become a hallmark of societal richness. Unfortunately, there also exists a tendency to oversimplify and assume cultural homogenization. This assumption can have profound consequences on social harmony, understanding, and the appreciation of diverse perspectives. Any discussion focusing on the characteristics of children and adolescents and their cultural backgrounds risks stereotyping and an overdependence on generalizations. The many differences resulting from cultural, intracultural, socioeconomic, geographic, generational, gender, sexual orientation, and individuality factors among people contribute to their diversity and to the difficulty of describing individuals of various cultures. Although the author based this text on current and objective information, it remains crucial for educators to understand individual children and adolescents within a culture through conscientious study and first-hand contact.

Especially when reading throughout Part II of this book, the author wants to alert readers to avoid the assumption of cultural uniformity. Failing to understand individuals and failing to consider crucial differences may result in assuming too much cultural homogeneity—for example, that all Hispanic cultural groups share identical values, problems, and cultural expectations or that all Asian Americans fit the "model minority" label. In addition, although readers will encounter a chapter entitled, "Understanding European American Children and Adolescents," there is no one type of cultural characteristic for European Americans. This chapter explores systems and characteristics and experiences that are common to Europeans, such as socioeconomic status, family, immigration, education, and political instability. However, the findings cannot and should not be generalized to all European Americans. For instance, Albanian Americans who left their country do not necessarily have the same culture and values as British Americans. Readers therefore need to consider the cultural backgrounds and experiences of various sub-groups within the European American population and avoid making broad generalizations that overlook the complexities of unique historical, cultural, and social structures.

The Organization of the Book

Multicultural Education of Children and Adolescents is divided into three parts and 13 chapters. Part I introduces multicultural education as a concept and documents the increasing cultural diversity of the United States. Part II provides a cultural portrait of children and adolescents in the African American, American Indian, Arab American, Asian American, European American, and Hispanic cultures. Part III focuses on topics that educators should consider when planning and implementing programs that teach acceptance and respect for cultural diversity, and also examines issues that will continue to challenge educators in the twenty-first century.

New to the Seventh Edition

Content and features new to the seventh edition include the following:

- ◆ An expanded and updated information on socioeconomic status, demographics, and current conditions of marginalized youth.
- ◆ Increased emphasis on social justice—the need has never been greater. America and its educators in multicultural schools need to accept the ethical, moral, and professional responsibility to promote social justice in all aspects of schools and society.
- ◆ Updated emphasis on white privilege and Critical Race Theory, including its effects on all people.
- ◆ Increased and updated information on diverse gender identities such as equity and rights of transgender and gender non-conforming individuals.
- ◆ New section on culturally relevant and culturally sustaining teaching, with the ultimate goal of promoting and nurturing linguistic, literary, and cultural diversity in schools.
- ◆ New topics on racial literacy for teachers to support a diverse student population.

- Expanded discussion on the challenges teachers face with linguistically diverse students and proposed solutions to support them.
- New topics on supporting multilingual learners and promoting heritage language teaching with bilingual and multilingual education and its benefits to students.
- New discussion on teachers' cultural biases and understanding Critical Race Theory.
- New discussion of racial issues through the globally prevalent new racism, Asian hate, and the Black Lives Matter phenomenon.
- New section on the changing landscape of America today with current demographic data on multiracial children and adolescents.
- New studies incorporated into "implementing research" sections.
- Updated references, additional readings, and current websites for "expanding your horizons."

Acknowledgments

An author's only chance and hope for making a valuable contribution lies in the willingness of others to offer advice and share their expertise.

The author's special thanks to Dr. M. Lee Manning and Dr. Leroy G. Baruth

I would like to extend my deepest thanks and appreciation to Dr. M. Lee Manning and Dr. Leroy G. Baruth, for their expertise, dedication, and contribution to previous editions of this book. I am especially grateful for Dr. Manning and Dr. Baruth's mentorship and encouragement that they have provided endlessly for me to successfully complete this seventh edition. Without their advice, support, and friendship, this important new edition would not be possible.

Dr. M. Lee Manning, Eminent Scholar Emeritus and Professor Emeritus of the Teaching and Learning at Old Dominion University, taught fifth, sixth, and seventh-grade language arts for five years in the public schools of South Carolina. His professional expertise includes middle-school education, multicultural education, and classroom management. He has authored or coauthored 24 books and over 200 journal articles. Selected books include *Multicultural Counseling and Psychotherapy: A Lifespan Approach* (Pearson Education, with Leroy G. Baruth), *Teaching in the Middle School* (Pearson Education, with Dr. Katherine T. Bucher), and *Classroom Management: Models, Applications, and Cases* (Pearson Education, with Dr. Katherine T. Bucher).

Dr. Leroy G. Baruth, Professor Emeritus of the Department of Human Development and Psychological Counseling at Appalachian State University, has authored/edited more than 35 books and numerous articles. Dr. Baruth received his doctorate at the University of Arizona and has a Bachelor of Science degree and Master of Science degree from Minnesota State University–Mankato. Prior teaching and counseling experience includes the University of South Carolina, the Minnesota Department of Manpower Services, and the Byron (Minnesota) Public Schools. He has devoted most of his five decades of professional career to the education of children and adolescents.

Part I

Multicultural Education and Its Response to Our Nation's Increasing Diversity

Part I introduces multicultural education as a concept and documents the increasing cultural diversity of the United States. Chapter 1 examines the multicultural education movement and its role in elementary and secondary schools. Chapter 2 looks at the United States' increasing diversity and the ways that people's differences enrich our schools. These chapters reflect a belief that educators have a professional responsibility to teach respect for diversity as well as to teach all students the concepts of social justice, equality, and democracy.

DOI: 10.4324/9781003429531-1

1

Multicultural Education

Understanding the material and activities in this chapter will help the reader to:

- ◆ Define multicultural education and explain its fundamental purposes, including the integration of cultural perspectives into curriculum and teaching practices.
- ◆ Identify the characteristics of the stages of multicultural education.
- ◆ List several goals, assumptions, concepts, and principles of multicultural education.
- ◆ List several myths and misconceptions about multicultural education.
- ◆ Explain briefly the historical milestones and legal precedents of multicultural education.
- ◆ Explain interdisciplinary approaches and how multiculturalism can be integrated through curricular experiences.
- ◆ Explain the Developmental Model of Intercultural Sensitivity and how it helps teachers to create effective multicultural education.
- ◆ Describe the concept of nonbinary gender identity and intersectionality including various dimensions of a person's identity.

DOI: 10.4324/9781003429531-2

Opening Scenario

Toward a Comprehensive Definition of Multicultural Education

Led by Mr. Taylor, the administrators and staff at Public School (PS) 105 met to plan and implement their multicultural education program. Two goals emerged from their deliberations: (1) they want a comprehensive, all-encompassing program; and (2) they want an interdisciplinary program.

Rather than address only cultural backgrounds, this group agreed that their program should direct attention to a broad range of differences: ethnicity, race, gender, social class, sexual orientation, and individuality. They wanted a program that recognized the vast differences among children and adolescents, such as the many different cultures that make up the Hispanic American population, the vast differences among Asian Americans, and the diversity among African Americans.

Goal 1: A program that addresses as many differences as possible. The decision was made to examine each difference, including its influence on learning and other school-related activities, and then to look at the curriculum, instructional approaches, print and nonprint media, school policies, extracurricular activities, and the cultural composition of the administration, faculty, and staff. Although this constituted a task of some magnitude, the group recognized the advantages of having a multicultural education program that genuinely addresses diversity in its broadest definition.

Goal 2: A program that demonstrates a total commitment to an interdisciplinary effort, one in which multiculturalism permeates the school day. Although the committee recognized the legitimacy of unit approaches and that multicultural education was one subject, it also recognized that an interdisciplinary approach would be most effective for several reasons. Specifically, the interdisciplinary approach could achieve the following:

1. Provide a means of including multicultural education experiences in all subject areas—for example, showing the contributions of all cultural groups in the various disciplines.
2. Ensure broad involvement of all educators responsible for the various discipline areas.
3. Show students from culturally different backgrounds as well as majority-culture learners that the school is committed to serious multicultural education efforts.
4. Provide a wide variety of instructional approaches and learning experiences.

5. Make all school personnel feel that they are a part of the multicultural education program and responsible for its success.

The educators at PS 105 felt good about their multicultural education efforts: Everybody was involved. Teachers and administrators examined curricular and instructional practices and reconsidered school policies, and their efforts crossed disciplinary lines.

Overview

The tremendous cultural, ethnic, religious, and socioeconomic diversity in schools today calls for multicultural education programs that reflect understanding and respect for children's and adolescents' differences. The multicultural education movement has particular relevance for the new century because of the continuing influx of people into the United States and because of the enlightened and more humane perspective that diversity enriches, rather than weakens, a nation. This chapter examines the fundamentals and principles of multicultural education and considers the various aspects that make programs successful.

The population of the United States is ever-growing and increasing in cultural diversity. Overall, nearly 47 million, or approximately 14.1 percent, of the population are foreign-born, representing those born in other parts of the world (Passel & Krogstad, 2023). This reflects an increase from the 40 million (13 percent) foreign-born individuals a decade ago. There is a great deal of attention paid to the growing number of immigrants to the United States. Educators need to understand that their classrooms will contain great diversity. Although it will vary by location, all states are certain to have some degree of increased diversity in their student population (Rodriquez & Lamm, 2016). Most people in the United States believe immigration reform is a primary issue and it is constantly present in national discussions (Gallup, 2023) because immigrant children deserve the best educational experiences possible.

According to the National Center for Education Statistics wing of the U.S. Department of Education (2023e), white student enrollment in public schools has decreased from 52 percent in 2010 to 45 percent in 2021, or 22.4 million students. By contrast, the percentage of Hispanic public school students has increased from 23 percent to 28 percent in that time, or 14.1 million students. African American enrollment has dropped marginally from 16 percent to 15 percent and Asian student enrollment has gradually increased from 4.6 percent to 5.4 percent. Because of immigration trends in the United States, both Hispanic and Asian student population increases are expected to continue.

Not all foreign-born people are in the country illegally, of course. Many have the right to work and live in the United States. As of 2021, the nation's 10.5 million unauthorized immigrants represented 22 percent of the U.S. foreign-born population and 3 percent of the total U.S. population (Passel & Krogstad, 2023). These 2021 figures are moving in the appropriate direction as unauthorized immigrants reported in 2011 were 11.5 million. It is interesting to note that unauthorized immigrants come from many parts of the world. While Mexico is still the most common country of origin and accounted for 39 percent (4.1 million) in 2021, Mexicans are no longer a majority with respect to unauthorized immigrants living in the United States.

Multicultural Education for Culturally Pluralistic Schools

This section describes the author's preferred definition of multicultural education and examines the principles, concepts, goals, and assumptions that form the basis for responsive multicultural education programs. It then looks at several myths and provides an overview of historical events and court decisions that have contributed to multicultural education.

Definition

Various groups and individuals define multicultural education in numerous ways. Some definitions address the perspectives of specific disciplines, such as education, anthropology, sociology, and psychology. Other definitions represent the views of accrediting agencies and professional organizations that are concerned with what teachers need to teach and what students need to learn.

The author thinks that the following definition most effectively meets the goals and purposes of multicultural education for children and adolescents. Multicultural education is both a concept and deliberate process designed to do the following:

◆ Teach learners to recognize, accept, and appreciate differences in culture, ethnicity, social class, sexual orientation, religion, special needs, and gender.
◆ Instill in learners during their crucial developmental years a sense of responsibility and a commitment to work toward the democratic ideals of justice, equality, and democracy.

Over two decades ago, Mulvihill (2000) maintained that multicultural education has always been a contested terrain because of tensions and debates over what the field includes and does not include. Although theories of multicultural education have been developed, they have not always taken into account the debates surrounding the terms *gender* and *sex* or the multiple feminist theories that focus on the more critical aspects of social justice. In fact, some believe multicultural education's influence as a change agent depends on the tensions it creates and on its success in working to resolve conflicts among various groups. In her article, Mulvihill (2000) looked at some of the tensions between gender studies and multicultural education, such as understanding gender as a category of analysis, theoretical constructions of feminism, and building an educational agenda for social justice.

Principles

Appropriate multicultural education requires more than simply providing cultural information about ethnic groups. Several fundamentals necessary to the promotion of effective multicultural education allow learners and teachers of various cultures to maintain integrity and dignity.

First, students need curricular materials appropriate to their cultural backgrounds. These materials should enhance students' self-concept, engage student interest in classroom learning, and provide examples, vocabulary, and models that relate to students' cultural backgrounds. Second, major curricular focuses should include skills in analysis and critical thinking. Third, materials, activities, and experiences should be authentic and multidimensional to help students understand ethnic differences and cultural diversity. They should include both cognitive and affective skills.

POINTS TO PONDER 1.1

Determining Differences to Include in Multicultural Education

Consider the differences and characteristics we included in our definition. Some might disagree with nontraditional views on sexual orientation, ability/disability, and gender. What do you think? Do people whose views are nontraditional have a culture of their own? For example, each person has his or her own cultural background, but wouldn't he or she also have a culture of sexual orientation, a culture associated with a disabling condition, or a culture associated with being either male or female? How inclusive do you think multicultural education should be?

Concepts

It is especially important for teachers to understand three concepts of multicultural education, because it is the educator's concept of the term that determines his or her program's direction and issues.

First, multicultural education is a product in which there is emphasis on the study of ethnicity—for example, the contributions or characteristics of a group of people. This concept, which addresses teaching about different ethnic and cultural groups, may be best described as *ethnic studies.*

Second, multicultural education emphasizes the role of oppression of one group by another and the oppressors' atonement or compensation for past injustices. Dealing primarily with targeted oppressed groups (and possible solutions to their problems), this concept considers multicultural education a concern only of minorities.

The third concept views multicultural education as a teaching process that emphasizes the intrinsic aspects of culture and its influence on teaching and learning processes. Such a concept of multicultural education recognizes the belief that to obtain what one is entitled to requires a fair system and an equal chance to acquire social and academic skills. It incorporates that (1) certain historical facts and events must be taught and (2) an adequate understanding of present conditions, as well as general human behavior, comes about with knowledge of historical facts.

As multicultural education is essential in preparing students for active participation in our diverse global society, educators should ensure that all students, no matter their race, ethnicity, gender, or other identity markers, such as social class, religion, special needs, and sexual orientation, have the same chances for a quality education and life.

Four Levels of Multicultural Education

James Banks (1993) played a key role in the conceptualization of multicultural education and the integration of cultural perspectives into teaching practices. Banks identified four levels of multicultural education to guide educators in making progress in effectively integrating diverse cultural content into their lessons. The four levels emphasize that multicultural education goes beyond just displaying cultural symbols. It involves changing the curriculum and engaging students in actions that contribute to making schools and society more equitable (Banks, 2007; 2013).

As explained below, educators move from using basic methods to more complex ones to integrate diverse perspectives into their teaching. Starting with showing culturally relevant video clips, for example, educators gradually move toward incorporating deeper discussions that not only enhance understanding but also encourage action to promote social justice. Through the four levels of multicultural education, teachers seek to foster understanding and respect for cultural diversity, value the contributions of different cultural groups, recognize and address issues of social justice, and promote equitable opportunities for all, regardless of cultural background.

The Four Levels of Multicultural Education:

1. Contributions: Educators highlight the positive aspects of specific cultural artifacts, celebrations, and characteristics. During Asian Heritage Month, for instance, a teacher can introduce the contributions of K-pop and K-culture and encourage students to appreciate cultural differences.
2. Additive: At this level, the curriculum is not changed, but educators add content and concepts from diverse ethnic, racial, cultural, and religious groups to the curriculum. A teacher can add a unit on Asian civilizations to a history class to extend students' understanding of diverse perspectives.
3. Transformative: Educators are more involved and change the curriculum to reflect diverse perspectives and challenge existing stereotypes. At this level, teachers try to change the way students understand world events. For example, teachers may update social studies content to include important contributions from Asia and Africa. This will be useful for students to understand how other countries have influenced historical events in North America, giving them a broad perspective on history.
4. Social action: At the highest level, multicultural education leads to change outside of school. Teachers can empower students to apply the lessons learned inside the classroom to their lives outside the classroom and encourage them to make decisions on social issues and take age-appropriate actions, such as posting a short video on a social media platform or writing a letter to legislators.

Developmental Model of Intercultural Sensitivity

Milton Bennett's Developmental Model of Intercultural Sensitivity outlines the different stages that individuals typically go through as they become more competent in intercultural interactions. In this instance, "stage" refers to sequential positions along a continuum, not discrete conditions. The first three stages—*denial, defense, and minimization*—are ethnocentric, with *denial* being the most so. The last three stages—*acceptance, adaptation, and integration*—are ethnorelative perspectives that can be gained through experiencing and learning about all cultures (Bennett, 1986; 2017).

Teachers who understand this model can develop multicultural learning experiences that are useful for students to gain greater sensitivity toward different cultures and reduce ethnocentric perspectives. Educators can help students recognize and appreciate cultural differences (acceptance) and then adapt their behavior based on cultural knowledge (adaptation), when they are in early stage of "deny, defend, or minimize cultural differences." At the *integration* stage, students gain a deep appreciation of multiple cultures and incorporate blended cultural practices into their lives. Through multicultural education, students adapt their behaviors in culturally appropriate ways, interact effectively with people from different backgrounds, and live harmoniously in an inclusive society.

Intersectionality Perspectives

Intersectionality is a concept regarding the overlap of a person's identity characteristics. The term and concept is attributed to legal scholar Kimberlé Crenshaw (2013), who shone a spotlight, through the dual lenses of gender and race discrimination, on the treatment of African American women in the U.S. legal system. As the reader progresses through this text, it is important to remain mindful of the many facets of our own identity, such as class, career, gender, sexuality, and religion, and how they can intersect with race and ethnicity to compound either discrimination or privilege. When educators understand the concept of intersectionality, they can better recognize the unique vulnerabilities and challenges each student brings to the classroom (Cho et al., 2013).

Nonbinary Perspectives

More and more, in today's schools, some students are gravitating to a nonbinary gender identity. Which is to say, they do not exclusively identify as either male or female. Their gender identity may be a blend of both or something completely outside of the traditional gender binary. Teachers can support students who identify as nonbinary by using preferred pronouns, respecting gender choices, and using the names that students provide. The reader should be open to considering student gender identities that may be beyond either male or female. Even though the chapters in Part II discuss particular differences that distinguish females from males, the reader should understand that individual variations exist. When students are supported in school they can more easily focus on learning.

POINTS TO PONDER 1.2

Incorporating Social Action into Teaching Practices

Implementing diversity, equity, and inclusion in schools is a dynamic process and creative approaches may continue to emerge in response to changing social, cultural, and educational contexts. Teachers should foster inclusivity and equitable schools by incorporating practical approaches for social action into their teaching practices. Think of four to five creative social action initiatives and strategies that you may want to implement into your teaching practices.

What problems might teachers face when trying to use the transformation and social action methods? How can they solve these problems? Do you think a veteran teacher would be more or less inclined to use a higher level approach than a newly licensed teacher? Observe other teachers and identify any practical social action strategies they are incorporating into their classrooms to promote awareness, empowerment, and a commitment to positive change, while working toward justice and equality in both schools and society at large.

Goals

Effective multicultural education programs have well-defined goals—ones for which educators can plan and implement multicultural experiences. Readers will recall that educators at PS 105 in the Opening Scenario agreed to two major goals: A comprehensive program and interdisciplinary efforts. While goals vary with respective school environments, several goals should provide a foundation for all effective multicultural efforts.

POINTS TO PONDER 1.3

Surveying for Gender Bias

Visit several elementary or secondary schools to determine gender bias. Prepare a survey that examines (but is not limited to) such items as teacher–student interactions, instructional methods, grouping strategies, questioning strategies, and classroom environment. What evidence do you see that teachers recognize and address gender differences? Are boys and girls being treated equally and equitably? How might multicultural education address the bias in treatment of boys and girls (if, in fact, you find evidence of bias)?

First, a basic goal of all multicultural education should be the development of the knowledge, skills, and attitudes necessary to function in a culturally diverse society and to promote social justice for all people. Sometimes called *cross-cultural* or *multicultural skills*, these three attributes (knowledge, attitudes, and skills) lead to an awareness, understanding, and acceptance of all types of diversity. Developing these skills also helps people better understand their own and others' differences.

Second, an important goal is to change the total educational environment so that it promotes a respect for a wide range of differences, enables all cultural groups to experience equal educational opportunities, and promotes social justice for all learners. Providing a multicultural educational experience in the classroom requires more than posting a collection of pictures or posters and ethnic food tasting events—it requires the implementation of diversity, equal opportunity, and inclusion of all students.

A third goal should be educators' enlightenment of the social, political, and economic realities encountered in a culturally diverse society. For example, students benefit when teachers respect differences and similarities; understand intracultural and individual differences; develop a better understanding of the impact of social injustices of students' motivation to learn and willingness to demonstrate positive behavior; and develop a positive attitude toward one's own cultural background.

Again, goals will vary with each respective school situation. For example, while one school might choose to adopt broad goals, another school might choose to have more specific goals, such as these: (1) Teach from multicultural perspectives to promote positive gender, racial, cultural, class, and individual identities as well as promote the recognition and acceptance of membership in many different groups. (2) Encourage social relationships to promote openness to and interest in others' differences and a willingness to include others in school and social activities. (3) Work to provide positive, healthy family–school relationships (which is a major focus of this text) and to promote the inclusion of immediate and extended families and caregivers.

Assumptions

Several assumptions underlie multicultural education and are, in fact, the philosophy on which this book, *Multicultural Education of Children and Adolescents*, is based.

Assumption 1

Cultural diversity is a positive, enriching element in a society because it provides individuals increased opportunities to experience other cultures as well as to understand their own. Rather than perceive it as a weakness to be remediated, educators should view cultural diversity as a strength with the potential for helping individuals better understand their own cultures. Similarly, as people reach higher levels of understanding and acceptance of other cultures, we hope that they will achieve similar heights of understanding and sensitivity in areas such as racism, sexism, and classism.

Assumption 2

Multicultural education is for all students. Some people believe that multicultural education is only for minority children and adolescents based on the odd notion that only minority youngsters need multicultural education. This notion completely fails to recognize that majority cultures can benefit from a better understanding of cultural differences and, eventually, of their own cultural backgrounds.

Assumption 3

Teaching is a cross-cultural encounter. All teachers and students have their own cultural "baggage"—their backgrounds, values, customs, perceptions, and, perhaps, prejudices. These cultural aspects play a significant role in teaching and learning situations and can have a substantial effect on behavior and learning. Socioeconomic status, ethnicity, gender, and language have a powerful and dynamic effect on one's outlook and attitude toward school and on one's actual school achievement.

Assumption 4

As demonstrated in the Opening Scenario about PS 105, multicultural education should permeate the total school curriculum, rather than be doled out in a one-course or a teaching-unit approach. Responsive multicultural education programs cannot accomplish lasting and worthwhile goals through "one-shot" approaches. The school must be genuinely multicultural. Multiculturalism must embrace the curriculum, as defined in the broadest sense (every aspect of the school with which learners come in contact); the composition of the administration, faculty, and staff; expectations that reflect an understanding of different cultural groups, their attitudes toward school success, and their learning styles; and the recognition of all other aspects that may affect both minority- and majority-culture learners. A school that appears to address only majority needs and expectations will cause learners from culturally different backgrounds to feel like intruders or outsiders.

Assumption 5

Generally speaking, members of minority groups, students from low-income families, and students who are culturally different or speak a language other than English have not fared well in U.S. school systems. Any number of reasons may account for such students' lack of achievement: differing achievement orientations; problems resulting from language barriers; differing learning styles; curricula and school policies that are unresponsive to minority student needs; testing and assessment procedures that may be designed for middle-class white students; and a lack of understanding or acceptance of cultural differences. In any event, the high dropout rate among American Indians, African Americans, and Hispanic Americans substantiates the position that learners from culturally different backgrounds often do not succeed in U.S. schools.

Assumption 6

Schools will continue to experience and reflect increasing cultural diversity because of influxes of immigrants and refugees, and the high birthrates of some cultural groups. To say that U.S. society continues to grow more diverse is an understatement. The arrival in the United States of increasing numbers of people from culturally different backgrounds is one example. Increasing recognition of differences in gender, religion, socioeconomic group, sexual orientation, and geography are others. Multicultural education programs have the responsibility to reflect the rich diversity that characterizes U.S. society.

Assumption 7

Elementary and secondary schools have a responsibility to implement appropriate multicultural education programs. These programs must contribute to a better understanding of cultural differences, show the dangers of stereotyping, and reduce racism, sexism, and classism. Families are unquestionably children's first teachers of values, opinions, and attitudes. Ideally, families teach acceptance and respect for all people and their differences. Realistically speaking, however, children may learn that their culture, race, or ethnic backgrounds are "right" but that those of others are "wrong" or "inferior." Because considerable cultural diversity characterizes the U.S. educational system, the transmission of understanding and respect for cultural diversity is most feasible in elementary and secondary schools. Responsive programs must teach genuine respect, and must work toward reducing racism, sexism, and classism. Admittedly, this is an undertaking of considerable magnitude; the teaching and modeling of respect for all people, however, may have the most dramatic impact during children's formative years.

Social Justice

One common definition of social justice focuses on human rights abuses and includes issues of minority groups, especially international justice, women's and children's issues, and war crimes and crimes against humanity. Another definition refers to the concept of a just society, where justice refers to more than just the administration of laws. It is based on the idea of a society that gives individuals and groups fair treatment and a just share of the benefits of society. While definitions vary, we feel that an emphasis on social justice should be a mainstay of any multicultural education programs. Walker (2006) offers several characteristics of social justice:

◆ Educators employ democratic policies, nurture relationships with all the constituencies, and involve the larger community for a more democratic society.

◆ Educators emphasize inclusion and exercise ethical decision making at all levels of the system.

◆ Educators transform the school culture and the policies and practices that are part of the culture in an equitable society.

◆ Educators view social justice as a process and a goal, whereby the process leading to social justice is democratic, participatory, and inclusive, and the goal is full and equal participation of all groups in a society, where resources are distributed equally, members are physically and psychologically safe, and members interact in a self-determining and interdependent manner.

Speaking primarily of principals and counselors, Walker (2006) maintains that despite our ideological dedication to equality and social justice, schools continue to be shaped by an educational system challenged by changing demographics and characterized by blatant inequality and failure. For well over a century, educators in the United States have confronted the issue of organizing the schools to support an increasingly diverse population and provide a socially just environment.

Howard and Solberg (2006) advocate for educators to become agents for social justice when creating, implementing, and supporting school-based interventions designed to promote school success, especially culturally relevant interventions that target youth from diverse and low-income backgrounds. Different advocates of social justice have developed different interpretations of what constitutes receiving fair treatment and a just share.

It can also mean an equitable distribution of advantages and disadvantages within a society or community.

In summary, educators who foster equity and social justice use culturally relevant pedagogy (Ladson-Billings & Tate, 1995: Lau & Shea, 2022) that connects learning to students' lived experiences and cultural backgrounds in order to make learning meaningful and successful for all students.

Myths and Misconceptions

At one time or another, most people have probably heard someone voice dire consequences about the results of multicultural education. Readers can probably make their own list of concerns, and in all likelihood, some educators at PS 105 in the Opening Scenario had doubts about multicultural education. This section will look at several myths and explain why multicultural education does not pose a threat.

Misconception 1: Multicultural Education Is for Others

Some people argue that multicultural education is an entitlement program and a curriculum movement for African Americans, Hispanic Americans, the poor, women, and other marginalized groups (e.g. gays, lesbians, and bisexuals). The author's definition of multicultural education is broad and all-encompassing, so it should be clear that I do not believe multicultural education is for only one group or type of diversity. In fact, the author's perceptions of multicultural education promote all groups and call for both learners and educators to acquire the knowledge, skills, and attitudes necessary to function effectively in a culturally diverse nation. Rather than focus only on specific gender and ethnic movements, multicultural education tries to empower all people to become knowledgeable, caring, and active citizens.

Misconception 2: Multicultural Education Is Opposed to Western Traditions Such as Individualism, Competition, and Goal Setting

In fact, multicultural education grew out of the Civil Rights Movement of the 1960s, which was grounded in such democratic ideals as freedom, social justice, and equality.

Misconception 3: Schools Can Create Unity by Assimilating Students from Diverse Racial and Ethnic Groups into a Majority Culture

Unfortunately, in some cases, even when students from different backgrounds engage in cultural assimilation, they continue to experience exclusion (and racism, prejudice, and injustice) from others of culturally different backgrounds. Furthermore, the assimilation approach traditionally used by U.S. society and schools required a process of self-alienation.

Birkel (2000, p. 22) maintains that *multicultural* has many meanings. To some, it means the acceptance and appreciation of diversity (an opinion emphasized throughout this book); to others, it means, an association with "political correctness" (Birkel, 2000, p. 22). The term is also misunderstood as a program on race relations, as an affirmative action vehicle, and as a civil rights movement. It has also been charged as an attack on Western thought. Birkel sought to clarify the true meaning of multicultural education and to refute some of the fallacious ideas that have limited its success.

Birkel's (2000) major points include that multicultural education is neither political nor an attempt to establish blame or instill guilt. Such actions would negate the purpose of the movement, which is to promote unity rather than division among the American people. Another point is that rather than advocating the eradication of ethnicity and diversity, multicultural education advocates the teaching of factual and complete knowledge about the cultural groups that comprise the United States.

According to Birkel (2000), multicultural education is, first of all, education concerned with the teaching/learning processes and the acceptance and appreciation of diversity. Primarily, multicultural education is a way of teaching and learning. Elements include the skills of intercultural understanding and interaction, the integration of cultural content, and the building of positive attitudes.

Birkel (2000) thoughtfully explains what multicultural education is and what it is not. Some may argue with a few of the misconceptions (e.g. multicultural education promotes unity rather than division among the American people), but Birkel proposes a sound defense of multicultural education as a movement to promote the acceptance and appreciation of diversity.

A Brief Historical Overview

Before the 1980s, scholarly literature had almost no focus on multicultural education in its listings; few pedagogical journals addressed the topic. During the 1980s, however, increasing numbers of articles and books focused on multicultural education. Three forces contributed to the emergence of the multicultural education movement: (1) the Civil Rights Movement came of age; (2) school textbooks came under critical analysis; and (3) assumptions underlying the deficiency orientation were changed to a more positive perspective.

The Civil Rights Movement began as a passive, nonviolent means of changing laws that oppressed specific racial groups. By the late 1960s, the movement had matured into an energetic coalition uniting all Americans of color and directed toward self-determination and power. The movement severely criticized the U.S. school system because of curricula that focused attention only on Western culture. Similarly, few teachers knew about minority groups, their individual strengths and weaknesses, and their learning styles. In fact, schools considered cultural differences primarily weaknesses in need of remediation.

The 1970s saw the development of multicultural education into a more comprehensive approach. With cultural diversity and equal opportunity serving as an impetus, the multicultural education movement encouraged educators to examine and consider the relationships among culture, ethnicity, language, gender, disabling conditions, and social class in developing educational programs. Multicultural education that takes a social reconstructionist tack is a recent and controversial approach that represents an extension of multicultural education toward more definitive social action. This approach incorporates a curricular emphasis on (1) active student involvement in social issues such as sexism, racism, and classism; (2) the development of problem-solving ability and political action skills; and (3) the implementation of curricular adaptations, cooperative learning, and decision-making skills (Hernandez, 1989).

The two world wars, mass immigrations to the United States, the intercultural movements, and racial disturbances all contributed to the emergence and development of multicultural education.

The Influence of Court Decisions

Ruling in favor of equal opportunity and human rights, several court decisions and laws also contributed to the present multicultural education movement. The U.S. Supreme Court, in *Brown* v. *Topeka Board of Education* (1954), ruled unconstitutional the segregation of black and white learners. In 1957, the U.S. Commission on Civil Rights was established to investigate complaints that alleged the denial of civil rights. In 1968, the federal Bilingual Education Act was passed as part of Title VII of the Elementary and Secondary Education Act. The U.S. Commission on Civil Rights issued a report in 1975 called *A Better Chance to Learn: Bilingual-Bicultural Education*, designed for educators as a means of providing equal opportunity for language-minority students. This report provides only a brief listing of a few representative events that recognized cultural diversity and equal rights. These and other events, however, were the forerunners of the movement to recognize and teach respect for people from culturally different backgrounds.

Interdisciplinary Approaches

Multicultural education should be an integral aspect of all curricular areas, rather than just be administered through the social studies course. Likewise, a once-a-year multicultural week or unit focusing on African American history, tacos, and Asian dress and customs will not suffice. Such approaches have not worked and will not work, because diversity awareness does not necessarily result in acceptance of and respect for individuals within a cultural group. The curriculum, learning environments, and mindset of learners, faculty, and staff should become genuinely multicultural in nature and should reflect the cultural diversity of the school. Second, well-meaning multicultural education programs may serve only cosmetic purposes if students and school personnel harbor long-held cultural biases and stereotypes. In essence, to be effective, responsive multicultural education programs must recognize the need both to inform and to change negative attitudes and long-held prejudices.

The Effective Multicultural Educator

Competencies for effective multicultural educators fall into three categories—knowledge, skills, and attitudes—and each is necessary to the existence of the other. The author briefly examines several examples here. Chapter 10 takes a more in-depth look at knowledge, attitudes, and skills, and more specific teaching behaviors.

Knowledge includes an understanding of individual learners' cultures. American Indians, for example, place great importance on the concept of sharing. African Americans value the extended family and have a unique language usage. Asian Americans have a unique concept of generational and family relationships. *Machismo* is an integral part of Hispanic American culture, as is commitment to the Spanish language.

Skills include recognizing and responding appropriately to learners' strengths and weaknesses, and responding to the relationship between learning styles and culture. Skills-based teaching provides school experiences that embrace learners' orientations toward school and academic success. It requires teachers to select standardized tests and evaluation instruments with the least cultural bias, and to use teaching methods that have proven especially appropriate for children and adolescents from culturally different backgrounds.

Attitudes include developing positive outlooks and values, creating culturally appropriate learning environments, and modeling for children respect and concern for all people. See Chapter 10 for a more detailed analysis of effective teaching behaviors in multicultural settings.

POINTS TO PONDER 1.4

Planning Interdisciplinary Approaches

Talk with several teachers who are experienced with interdisciplinary curricular approaches. (In fact, several might be in the class.) Ask these teachers to offer suggestions for integrating multiculturalism throughout the curriculum. For example, specific questions should focus on culturally appropriate topics, materials that offer diverse perspectives and show respect for diversity, instructional methods that cater to diverse learning styles, and culturally appropriate assessment techniques.

Summing Up

Educators planning and implementing multicultural education programs should remember to:

1. Address the wrongs of the past, such as racism, prejudice, and discrimination, but maintain the primary focus on the present understanding, respect, and acceptance of people of differing cultural backgrounds.
2. Consider multicultural education as an emerging concept that will continue to evolve as necessary to meet the needs of a society that is becoming increasingly diverse culturally.
3. Transmit facts and knowledge (including an awareness of cultural diversity) to help learners develop the skills necessary to interrelate positively with people of culturally diverse backgrounds.
4. Consider a total school curricular approach that integrates multicultural education in all teaching and learning situations.
5. Recognize multicultural education as an endeavor that has received considerable recognition and respect. Several areas of controversy and criticism continue to exist, however, and deserve attention.
6. Direct attention to issues such as sexism, agism, and classism, create more positive attitudes toward the disabled, and eliminate the racism, prejudice, and discrimination that plague U.S. society.
7. Address the ethnocentrism of learners and educators both.
8. Insist on multicultural education programs in all schools, rather than just in schools that have a culturally diverse student population.
9. Expect that all students reach the most advanced level of the Developmental Model of Intercultural Sensitivity.

10. Understand the inclusion of gender within multicultural education helps in understanding the complexities and intersectionalities of identity and oppression.

Suggested Learning Activities

1. Outline a multicultural education program for a school that has a population 50 percent European American, 25 percent African American, 20 percent Hispanic American, and approximately 5 percent other culturally diverse groups. Respond specifically to such areas as the extent of emphasis on each culture; a determination of the content of the program and examination of attitudes; appropriate in-service sessions for administration, faculty, and staff; appropriate curriculum and instruction methods and materials; and methods of assessing the program.
2. Read several definitions of multicultural education, and then, on the basis of these definitions and your opinions, write your own definition of multicultural education. Should multicultural education include more than just culture, for example, and should the definition include diversity in religion, gender, social class, and sexual orientation?
3. Interview someone who embodies the integration stage of the Developmental Model of Intercultural Sensitivity. This could be a person involved in international business, education, or community relations of multiple cultural backgrounds. How do they manage the different cultural norms and values in their daily life? What challenges do they face when integrating different cultural perspectives? What are some benefits they receive from embracing a multicultural identity? Document the interview responses, maintaining confidentiality and ethical standards.

Implementing Research

Teacher Perceptions of Culturally Responsive Practices in the Classroom

The study analyzed interviews with 13 exemplary teachers, focusing on their classroom behavior and practices, to explore their definition and implementation of culturally responsive teaching (Debnam et al., 2023). The researchers stressed that there is no one correct way to use culturally responsive teaching, which views students' cultural backgrounds as valuable resources in the classroom and empowers them by incorporating their cultural experiences into learning. Culturally responsive teachers acknowledge linguistic and cultural influences on student behavior, such as some African American students' expressive energy and some Asian students' indirect communication preferences which may make them less inclined to speak up in class. Understanding these nuances is crucial for creating an inclusive classroom environment. It is imperative that teachers develop intercultural sensitivity and familiarize themselves with these cultural variations so their students feel comfortable being their genuine selves while learning at school.

Implementing the Research

1. Culturally responsive teachers foster genuine connections with every student, investing time to understand their interests, backgrounds, strengths, and challenges. This personalized approach demonstrates care and inspires students to excel.
2. Teachers need to value their students' diverse experiences and backgrounds and customize the curriculum to ensure all students feel represented.
3. Incorporate students' outside interests and experiences into the classroom, discussing culture and using relevant materials. For example, if students are interested in music, teachers can use musical examples to teach mathematical concepts like fractions (rhythms and beats).
4. Use project-based learning where students can choose activities that align with their interests to engage deeply with meaningful topics while also learning essential academic skills.

Source: Debnam, K. J., Smith, L. H., Aguayo, D., Reinke, W. M., & Herman, K. C. (2023). Nominated exemplar teacher perceptions of culturally responsive practices in the classroom. *Teaching and Teacher Education, 125*(1). https://doi.org/10.1016/j.tate.2023.104062

Suggestions for Collaborative Efforts

Form groups of three or four that, if possible, represent the United States' cultural and gender diversity. Working collaboratively, focus your group's attention toward the following efforts.

1. In your group, discuss the following statement: "There are more differences in social class than there are differences in culture. For example, middle- or upper-class people of various cultures may be more alike (e.g. in terms of preferences in food, clothing, customs,

traditions, and religion) than people of a given culture or race. In essence, social class may be the distinguishing factor among people." Have several members of your group interview people from different social classes and several people from different cultural backgrounds to compare and contrast differences and similarities.

2. Have one or two of your group members visit a school to examine and compare the multicultural education programs. How do schools differ in philosophy, commitment, approaches (unit or total curriculum integration), goals and objectives, treatment of holidays, and overall attempts to have a truly multicultural school?

3. Select a school known for its diverse student population. Have your group formulate an instrument (survey or checklist) to assess the school's efforts in multicultural education. Make sure it examines the cultural, racial, and ethnic composition of faculty, staff, and other professional personnel; whether organization and grouping methods segregate learners by race; and whether the curriculum and instruction materials reflect cultural diversity.

Expanding Your Horizons

Additional Books and Journals

Buzzai, C., Muscarà, M., Romano, A., Passanisi, A., & Pace, U. (2023) The relationship between socio-cognitive skills and ethnic prejudice in preservice special education teachers. *International Journal of Inclusive Education*, 1–16. https://www.tandfonline.com/doi/abs/10.1080/08856257.2022.2107679
The study revealed that teachers' positive attitudes toward multicultural education mediated the relationship between their confidence in inclusive practices and their motivating or demotivating teaching styles. The findings underscore the significance of educators' attitudes toward multicultural education and their belief in their ability to promote inclusivity in the classroom as key factors shaping teaching approaches in diverse settings, with practical implications for schools.

Griffin, C. B., Harris, J. N., & Proctor, S. L. (2024). Intersectionality and school racial climate to create schools as sites of fairness and liberation for Black girls. *Journal of School Psychology*, *104*, 101282. https://doi.org/10.1016/j.jsp.2024.101282
The study explores systemic discrimination and its impact on experiences of African American girls in educational settings. Intersectionality and school racial climate to create schools as sites of fairness and liberation for African American girls is examined.

Kilag, O. K., Diano, F., Bulilan, R., Moralista, R., Allego, L., & Cañizares, M. C. (2024). Leadership strategies for building inclusive school communities: The challenges of managing diversity in schools. *International Multidisciplinary Journal of Research for Innovation*, 1(1), 92–100. https://risejournals. org/index.php/imjrise/article/view/10
This study identified four key dimensions of effective leadership strategies for managing diversity in schools: building inclusive school culture, promoting collaborative leadership, addressing educational equity, and fostering effective communication.

Websites

Center for Research on Education, Diversity, and Excellence (CREDE) – www.cal.org/projects/crede/
CREDE produces research and educational practice reports focused on linguistically diverse students. Their site includes webinars, databases and publications.

Ed Change – www.edchange.org/multicultural/papers/keith.html
This site discusses multicultural education, as well as training and educational practices.

National Association for Bilingual Education – www.nabe.org
This site promotes bilingual education, provides information, and sponsors an annual conference.

National Association for Multicultural Education – www.nameorg.org
This site provides information on the purposes, design, and implementation of effective multicultural education programs.

Quality Education for Minorities (QEM) Network – https://qem.org/
QEM's goal is to strengthen educational opportunities for historically underrepresented groups in science, technology, engineering and mathematics (STEM) fields. Their site promotes culturally responsive teaching and includes reports and studies on multicultural education.

Teaching for Change – www.teachingforchange.org/
Teaching for Change focuses on issues of equal opportunity in schools, conducts training institutes on topics such as racism, and produces materials and a newsletter.

Teaching English to Speakers of Other Languages – www.tesol.org/
TESOL aims to improve ELL education through professional learning, research, standards and advocacy. Their site has research and resources on the issue.

Diversity

Understanding the material and activities in this chapter will help the reader to:

- ◆ Grasp the historical and contemporary perspectives toward cultural diversity—that is, the melting-pot and salad-bowl ideologies, respectively.
- ◆ Explain concepts such as culture, racial literacy, race, ethnicity, socioeconomic status, and gender diversity, and explain why understanding these concepts is important when working with children and adolescents from various cultures.
- ◆ Explicate perspectives toward cultural diversity such as cultural deficit and cultural mismatch, and provide a rationale for adopting a positive and enriching perspective that appreciates cultural difference or cultural diversity.
- ◆ Explain how racism, discrimination, and stereotypes can harm children and adolescents from diverse cultures, and discuss strategies for elementary and secondary schools to address these issues effectively.

Opening Scenario

Toward a Salad-Bowl Perspective

Mrs. Rowe detected relatively easily that the school expected all learners to assimilate to middle-class European American values and customs. Textbooks

DOI: 10.4324/9781003429531-3

emphasized middle-class characters while downplaying members from other cultural groups; teaching styles and instructional strategies addressed the needs of middle-class learners; school rules and policies applied to all learners; school environments did little to celebrate cultural or gender diversity; and the administration, faculty, and staff provided little evidence that the school system had tried to employ professionals from various cultures. Learners with culturally different backgrounds who were unable or unwilling to adopt mainstream values suffered the consequences of lower achievement, poorer self-esteem, and a feeling of nonacceptance in the school.

Mrs. Rowe thought of ways to move the school toward a more "salad-bowl" perspective, one in which learners from all cultures could retain their cultural values and traditions and in which the school could address the needs of all learners. Mrs. Rowe asked for the administration's advice and support. The administration then formed a committee consisting of Mrs. Rowe, a speech therapist, a special educator, a guidance counselor, several classroom teachers, and several parents representing different cultural groups. The committee decided to take deliberate action to make the entire school more responsive to learners with differing cultural and ethnic backgrounds. They made plans to examine all phases of the school: textbooks and other curricular materials, the overall curriculum, instructional strategies, the efforts of special school personnel, the school environment, and efforts designed to celebrate diversity.

Mrs. Rowe and the committee realized they needed to be realistic. Changing the school would take time, commitment, and the efforts of all educators. They did achieve, however, two crucial steps: The school had realized the need for change and decided to take planned and deliberate action toward making all students feel accepted.

Overview

The increasing cultural diversity of the United States challenges elementary and secondary school educators to understand differing values, customs, and traditions, and to provide responsive multicultural experiences for all learners. The melting-pot theory, once thought to be a model of the assimilation of immigrants into the United States, obviously is not valid. People do not lose their differences when they immigrate to the United States. The melting-pot theory is no longer considered a model, much less a means of achieving a just, equal, and accepting society. Educators need a sound understanding of cultural, ethnic, racial, socioeconomic, gender, and individual differences, especially in light of the wealth of cultural diversity of the nation that increases daily. This chapter examines cultural diversity in the United States and suggests that responsive multicultural education programs can address many challenges.

A Word of Caution

As prominently mentioned in the Preface, anyone writing and talking about diversity should use extreme caution and pay close attention in order to avoid the assumption of stereotypes. Mrs. Rowe realized the need to recognize diversity and take deliberate action to accept all cultures and ethnicities in the Opening Scenario.

As we look at diversity in this chapter, we cannot overemphasize the importance of recognizing individual differences. For instance, all Asian Americans are not alike. Differences exist due to differences in social class, acculturation, time in the United States, as well as a wealth of individual differences. Similarly, whenever possible, we need to specify a specific culture. That is, instead of using the term *Asian American*, we need to specify Korean American, Nepalese American, Chinese American, Bhutanese American, or whatever the Asian culture might be. When it is not feasible to name a specific culture, we should always remember that overgeneralizing can result in relying on stereotypes.

As you read this chapter, remember the vast diversity among cultures, ethnicities, social classes, and learners with different sexual orientations. This variety represents experiences, perspectives, and characteristics that can significantly differ from one person to another even within any group. Also, keep in mind that *knowing* individuals requires conscientious study and first-hand contact. It's important not to overlook the diversity that exists within a culture. Recognizing that cultures aren't simple, but often complex with differences and degrees, will help in realizing meaningful cross-cultural exchanges. By learning about and embracing the diversity that exists within cultures, meaningful dialogue, mutual respect, and acceptance will be more easily obtained. Cultural homogenization, however, can lead to the perpetuation of stereotypes and biases which will hinder social harmony and reinforce hate and discrimination.

Diversity

Culture

Culture can be defined in a number of ways, but recent definitions, while worded differently, basically connote similar meanings. We define *culture* as people's values, language, religion, ideals, artistic expressions, patterns of social and interpersonal relationships, and ways of perceiving, behaving, and thinking. People's basis for perceptions, as well as their actual perceptions, differ culturally. How we feel, think, respond, and behave reflects our cultural background.

It is important to say that all people have culture. Such a statement might appear strange, but a century or so ago, culture was thought to be the province of only educated people who were well read, literate, and knowledgeable in areas such as music, the arts, and drama. Today, we recognize that all people have culture. People referred to as *bicultural* have competencies and can function effectively in two cultures.

POINTS TO PONDER 2.1

Determining Culture

Consider your culture—how many do you have? You have a cultural background, but you also have a culture of region, sexual orientation, gender, socioeconomic status, and professional status: Are you a pre-service or an in-service teacher?

Race

Although the term *race* refers to biological differences among people, it has long been used to differentiate groups of people. Determining racial categories often proves difficult because of the wide variety of traits and characteristics people and groups share. Society has generally recognized differences between races (e.g. physical differences), but these differences satisfy only biological aspects and do not explain differences in social behavior.

There are several important points concerning race. First, despite the movements of large numbers of people from one geographic region to another and the influence of intermarriage across racial groups, the concept of race today still has a significant social meaning. Second, race contributes few insights to cultural understanding. There is seldom cultural correspondence between a person's nationality, geography, language, and religion, and his or her racial category. Therefore, knowledge of a person's racial identity does not reveal much about his or her nationality, religion, and language.

Difficulties the U.S. Census Bureau experienced in its documents show the confusion regarding race and ethnicity. For example, the census may ask people to define themselves in categories that are not mutually exclusive—that is, a person can have more than one racial or ethnic designation.

Weiner (2006) suggests that teachers should integrate race and racial experiences into their classrooms in her review of Jane Bolgatz's book *Talking Race in the Classroom* (2005). These can be sensitive topics and often uncomfortable for both students and teachers. However, Bolgatz encourages teachers to discuss with students how they encounter race in their daily lives. Teachers should examine and critique their own attitudes on race as well. When teachers have reflected on their own opinions, attitudes, and biases they will be better prepared to create a classroom environment that is conducive to learning and discussion about race.

Racial Literacy

Racial literacy encompasses the ability to comprehend, analyze, and navigate issues surrounding race and racism (Guinier, 2004). It requires a critical understanding of how racial background functions in society and historical and structural factors contributing to racial disparities which cultivates skills for frank conversations about race. By fostering racial literacy in schools and involving families, teachers can create an environment where all feel comfortable in exchanging new ideas and offering solutions to reduce conflict. Racially literate individuals go beyond recognizing diverse groups to a deep comprehension of the complex dynamics surrounding race, including systemic racism.

Racial literacy is valuable and empowers teachers and students to discuss race openly and with sensitivity, understand consequences of inequality, and reduce racial barriers. Similarly, Daly (2023) suggests that discussion in the classroom, where teachers lead students through caring conversations designed to increase awareness of the ramifications of racism in the United State, can help build mutual understanding. After examining how a white teacher addresses challenges during race-related conversations while reading shared texts in her multiracial fourth-grade classroom, Daly found that instead of viewing tensions as hindrances and avoiding them, both the teacher and students can manage these tensions effectively through the application of racial literacy practices. These included learning the history of racial inequality in the United States, viewing racism as a structural rather than a personal issue, and engaging in ongoing discussions and critical self-reflection through question-and-answer sessions using informational texts, current news footage, and literature.

Both teachers and parents of marginalized students need to work together in combating racial issues and promoting equitable and inclusive teaching approaches. They should be sympathetic to the impact of discrimination such as feelings of alienation, and seek therapeutic support to help those students heal and develop effective coping strategies (Osborne et al., 2023). Through the efforts of caregivers and teachers, schools can create a more comfortable environment to constructively discuss stereotypes and racial conflicts in pursuit of equity and justice in any context.

Ethnicity

The definition of *ethnicity* takes into consideration people's national origin, religion, race, and any combination thereof. Attributes associated with ethnicity include group image and sense of identity derived from contemporary cultural patterns; shared political and economic interests; and involuntary membership, although individual identification with the group may be optional. The extent to which individuals identify with a particular ethnic group varies considerably, and some may identify with more than one. Strong ethnic identification suggests a sharing and acceptance of ethnic group values, beliefs, behaviors, language, and ways of thinking.

Gender

The term *gender* describes masculinity and femininity—the thoughts, feelings, and behavior that identify one as either male or female, or transgendered male or transgendered female—topics that have been explored only recently with any intensity. A multicultural education text would be remiss if it failed to address gender or transgender differences. Although many similarities exist between males and females, differences also exist, which educators should recognize and for which they should plan gender-appropriate educational experiences. Likewise, educators have a responsibility to clarify stereotypical beliefs about males and females or transgender people.

How might females differ from males? Research on gender and its effects has focused mainly on health concerns, social networks, self-esteem, achievement, self-image, and sex-role attitudes and behaviors: Some generalizations can be offered—with great caution.

1. Females and males report the same number of best friends; attributes they considered important in themselves and their same-sex friends differed according to sex. Males had larger social networks than females.
2. Females feel less positive about their bodies than males feel about theirs and assign different values than males do to different aspects of their bodies. Changes affecting the female body may make girls disappointed in their bodies. Boys, by contrast, may be less concerned with physical appearance and more interested in task mastery and effectiveness.

3. Females who have curricular choices often choose fewer mathematics courses than do males. The reason for this difference, however, is attributed to educators and counselors who steer females away from mathematics and science, not to actual weaknesses in females' native ability.
4. Females benefit more from group-oriented collaborative learning projects (e.g. cooperative learning), rather than individualistic and competitive projects, which many males prefer.

Again, extreme caution is warranted when discussing gender differences such as friendships, body image, curricular choices, and collaboration versus competitive activities.

While significant changes to improve gender equity have been made, it would be unrealistic to say educators always treat boys and girls the same way. Gender inequities still exist. Schools sometimes promote exclusionary practices and exclude (perhaps not intentionally) girls from activities. While schools' tactics may be subtle, they sometimes discourage girls from participating in specific activities, clubs, and learning activities, and the same holds true for boys. Over the decades, some educational experiences have become gender specific. Educators will be wise to have nondiscrimination as a goal and to comply with all legal mandates of nondiscrimination by examining both curricular and extracurricular activities, reviewing policies that might unintentionally discriminate, and seeking changes in school policy and practice to reduce discrimination.

Sexual Orientation: Lesbian, Gay, Bisexual, Transgender, Queer, Questioning, Intersex, Asexual, Plus (LGBTQIA+) Students

The author believes that multicultural education should include people of differing sexual orientation. LGBTQIA+ students share specific cultural characteristics, experience injustices and discrimination the way racially and ethnically marginalized people do, and deserve educators capable of providing effective educational experiences. The acronym continues to evolve as evidenced by LGBTQIA+ and the recognition of IA+ which represents intersex, asexual, while the "+" symbolizes more space for gender identities that may emerge in the future.

Such a position does not imply that LGBTQIA+ students do not share many similarities with others. It simply implies that, because of differences and potential as targets of injustice, they should be included in the definition of multiculturalism and in multicultural education programs.

> **POINTS TO PONDER 2.2**
>
> **School Practices and Gender**
>
> Make a list of school practices or education-related issues that might fail to address gender differences. Why do you think educators sometimes use school practices and harbor expectations that fail to address gender differences?

Educators teaching LGBTQIA+ students need to understand the special challenges—e.g. loneliness, bullying, isolation, and ridicule. The author feels that sexual orientation should be perceived as a cultural difference, just as gender, race, ethnicity, and social class. Teaching LGBTQIA+ students requires trying to understand these students' worldviews and perspectives on life.

Students are becoming more visible each day through increased numbers of referrals to school counselors, school social workers, substance-abuse personnel, and various other support staff. Individual reasons for these referrals are diverse, but among the most common are efforts to clarify sexual orientation, anxiety, suicide attempts, substance abuse, low self-esteem, family conflict, and emotional isolation.

Educators should (1) provide factual information about youth sexuality, (2) abandon the myth that discussing homosexuality will cause young people to grow up to be LGBTQIA+ people, (3) promote and protect the human and civil rights of all people in the classroom, and (4) encourage the hiring of and supporting LGBTQIA+ educators who can provide healthy role models.

The document *GLAAD Media Reference Guide—Transgender Issues* (Glaad, 2016) offers definitions and significant information on transgender students.

> **Gender Identity** can be defined as one's internal, deeply held sense of one's gender. For transgender people, their own internal gender identity does not match the sex they were assigned at birth. Most people have a gender identity of man or woman (or boy or girl). For some people, their gender identity does not fit neatly into one of those two choices. Unlike gender expression (see below) gender identity is not visible to others.
>
> **Gender Expression** is the external manifestations of gender, expressed through one's name, pronouns, clothing, haircut, behavior, voice, or body characteristics. Society identifies these cues as masculine and feminine, although what is considered masculine and feminine changes over time and varies by culture. Typically, transgender people seek to make their gender expression align with their gender identity, rather than the sex they were assigned at birth.

Sexual Orientation describes an individual's enduring physical, romantic and/or emotional attraction to another person. Gender identity and sexual orientation are not the same. Transgender people may be straight, lesbian, gay, or bisexual. For example, a person who transitions from male to female and is attracted solely to men would identify as a straight woman.

Glaad (2016) also offers transgender-specific terminology:

Transgender (adj.) An umbrella term for people whose gender identity and/or gender expression differs from what is typically associated with the sex they were assigned at birth. People under the transgender umbrella may describe themselves using one or more of a wide variety of terms—including *transgender*. Some of those terms are defined below. Use the descriptive term preferred by the individual. Many transgender people are prescribed hormones by their doctors to change their bodies. Some undergo surgery as well. But not all transgender people can or will take those steps, and a transgender identity is not dependent upon medical procedures.

Transsexual (adj.) An older term that originated in the medical and psychological communities. Still preferred by some people who have permanently changed—or seek to change—their bodies through medical interventions (including but not limited to hormones and/or surgeries). Unlike *transgender, transsexual* is not an umbrella term. Many transgender people do not identify as transsexual and prefer the word *transgender*. It is best to ask which term an individual prefers. If preferred, use as an adjective: transsexual woman or transsexual man.

Trans Used as shorthand to mean *transgender* or *transsexual*—or sometimes to be inclusive of a wide variety of identities under the transgender umbrella. Because its meaning is not precise or widely understood, be careful when using it with audiences who may not understand what it means. Avoid unless used in a direct quote or in cases where you can clearly explain the term's meaning in the context of your story.

Transgender man People who were assigned female at birth but identify and live as a man may use this term to describe themselves. They may shorten it to trans man. (Note: *trans man*, not "transman.") Some may also use FTM, an abbreviation for female-to-male. Some may prefer to simply be called *men*, without any modifier. It is best to ask which term an individual prefers.

Transgender woman People who were assigned male at birth but identify and live as a woman may use this term to describe themselves. They may shorten to trans woman. (Note: *trans woman,* not "transwoman.") Some may also use MTF, an abbreviation for male-to-female. Some may prefer to simply be called *women,* without any modifier. It is best to ask which term an individual prefers.

The author recommends the Glaad's (2016) report to readers who want more detailed information (e.g. transition, sex reassignment surgery, gender non-conforming, and gender-queer). Specific suggestions for working with transgendered students include:

Always use a transgender person's chosen name. Many transgender people are able to obtain a legal name change from a court. However, some transgender people cannot afford a legal name change or are not yet old enough to change their name legally. They should be afforded the same respect for their chosen name as anyone else who lives by a name other than their birth name (e.g. celebrities).

Whenever possible, ask transgender people which pronoun they would like you to use. A person who identifies as a certain gender, whether or not that person has taken hormones or had some form of surgery, should be referred to using the pronouns appropriate for that gender. If it is not possible to ask a transgender person which pronoun is preferred, use the pronoun that is consistent with the person's appearance and gender expression. For example, if a person wears a dress and uses the name Susan, feminine pronouns are usually appropriate.

The U.S. Departments of Education and Justice released a joint guidance to help provide educators the information they need to ensure that all students, including transgender students, can attend school in an environment free from discrimination based on sex (U.S. Department of Education, 2016). The reports focus on how to best ensure these students, and nontransgender students, can all enjoy a safe and discrimination-free environment. Under Title IX of the Education Amendments of 1972, schools receiving federal money may not discriminate based on a student's sex, including a student's transgender status. The guidance makes clear that both federal agencies treat a student's gender identity as the student's sex for the purposes of enforcing Title IX.

The guidance explains schools' obligations to:

◆ Respond promptly and effectively to sex-based harassment of all students, including harassment based on a student's actual or perceived gender identity, transgender status, or gender transition.

- Treat students consistent with their gender identity even if their school records or identification documents indicate a different sex.
- Allow students to participate in sex-segregated activities and access sex-segregated facilities consistent with their gender identity.
- Protect students' privacy related to their transgender status under Title IX and the Family Educational Rights and Privacy Act.

At the same time, the guidance makes clear that schools can provide additional privacy options to any student for any reason. The guidance does not require any student to use shared bathrooms or changing spaces, when, for example, there are other appropriate options available; and schools can also take steps to increase privacy within shared facilities.

The U.S. Department of Education of Elementary and Secondary Education Office of Safe and Healthy Students (2016) released *Examples of Policies and Emerging Practices for Supporting Transgender Students*, based upon the belief that many transgender students (i.e. students whose gender identity is different from the sex they were assigned at birth) report feeling unsafe and experiencing verbal and physical harassment or assault in school, and that these students may perform worse academically when they are harassed. While the document is too long to describe in detail, it provides a detailed Table of Contents and approximately 18 pages of examples currently being implemented by school districts across that nation.

More recently, the U.S. Department of Education (2021) released a statement of support for transgender students and provided ways schools can support them with respect to discrimination. It also provided information on steps a student can take if they experience discrimination at school. Following the guidelines, school districts should support transgender students who experience discrimination and create inclusive school policies. Schools can also provide training to teachers and staff on the use of welcoming and inclusive language.

Socioeconomic Conditions

Health disparity generally refers to a higher burden of illness, injury, disability, or mortality experienced by one population group relative to another group. Hill et al. (2024) provide a wealth of information on health and healthcare coverage among population groups. A healthcare disparity typically refers to differences between health and coverage, access to healthcare, and quality of care. Disparities are commonly considered in terms of race and ethnicity, socioeconomic status, age, location, gender, disability status, and sexual orientation.

Disparities in health and healthcare limit continued improvement in overall quality of health and healthcare. While exceptions exist, medical costs for African Americans, Hispanic Americans, and Asian Americans result from health inequities. As the population becomes more diverse, with people of color projected to account for over half of the population by 2050, it is increasingly important to address health disparities.

Hispanics, blacks, and American Indians/Alaskan Natives as well as low-income individuals all are much more likely to be uninsured relative to whites and those with higher incomes. Low-income individuals and people of color also face increased barriers to accessing healthcare, receive poor quality care, and ultimately experience worse health outcomes.

Recognizing the continuing problem of disparities, the U.S. Department of Health and Human Services (2022) developed an action plan to reduce racial and ethnic health disparities. The HHS Equity Action Plan sets out a series of priorities, strategies, actions, and goals to achieve equitable access to health resources. Actionable items in the report include developing civil rights protections, using grants to support equity considerations, and prioritizing maternal mortality by working with states to extend health insurance coverage.

In conclusion, health and healthcare disparities remain a persistent problem in the United States, leading to certain groups being at higher risk of being uninsured, having more limited access to care, experiencing poorer quality of care, and ultimately experiencing worse health outcomes. While health and healthcare disparities are commonly viewed through a lens of race and ethnicity, they occur across a broad range of dimensions and reflect a complex set of individual, social, and environmental factors. Disparities limit continued improvement of care and population health and result in unnecessary costs, and are increasingly important to address as the population becomes more diverse. For the past decade, there has been an increased focus on reducing disparities and a growing set of initiatives to address health disparities at the federal, state, community, and provider level. The Affordable Care Act (ACA) includes provisions that advance efforts to eliminate disparities. As the population grows more diverse, it will be important to recognize disparities and address such factors as social and environmental factors that extend beyond the healthcare system.

Health Insurance Coverage

Health insurance coverage facilitates timely access to healthcare. People may receive health insurance coverage as a fringe benefit through their job, may be eligible for publicly financed coverage, or may purchase it on their own.

Health status is a function of several factors, including access to care and insurance coverage, socioeconomic conditions (education, occupation, income, and place of residence), genetics, and personal behavior. Racial and ethnic marginalized population groups (other than Asian Americans) rate their overall health worse than non-Hispanic whites. Marginalized Americans frequently report a higher prevalence of specific health problems, such as diabetes and obesity, which can have serious consequences for health and longevity.

A significant aspect of one's overall health condition is access to adequate and affordable healthcare. Unfortunately, this access to healthcare is often influenced by one's race and ethnicity.

Table 2.1 shows the makeup of the U.S. population.

In contrast to the percentage of the population by race, when one examines poverty rates by race and ethnicity, as shown in Table 2.2, a much more serious picture becomes evident, especially when one considers the cost and availability of health insurance. The U.S. poverty threshold for a family with two adults and one child was $23,556 in 2022 (Kaiser Family Foundation, 2022). This income line is used to measure poverty data by the Federal Government and State Health Facts.

A major goal of the ACA was to make health insurance more available and affordable, especially to those with low incomes. Under the coverage expansions, Medicaid and subsidized Marketplace insurance are available to low-income individuals, and those who have gained coverage are experiencing improved access to care and increased financial protection against medical expenses. In addition, because this new coverage is not linked to employment, it allows individuals in various types of work situations to gain

Table 2.1 U.S. Population by Race

White	Black	Hispanic	Asian	Other	Total
58.9%	13.6%	19.1%	6.9%	1.5%	100%

Source: U.S. Census Bureau (2023g)

Table 2.2 Poverty Rate by Race and Ethnicity

White	Black	Hispanic	Asian	Two or more races	American Indian/ Alaskan Native
9.5%	21.4%	16.7%	10%	13.8%	24.5%

Source: Kaiser Family Foundation (2022)

Table 2.3 Percentage of Uninsured Americans by Race and Ethnicity

White	Black	Hispanic	Asian	Native Hawaiian and Other Pacific Islander	American Indian and Alaska Native
6.6%	10%	18%	6%	12.7%	19.1%

Source: Hill et al. (2024)

and maintain coverage, including entrepreneurs and small-business owners, those who are in school or transitioning to new careers, individuals who work one or more part-time jobs, and the millions who have shifted to other types of labor arrangements, by choice or necessity.

While significant numbers of Americans continue to be uninsured (usually no fault of their own), as shown in Table 2.3, the percentage change in the number of uninsured by race and ethnicity has definitely decreased. Such information shows that the ACA has benefited many people and has contributed significantly to the overall health and well-being of many races and ethnicities residing in the United States.

National School Lunch Program

Another excellent indication of socioeconomic conditions among communities of color is the National School Lunch Program (NSLP) that provides free or reduced-price meals across the United States. It is an important child nutrition and development program that covers meal costs of approximately $14 billion annually for students who are at risk of food insecurity. According to the current NSLP report (U.S. Department of Agriculture, 2024), 28.5 million students participated in the NSLP on an average school day in 2023, a decrease from a high of 31.8 million students per day in 2011. However, it is up from a record low in 2021 of 11 million students per day on average, which was during the remote education period of the COVID-19 pandemic.

The numbers do not suggest students of color receive free lunches— quite the contrary—they only suggest that students' lower socioeconomic conditions contribute to their likelihood of receiving free lunches. Blad (2015) maintained that declining participation in the NSLP was not caused by more stringent nutrition standards. Some factors may contribute to slightly declining participation in the NSLP, including changes in eligibility criteria, changes in student preferences for school meals, and economic conditions affecting the eligibility of students. Some who don't agree with standards make the point that they cause schools to prepare meals that students don't find appealing and therefore won't eat.

To implement the NSLP, schools use data on students' family income to measure eligibility for subsidized meals. As a result, schools accentuate social class closely linked to family socioeconomic status. Consequently, lunch in school is linked to family income-based criteria such as free lunch and meal tickets which become clearly visible to both students and teachers (Best, 2017). As a result, students who receive free school meals face a stigma or avoid participating in the NSLP program to avoid embarrassment.

In addition, while the NSLP offers nutritious meals and can prevent youth malnutrition, the association with lower socioeconomic status often affects teacher expectations of student behavior and academic ability even before they interact substantially with those students (Domina et al., 2024). Teachers, counselors, and school administrators, therefore, need to actively combat the NSLP stigma and maintain high expectations for all students; focusing on each student's individual strengths and talents to mitigate the biases related to socioeconomic status.

Effects on Motivation and School Achievement

What can we learn from the socioeconomic conditions of marginalized communities? We should not blame them for having lower incomes, lower levels of health insurance, more medical challenges, more free lunches, and, in some cases, lower academic achievement. Rather, we should look at the conditions that have led to these disparities and try to address each condition, whether racism, discrimination, or some other social ill. In addition, we need to look at the many Asian Americans who have achieved tremendous success in the United States. Our conclusion is that we (individuals and the nation) should assist all people to raise their incomes, to increase their levels of health insurance, to reduce their medical problems, and to improve their educational aspirations and achievement.

Specifically, the educational difficulties stem from socioeconomic problems. Socioeconomic differences play a significant role in determining how a person acts, thinks, lives, and relates to others. Differences in values between students and educators basically represent social class differences, because many underprivileged-group learners come from the lower socioeconomic classes. Educators coming from middle- or upper-class backgrounds may have difficulty understanding the social and economic problems facing children and adolescents from lower socioeconomic homes. Many educators are far removed from poor people's experience of poverty, low wages, lack of property, and indeed of the most basic needs. The accompanying differences in values, attitudes, behaviors, and beliefs among the various socioeconomic groups warrant the professional's consideration.

A person's social class is sometimes thought to indicate his or her ambitions or motivation to achieve. It is a serious mistake, however, to stereotype people by social class—to assume, for example, that people from the lower classes lack ambition and do not want to work or improve their education status. It is not unreasonable to suggest that lower-class families, regardless of cultural background, want to improve their social status in life but meet with considerable frustration when faced with poverty and its accompanying conditions.

Language

Language diversity is one of the most significant challenges facing U.S. schools. The number of students who speak a language other than English has grown dramatically. Almost simultaneously, the number of English-only advocates has increased. English is the language spoken by most people in the United States. The official language of most states is English and it is the language used in nearly all governmental functions. Despite this predominance, many people speak languages other than English, and there has long been an interest in these groups and in how well they are able to participate in civic life and interact with the English-speaking majority. The number of people who speak a language other than English at home has gone from 23.1 million in 1980 to 67.8 million in 2019 (Dietrich & Hernandez, 2022b); approximately one in five people. At roughly the same time, 1989 to 2019, the number of people speaking only English at home increased from 187.2 million to 241 million. The majority of immigrants to the United States arrive with little to no command of English, just 17 percent spoke English upon arrival (Pew Research Center, 2020). In contrast, 42 percent of immigrants spoke Spanish upon arrival and 6 percent spoke Chinese.

The languages other than English spoken most frequently in the United States in 2019 were Spanish, Chinese, Tagalog, Vietnamese, and Arabic. Sixty-two percent of the U.S. population that spoke a language other than English at home spoke Spanish. Major urban hubs are significant in that they contain large numbers of people of different backgrounds and cultures. They attract people from many different parts of the world and are centers of immense language diversity. The U.S. Census Bureau (2015) reports at least 350 different languages are spoken in U.S. homes.

This section looks at the number of non-English-speaking students and the challenges both they and their supporters face.

The increase in the number of students who speak a language other than English should be seen as a call for planned action. Consider these highlights for the ten largest metropolitan areas:

- New York metro area: At least 192 languages are spoken at home.
- Los Angeles area: At least 185 languages are spoken at home.
- Chicago metro area: At least 153 languages are spoken at home.
- Philadelphia metro area: At least 146 languages are spoken at home.
- Houston metro area: At least 145 languages are spoken at home.
- Washington metro area: At least 192 languages are spoken at home.
- Miami metro area: At least 128 languages are spoken at home.
- Atlanta metro area: At least 146 languages are spoken at home.
- Boston metro area: At least 138 languages are spoken at home.
- San Francisco metro area: At least 163 languages are spoken at home.

The multitude of languages spoken in the largest cities contribute to their cultural richness. While linguistic diversity can be a source of strength and opportunity, it also presents challenges in education, community unity, and provisions for public services. According to Dietrich and Hernandez (2022), 52 percent of people who spoke Chinese and 57 percent of people who spoke Vietnamese at home spoke English "less than very well" because English is not a primary language in their home countries. This is most likely due to the recent high influx of Asian immigrants who have not yet had time to master English. Of the other three most common immigrant groups, 39 percent of Spanish-speakers, 30 percent of Tagalog-speakers and 35 percent of Arabic speakers reported their ability to speak English as "less than very well."

English-speaking ability is an important topic surrounding immigration in the United States. For the foreign born, fluency in English is associated with earnings and occupational mobility. Conversely, the presence of many people with limited English ability requires state and local governments to make costly adjustments, such as providing English as a Second Language (ESL) classes in schools and translating official forms into multiple languages.

English is not the native language of most immigrants in the United States. However, many do arrive knowing how to speak English, especially from countries where English is widely used. These include not only countries such as Canada, Jamaica, and the United Kingdom, where English is the primary language, but also countries where English is an official language, such as India, Nigeria, and the Philippines. Many others learn English through years of study or practice prior to immigrating to the United States or while living in the United States.

Identity Formation

Identity formation involves questions such as "Who am I?" and "Who am I to be?" Identity is our sense of place within the world or the meaning that we attach to ourselves in the broader context of life. It is important that educators show children and adolescents that people may have several identities at once—that is, an individual might be Hispanic American, a member of any of the Spanish-speaking cultures, someone's brother, a Catholic, and an inhabitant of a specific geographic region in the United States.

The educator's first challenge is to view students as different and unique individuals rather than as a homogeneous group. Educators who assume too much homogeneity among students often fail to address individual and cultural differences and then fail to provide experiences that lead to forming positive cultural identities.

The second challenge for multicultural educators becomes clear as they understand that all individuals need to clarify personal attitudes toward their cultural and ethnic backgrounds. Educators' goals can be to teach self-acceptance, to instill in learners an acceptance and understanding of both the positive and negative attributes of their cultural groups, and to teach learners the importance of working toward social justice and an equitable environment. Students both desire and have the ability to take actions that will support and reinforce the values and norms of their ethnic, national, and global communities.

In some situations, people of differing cultural backgrounds might feel a need to forsake their identities in order to feel accepted and to experience success. Still, people of differing cultural backgrounds might not view the attitudes and behaviors of the dominant group appropriate for them. People who adopt the attitudes and behaviors of the dominant group might experience an identity crisis or an internal opposition to giving up their cultural beliefs.

POINTS TO PONDER 2.3

Clarifying Multiple Identities

Ask children and adolescents to consider their identities. For example, a child or an adolescent may have a number of different and changing identities, such as the following:

African American, Asian American, European American or Hispanic American or American Indian (just to mention cultures mentioned in this book);

a person of the specific cultural background;
a member of a marginalized group;
male or female;
gay, lesbian, or bisexual or heterosexual;
a member of a particular school and grade;
a son, grandson, or nephew;
a best friend;
a person with disabilities.

To prevent students from feeling they must like any specific culture, educators need to design teaching–learning experiences in such a way that students feel they can maintain their cultural identities and still experience school success. While such a task will be difficult, educators need to demonstrate their respect for students' cultural identities, understand that students' perceptions of motivation may vary with culture, allow students to learn in the way they consider culturally relevant (i.e. working collaboratively, rather than competitively), provide curricular content and learning materials that show the contributions of various cultural groups, and help students to feel they are accepted in the majority culture school system.

Exceptionalities

Nationwide, 7.3 million students, or approximately 15 percent of all public school students, had a disability of some kind in 2021–2022. The most common category of disability was specific learning disabilities at 32 percent of all disabilities (National Center for Education Statistics, 2023f).

Although each state must comply with federal mandates, the level of inclusiveness and support varies with the will of and budget of the local school district as well as the degree of parental advocacy.

There is a broad range of disabilities, such as specific learning disabilities, speech and language impairments, mental retardation, emotional disturbances, hearing disabilities, and several others covered by the Individuals with Disabilities Education Act (IDEA). Exceptional students (also referred to as *special-needs students*) include those with disabling conditions in any one or more of the following categories: Mental retardation, hearing, speech or language, visual, emotional, orthopedic, autism, traumatic brain injury, other health impairment, and specific learning disabilities. To the maximum extent possible, students with special needs must be educated with their peers in the regular classroom, whether for the entire school day (full inclusion) or for part of the day (partial inclusion). General and special educators collaborate to provide instruction in the regular classroom. Providing effective instruction to special-needs students requires more attention to individual needs, better diagnosis of the child's strengths and weaknesses, and an understanding of the child's characteristics, especially those that affect instruction.

Sometimes educators are challenged to have their curricular and instructional experiences reflect the objectives stated in the student's individualized education program (IEP). With the reauthorization of the IDEA comes additional pressure for schools to demonstrate that all students, including students with disabilities, are meeting established learning outcomes. However, there has been some concern over both the failure to link specially designed instruction with the general education curriculum and the inadequate attention given to documenting the effectiveness of services specified on the IEP.

Among the students with exceptionalities are those who are gifted and talented. These students are sometimes neglected in the regular classrooms because there is no singular method to identify them. Gifted students can be very diverse and characterized as antisocial, creative, high achieving, divergent thinkers, or perfectionists. They can also have some special-needs characteristics, such as attention-deficit disorder, dyslexia, and other learning disorders. A number of developmental characteristics that apply to most other students apply to gifted students, as well, particularly rapid physical growth, varying levels of cognitive operation, sporadic brain growth, affective ambivalence, and capacity for introspection. Like all learners, gifted students have to deal with achieving independence, developing identity as a person, exploring and accepting sexuality, developing meaningful interpersonal relationships, and establishing personal values.

Students who are exceptional and diverse may face even more challenges. Building an identity influenced by both exceptionality and diversity could create a feeling of double jeopardy. Also, some people in society equate language differences (e.g. speaking English as a second language or a dialect) with limited intelligence, while others equate physical exceptionalities with deficient mental abilities. There appears to be a disproportionate number of African American students in special-education classes. Similarly, African American students are disproportionately referred for and placed in special classes for mental retardation, emotional and behavioral problems, and learning disabilities. Such treatment too often leads to segregation of students by race and ethnicity as well as to African American students receiving a less demanding general education.

Challenges to Diversity

Historical perspectives reveal that many people have been the recipients of cruel and inhumane treatment, mainly because of their differences. Just a few examples include the injustices imposed on American Indians in seizing their land and destroying their culture; the racism and discrimination in education, employment, and housing that have affected the progress of African American and Hispanic Americans for centuries; and Asian Americans' cruel treatment upon immigrating to the United States. Educators have the challenge of molding a more humane and equitable society by providing responsive multicultural education programs that reduce racism, prejudice, and ethnocentrism, and promote social justice, as discussed in Chapter 1.

White Privilege

Often defined as the domination of one social or ethnic group by another, *racism* is an ideological system used to justify the discrimination of some racial groups against others. Although we continue to hope for greater acceptance and recognition of cultural diversity, we must report that socioeconomic and societal inequities, racism, prejudice, and ethnocentrism continue in the United States. Whether due to overt racism and discrimination or the more covert forms often found in employment and housing, many people of color continue to experience inequities and inequalities. Although overt acts of discrimination and Jim Crow attitudes are not as visible today as they were several decades ago, racial injustice continues to affect people's progress and well-being. Educators of all cultures may have to deal with problems resulting from these realities in the United States and may have to sort through their own personal biases and long-held cultural beliefs.

Racism and its negative effects have been with us for centuries and, unfortunately, little evidence suggests that this evil will ever be eliminated. Educators are challenged to implement effective multicultural education programs that reduce the ignorance that breeds racism and to develop the understanding and actions people need to become antiracist. Undoubtedly, students of all cultures benefit when educators focus on reducing racial and ethnic prejudice and discrimination; teach certain humanistic values, such as the negative effects of racism, prejudice, and discrimination; provide appropriate educational experiences; and continue efforts toward realizing social justice.

White privilege, an important topic in multiculturalism, refers to white people having a whiteness that offers them specific advantages—some think whiteness implies correctness or the way thoughts and actions should be. In reality, such whiteness can result in employment or educational opportunities. For example, white men earned more than any income group until they were surpassed by Asian men at the beginning of the twenty-first century. White privilege can also result in only white people's standards and opinions being considered accurate. Educators should recognize the impact of interlocking oppression and privilege, including the assertion that whiteness and white privilege are used to position others as inferior, with compelling effects on people's lives, and the need to address institutionalized racism by creating spaces for whites to examine their identity.

Privilege can also be considered in terms of power, access, advantage, and majority status. Power is having control, choice, autonomy, and authority or influence over others. Access is having money, opportunities, and/or material possessions. Advantage is having connections, favorable treatment, entitlement, social support, and lack of concern for others. Majority is simply being part of the majority in number, social standing, and/or social norms.

An emphasis on white privilege is fundamental to understanding the oppression of minorities and raising self-awareness about practitioners' roles and responsibilities with culturally diverse groups and communities. An additional benefit is that white students would have an opportunity to explore their own racial and ethnic backgrounds.

What does all this have to do with educators developing multicultural education programs and working toward an overall sense of social justice? White educators respond to white privilege and oppression with varying levels of awareness. Depending on their level of awareness, white professionals report anger, guilt, confusion, defensiveness, sadness, and a sense of responsibility and need for advocacy when discussing these topics.

Stereotypes

A *stereotype* can be defined as an attitude toward a person or group that supposedly characterizes or describes an entire group, gender, race, or religion. A stereotype produces a generalized mental picture that usually results in a judgment (negative or positive) of a person or an entire culture.

Although a stereotype might be partially valid, it is imperative that educators approach all stereotypes with skepticism and acknowledge that most result in prejudice, like or dislike, or approval or disapproval of a cultural group. Recognizing that stereotypes all too often contribute to people being beneficiaries or victims of racism, sexism, ageism, and so on, effective multicultural educators seek to understand and respond appropriately to others' and their own beliefs about people.

How can educators' counter biases and stereotypes? How can teachers design multicultural education programs that respond to U.S. schools' diverse population?

POINTS TO PONDER 2.4

Clarifying Stereotypes

List several stereotypes that people might harbor about cultural groups. How do you think these stereotypes originated? Is there any objective basis for these stereotypes? How might such stereotypes affect educational decisions? List several ways educators can gain a better understanding of people, rather than rely on stereotypes.

---

1. Educators should be aware of their own biases and stereotypes.
2. Educators should expect achievement of all students, regardless of diversity.
3. Educators should examine and confront biases and stereotypes that students hold.
4. Educators should ensure that library materials and other instructional materials portray characters in a realistic, nonsexist, nonracist, nonstereotypical manner.
5. Educators should provide heterogeneous classes that allow students opportunities to build interethnic and interracial relationships with one another.
6. Educators should provide role-playing situations and simulation activities that help students gain better understanding of stereotyped groups.

Stereotypes and other generalizations that surround cultures have the potential for severely damaging interpersonal counseling and the outcomes of educational efforts. Whether one believes that all learners from different cultural backgrounds are underachievers or that all adolescents are involved in drugs and sex, stereotypes and generalizations can be detrimental to learners and educators, as well as teaching and learning relationships. For example, a teacher who bases educational decisions on the images the mass media present might conclude that all African Americans are dealing in drugs or survive only as welfare recipients. Too often, cultural stereotypes and generalizations are considered rooted in facts and become the basis for professional decisions affecting personal lives.

Ethnocentrism

Ethnocentrism is the belief that one's own culture is superior to that of others. People also use ethnocentric beliefs to evaluate and judge human behavior.

Persons with strong ethnocentric attitudes and beliefs may have difficulty appreciating and accepting the range of cultural differences that exist in society. Because our culture influences the way we think, feel, and act, it becomes our means of judging others and their actions. Our own ethnic background becomes the norm or the expectation for other cultures of the world. The result is that we evaluate other people by our cultural standards and beliefs, thus making it virtually impossible to view another culture as separate from our own.

The challenge for educators in multicultural situations is to understand ethnocentrism and to realize we judge others by our own values and beliefs. For example, textbooks and other instructional materials can perpetuate ethnocentrism in subtle ways that educators may find difficult to recognize. Since we will likely accept without question a perspective consistent with our own vantage point, attitudes, and values, educators might not even be aware that another cultural perspective exists.

The following educational accommodations can be made to address ethnocentrism:

- Instill in children and adolescents the idea that they should not consider cultural differences as right or wrong, superior or inferior.
- Arrange teaching and learning situations (e.g. cooperative learning and cross-age tutoring) so that learners of varying cultures can have first-hand experiences with each other.
- Model acceptance and respect for all people.
- Respond appropriately to statements indicating a lack of understanding or acceptance of cultural differences.
- Encourage respect for all differences—cultural and ethnic, socioeconomic, sexual orientation, disabling conditions, gender, and other characteristics that contribute to diversity among individuals.

Responding appropriately to ethnocentrism is a significant challenge, because one of the primary goals of any multicultural program is to encourage and instill an acceptance of others' cultures and cultural backgrounds. First, it is crucial for educators to recognize their own ethnocentrism and its potential for clouding their objectivity. A second challenge is to convince children and adolescents that while they view their cultural beliefs as right, people from other cultures also consider their beliefs to be right. Convincing learners of the dangers of ethnocentrism and teaching them to perceive others' cultural differences and beliefs in a more positive light may be a major undertaking.

In some cases, the educator may be challenging long-held beliefs that the learner's family may have taught or encouraged.

Cultural Models

Educators and other professionals need to examine their perspectives toward diversity and to determine if diversity appears as a *cultural deficit* (implying the need for change), a *cultural mismatch* (implying that learners from different cultural backgrounds fail because their traits are incompatible with schools' teaching practices), or as *culturally different* (implying that differences enrich the classroom and make individuals unique). This is more important than just an academic question; educators' perception of diversity determines their philosophical beliefs toward learners and toward their own instructional practices.

The Cultural Deficit Model

In the cultural deficit model, students who are culturally different are thought of as "deprived," "disadvantaged," and "socially deprived" only because their behavior, language, and customs are different from those with middle-class values. The notion that some cultures do not seek to advance themselves because of a cultural deficit results in "blaming the victim." The individual is at fault for not being more successful (educationally, socially, etc.). The cultural deficit model has failed to address the implicit cultural biases that shape negative perceptions and inhibit the understanding of the roles of sociopolitical forces. Marginalized students who come from different backgrounds historically have had difficult experiences and suffered trauma at school because of systematic deficit views. Being aware of the risks of reinforcing deficit perspectives, knowing the dangers of perpetuating negative views, and trying to advocate for the integration of antiracist and equity-focused practices in the classroom will support those disadvantaged students. Abdou et al. (2023) assert that instead of ignoring these difficulties and challenges, the entire school can, with trauma-informed approaches, work together to identify difficulties that affect learning and behavior, and help students feel supported. Neglecting the impact of cultural deficit views on youth with diverse cultural and linguistic backgrounds can lead to a generic, one-size-fits-all approach that is not conducive to the specific needs of under-represented students. Teachers, staff, and counsellors need to listen to what each student needs to learn. Using caring approaches, such as one-on-one counseling, they can then provide a safe learning space where diverse cultural backgrounds are respected. The well-being of youth, impacted by both racism and the COVID-19 pandemic, deserves careful consideration (Butler-Barnes, 2023). It is essential to approach the support of underprivileged adolescents with a strength-based perspective rather than a cultural deficit approach.

Principles of Critical Race Theory

Critical Race Theory (CRT) is an intellectual framework that examines the intersection of race, law, and power, and challenges systemic racism. It views racism as normal in the United States. Teachers should realize that CRT is intended to eliminate suppression and is committed to social justice. They should understand the aspects of CRT that are applicable in curriculum and instruction as they are an important part of teaching diversity and human rights. The five tenets of CRT are counter-storytelling; the permanence of racism; whiteness as property; interest conversion; and the critique of color-blindness (DeCuir & Dixson, 2004; Ladson-Billings, 1998).

Educators should advocate for marginalized students. Teachers can begin discussion in the classroom around the topic of how policies claiming to be colorblind may inadvertently perpetuate systemic inequalities. CRT explores how being white is treated as a valuable social asset, similar to property, providing advantages. Teachers can introduce news reports showing how certain rights and advantages are associated with perceived "whiteness" in society.

The Cultural Mismatch Model

In contrast to the cultural deficit model, the cultural mismatch perspective assumes that cultures are inherently different but not necessarily superior or inferior to one another. It assumes that people from culturally different backgrounds fail to achieve academically because their cultural traits do not match those of the dominant culture reflected in schools. Thus, in the mismatch model, the educational performance of diverse groups is related to the degree of incongruence between group values and traits and those of the educational system: The better the match, the greater the likelihood of academic success.

The Culturally Different Model

The culturally different model recognizes differences as strengths that are valuable and enriching to schools and to society as a whole. Its proponents believe nonetheless that all children and adolescents need to learn mainstream cultural values and knowledge. Researchers have begun to establish a research base documenting that differences in learning styles and language are not deficiencies. The differences can be a foundation to facilitate learning.

POINTS TO PONDER 2.5

Determining School Opinions toward Differences

Visit an elementary or secondary school to learn about its educational philosophy, grouping practices, curricular and library materials, and extracurricular activities. Do you think the school's practices and policies indicate an acceptance of a cultural deficit, mismatch, or difference model? What are the implications of the model the school has chosen?

A certain degree of cultural compatibility is necessary as teachers and students become increasingly aware of others' cultural differences, whether differences relate to school or home expectations. The situation for children and adolescents might be even more acute than for teachers, especially because learners must switch from home to school cultures and vice versa.

Summing Up

Educators who wish to plan an appropriate response to the United States' cultural diversity and to provide effective multicultural education programs should:

1. Understand the melting-pot ideology and the more realistic contemporary perspectives toward cultural diversity.
2. Understand that cultural differences have value and are enriching to the United States.
3. Understand terms such as *culture, ethnicity, race, social class, gender,* and *sexual orientation.*
4. Address and stand against racism in all forms, regardless of the victim's cultural and racial backgrounds.
5. Form a perspective on culture and cultural diversity that perceives differences as positives rather than disadvantages that must be eliminated.
6. Know that ESL programs may inadvertently contribute to the erosion of students' heritage languages through emphasizing only the gaining of English proficiency without recognizing the linguistic richness that students bring from their cultural backgrounds.

7. Comprehend the principles and debates surrounding CRT to raise awareness, challenge stereotypes, and work towards creating a more just and equitable society.
8. Recognize systematic discrimination. dismantle biased practices, and foster racial literacy involving families to promote diversity, equal opportunities, and inclusivity in schools.

Suggested Learning Activities

1. Suggest several methods of helping children and adolescents develop positive individual and cultural identities. What would be your response to an educator who stated, "My work is teaching content—improving cultural identities is not my job!"?
2. Give at least four examples of racist acts and offer a solution (a difficult task indeed) to each racist act. To what extent should reducing racism be a role of the school?

Suggestions for Collaborative Efforts

Form groups of three or four that, if possible, represent the United States' cultural and gender diversity. Working collaboratively, focus your group's attention on the following:

1. Survey a number of elementary, middle, or secondary schools to determine the cultural composition of the student body. What has been the school's response to meeting the needs of students' cultural differences? What efforts has the school made to teach majority cultures about marginalized cultures and vice versa?
2. Increasingly, gender and gender differences are important topics in multicultural education programs. Does your group feel that gender should be a minor or major emphasis in multicultural education programs? Does your group feel that there is a "culture of gender" or that there is an overemphasis of gender differences? What role should educators play (or not play) in making gender an integral component of multicultural education programs?
3. How inclusive should multicultural education be? Originally, the idea prevailed that the term *multicultural education* included only culture, ethnicity, and race. Now, it has been expanded to include

cultures of gender, sexual orientation, and ability/disability. How inclusive does your group think multiculturalism should be? Have scholars taken the inclusiveness idea too far? Or do we need to make multiculturalism even more inclusive?

Expanding Your Horizons

Additional Books and Journals

Castillo, S. (2023). The battle for trans rights: Political spectacle theory and its implications for education policy. *Sexuality, Gender and Policy*, 6(1), 8–15. https://onlinelibrary.wiley.com/doi/10.1002/sgp2.12057
This article discusses how the growing political polarization and focus on cultural conflicts have led to a rise in legislation and policies specifically directed at transgender and nonbinary students within public education systems.

Nierenberg, A. A. (2023). Hateful and cruel policies will harm trans people. *Psychiatric Annals*, 53(4), 150–151. https://doi.org/10.3928/00485713-202 30321-01
This author discusses how transgender individuals face a multitude of challenges, encompassing issues such as gender dysphoria, depression, elevated suicide rates, and being vulnerable to violence and tasks society with the responsibility to provide support and assistance to address these challenges.

Schuman, J. G. & Reynolds, D. (2023). Attempts at anti-racist teaching by white English teachers of black students. *English Teaching: Practice and Critique*, 22(4), 418–432. www.researchgate.net/publication/372513913_ Attempts_at_anti-racist_teaching_by_white_English_teachers_of_black_ students
The authors examine narratives featuring white English teachers instructing significant numbers of black students, all of whom express antiracist intentions but ultimately fail to fully realize those goals.

Websites

Edutopia – www.edutopia.org/blog/preparing-cultural-diversity-resources-teachers
Discusses cultural and diversity issues within educational settings, and provides resources for teachers to prepare for cultural diversity.

Let's Fight Racism – www.un.org/en/letsfightracism/
Provides real-life stories of racism, xenophobia, and intolerance that are prevalent in all societies.

NAACP – https://naacp.org/
The NAACP is a prominent civil rights organization whose website has resources regarding contemporary issues related to racial injustice, inequality, and discrimination.

Tolerance.org – www.tolerance.org/culture-classroom
This site focuses on stereotypes, tolerance, and diversity within classroom settings.

Part II

Understanding Learners and Their Cultural Backgrounds

Understanding, accepting, and respecting learners from all cultural backgrounds is of primary importance, as is providing them with culturally relevant educational experiences. Part II provides a portrait of children and adolescents in African American, American Indian, Arab American, Asian American, European American, and Hispanic American cultures.

DOI: 10.4324/9781003429531-4

Understanding African American Children and Adolescents

Understanding the material and activities in this chapter will help the reader to:

- Describe the cultural, gender, socioeconomic, familial, and language characteristics of African American children and adolescents.
- List several stereotypes of African American children and adolescents, and explain how these beliefs affect curriculum and school practices.
- Describe the educational achievement of African American children and adolescents, and be able to explain the importance of self-esteem to learning achievement.
- Understand African American English dialect as a valued cultural trait, and be able to explain its importance to achievement in school.
- List several points educators should remember when planning educational experiences for African American children and adolescents.
- Explain the Black Lives Matter movement as well as the violence toward African Americans.

Opening Scenario

Cultural Portrait: Paul: An African American Learner

Paul J., a 16-year-old African American learner, lives with his mother, father, grandmother, one older brother, and two older sisters in a lower middle-class

DOI: 10.4324/9781003429531-5

neighborhood in a large city. Several aunts and uncles and six cousins also live in the immediate neighborhood. William, Paul's father, has completed 11 years of schooling and works in a local manufacturing plant. His mother, Sheila, has had a similar education. She works as a hospital aide.

Paul attends a large urban school, which is approximately 50 percent African American, 30 percent European American, and 20 percent Hispanic American. He is a low achiever and speaks a dialect of English. Paul's neighborhood is predominantly African American, although several Puerto Rican and Cuban families have recently rented houses in the area. Paul already realizes that people of different ethnic backgrounds have different customs and lifestyles.

Paul's teachers are predominantly middle-class African Americans, but he also has Mrs. Smith, a teacher who is middle class and European American. Although Paul tries hard in school, his achievement scores and performance place him below average. His teachers assume that his problems stem from a poor home environment, and they blame Paul and his parents for his difficulties. Although his dialect works well with his parents and in his neighborhood, it is not viewed favorably at school. Sometimes, he does not understand his teacher or the class materials. Mrs. Smith frequently corrects Paul's speech because, she says, students will need to use correct English when they enter the real world.

Paul has experienced several identity crises. He has questioned his success in developing from childhood to adulthood, and he has also questioned the significance of being African American in a predominantly European American society. Although he has learned much about his cultural heritage and is proud to be African American, he also realizes the harmful effects of racism and discrimination. Also, being an adolescent has not been easy. Even though Paul's parents and siblings view him as not yet grown, his peers think he is ready for adult activities. Should he listen to his family, or should he go along with his friends?

Another problem confronting Paul is his education. He is not sure that he will graduate from high school. His grades in middle school were below average, but they are even lower now, and this is his second year in the ninth grade. Paul thinks he can do the work, but his recent academic record discourages him and he admits to having many outside interests. He does not have many behavior problems in school (except perhaps talking with his friends too much at times), but he thinks his teachers are not too interested in him. Also, although he has both African American and European American teachers, he doubts whether any of them really understand what it is like being an African American adolescent in a large urban school. His parents talk with him often about the importance of education and encourage him to do his best work.

When speaking of Paul's lower academic achievement, Mrs. Smith, one of his teachers, feels he does not listen. She says, "I have tried to get him to look at me, but he looks away when I talk to him." Paul claims he is listening, even though he does not look directly at Mrs. Smith as she speaks. Regarding his language, Paul knows Mrs. Smith does not approve of his dialect, but his language works fine at home and with his friends, so he doesn't see any need to change.

Paul feels he is in a bind: He tries to make higher grades, but he just can't seem to do it. He sees himself in the middle. Some African American students make better grades than he does, and others make worse grades. Paul feels the frustration of coping in a school that appears to cater to white students and to expect African Americans to conform to European American expectations.

Although Paul has not confided in his friends, he has several concerns: What will he do if he cannot improve his grades? If his teachers insist that he speak a more standard form of English, will he be able to maintain his cultural heritage? Will he be able to accommodate his parents' insistence on academic achievement, his own motivation, and the expectations of his peers? Sometimes, Paul actually wishes that the adolescent years would end so that he could begin his adult life.

Overview

A responsive multicultural curriculum recognizes the cultural diversity of African American children and adolescents, and provides appropriate educational experiences based on an understanding of both the individual and the culture. The culture of African American children and adolescents, as well as socioeconomic class, family, and language, play significant roles and interact in a complex fashion to create unique learners with individual strengths and needs. Providing appropriate teaching and learning experiences for African American learners requires an understanding of the individual's development, achievement level, and self-esteem. This chapter examines African American children and adolescents and explores educational issues germane to them as learners.

Origins

African American people have lived in the United States for many centuries. Arriving in North America either as explorers or as slaves, African American people have experienced a long history of struggle. The first Africans in the Americas were explorers: Columbus's last voyage to the Americas included an African man, Balboa's crew brought an African man, and an African explored the territory that is now Kansas with Coronado. Africans were among the first non-native settlers. African people were part of the ill-fated South Carolina colony, San Miguel de Guadalupe, in 1526, and African people helped to establish Saint Augustine, Florida, in 1665.

One important distinction deserves understanding: Many multicultural groups elected to immigrate to the United States in hopes of improving their lives, to seek religious freedom, or to get away from oppressive conditions or war-torn areas. Most Africans, on the other hand, were transported against their will to a foreign land and forced to work and live in cruel and inhumane conditions.

African Americans Today

The latest population estimates for the United States indicate that the African American population is more than 50 million (U.S. Census Bureau, 2024b) with most residing in metropolitan areas. Of the U.S. suburban population 20.2 percent were African American according to the 2020 census data (Frey, 2022). This is an increase from the 1990 number of 9 percent. Educators in city schools work with significant numbers of African Americans, but educators in suburban schools will increasingly work with African Americans as more and more move away from the inner city.

Decades after the Civil Rights Movement forced the United States to confront racial inequities, disturbing disparities remain on one of the most basic human levels: blacks get sick more easily, stay sick longer, and die sooner than whites. From birth, a black baby's life expectancy is six-and-a-half years shorter than a white baby's. The black population is more likely to be born weighing too little and less likely to survive their first year. Blacks face a higher risk of asthma, hypertension, and cancer. They are nearly twice as likely as whites to die of a stroke, more likely to die of heart disease, and they face a higher cancer rate than whites.

African Americans cite many reasons for their health predicament: African Americans face extra stresses, have an unhealthy diet (it can be difficult to find fresh vegetables and produce in many inner-city grocery stores), and often mistrust doctors and other healthcare providers (Caraballo et al., 2023). The cumulative effects of health disadvantages and the tendency to avoid medical visits until conditions are critical predispose African American adults to higher incidences of chronic disability and illness. Consequently,

African Americans experience poorer health outcomes and shorter life spans compared to their white counterparts. Although the poverty and low-income factors cannot be ruled out, African Americans' healthcare should be changing and improving with the Affordable Care Act.

African Americans have not shared equally in the nation's prosperity. They earn less than whites and they possess far less wealth. The black-to-white American median income ratio has remained between 50 and 60 percent for the past 20 years. Fluctuations have been minor. In some respects, Americans have grown accustomed to this benchmark of inequality or are not sure how to correct the problem. The median household income in the United States increased from $51,570 in 1967 to $74,580 in 2022 (O'Neill, 2023). In 2022, the median black American household income was $53,500, and $81,060 and $109,400 for whites and Asians, respectively. African Americans have consistently been at the lowest median income levels while Asian Americans have been consistently at the highest. The median household income for Asian Americans has typically been double that of black American households.

Black Lives Matter Movement

Black Lives Matter, or BLM, is a global organization advocating for racial justice and equality, focusing particularly on addressing systemic racism and violence toward black individuals. The BLM organization was founded in 2013 after George Zimmerman was found not guilty in the Florida case of the shooting death of Trayvon Martin, an unarmed African American teenager. The movement has since become the largest mass movement seeking racial justice in US history (Francis & Wright-Rigueur, 2021), and has greatly increased public awareness of the injustice in the criminal justice system, inspiring African American people to seek racial justice. Police brutality and violence toward black Americans catalyzed BLM and triggered nationwide protests across all 50 states in 2020 (Wright et al., 2023). It gained significant traction following the deaths of other black individuals such Michael Brown and Breonna Taylor. BLM was magnified by the last words of George Floyd, "I can't breathe," and "Mom," calling for his protector. He was also video-recorded with a crowd watching, pinned under the knee of a white police officer minutes before his death in 2020 in Minneapolis, Minnesota. It was a pivotal moment for racial justice efforts in the United States and garnered global attention. The BLM movement pushes for policy changes, police reform, and social transformation to ensure that all lives are valued and protected. It specifically highlights the racial biases that African Americans encounter in educational settings and the workforce, revealing their significant underrepresentation in advanced academic programs and leadership positions. By integrating discussions on racial inequality, social justice, and the representation of BLM into the curriculum, teachers can educate all students about the importance of fostering fairness, building an equitable society, and rewarding school environments for African American students.

Stereotyping of African American Children and Adolescents

To be a child or adolescent as well as an African American in a predominantly European American society is to bear a double stigma. Stereotyping has produced negative images of the African American culture and its young people. Youth is the time of identity formation; for this reason, it is especially important that everyone objectively accept social, cultural, and age differences among young people. Young African Americans need fair opportunities to develop identities appropriate for their culture and age. Categorizing African American young people as language deficient because they speak dialectical English or as low achievers with behavior problems negates diversity and individual differences.

Educators must take a closer and more objective look at the child and the adolescent in the African American culture to improve their understanding of the learner and the world in which she or he lives. Such knowledge and understanding gives educators an objective and sound foundation for a multicultural curriculum. Teacher biases can lead to unfairly lower evaluations of students who are black compared to white counterparts, even when their test scores are similar. Childs and Wooten (2023) examined the correlations and consequences of teacher biases experienced by primary and secondary students in the United States. They found that teacher bias was associated with student race, ethnicity, immigration status, as well as other characteristics, and plays a significant role in teachers' perceptions of and attitudes toward African American students. Examples of teacher bias include exclusionary and unfair discipline, microaggressions, name mispronunciations, and disproportionate special education referrals. Teacher bias has created a discipline gap with African American students being suspended and expelled at a much higher rate than their white peers (Baker, 2019; Zhu, 2024). This consequently affects academic performance gaps as students with more missed school days generally have lower scores than students with fewer.

As you recall from the Word of Caution at the beginning of Chapter 2, we must always consider the *individual* child or adolescent. Chapter 3 makes the same point. As we look at African American children and adolescents, we have a professional obligation to consider the individual. As you consider cultural characteristics, gender, socioeconomic status (SES), and other differences, remember that cultural and intracultural differences exist. We cannot speak of a typical African American any more than we can discuss a typical Asian American or Hispanic American. Generalizing about African American culture requires extreme caution and avoidance of stereotypes. The opening cultural portrait describes Paul, an African American adolescent. Paul, like all other students, is unique and deserves to be considered as an individual.

Cultural Characteristics

African American children and adolescents are considerably diverse. Differences exist between lower, middle, and higher socioeconomic groups; between younger and older generations; between African Americans residing in the various geographic locations of the United States; and between urban and rural African Americans. An educator who understands this diversity among African American children and adolescents can make a valuable contribution to the multicultural curriculum and base choices on objective and factual information.

African American children daily face two cultures: The African American culture of the home and neighborhood, and the cultures of schools and other social institutions. African American children and children from other cultures need opportunities to learn about one another's cultures and to understand that *different* does not imply *wrong*.

Education has focused for many years solely on historical and contemporary whites. Educators sometimes justifiably complain that their education did not provide them with examples of the contributions of African Americans. During the past several decades, attempts to instill pride and a better understanding of African American culture have given rise to learning materials that emphasize the many positive aspects and leaders of the culture.

Although educators should make cultural generalizations cautiously, African Americans *tend* to have large families and respect for immediate and extended families. They also *tend* to have a nonverbal communication style that differs from that of European American culture. (For example, an African American feels comfortable interrupting a speaker to show support and does not find it necessary to look the speaker in the eye.) African American children are generally highly expressive emotionally, assertive, and verbal in dealings with peers and adults. African American children and adolescents are taught respect for the elderly, kinship and extended family bonds, and authoritarian child-rearing practices. Once again, the author reminds readers that individuals within a culture differ and that cultural characteristics vary with SES and geographic region.

POINTS TO PONDER 3.1

Identifying Cultural Differences

Make a list of the cultural differences of African Americans. Then, keeping in mind the characteristics you listed, make another list of social class differences. How are the two alike and different? Are the social class differences more alike or different?

A difficult situation exists when African Americans want to retain their cultural heritage, the culture of their ancestors, and the culture with which they can relate and feel comfortable. Some African Americans, however, may also feel that some acculturation with the European Americans is necessary for economic and psychological survival. It is important to attain a middle ground on which African American adolescents can not only retain their African heritage, but also feel successful in contemporary society.

Gender

The recent emphasis on gender differences and gender-appropriate education suggests educators should consider African American females and males from different perspectives. Undoubtedly, educators need to consider females' different learning styles, perceptions of motivation, and ways of responding to educators' efforts. Females, however, may need to give special attention to socially acceptable behaviors such as modulating their voices, proper grooming, and developing assertive demeanors. Such a proposal does not suggest that African American males (as well as males from other cultures) do not need educational experiences in similar areas; when addressing these points, however, educators need to consider the female perspective.

Teachers also should consider gender differences when planning actual educational experiences for African American females. For example, African American females might learn better through cooperative efforts rather than in competitive atmospheres. Also, they might benefit more from behavior management systems promoting positive consequences rather than negative ones. Positive environments also contribute to African American females' academic achievement and social development.

POINTS TO PONDER 3.2

Helping African American Urban Males

Design a strategy to help African American urban boys in either elementary or secondary school. First, decide on a method of determining their needs (either a case study, some diagnostic device, interviews, or observation); second, select instructional methods that reflect their learning styles; third, select curricular materials to which they can relate; fourth, select culturally appropriate assessment devices; and fifth, decide what other guidance or advising topics might address their needs. In addition to these five approaches, what else might you suggest to help African American urban boys?

Gale et al. (2023) maintain that the plight of African American males calls for school-based intervention to combat systematic issues they face in the United States. This is in response to the disturbing statistics that exist about black males. African Americans account for just 13 percent of the total population, yet they account for 39 percent of the prison population (Klein et al., 2023). The unemployment rate among African American males is twice that of people who are white (Mitchell et al., 2002; Moore, 2023). These disturbing statistics have been valid for more than 20 years. Black males have higher suspension, expulsion, retention, and dropout rates as well as dramatically lower grade-point averages. The key strategies in school-based interventions aimed at supporting black males to avoid these dire consequences include using family and community resources, making education more accessible to black youth, and ensuring that learning activities are personally and culturally relevant to their lives (Gale et al., 2023). Still, while alternative schools have their place, we need to be careful that alternative schools do not result in segregation that the United States experienced for decades.

As early as 1790, Africans in the United States created alternative ways to school themselves. Reasons included lack of access to public schools, a threat of miseducation, and a belief that they were responsible for their own education. More recent impetuses to the independent schooling tradition and the black studies movement of the 1960s and 1970s included the Black Power, civil rights, and pan-American movements. The result has been an emergence of schools designed to focus on African American students, such as African American-centered public schools, African American immersion academics, and black male academies (Mitchell et al., 2002).

The National Urban League (2022) calls for greater experimentation with all-male schools, longer school days, and mentoring. All-male schools, such as the Eagle Academy and Enterprise School in the New York City area, combined with mentoring and longer school days, help keep young boys focused on education and away from distractions that might lead to trouble. Mitchell et al. (2002) also recommend alternative schools for African American males. Such schools emphasized academic achievement, study skills development, cultural enrichment activities, counseling and mentorships, parent-education workshops, and sports-related activities to promote healthy development and adult mentors.

Socioeconomic Status

Six key factors determine SES: income, wealth, occupation, education, prestige, and power (Gollnick & Chinn, 2006). In the context of children's home environment, crime, barriers to housing and services, and overall living conditions also have become factors (Dalmaijer et al., 2023). It has been increasingly acknowledged that this oversimplifies the term, and fails to consider each child's individual experience and the variability in developmental outcomes associated with different aspects of SES (Murtha et al., 2023). Notably, there exist racial discrepancies in neighborhood quality. Middle-class African American families often reside in more disadvantaged neighborhoods than their white counterparts. In cities like New York, for instance, neighborhoods vary greatly with respect to resources and safety. Middle-class black families are more likely to live in an area with fewer resources and a higher crime rate than white middle-class families. This circumstance often is due to unfair policies, ideologies, and institutional practices that perpetuate systemic inequality among people of color. Such disparities in living environment can contribute to differences in educational achievement between African American and white students, highlighting the impact of SES on daily life and future opportunities.

SES continues to be a powerful indicator of academic success for American children. Children from higher SES backgrounds score higher on standardized achievement tests, are more likely to finish high school, and are more likely to attend college and do postgraduate work than their less advantaged peers. Because poor children are less likely to pursue higher education, it is difficult to break them out of the cycle of poverty. The relationship between poverty and academic achievement is complicated by ethnicity; a disproportionate number of the poor are members of ethnic marginalized groups. The National Urban League's (2022) *State of Black America* report introduced the most recent equality index, a quantitative tool for tracking racial equality in

America which compares the progress of black and white Americans' equality over time, focusing on economics, health, education, social justice, and civic engagement.

This index shows that African Americans achieve 74 percent of what whites do in SES, indicating a 26 percent gap in achieving equality. Similarly, Hispanic Americans have an equality index of 80 percent, meaning they lack 20 percent of the equality measures compared to whites (National Urban League, 2020). The equality index offers evidence of how slowly change happens, and highlights the need for policies that fight inequality.

The National Urban League proposes a sweeping and decisive solution to the nation's persistent social and economic disparities. The United States needs investments in the following:

◆ Universal early childhood education.
◆ A federal living wage of $25.02 per hour, indexed to inflation.
◆ A plan to fund comprehensive urban infrastructure.
◆ A new Main Street small- and micro-business financing plan focusing on minority- and women-owned businesses.
◆ Expansion of summer youth employment programs.
◆ Expanded homeownership strategies.
◆ Expansion of the Earned Income Tax Credit (EITC).
◆ Targeted re-entry workforce training programs administered through community-based organizations.
◆ Doubling the Pell Grant program to make college more affordable.
◆ Expansion of financial literacy and homebuyer education and counseling.
◆ Expansion of the low-income housing voucher "Section 8" program.
◆ Establishment of Green Empowerment Zones in neighborhoods with high unemployment.
◆ Affordable high-speed broadband and technology for all.
◆ Increased federal funding to local school districts to help eliminate resource equity gaps as America's urban communities continue to struggle socially and economically.

When working with African American learners, elementary and secondary educators should understand the following:

1. the effects of being a member of a lower socioeconomic group;
2. that children from lower socioeconomic groups might not understand words like *physician, lavatory, wraps,* and *pens* (*pens* for writing versus *pens* for confining animals);
3. that language differences are "differences," not "deficits";

4. the need to work first on concrete learning and then move on to abstract learning;

5. the need to provide positive reinforcement during the learning process, rather than expect learners to stay motivated by focusing on some faraway goal;

6. the need to involve parents and extended families in the learning process;

7. each learner's individual strengths and needs, and how to plan teaching and learning experiences that always challenge and instruct.

Today, African Americans have more equality of opportunity, better access to education, and more equitable salaries. Through civil rights legislation, affirmative action programs, and equal employment opportunity, African Americans are able to obtain an education and seek employment. Hopefully such gains will result in improved conditions for children. The problem of poverty, however, continues for many people and requires the attention of government, school, and other organizations concerned with the welfare of children.

Families

Educators who work with African American learners need a historical understanding of and perspective on the African American family. To gain such knowledge might prove difficult, because U.S. scholarship has mistreated, ignored, and distorted the African American family. Often, the misconceptions of majority-culture educators may cause them to question African American cultural traditions. Throughout centuries of cultural oppression and repression, for example, African Americans have developed, perhaps as much through necessity as choice, a network of "significant others" who have close ties to and are willing to assist the individual family. Understanding and accepting this African American family tradition continues to be a prerequisite for educators to help students make effective educational decisions.

Many African American children grow up in homes that are very different from the homes of children and adolescents from other cultures. Extended families of people of color function on the principles of interdependence and an extensive reliance on networks of people, including blood relatives and close friends called *kinsmen*. A young African American child might be taken into the household of elderly grandparents. In such arrangements, children have a sense that they belong to an extended family clan, not merely to their parents. Uncles, aunts, cousins, and grandparents have considerable power within the family unit, and may take responsibility for the care and rearing of children, and for teaching appropriate skills and values.

Religion

Religion is a powerful aspect of the African American family orientation that has almost never had empirical documentation. Rather than study the Church and religion in relation to children, writers usually focus attention on the role of religion in the Civil Rights Movement, economic leadership, and the quest for equal opportunity. Children, however, undoubtedly perceive the African American Church as a socializing and peer-group institution, a hub of social life, and a means to aspire to community leadership. Rather than simply a Sunday morning experience, Church membership for children is an integral aspect of African American family life.

The most rapidly growing religion in the United States is Islam. In 1960, there were no mosques in this country. Now, mosques are relatively common and the religion's membership is growing daily. Muslims are a rapidly increasing part of the American religious scene. The United States needs to appreciate the gifts—their culture, their music, their food, and their philosophy—they bring to U.S. society. It is in schools that people first start adapting to Muslim cultures and Muslims begin adapting to other U.S. cultures.

Language

The language of African American children is a function of their culture and plays a significant role in their cultural identity, school achievement, and social and psychological development. Although the child may not experience communication difficulties at home or in the neighborhood, language differences may cause problems when significant variations exist between home and neighborhood and school languages. Children's language skills are crucial in their education, and much of what educators measure as intelligence and achievement is actually skill in language and communication.

Aspects of African American oral tradition are observable in African American student behavior. In telling stories, African Americans render abstract observations about life, love, and people in the form of concrete narrative sequences that may seem to meander from the point and to take on an episodic framework. In African American communication styles, we often find overt demonstration of sympathetic involvement through movement and sounds; a prescribed method for how performer and audience react; total involvement of the participants; the tendency to personalize by incorporating personal pronouns and references to self (African American students tend to use first-person singular pronouns to focus attention on themselves); and the use of active verbs coupled with adjectives and adverbs with potential for intensification (called *features of elongation* and *variable stress*). Prosodic structure of speech often reflects the way information is organized for presentation. All of these observable aspects of the African American communication style provide leads for teaching innovations (Anokye, 1997). Despite facing assimilation into mainstream society and enduring cultural and linguistic oppression in the United States, many African Americans have upheld their cultural identity and communication style by speaking African American Vernacular English, or AAVE (Lyn, 2022). Linguists and cultural anthropologists support the theory that AAVE represents a fusion of West African language traditions and English vocabulary. When African Americans were forcibly taken from Africa, where many languages were spoken, they developed a hybrid language to effectively communicate in the United States. This amalgamation reflects the creolization process, wherein African descendants created new cultural and communicative forms. Additionally, black Americans devised distinct linguistic traditions for private and public discourse as a form of resistance. For instance, enslaved black people utilized coded language to conceal messages of solidarity and rebellion from their white enslavers. Similarly, AAVE serves as a deliberate and culturally significant mode of expression to assert their emotions privately and publicly.

Educators can benefit from objective and reliable information about African American language. Although the child may not experience difficulty at home or in the neighborhood, language differences may cause problems when the child gets to school. The dilemma for African American children is that their language, which is worthy at home, may be different and unworthy in school.

Considerable diversity exists in the degree to which children speak an English dialect. Dialect use varies with SES, geographic location, and the acculturation of the child and the parents. Children of educated and socially mobile urban African American parents may not speak the dialect of rural and less fortunate parents. African American English is used in varying degrees depending on the individual and the situation.

African Americans have developed effective nonverbal communication that other cultures may question. For example, African American children may learn early that active listening does not always require looking the speaker in the eye. Nor is it necessary to nod one's head or make little noises to show that one is listening.

The language of African American children, albeit an excellent means of communication in the African American culture, may result in communication difficulties and other problems generally associated with not being understood outside one's social community. Furthermore, children who hear negative statements about their language and who are urged to change to a more standard form of English will undoubtedly have lower self-esteem and opinions of their own cultural backgrounds.

The grammatical structure of African American speech patterns frequently leads listeners to conclude that a genuine structural pattern does not exist. Linguists acquainted with the various vernaculars of African American English realize the fallacy of such thinking. African American speakers who say "Carl hat" and "she book" might have knowledge of possessives in grammar like the speaker who says "Mary's hat" and "his book."

Achievement Levels

Objectivity is fundamental in considering the African American child's achievement. There is no room for stereotypes of achievement expectations.

A key concern arising from these findings is that teachers' perceptions of student achievement may be influenced by factors other than student performance, such as negative stereotypes or biases towards certain groups along gender or race lines. This underscores the importance of understanding the nature of biases in student assessment. Existing studies looking at racial discrepancies in teachers' evaluations of student achievement have found that teachers assess black students as lower performing compared to white students, conditional on standardized test scores (Botelho et al., 2015; Burgess & Greaves, 2013).

The National Assessment of Educational Progress (NAEP) provides, on a large scale, scores on how American students are performing across time in various grades and subjects. It measures achievement gaps by comparing scores across race and ethnic groups such as African American and white students.

In 2022, the NAEP reading assessment was administered to representative samples of fourth- and eighth-grade students across the nation. The reading assessment of grade 12 students was last administered nationally in 2019. Students also were given survey questions addressing the opportunities they had to read in and out of school. Literary as well as informational content to assess reading comprehension skills were included in the 2022 assessment.

The COVID-19 pandemic led to a drop in advanced academic achievements across all racial and ethnic groups, and among students from higher SES as well. Results showed that 2022 reading scores had decreased by three points from 2019 for both fourth- and eighth-grade students. Students of lower SES and those already struggling academically were most negatively affected by the COVID-19 pandemic.

Specifically, the NAEP results show that reading scores for African American students are much lower than those of their white counterparts; by 28 points for fourth- and eighth-grade students. This is a continuation of a pattern first recorded in 1992, with the gap ranging from 26 to 32 points. African American students score consistently lower than their peers from other racial groups as well (National Assessment of Educational Progress, 2022).

The NAEP data shows that students from higher SES within each racial/ethnic group tend to score at advanced levels more often. As SES decreases, so does the percentage of students reaching advanced levels in their achievement (Coffey & Tyner, 2023). The data also reveals a concerning trend in the disparities in educational achievement between black and white students, reflecting broader SES gaps between them and highlighting the inequality in access to quality instruction, resources, and a supportive learning environment. Educators are increasingly concerned about the trend of school resegregation and its impact on student achievement gaps. Schools with a higher percentage of African American students, especially in urban areas, show lower academic achievement for both African American and white students than those with fewer African American students (Bohrnstedt et al., 2015).

However, when accounting for factors such as student SES and other student, teacher, and school characteristics, the analysis found:

◆ White student achievement in schools with the highest black student density did not differ from white student achievement in schools with the lowest density.
◆ For black students overall, and black males in particular, achievement was still lower in the highest density schools than in the lowest density schools.
◆ The black–white achievement gap was larger in the highest density schools than in the lowest density schools.
◆ Conducting analysis by gender, the black–white achievement gap was larger in the highest density schools than in the lowest density schools for males but not for females.

  In summary, the size of the achievement gap within each category was smaller when the analysis accounted for SES and other student, teacher, and school characteristics, which suggests that these factors have a considerable impact.

Selected instructional strategies for African Americans include the following:

- Validating the African American culture and worldview, moving away from a cultural deficit model and supporting a sense of social justice.
- Showing appreciation for the African American dialect and for its tradition of oral discourse.
- Showing children and adolescents the value of African Americans' informal language interactions and writings.
- Instilling a sense of trust, community, and social justice among students and teachers.
- Using group projects that demonstrate an appreciation for collaborative efforts.
- Fostering a school and class climate of cooperation, collaboration, empathy, and social consciousness.

Although statistics reveal lower academic achievement among African Americans, it is important to understand the situation in its historical perspective. For years, many African Americans attended segregated schools in which instruction and materials were often substandard. Substantial progress has been made toward the provision of educational resources to African Americans, but educational opportunities are still not always equal.

African American learners face a brighter and more optimistic future. First, African Americans now receive more equitable educational opportunities. Second, more opportunities in employment, education, and housing will allow their families an improved standard of living. Third, educators are better trained in diagnostic and remediation approaches and individualized education. Fourth, educators are translating the research on effective teaching, which has grown considerably during the past 20 years, into practical application.

The following are some suggestions for working with elementary and secondary learners:

1. Get to know individual children and their strengths and weaknesses. Hold high expectations for *all* your students.
2. Disregard stereotypes about African American behavior and academic achievement.
3. Administer interest inventories to determine needs and areas in which instruction might be most effective.

4. Administer culturally appropriate diagnostic tests to determine which areas require remediation.
5. Work to convince learners that they can learn and achieve.
6. Work to improve learners' attitudes about the African American culture.
7. Teach, evaluate, and reteach basic skills.

POINTS TO PONDER 3.3

Instructional Strategies for African Americans

Consider the instructional strategies just mentioned for African Americans. What other methods do you suggest for developing a sense of trust, community, and social justice? How can we develop classes and schools that do not reflect the cultural deficit model? This effort should not be a matter of improving self-esteem; it should be an effort to change the mindsets of both students and teachers.

Other suggestions include improving teaching practices and creating a more credible education system for African American students.

- Use parents as resources to learn about their children, and use their expertise to provide a culturally relevant curriculum.
- Consider classroom materials to ensure that students experience learning materials that reflect positively on their culture.
- Facilitate learning by increasing variety, space, and opportunity for social interaction and movement.

School Practices Promoting African Americans' Progress

Educators sometimes develop and implement curricula that either overlook or ignore cultural diversity. African American learners may find themselves in a world of unfamiliar rules, expectations, and orientations. Rather than recognize cultural diversity and teach learners as individuals, educators often treat learners as groups with homogeneous characteristics.

Conversely, school practices should promote learning achievement and appropriate behavior such as the following:

1. Understanding African American learners and expecting all learners to conform to specific standards and expectations.

2. Grouping by heterogeneous ability, which does not result in the segregation of learners by culture and by social class.
3. Providing sufficient and appropriate positive reinforcement.
4. Understanding learners who speak English dialects.
5. Basing academic and behavior standards and expectations on objective expectations.

School practices related to the assessment of children and adolescents is another area that can impede African American learners' progress. Assessment devices designed primarily for middle-class learners do not always provide an accurate assessment of African American learners.

Promoting Cultural Identities

Several studies have sought to ascertain the effects of minority group status on personality development during identity formation. These studies provide concrete evidence for long-held opinions that the society and the culture in which African Americans live adversely affects their personality development, and educational achievement.

The African American child or adolescent's self-perception influences not only his or her academic achievement, but also many other social and psychological aspects of development. Distinctive aspects affecting self-esteem include children's perception of themselves, how others perceive them to be, and how they perceive others. Historically, African Americans have experienced much to lower their self-esteem, but civil rights efforts and recent decades of progress have helped raise it.

The identity formation of the African American adolescent has been a source of considerable concern, especially in poverty-ridden households and single-parent homes. Specifically, single mothers do not usually perceive their families as "broken," because fathers and the extended family and kinship network continue to play a role in their lives. The physical presence or absence of adult males in the home says little about the availability of other male role models.

Suggestions for educators working with African American children and adolescents include the following:

1. Be open and honest in relationships with African American children.
2. Seek to respect and appreciate culturally different attitudes and behaviors.
3. Take advantage of all available opportunities to participate in activities in the African American community.

4. Keep in mind that African American children are members of their unique cultural group and are unique individuals as well.
5. Implement practices that acknowledge the African American culture.
6. Hold high expectations of African American children, and encourage all who work with African American children to do likewise.
7. Develop culture-specific strategies, mechanisms, techniques, and programs to foster the psychological development of African American children.

As mentioned in Chapter 2, LGBTQIA+ African American youths (ages 14–19) have a unique set of stressful life events, low self-esteem, emotional distress, and multiple problem behaviors (alcohol use, drug use, and risky sexual behavior). Admitting their sexual orientation or having it discovered by others can expose LGBTQIA+ learners to ridicule. LGBTQIA+ youths cannot anticipate how others may respond to knowledge of their sexual identity. Stressful events related to being LGBTQIA+ have been shown to cause significant emotional distress and multiple problem behaviors.

CASE STUDY 3.1

Responding to Parents' Demands

A vocal group of African American parents presents to the school board a list of demands for improving the school. They feel that the education their children are receiving does not meet the needs of African Americans. Two of their demands are to create all-male African American classes and to have African American male teachers for kindergarten through grade 3. Concerns also include the high rate of special-education placements of African American students.

Clearly, some action is necessary to change the attitudes of these parents toward the schools and to create schools that better meet the needs of African American learners. Failing to listen and respond appropriately to the parents' concerns will only result in frustration for the parents, school officials, and children attending the schools.

Recall from the Gender section of this chapter that the National Urban League (2022) has also recommended separate schools for African American females and males. Another concern focuses on students like Paul in the opening scenario—African American males who do not seem to fit in the public school system. Also, as we look at this Case Study, we should recall Ford et al.'s (2023) concern that African American boys are too often placed in special-education classes yet underrepresented in gifted classes.

Questions for Discussion

1. As a school board member, how would you respond to the parents' concerns? If you intend to give them what they want, then what will you do when another cultural group wants gender-specific and cultural-specific classes (which can lead to segregation)? If you cannot give them what they want, how will you somehow compromise to help the students and their parents?
2. What do you think about all-male and all-female schools? What are the advantages and disadvantages? What would be the likely effects on academic achievement and social development?
3. Why do you think African Americans are overrepresented in special-education classes and underrepresented in gifted classes? Think beyond the cultural deficit model and consider social justice (discussed in Chapter 1). Is this a violation of social justice? How can we resolve these placement problems and promote social justice?

Summing Up

Educators planning a culturally responsive curriculum and school environment for African American learners should:

1. Understand the African American culture and its people from both historical and contemporary perspectives.
2. Understand the close correlation between SES and academic achievement among African American learners (and learners of other cultures).
3. Address the dilemma of African American English, which needs understanding and appropriate action: African Americans understand one another in home and community situations, yet they sometimes experience difficulty in school and teaching and learning situations. Remember that *different* does not equate with *wrong* or *inferior*.
4. Promote cultural identities that are crucial to African American learners' academic achievement, psychosocial development, and general outlook on life.

5. Consider and address African American students' learning styles when planning teaching and learning experiences.
6. Consider intracultural, geographic, socioeconomic, urban and rural, and other differences that result in individuality, rather than categorizing all African American learners as a homogeneous group.
7. Understand several factors (appropriate diagnostic and remediation procedures, improving self-esteem, basic skills instruction) that have the potential for improving African American academic achievement.
8. Adhere to the commitment that educators should not stereotype African American learners or label them as slow learners. Educators also must not group learners in organization patterns that result in segregation by either culture or social class.

Suggested Learning Activities

1. Complete a case study of two African American learners, each from a different social class—for example, one from a lower class and one from a higher social class. Compare and contrast differences in culture, language, familial traditions, food, and life expectations.
2. The family, both immediate and extended, is a valued aspect of the African American culture. How can educators use this resource? What can educators do to involve African American families? What special concerns should educators keep in mind during parent conferences?
3. Debate the role of standardized testing and the Common Core Standards in educational equity. Make a presentation on how standardized tests impact African American males' placement in special education and gifted programs.

Implementing Research

Race, Disability, and Giftedness

This implementing research focuses on African American students being placed in special education (SPED) classes. Ford et al. (2023) highlight the unique challenges and biases that African Americans face and discuss the disproportionate representation of black male students in special-education programs versus gifted and talented programs and Advanced Placement (AP) courses. While comprising 7.7 percent of all students in the United States,

African American boys make up 11.8 percent of SPED placements; specifically, they are overrepresented in "high-incidence, subjective, and test-driven categories" such as developmental delays, learning disabilities, emotional and behavioral disabilities, and ADHD. This is likely a result of schools' over-reliance on standardized test scores that often result in mislabels for African American male students. Their low test scores also bar them from participating in gifted and talented programs and AP courses. Black students of all genders make up 17 percent of the K–12 students in the United States, however, they are only 7.3 percent of the gifted and talented student body. Thirty-five percent are in special education which impacts them negatively. This erodes the academic opportunities and potential of black students who suffer from the vicious cycle of deficit thinking and standardized testing inequities.

Implementing the Research

1. Vigilantly identify and address factors that impede the academic performance of black students such as test biases or personal biases.
2. Investigate alternative testing options that allow students of all backgrounds to thrive and showcase their strengths.
3. Practice culturally responsive teaching methods to create an inclusive classroom environment.

Source: Ford, D. Y., Hines, E. M., Middleton, T. J., & Moore, J. L. (2023). Inequitable representation of Black boys in gifted and talented education, Advanced Placement, and special education. *Journal of Multicultural Counseling and Development*, *51*, 304–314. https://doi-org.proxy.lib.odu.edu/10.1002/jmcd.12283

Suggestions for Collaborative Efforts

Form groups of three or four that, if possible, represent the United States' cultural and gender diversity. Working collaboratively, focus your group's attention toward the following efforts:

1. Conduct an in-depth study of English dialects. Divide learning assignments in such a manner that each group member has an individual task, such as providing specific examples of dialectical differences, providing names of textbooks and other curricular materials that positively reflect dialects, and reviewing the literature on dialects. Working collaboratively, discuss how children and

adolescents who are able to communicate in home and community situations may experience difficulties communicating in school.

2. Design a study (case studies, interviews, anecdotal records) to learn more about several African American families. Determine cultural, intracultural, and socioeconomic differences. How do these families differ in dress and food preferences, customs, and family behaviors? What other evidence can you find of tremendous diversity among African American families? How can the school provide a curriculum that responds to the African American family?

3. Reread the opening scenario about Paul and his academic difficulties. Also review the section on Gender, in which the National Urban League (2022) suggests all-male schools for African American boys, and reconsider the Case Study, in which parents want all-male schools and all-male teachers in kindergarten through grade 3. In your group, make a list of the advantages and disadvantages of all-male schools for African Americans. Why would the National Urban League make this recommendation? Does this sound like just another form of segregation? Will such schools prepare African Americans to live and work with people of other cultures?

Expanding Your Horizons

Additional Books and Journals

Adler, R. M., Rittle-Johnson, B., Hickendorff, M., & Durkin, K. (2024). A longitudinal examination of the relations between motivation, math achievement, and STEM career aspirations among Black students. *Contemporary Educational Psychology, 76*, 102–240.

The study investigated math motivation and science, technology, engineering and mathematics (STEM) career aspirations of tenth-grade African American students. While early math motivation predicted math achievement, it did not influence students' interest in STEM careers, suggesting the need for more research to understand how to nurture black students' STEM aspirations.

Egalite, A. (2024). What we know about teacher race and student outcomes: A review of the evidence to date. *Education Next, 24*(1), 42–49.

Policymakers, using federal grants to HBCUs, are actively working to increase the number of black teachers in public schools. This initiative is informed by research suggesting students of color benefit from being taught by teachers of the same race.

Williams III, O., Davis, J., & Cox, M. (2023). Partnership with a school system to implement an Africentric rites of passage program for middle school Black boys. *Psychology in the Schools*, *60*(12), 5099–5114. https://doi-org.proxy.lib.odu.edu/10.1002/pits.23092

This text describes a school-based intervention aimed to "socialize, educate, and nurture Black male students in their journey toward manhood, utilizing Afrocentric principles."

Websites

About.com: African American history – https://afroamhistory.about.com
Major topics on this site include Arthur Ashe, radical reconstruction, *Brown* v. *Board of Education*, Louis Armstrong, and the Montgomery bus boycott.

Black Educational Advocacy Coalition – www.thebeac.org/
This organization aims to secure high quality educational experiences for black students by focusing on academic achievement, leadership, voice, collaboration, and student safety and well-being.

History.com – www.history.com/topics/black-history/black-history-facts
Provides historical highlights of African American history including articles, videos, and speeches.

National Urban League – https://nul.org/
This organization develops social programs, conducts public policy research, and advocates for policies and services that close the equality gap.

Understanding American Indian Children and Adolescents

Understanding the material and activities in this chapter will help the reader to:

◆ Describe the cultural, socioeconomic, and familial characteristics of American Indian children and adolescents.

◆ Explain special problems and challenges that confront American Indian children and adolescents.

◆ Describe American Indian learners and their development and achievement levels.

◆ List several educational practices that impede the American Indian learners' educational progress.

◆ Offer several suggestions and strategies for improving American Indian learners' cultural identities.

◆ List several points that educators of American Indians should remember when planning teaching and learning experiences.

Opening Scenario

Cultural Portrait: 14-Year-Old John

John attends a school off the reservation. The student population is a mixed group of American Indians, some Hispanic Americans, a few African

DOI: 10.4324/9781003429531-6

Americans, and some European Americans. Although the school includes several culturally diverse groups, most of the teachers are European American, and the school environment and educational program are oriented toward traditional white expectations.

John has several problems that result, at least in part, from his lack of proficiency in English. He must be able to function in a bilingual world. While his family continues to use the native language it has spoken for centuries, he must speak English at school. (Some of his friends have been punished for not speaking English.) Meanwhile, his grades are failing, he does not always understand the teacher (and vice versa), and he experiences difficulty as he ventures outside the social confines of his native culture.

John also has several academic and social problems: He makes below-average grades, feels he does not have many friends, and generally feels uncomfortable while in school, perhaps due to his language problems. Everything seems rushed, and cooperation is second to competition. His teachers feel he is not trying, and the overall curriculum makes little sense to him. John is interested in the ancient traditions of his people, yet his teachers rarely address his cultural interests or, in fact, any of his interests. He realizes that his grades need to improve, yet he does not always understand the teachers or the way they teach. Although John has American Indian friends, he has few friends among the students of other cultures. School is often frustrating for John, as he strives to make it through another day.

One of John's teachers, Ms. Lawler, recognizes his problems and potential and has made an effort to help. She has decided to do the following:

1. Arrange for John to visit the language specialist or a bilingual teacher, who can determine the extent of his difficulty and plan an appropriate course of action.
2. Arrange for John to visit the guidance counselor, who may be able to help him widen his circle of friends.
3. Spend some time alone with John to determine his strengths, weaknesses, and interests.
4. Reassess her teaching to see whether her methods match John's style of learning and knowing.
5. Build on John's interest in his cultural heritage through appropriate reading and other curricular materials.

Ms. Lawler also has another idea that she wants to try. Having John read and study about his own cultural background might show him that the curriculum values his American *Indian* culture and recognizes his individual needs and interests. Just as important, Ms. Lawler will provide a curriculum that gives other learners an appropriate multicultural understanding of the

American Indian culture. There are many possible ways to help John and improve his feelings about school and himself. All John's teachers should recognize the importance of showing interest in him and providing first-hand and individual help in improving his academic and social progress.

Overview

American Indian children and adolescents have special needs that warrant educators' understanding: Cherished and unique cultural characteristics, language problems, familial traditions, and learning problems, all of which present schools with special challenges. Yet teacher-education programs traditionally have not prepared prospective teachers to understand multicultural populations and the special characteristics and learning problems of American Indian learners or, in reality, any other multicultural group. This chapter examines American Indian learners—their culture, language issues, families, achievement levels, and overall school programs.

Origins

Scholars do not know exactly when people first came to the Americas. While many archaeologists have concluded that the lack of fossils rules out the possibility of men and women having evolved in the Western hemisphere, some American Indians believe that they originated in the Americas. Archaeologists believe that the ancestors of American Indians came from Asia.

Portman and Herring (2001) offer an excellent description of American Indian history. (It is important to note that Portman and Herring preferred the term *Native American Indian* rather than *Native American* or *American Indian*.) The long history of interaction between Native American Indians and European Americans can be divided into five time periods, which have been determined largely by the interaction of the federal government with Native American Indians: (1) removal (seventeenth century to the 1840s), characterized by the saying "The only good Indian is a dead Indian" (Portman & Herring, 2001, p. 186); (2) reservation (1860s to 1920s), characterized by the saying "Kill the Indian, but save the person"; (3) reorganization (1930s to 1950s), when schools were allowed on the reservation, which eased cultural repression; (4) termination (1950s to 1960s), characterized by attempts at sociocultural integration and the end of dependence on the federal government, which led to the sale of large tracts of Native American Indian lands and increased poverty; and (5) self-determination

(1973 to present), characterized by increased tribal sovereignty due mainly to the militant struggles of many Native American Indians in the early 1970s. Portman and Herring (2001) maintain that these time periods cannot be considered exclusive of each other because of the oral histories that were passed from one generation to the next in Native American Indian cultures. The experiences of past generations are continued in some degree by those Native American Indians who have maintained cultural and familial ties (Portman & Herring, 2001). Cooke (2023) questioned traditional research that oversimplified the history of Indian removal by interpreting it from a perspective that focused solely on conflicts between Indians and Anglo-Americans. In U.S. history books, Indians have often been portrayed inaccurately and presented through a negative lens that reinforces stereotypes by portraying them as violent savages in contrast to supposedly civilized Anglo settlers to explain the control and dominance of settlers over the land. With biased views, settlers justified their claims to the land and worked to undermine the legitimacy of Native Indians' ownership of the land they occupied by depicting Indians in a negative light. Cooke (2023) underscores the need for researchers to rectify past inaccuracies in historical representations by highlighting Native American cultures, their rich traditions, and their vibrant contributions to society. He argues that there are deeper issues of identity maintenance, power dynamics, and justice—far beyond just a Native Americans–white settlers conflict.

American Indians Today

American Indians number more than 500 tribes of varying sizes. The larger tribes include the Cherokee, Navajo, Chippewa, and Sioux. Fourteen tribes have populations between 10,000 and 21,000. Many tribes have less than 10,000. Nearly one-half of American Indians today live west of the Mississippi River. In fact, more than half of the American Indian population lives in just six states: Oklahoma, California, Arizona, New Mexico, Alaska (with large numbers of Aleuts), and Washington. The population is diverse in terms of tribes, clans, reservation and off-reservation living, and socioeconomic status. There is, in fact, no "typical" American Indian. The American Indian population is young and growing as well, which indicates that it will continue to increase. Per the most recent U.S. Census Bureau (2023b) data, the American Indian and Alaska Native (AI/AN), both alone and in combination with other races, numbers approximately 6.3 million, or roughly 2.9 percent of the total U.S. population. This reflects a significant increase from earlier counts and highlights a trend of growth of the

AI/AN population. Nationwide, there are approximately 459,000 American Indian and Alaska Native (AI/AN) K–12 students and 180,000 Native Hawaiian and Other Pacific Islander (NHOPI) K–12 students enrolled in public schools (National Center for Education Statistics, 2021). This represents approximately 1 percent and 0.4 percent of all K–12 public-school students, respectively.

The U.S. Census Bureau (2023b) provides some interesting characteristics of the American Indian population:

- The educational attainment of American Indians continues to improve, although educators' jobs are far from done. An extremely low portion of the American Indian population holds college and advanced degrees. Among those aged 25 and over, only 15.5 percent of American Indians hold a bachelor's degree or higher and just 5.3 percent have a graduate or professional degree.
- The vast majority, 93 percent of AI/AN students and 92 percent of NHOPI students, attend public schools. This is encouraging.
- Among the AI/AN population aged three and over enrolled in school, 43.8 percent were in grades 1–8.
- Among American Indians aged five and over, 32.1 percent spoke a language other than English at home.
- Among those aged 16 and over, 58.9 percent were in the labor force.
- Veterans accounted for 6.3 percent of the civilian population aged 18 and over.
- Median household income was $50,183. Many American Indians live below the poverty line. Native Indian youth are especially affected by poverty. The child poverty rate for American Indians is 31 percent, 27 percent for Native Hawaiian, and just 11 percent for white children. In addition, a substantial percentage of Native American students attend high-poverty public schools: more than one-third (37 percent) of AI/AN students and one-quarter (25 percent) of NHOPI students, compared to only 8 percent for their white counterparts.

Over the past several decades, American Indians have been progressively moving off reservation lands. As a result, many American Indians live in non-Indian communities. Movement from reservation to off-reservation settings can harm family relationships and increase the likelihood of risk-taking behaviors that endanger health and well-being. Because educational behaviors and attitudes may result from other stresses in students' lives, off-reservation adolescents may be even more prone to educational problems than their on-reservation peers.

POINTS TO PONDER 4.1

Learning about American Indians: Their Tribes and Individuals

The American Indian population represents many different tribes and peoples—it is difficult to offer generalizations and conclusions. Bearing in mind tribal and individual differences, suggest four or five ways you could learn about the American Indian students in your class.

Stereotyping of American Indian Children and Adolescents

Although stereotypical images often accompany the term *American Indian*, this culture and its developmental periods constitute a highly diverse group. Differences in developing children and adolescents vary significantly. Not all American Indians are slow learners, shy, and undependable; likewise, not all adolescents are rebellious and experience difficult and stressful times. Although some common characteristics emerge from the study of American Indian children and adolescents, we must use caution not to oversimplify or ignore individual differences.

As the author has emphasized thus far, we need to be careful to speak of *individuals* in a culture. While some American Indians experience poverty on a daily basis, others have been successful in their educational and financial endeavors. A multitude of differences exists among tribes, clans, and geographic regions, as well as among American Indians living on reservations and off reservations. For too long, American Indians have been stereotyped without regard for differences in gender, social class, and sexual orientation. As we explore the American Indian population, the author wants readers to always remember the diversity of this culture.

American Indians might be the most misunderstood cultural group in the United States, mainly because many people have such limited knowledge of the American Indian culture. Even in areas where the concentration of American Indians is high (e.g. the West), most people do not know much about American Indian history and culture. Thus, many people adopt negative stereotypes, such as that American Indians are drunks, get free money from the government, and receive large sums of money from their casinos. Others assume all American Indians are at one with nature, deeply religious, and wise in ways of spirituality.

Cultural Characteristics

American Indian culture plays a major role in the shaping of children and adolescents. Educators must make the extra effort to seek accurate information and to understand American history and the American Indian culture from the point of view of the American Indian child and adolescent. Educators should also think through their own cultural beliefs and realize the dangers of *cultural substitution*, in which American Indian learners are expected to change cultural viewpoints.

American Indians have some values and beliefs that differ from those of other cultures. Some Americans believe that individuals have freedoms as long as their actions remain within the law; American Indian children are taught that all actions must be in harmony with nature. Other values conveyed to children and adolescents include a degree of self-sufficiency and being in harmony with knowledge they gain from the natural world. Adults teach youth to respect and protect the aged, who provide wisdom and acquaint the young with traditions, customs, legends, and myths.

Societal and cultural beliefs and traditions of the American Indian people particularly influence developing adolescents and their evolving identities. Adolescents living in American Indian families and attending European American schools, whether on or off the reservation, experience degrees of cultural confusion and often question allegiance to a cultural identification. Such a dilemma can pose a particularly serious problem for adolescents who want to retain their rich cultural heritage while seeking acceptance in European American schools and society.

American Indian adolescents must also resolve cultural differences surrounding the concept of sharing. Sharing represents a genuine and routine way of life in the American Indian culture. Yet this cultural belief, which is so deeply ingrained in the American Indian culture, does not equate with the European American custom of accumulating private property or savings. The accumulation of material possessions is the measure of most people's worth and social status, but the American Indian considers the ability and willingness to share to be most worthy. While younger children may wish to share only with adults, acceptance of and allegiance to the cultural tradition of sharing increase as the child or adolescent develops. Adolescence is a unique time to develop a concept of sharing that is congruent with American Indian cultural expectations.

Several reasons exist for adolescents becoming increasingly cognizant and accepting of this cultural expectation. Adolescents have more advanced intellectual abilities that enable them to recognize that it is possible for two people to want the same thing at the same time, that shared possessions often return, and that sharing can be reciprocal. Developing intellectual skills allows an adolescent to understand the difference between sharing temporarily and donating permanently. The adolescent can understand, as well as make clear to others, his or her intent. Other notable cultural characteristics of

American Indians that become an integral part of children's and adolescents' evolving identity are the tendencies toward patience and passive temperaments. American Indians are taught to be patient, to control emotions, and to avoid passionate outbursts over small matters. As the American Indian adolescent develops an identity, cultural characteristics such as poise and self-containment become ingrained.

POINTS TO PONDER 4.2

The American Indian Concept of Sharing

Mrs. Jason was upset with eight-year-old Bill, an American Indian, when she learned that he had taken a pencil off another child's desk. The week before, he had taken a pencil off her desk. "What's wrong with Bill?" she wondered. She asked a friend, "I told him about taking other people's things. I just cannot understand him. Why does he continue to take things that don't belong to him?"

How would you handle Bill's situation? Is he stealing or sharing? What would you say if a teacher accused him of stealing yet he said he was just borrowing it? This can be a complex issue because of the cultural differences on what constitutes *sharing* versus *stealing*.

Such characteristics often lead to a mistaken perception that the American Indian is lazy, uncaring, and inactive. This demeanor or personality trait is also demonstrated in American Indians' tendency to lower their voices to communicate anger, unlike European American adolescents, who learn to raise their voices to convey a message.

Noninterference with others and a deep respect for the rights and dignity of individuals constitute basic premises of American Indian culture. Although such practices may have allowed people of other cultures to think of American Indians as uncaring or unconcerned, the actual case is quite the contrary. American Indians are taught early to respect the rights and privileges of other individuals and the responsibility to work together toward a common goal in harmony with nature.

Gender

Gender is another difference that makes American Indian children and adolescents unique. As in other cultures, American Indian females differ from males in their ways of thinking, behaving, and learning. Undoubtedly, American Indian females are also taught certain cultural and tribal beliefs from birth that influence their roles. Educators working with American Indians need to address females' particular gender differences, rather than assuming too much homogeneity between males and females. While research studies focusing specifically on American Indian females are virtually nonexistent, it is obvious that gender differences exist. As with other differences that multicultural educators work to address, gender differences also deserve consideration.

Portman and Herring (2001) offer several generalizations about American Indian women today. While these generalizations are useful in providing a glimpse of Native American Indian women, it is also important to consider tribal and other differences. First, Native American Indian women continue to maintain a respect for the power of words. They are socialized to use words positively (e.g. to inform, think, reconcile others) as well as negatively (e.g. to insult or threaten). Many also use disclaimers about their humbleness and limitations prior to expressing an opinion. Native American Indian women also are encouraged to be strong and resilient in the face of tragedy.

Second, Portman and Herring (2001) also maintain that there are some indications of a positive correlation between the number of Native American Indian women in the labor force and the suicide rate of Native American Indian women. As more American Indian women entered the labor force, their suicide rates increased. Comparative data indicates that American Indian females are more likely than males to have attempted suicide, and young adults face the highest risk of suicide death.

Third, the effects of forced assimilation have destroyed the complementary nature of female–male relations and have resulted in a general increase of Native American Indian male control over women. Women held many complementary positions in the tribes, as did men. When European men colonized the New World, they imposed a male-dominated system of "gynocide" (Portman & Herring, 2001, p. 193).

Socioeconomic Status

Statistically, American Indians in the United States are among the poorest economically, the least employed, and the unhealthiest. Their education and income levels are low, and they are among the worst-housed ethnic groups. There are, however, signs of improvement in each area.

Civil rights legislation and the strong will and determination of the American Indian population are enabling these people to improve their lot in life. Some of their lands contain rich energy resources. Specifically, the Southern Utes in Colorado, the Uinta-Ouray Utes in Utah, and the Blackfeet in Montana have gas and oil reserves, as do the Shoshones and Arapaho in Wyoming. Similarly, the Bannocks and Shoshones, whose reservations are in Idaho, own one of the largest phosphate deposits in the West. The Navajo and Hopi reservations in the Southwest contain vast oil and gas fields as well as uranium reserves.

Attempting to break the bonds of poverty, other American Indians today are making notable achievements. Some American Indians have engaged in business ventures that have had considerable successes. The Navajo Nation produces electronic missile assemblies for General Dynamics; the Choctaws of Mississippi build wire harnesses for Ford Motor Company; the Seminoles in Florida own a 156-room hotel; and the Swinomish Indians of Washington state plan a 60-acre boat basin, an 800-slip marina, and a three-story office and commercial headquarters.

As such, indigenous communities, including American Indians, Alaska Natives, and Native Hawaiians, boast a rich tradition of entrepreneurship and small business ownership. According to the U.S. Small Business Administration (2020), there are approximately 300,000 Native American-owned small businesses in the United States, contributing an impressive $50 billion in annual revenue. Across diverse sectors such as tourism, gaming, energy, agriculture, forestry, manufacturing, and federal contracting, Native American business owners have contributed significantly to local economies, thereby sustaining communities, creating jobs, and fostering economic growth.

Families

American Indian adolescents place a high priority on both the immediate and the extended family. The immediate and extended families, tribe, clan, and heritage all contribute to the child's cultural identity and play a significant role in overall development.

Grandparents retain an official and symbolic leadership in family communities. Children seek daily contact with grandparents, who monitor children's behavior and have a voice in child-rearing practices. Although the adolescent's social consciousness and awareness doubtlessly cause a transition from a family-centered to a more peer-centered environment, the traditional American Indian respect and commitment to the family continue.

Adult perceptions of childhood and child-rearing practices also influence the developing person significantly. The American Indian family considers children to be gifts worthy of sharing with others, while the white perception holds that children constitute private property to be disciplined when necessary. In essence, children in the American Indian family have few rules to obey, but white children have rules with strict consequences. American Indian parents provide children with early training in self-sufficiency, and whereas European Americans prize individualism, the American Indian family places importance on group welfare.

Any crisis in the home or within the family precipitates an absence from school until the crisis ends and the family situation returns to normal. American Indian children and adolescents are taught obedience and respect for elders, experts, and those with spiritual power. They also learn the importance of the family as well as responsibility to family members. In fact, supportive nonfamily members are often considered to be an integral part of the family network.

American Indian child-rearing practices and differing cultural expectations for behavior can result in confusion and frustration for the children. American Indians who confront an incompatibility with their European American counterparts appear to demonstrate growing feelings of isolation, rejection, and anxiety, which can result in alienation, poor self-image, and withdrawal. Such feelings undoubtedly affect the behavior and aspirations of American Indian children and adolescents.

Young people seek social acceptance and approval from older members of the family as well as from younger family members. Unlike adolescents in European American culture, which emphasizes youth and the self, American Indian adolescents place family before self and have great respect for elders and their wisdom. The wisdom of life is received from the older people, whose task it is to acquaint the young with the traditions, customs, legends, and myths of the culture.

The early training in self-sufficiency that American Indians receive from their families and other significant adults continue to have an impact during the adolescent years. Although the adolescent continues to recognize the loyalty and dependence on the immediate and surrounding family, adolescents develop independence and confidence in their abilities to deal with the world outside the family. We must consider this attitude of self-sufficiency, however, from the American Indian point of view. For example, not sharing with one's fellows and accumulating great wealth and possessions would not be included in the American Indian self-sufficiency concept.

Religion

According to American Indian belief, the world is interconnected and everything, including humankind, lives according to the same process. Each being has its power, function, and place in the universe. Every part of nature has a spirit that many tribes believe possesses intelligence, emotion, and free will. Praying, in fact, is praying to one's own power. Because the Great Spirit is everything in all of nature, there is no need to question the existence of a god. Because nature is the essence of God, nature would stop if God no longer lived.

God is the great power above everything. God created man, nature, and the universe, and God instructs on how to live on the land. The inner spiritual power, or the word *God*, was *orenda* to the Iroquois, *manitou* to the Algonkian tribes, *alone* to the Powhatans, and *wakan* or *wakonda* to the Sioux. The Sioux also used the expression *wakan tanka*, meaning all of the *wakan* beings.

The spiritual God of the American Indians is positive, benevolent, and part of daily living. God's knowledge and advice are transmitted through traditional American Indian wisdom. Ideal action toward God is accomplished by helping others understand and get along with people and by comprehending the natural world of which everything (living and nonliving) is a part. The American Indian respects all of nature's objects equally as both physical and spiritual entities.

As in any other culture, the American Indian culture contains norms and standards for behavior, but American Indians are inclined to judge each person as a separate individual, taking into consideration the reasons for actions ahead of the norms of the society. Some societies judge behavior as right or wrong, good or bad, and consider how things "should" be and not necessarily how they are.

For American Indians, there exists a close relationship between spiritual realization and unity and their cultural practices. Catholic and Protestant clergy have sought to Christianize American Indians, but there has been a continuation of indigenous religious rituals and beliefs in the healing power of nature. Natural forces are associated with the life process itself and pervade everything that the believing American Indian does.

Community religious rites are a collective effort that promote this mode of healing and increase inward insight and experiential connection with nature. American Indian individuals can utilize the positive experiences resulting from ceremonial events, power-revealing events (omens, dreams, visions), and contact with a tribal medicine man in the healing process.

Language

Language and communication, whether verbal or nonverbal, may constitute the most important aspects of an individual's culture and characterize the general culture, its values, and its ways of looking and thinking. Educators should develop a consciousness and appreciation for the many American Indian languages and recognize the problems that may result when educators and school children have differing language backgrounds.

The cultural mannerisms and nonverbal communication the American Indian child demonstrates add another personal dimension to both culture and language. Professionals should recognize communicational differences (both verbal and nonverbal). American Indians tend to speak more softly and at a slower rate, to avoid direct identification between speaker and listener, and to interject less frequently with encouraging communicational signs such as head nods and verbal acknowledgments.

American Indian adolescents, like adolescents of all cultures, need the security and psychological safety that a common language provides, yet they experience significant language problems during this crucial period of development. Self-esteem and identity are formed during the transition from the family-centered world of the immediate and extended home. No longer is communication possible only with elders, parents, and siblings.

Achievement Levels

As stated earlier, several studies suggest that tests and teacher reports show that American Indian children function at the average-to-superior range until the fourth grade. After the fourth grade, academic functioning typically declines each year so that by grade 10, American Indian learners' academic achievement falls below the norm. Several complex factors may contribute to this predicament, such as growing feelings of isolation, rejection, and anxiety that American Indian learners feel as they confront the incompatibility of their cultural value system with peers. These feelings contribute to alienation, poor self-image, and withdrawal.

Teachers sometimes view some behaviors that American Indians exhibit as rude or insulting. For example, if these students avoid the teacher's gaze, do not volunteer answers, or delay response, as their cultural background has taught them to do, they are seen as lazy or uncomprehending.

American Indian students are sometimes thought to lack time-management skills or to be self-centered because of their present-time orientation. The American Indian concept of time is that what is happening now is more important than what is not happening now; that what is happening now deserves full attention; and that what one will be doing at this time tomorrow will be more important than what one is doing now or what one will not be doing tomorrow.

Adolescents' ability to reach out to a wider world depends greatly on their ability to speak and understand the language of the majority and other cultures. American Indian children and adolescents often have to decide which language to speak. This may be an even more difficult task for American Indians than for other cultures, because American Indians view language as a crucial aspect of the culture and a cherished gift that should be used whenever possible. Such a belief conflicts with the European American opinion that English is American Indians' means to success and that English should be the predominant language.

That American Indians speak about 2,200 languages further complicates language use. This broad and diversified language background, albeit personal and sacred to American Indians, has not provided the rich cultural and language experiences that contribute to European American definitions of school success. Wide-scale differences exist in American Indians' ability to speak English. In some cases, as few as 4 percent of American Indians speak "excellent" English; a far greater percentage speak either "good" or "poor" English. Children who have attended English-speaking schools, of course, speak better English than their elders.

Whether or not the educational problems American Indian adolescents experience are caused by *cultural teachings* or the *cultural differences* in European American schools, the result is the same: Americans Indians continue to have one of the highest dropout rates. The reasons for dropping out of school include: (1) school rules are not enforced uniformly; (2) factors pertaining to teacher–student relationships, for example, teachers not caring about students and not providing sufficient assistance; (3) disagreements with teachers; and (4) the content of schooling, which the students perceive as not important to what they want to do in life.

Perceptive educators should demonstrate genuine care, understanding, and encouragement with which American Indian learners can identify; ensure that the curriculum addresses American Indian needs and provides culturally relevant experiences; and understand the home problems of some American Indians, such as separations and divorces, unemployment, alcoholism, and child abuse.

Educators who understand American Indians' cultural characteristics can help prevent school failure in American Indian learners. A significant factor in American Indians' academic underachievement appears to be feelings of isolation, anxiety, and rejection as they confront the incompatibility of their cultural values with those of their mainstream classrooms. Often forced to renounce their own culture, these learners are torn between two worlds and often withdraw as a result.

Morris et al. (2006) argue that American Indian children experience an education system that is distinctly different; have a history of child-rearing and educational practices that is not congruent with the education system; experience shortages of sociopolitical and socioeconomic resources; and often are forced to learn a different language.

Powers (2005) offers several suggestions for educating American Indian students:

1. Teachers should strengthen connections with American Indian students. Having strong relationships between students and teachers promotes a sense of belonging, freedom to take academic risks, and investment in academic learning, and may help American Indian students negotiate cultural discontinuities between school and home.
2. Teacher training in native cultural competencies is a positive step toward increasing teachers' understanding and commitment to forming positive relationships with their students.
3. Schoolwide antibullying, anger management, and substance abuse programs also may contribute to academic achievement.
4. Schoolwide screening may be effective in identifying American Indian students when they first begin to fall behind in achievement or attendance. An individualized intervention plan can be devised based on factors such as individual assets, native cultural affiliation, and parental support for learning.

Nel (1994) offers several American Indian cultural characteristics that often conflict with mainstream school systems. Educators should be able to address the following:

◆ American Indians often place emphasis on generosity, sharing, and cooperation. These cultural characteristics sometimes conflict with mainstream school systems, which emphasize competition. Educators can take two directions: (1) reassure American Indian learners that mainstream society accepts and encourages personal achievement and that peers will not blame them or think less of them for excelling in classwork or even in the playground, and (2) provide teaching and learning experiences that emphasize teamwork and cooperation.
◆ American Indians often experience discomfort when teachers single them out for praise for accomplishments, because they often do not want to excel at others' expense. Educators can: (1) let students know that praise is a form of acknowledging accomplishments

and mainstream schools' students expect it; and (2) offer private recognition and praise for those learners who continue to feel uncomfortable.

◆ American Indians' sense of generosity and cooperative efforts makes it difficult not to help a friend in need—for example, a fellow student needing help on a test or graded exercise. Educators should understand American Indians' concept of generosity and should take special care in handling these situations. Educators can (1) avoid situations in which they strictly prohibit lending assistance and, for situations in which individuals must work alone, (2) try to explain the necessity of working alone, so they can determine individual achievement.

◆ American Indians have more flexible concepts of time than do some other cultures—that is, students might not arrive at class on time and might be late with assignments. They often do not regard time and punctuality as important concerns. Educators need to take several directions: (1) avoid judging American Indians using middle-class white perspectives by realizing that students being late or submitting assignments late might not be signs of laziness or unconcern; and (2) help students to understand that their cultural orientations are not wrong but that mainstream U.S. schools and society expect punctuality in many cases.

Educational and societal factors, as well as the clash of cultures, during these crucial developmental years have the potential for developing feelings of frustration and hopelessness that often result in alienation. Such alienation may have been a factor to the American Indians' general loss of confidence and decline in motivation. These feelings during adolescence may also result in considerable confusion in the classroom. The American Indian adolescent may demonstrate behavior that teachers perceive as excessive shyness, inactivity, or lack of motivation. Adolescents whose teachers misunderstand or culturally misconstrue these characteristics (along with the adolescent's usual steady decline in achievement) may develop feelings of hopelessness and alienation.

Educators can benefit from understanding these common characteristics of American Indians:

1. American Indians often harbor significant feelings of suspicion and distrust of professionals and institutions.
2. Communication problems may result in an inability to understand, trust, and build rapport with peers and professionals of other

cultures. Differences in home language and school language or American Indians' nonverbal communication might hinder educational efforts. American Indian learners may appear to be unconcerned with educational progress when, in fact, they may be painfully shy and oversensitive to strangers because of language problems.

3. American Indian adolescents develop in an often unique and difficult situation. They must reconcile allegiance to the values and customs of both the American Indian and other cultures. They also encounter the usual problems of adolescence—for example, the possibility of experiencing role confusion or differences associated with building a positive identity.

4. American Indian learners have to decide whether the Indian, other culture, or European American culture (or some "cultural combination") should provide the basis for their identity. They need to attempt proficiency in both the Indian language and English, and learn how to maintain harmony with family and nature while surviving in the European American world.

Suicide and Substance Abuse

Suicide is a pressing public health issue that affects American Indian communities disproportionately. Fetter et al. (2023) reported that American Indians show the highest suicide rates among all racial groups until age 45, at which point the rate for the white population is higher. Despite efforts to mitigate and prevent suicide, these disparities in rates are on the rise, with the data showing a 45 percent increase over the past five years (Fetter et al., 2023). Several risk factors, such as depression, childhood abuse, serious trauma, historical injustices, and exposure to violence or suicide within their community, increase Native American adolescents' vulnerability to substance abuse and suicide. Additionally, challenges such as family conflicts and difficulties at school further exacerbate susceptibility to these serious risks. Tingey et al. (2016) discuss an education program for American Indian youth living on a reservation. The program aims to address protective factors effective against substance use and suicide at individual, peer, and community levels. The study reviews such factors and evaluates their impact on youths' psychosocial and behavioral health, as well as educational and economic outcomes. Key protective factors integrated into the program include connectedness to caring adults, schools, and peers, along with elements of positive youth development such as hope, mastery, self-control, and entrepreneurship education.

Leading substance use and suicide prevention researchers working with North American indigenous communities have issued a call to action: To develop prevention models targeting key determinants of mental health and well-being at the community level situated within their larger socioeconomic contexts. Past substance abuse and suicide prevention research has been deficit based focused on problems. Researchers urge new initiatives that examine societal-level factors such as poverty and unemployment, and suggest a commitment to local capacity building and community health, with an overarching emphasis on resilience. Educators should prioritize initiatives that promote the well-being and mental health of Native American students. While previous approaches have focused on risk and utilized deficit-based approaches, calls are now for development frameworks that are strength-based and target change at individual and community levels.

1. Educators must first understand and accept the reality that many American Indian adolescents face serious alcohol and substance abuse challenges.
2. Educators should design programs that emphasize *connectedness* in all forms—connectedness with schools, peers, and caring adults. Other factors include hope, mastery and self-control, and positive youth development.
3. Educators should carefully plan and implement entrepreneurship education programs that build on the theme of *connectedness*.

POINTS TO PONDER 4.3

Promoting American Indians' Academic Achievement

Consider several ways to promote American Indians' academic achievement. Remember, American Indians generally meet academic expectations until the fourth grade. Then, many of them (just like John in the opening Cultural Portrait) begin a downward trend in academic achievement. What might cause this downward trend for American Indians? What can educators do to help American Indians maintain satisfactory academic achievement?

Promoting American Indians' Academic Achievement

Many American Indian students who are gifted are either not identified or not served in schools. Fairly and equitably representing diverse students with respect to culture, language, and socioeconomic status in gifted programs remains an important goal and significant concern in education. Native American students, both presently and throughout history, have been underrepresented in gifted programs while at the same time being over-represented in special education programs (Hodges & Gentry, 2021). Many factors contribute to this and include testing method biases, cultural biases that are disadvantageous to underrepresented groups, a lack of educational resources, and academic challenges that go beyond mere racial and ethnic differences. Combined, these act as barriers that prevent equitable representation in gifted programs.

Montgomery (2001) also asserted several changes need to be made to address the underrepresentation of American Indians in gifted programs: The need for appropriate measures, the need for cultural responsiveness, the need for appropriate language and relevant cultural responsiveness, the need to accommodate predominantly rural schools providing education to American Indian children, and the need to address alternative learning styles.

Consider several ways to promote American Indians' academic achievement. Remember, American Indians generally meet academic expectations until the fourth grade. Then, many of them (just like John in the opening Cultural Portrait) begin a downward trend in academic achievement. What might cause this downward trend for American Indians? What can educators do to help American Indians maintain satisfactory academic achievement?

Montgomery (2001) also maintains that rural schools traditionally have had difficulty offering a range of programs necessary to meet the needs of gifted American Indians. The main reasons for this difficulty include the heavy reliance on standardized achievement tests, and the limited number of culturally and linguistically diverse school professionals. Increasing the number of American Indian teachers, administrators, paraprofessionals, and psychologists may provide American Indian children with greater access to educational opportunity.

To address the challenges facing American Indians in gifted programs, Montgomery (2001) explains Project Leap, which includes four program initiatives: Leadership, Excellence, Achievement, and Performance. The program focuses on collaboration, identification, curriculum, and community and parent involvement, all designed to help gifted American Indian students discover and nurture gifts, talents, or high potential.

School Practices Promoting American Indians' Progress

Teachers need to keep in mind that the Native Americans' languages, literacies, histories, and cultural practices are assets and should not be viewed as flawed. Martinez (2023) recommended implementing culturally relevant pedagogies in the classroom that not only reflect indigenous identities and wisdom where they've been historically excluded, but also critique and challenge systems that misrepresent or undermine indigenous knowledge. Similarly, Guiberson and Vining (2023) highlighted the importance of integrating culture-based curriculums, employing traditional storytelling methods, and using authentic practices such as teaching about nature and connection to the land into educational settings to enhance Native American children's learning experiences. Guiberson and Vining (2023) suggested promising strategies such as using indigenous songs to preserve, document, and teach indigenous languages from preschool through grade 12 in language immersion programs. Other promising approaches involve caregivers teaching indigenous words, using indigenous language materials, applying the language in classroom activities, and incorporating bilingual and bidialectal instruction.

Culturally relevant pedagogies influence Native American educational policies in the U.S. Southwest where indigenous people's perspectives, lived experiences, and knowledge are emphasized in educational settings. They promise to promote home and school connection, educational sovereignty, and academic confidence. For example, the Indian Education Act in Arizona was established by the Office of Indian Education "to meet the needs of its Native American students." This Act covers Arizona's 22 federally recognized tribes including bands within Apache, Cocopah, Colorado River, Havasupai, Hopi, Hualapai, Maricopa, Mojave, Navajo, Paiute, Quechan, O'odham, Yaqui, and Yavapai Nations (Arizona Department of Education, 2022).

Because some techniques taught to educators are incompatible with American Indian cultural traditions, it is imperative that educators use strategies that are appropriate for the culture. What specifically should educators avoid?

1. Methods that increase positive self-talk, such as "something I like about myself" or "a sport I can play well," often work well with white and African American children but not with American Indian children.
2. Attempts to convince American Indians to be competitive (such as being the first, best, fastest, or smartest) are incompatible with their cultural values.

3. Educators often expect eye contact and perceive the American Indian's tendency to look the other way as a sign of withdrawal, embarrassment, or discomfort.

4. Educators and counselors often rely extensively on verbal participation by children in the class. Although verbal interaction is valued by Anglo, African, and Hispanic cultures, it is not valued by American Indians.

CASE STUDY 4.1

Avani: A 15-Year-Old American Indian Girl

Avani, a 15-year-old American Indian girl, demonstrated the usual accepted characteristics of the American Indian culture. With that said, American Indian cultures differ significantly so one must use considerable caution. Still, in this case, it is safe to say she was abiding by her elders' expectations. Avani had school problems that were impeding her progress and limiting her future ambitions. On the other hand, maybe she did not want to excel at the expense of her peers. Her American Indian school was on a reservation and held on to cherished American Indian values and customs. Several European American teachers had ventured into the school with "good intentions" of teaching American Indian students to think and act like "white people." Their intentions were well meant—changing would mean a better ease of transition off the reservation and into mainstream society. Avani felt torn between her own culture and so-called white people's culture. Some educational recruiters would visit the reservation to recruit the best and brightest students. Two results occurred: Avani did not want to stand out from her peers; and, second, recruiters were usually made to feel very unwelcome. Tribal elders did not want young people to leave the reservation. Students who left often lost their cultural values, languages, and traditions, and often never returned.

Avani feels she is in a bind—she thinks she can make better grades, but at what cost to her family and cultural traditions?

Questions for Discussion

1. What approaches (school environment, curriculum, instructional, management, etc.) should the educators take? They wanted the best for Avani, but they did not want to offend her beliefs or her tribal elders' expectations.

2. How could the educators get Avani to change her belief in "not excelling" with her peers? Is this a value they should have tried to change?

3. Should Avani's teachers reinforce the beliefs that her values and traditions would have to change in order to survive off the reservation?

Promoting Cultural Identities

Educators working with American Indian learners readily recognize the many personal and social factors that affect children's and adolescents' self-esteem and cultural identities. Injustice and discrimination, poverty, low educational attainment, and perhaps growing up on reservations, in foster homes, or in a predominantly white society may cause American Indian learners to question their self-worth and the worth of their culture.

What specific methods might educators use to promote cultural identities? Ask young American Indian children to make a drawing or a silhouette of an Indian child. Ask them to write words or draw symbols to illustrate their favorite foods, favorite games, favorite sports, and perhaps some things they like to think about.

Ask the American Indian children to explain their pictures to the other children in the group. Indian children may prefer to simply look at their pictures, together, as a group. They may look for some similarities in their pictures to identify their group's favorite foods or some things their group likes to think about.

After sharing, the children may combine their pictures to create a "group personality" collage. The purpose of this type of self-disclosing activity for American Indian children is twofold: First, they see a type of collective group personality emerge, and, second, they begin to think of themselves as a part of the group. They do not compare themselves individually with other members of the group. Instead, they gain a sense of their contribution to the group and of the ways in which they belong and identify, not with individuals in the group but with the group as a whole.

CASE STUDY 4.2

Mr. Thomas and Low-Achieving Students

Mr. Thomas pondered his class—the achievers, the low achievers, and those who seemed to be in a constant struggle just to make passing grades. As Mr. Thomas thought about his students, he also wondered whether his lack of knowledge of how American Indians learn actually contributed to their learning difficulties. He did not understand American Indians' short-term orientation, their concern for nature, and their sometimes strange cultural mannerisms. Mr. Thomas asked himself: "What should I know about the way American Indians learn, and how can I help to improve their academic achievement?"

Mr. Thomas went to several authorities on American Indian children and adolescents to seek advice on how he could better understand these learners, make his teaching more effective, and maximize teaching and learning efforts. The advice he received included the need to understand the short-term time orientation of many American Indians; to understand families and involve them in school activities and their children's learning; to understand how to improve American Indian learners' belief in their ability to learn; to understand the importance of genuinely positive and caring relationships between teachers and students; to understand the importance of designing curricula that reflect American Indians' backgrounds and contemporary needs; and to understand American Indians' ways of receiving and using knowledge.

Questions for Discussion

1. After the fourth grade, American Indians' academic achievement typically begins to decline. While understanding the reasons for the decline is important, it is even more important to think of strategies for preventing it. Suggest a number of steps (e.g. culturally appropriate diagnostic tests, curricular materials, and instructional procedures) that educators might take to increase American Indians' academic achievement.
2. Realistically speaking, what should Mr. Thomas do? Should he pursue another teaching job with students from his own socioeconomic group and culture? What is the possibility of his finding a teaching position with less diversity? If he continues at this predominantly American Indian school, what methods should he use to learn more about American Indian students?
3. Consider this suggestion: "Understand the importance of designing curricula that reflect American Indians' backgrounds and contemporary needs." How can such a suggestion be made a reality? What would be the first steps in designing such a curriculum? What are specific aspects of American Indians' backgrounds? Their contemporary needs?

Summing Up

Educators who plan teaching and learning experiences for American Indian children and adolescents should:

1. Remember that American Indian people have a proud history of accomplishments and notable contributions and that these should be part of school curricula.
2. Avoid providing curricular and instructional practices that indicate only white, middle-class expectations and that might seem alien to American Indian learners.
3. Remember that educators who understand American Indians and the possible cultural basis for educational problems must address achievement levels and school dropout rates.
4. Promote positive self-images and cultural images among American Indian learners, which may be one of the most effective means for improving academic achievement and school-related problems.
5. Adapt teaching styles and other school practices to meet American Indians' ways of knowing, demonstrating that educators are caring and interested in improving school achievement and overall school success.
6. Understand the American Indian culture and the learners' cultural characteristics, religious orientations, and socioeconomic backgrounds.
7. Provide learning experiences so that learners of other cultures can develop a better understanding of their American Indian peers.
8. Understand the learner's development, and provide school experiences based on developmental and cultural characteristics.
9. Consider American Indians as individuals who come from different nations, tribes, socioeconomic levels, and levels of educational attainment.

Suggested Learning Activities

1. Observe an American Indian learner and record the cultural mannerisms that might be contrary to the behaviors that schools expect. How might a teacher misinterpret the behavior of American Indians? How might educators better understand American Indian learners and their behaviors?
2. List several stereotypical beliefs about American Indians. What is the basis of these beliefs? How might these beliefs affect educators' perceptions of these learners? What steps can multicultural educators take to lessen the effect of stereotypical beliefs?
3. Consider the following Implementing Research section, which looks at a review and analysis of the research on American Indian students.

Implementing Research

Culturally Relevant Pedagogy for American Indian Students

Bryant (2023) explored the use of the formal education of American Indians as a weapon to strip indigenous peoples of their culture and language. He examined the history of American Indian education, which was marked by colonialism and cultural erasure, and detailed the abuse suffered by Native American children. Bryant suggests that education for American Indian youth, specifically Cherokee youth, should be reclaimed through culturally relevant pedagogy rooted in Cherokee values. The study examines the efforts of the Gadugi Partnership—a collaboration between Appalachian State University and Cherokee High School, and its efforts to reclaim formal education for Indian youth. The program focuses on education that emphasizes human potential and reflects indigenous values. The Cherokee term "Gadugi" means working together for the common good. One example of a course in this program is the Cherokee Culture and Leadership course, which incorporates service projects for community issues such as drug dependency. Bryant (2023) stresses that the inclusion and recognition of Cherokee culture within the education system sets a precedent for how education can serve as a vehicle for cultural preservation and respect.

Implementing the Research

1. It is important for educators to understand the value of Native American students' culture. Participating in professional development opportunities focused on culturally responsive teaching practices addressing historical contexts, cultural sensitivity, and instructional strategies that address diverse student backgrounds will assist in this.
2. Incorporate culturally relevant and culturally sustaining teaching strategies that include various customs, experiences, and perspectives of Native American students. This will foster a supportive and inclusive classroom where Native American children can thrive.
3. Establish relationships with the local Native American community and involve its members in classroom and curriculum planning to ensure culturally relevant and respectful content. Community members can suggest guest lectures, community projects, and cultural events.
4. Schools should provide resources and support to Native American students in addition to quality teachers, counselors, and specialized support staff.

Source: Bryant, J. A. (2023). Gadugi: Reclaiming Native American education through a culturally reflective pedagogy. *Athens Journal of Education*, *10*(4). https://eric.ed.gov/?id=EJ1414576

Suggestions for Collaborative Efforts

Form groups of three or four, which, if possible, represent the U.S. nation's cultural and gender diversity. Working collaboratively, focus your group's attention toward the following efforts:

1. Talk with several teachers of American Indian learners to see what first-hand experiences they have to offer. Specifically, learn their perceptions of cultural characteristics, the influence of families, achievement levels, and language problems. What advice can these teachers offer?
2. American Indians experience academic problems, including low academic achievement, low reading scores, and high dropout rates. Design a remediation plan to address American Indians' academic problems. Specifically, look at learning styles, curricular materials, instructional strategies, classroom environments, and motivation. (Be sure to consider that American Indian indicators of motivation might differ from others'.) In other words, how does your group believe schools can better address the needs of American Indian learners?

Expanding Your Horizons

Additional Books and Journals

Bradley, R. H. (2023). Home life and well-being among Cherokee adolescents. *Family Relations*, *72*(3). https://doi-org.proxy.lib.odu.edu/10.1111/fare.12643

Historical trauma and collective loss experienced by Native Americans can result in enduring emotional pain, challenges in coping, and struggles with effective parenting practices. Over time, Native American communities have endeavored to foster resilience among their youth, with many parents adapting their child-rearing methods to empower their children to thrive as healthy, well-adjusted individuals in a society that may not always align with indigenous values.

Day, A., Barton, E., Cross, S., Miller, C., & Gonzales, J. (2024). Experiences and service utilization of American Indian/Alaskan Native kinship care-givers in kinship navigator programs across Washington state. *Families in Society*, *105*(1), 19–36. https://doi-org.proxy.lib.odu.edu/10.1177/10443894231193779

In AI/AN communities, kinship caregiving, particularly the practice of grandparents assuming sole responsibility for their grandchildren's care, is more prevalent than in any other demographic group. This tradition, deeply rooted in AI/AN culture, underscores the significant role of grandparents in passing down skills, traditions, and actively participating in the upbringing and nurturing of their grandchildren.

Websites

Indians.org – www.indians.org
This Internet site provides various resources, such as indigenous literature, a tribal directory, and information on activism.

National Congress of American Indians – www.ncai.org/about-ncai
This organization works to protect and advance tribal governance and treaty rights, promote the economic development, health and welfare in Indian and Alaska Native communities, and educate the public toward a better under-standing of Indian and Alaska Native tribes.

National Indian Education Association – www.niea.org/
The NIEA collaborates with Native educators to enhance schools and the education of Native children, foster the preservation and growth of Native languages and cultures, and devise tactics for impacting local, state, and fed-eral policies and decision-makers.

Native American Resources – www.kstrom.net/isk/mainmenu.html
Covering over 300 Internet sites, this site provides maps, stories, art, astron-omy, and herbal knowledge, just to name a few topics.

Native American Studies – http://libguides.usc.edu/nativeamericanstudies/articles
This site provides information and useful databases for Academic Research with regards to Native American studies.

Shmoop Historical Overview – www.shmoop.com/native-american-history/
Provides historical information regarding Native Americans. Provides time-line, people, facts, and photo information.

5

Understanding Arab American Children and Adolescents

Understanding the material and activities in this chapter will help the reader to:

- ◆ Understand the Arab American people, their origins, and what they are like today.
- ◆ List several stereotypes of Arab American children and adolescents.
- ◆ Describe Arab Americans' cultural, gender, socioeconomic, familial, religious, and language diversity.
- ◆ Name several culturally responsive educational practices that promote Arab Americans' educational progress, self-esteem, and cultural identities.

Opening Scenario

Cultural Portrait: Abdullah Salaam

Abdullah Salaam is a 13-year-old Arab American boy whose parents had moved to the United States from Saudi Arabia. Abdullah's father worked for a company that wanted to expand its international operation. His family was reluctant to move to the United States, but then they realized the economic and other benefits of doing so. The family hated to leave behind their family and friends, as well as their cherished religious customs and traditions. Still, they knew their family could visit. Plus, places existed in the United States where they could practice their religion.

DOI: 10.4324/9781003429531-7

Abdullah faced several challenges, which his school addressed with varying degrees of success. First, his English-speaking skills were good, but he still had difficulty understanding the teacher and communicating with other students. Second, he received a little abuse from the other middle-school students, who sometimes mocked his language. They spoke to him using what they considered an Arab accent. Third, Abdullah's social development was lacking, perhaps because of his language proficiency and fear of others mocking him. He had few friends and usually stayed alone.

Most of the teachers, unfortunately, ignored Abdullah's school situation, but two realized that he needed help. After enlisting the aid of the guidance counselor to come up with a plan, they decided on a four-pronged approach. First, they asked the language specialist to work with Abdullah to improve his language abilities. Second, they decided to address mocking and other forms of harassment in the advisor–advisee program (an essential middle-school concept) to try to show the effects of such negative behaviors. Third, they decided to try cooperative learning activities that would bring Abdullah into social contact with other students. Fourth, they agreed to work informally with him to improve his self-esteem. Admittedly, the teachers had doubts about whether these approaches would have positive and long-term effects, but they thought Abdullah's problems deserved to be addressed in some way.

Overview

Although articles, books, and instructional materials may deal with the cultural heritages of African American, American Indian, Asian American, European American, and Hispanic American children and adolescents, Arab American learners and their cultures are often ignored. "The kids from the Middle East are the lost sheep in the school system. They fall through the cracks in our categories" (Wingfield & Karaman, 1995, p. 8). The author agrees wholeheartedly that Arab American children and adolescents are still often forgotten or ignored in U.S. schools.

Origins

Arab people emigrate from 22 countries in the Middle East and northern Africa. They possess a shared heritage, which typically includes Arabic as their native language, and they identify with key features of Arab culture, including the centrality of family and religion. Nevertheless, important social, political, and religious differences exist both within and among people from Arab countries. Notably, considerable variability exists among families in terms of the degree of acculturation to both Western and Arab countries. The Arab American demographic is relatively young; roughly 26 percent of the 3.5 million individuals of Middle Eastern or North African (MENA) heritage were below the age of 18 in 2020 (Marks et al., 2023).

According to Haboush (2007), Arabs are those people whose ancestry originates in Arabic-speaking countries, even though not all these individuals consider themselves Arabs. In the Middle East, Arab countries include Lebanon, Syria, Jordan, Iraq, Yemen, the United Arab Emirates, Kuwait, Saudi Arabia, Bahrain, Oman, and Qatar. These countries differ in terms of racial and ethnic mix, religious composition, and economic development. The racial/ethnic diversity of Arab American families is not well reflected in the U.S. Census because Arabs often identify themselves as white.

Like Hispanic Americans, Arab Americans are a linguistic and cultural community, rather than a racial or religious group. Arabs speak Arabic as their primary language and share in the culture and history of the Arab world, which stretches from Morocco to the Arabian Peninsula. Most Arabs are Muslim, which means they believe in the religion of Islam. However, most of the largest Muslim countries—including Indonesia, Pakistan, Bangladesh, Iran, Turkey, and Nigeria—are not Arab. As the fastest-growing religious group, Islam constitutes 24.1 percent of the global population (Bai, 2023; U.S. Census Bureau, 2024a). A common misconception is that all Muslims are Arabic, however, worldwide there are 276 million Arabs (U.S. Census Bureau, 2024a). They make up only 15 percent of the 1.8 billion Muslims; a relatively small percentage (Bai, 2023).

Table 5.1 provides a list of definitions to assist educators in understanding Arab Americans and the Arab culture.

Table 5.1 Terms and Definitions

Allah	Means God and is used by Arabic-speaking Christians, Muslims, and Jews.
Arab	A person whose native language is Arabic and who lives according to Arab cultural traditions and values.
Arab Americans	Immigrants and their descendants with ethnic roots in Asian and African Arabic-speaking lands.
Arab nation	All peoples who speak the Arabic language and claim a link with the nomadic tribes of Arabia, whether by descent, affiliation, or by appropriating the traditional ideals of human excellence and standards of beauty.
Bedouin	A nomadic desert-dwelling Arab.
Collective or collectivism	People who are more oriented toward the group.
Fundamentalist	One who follows the fundamentals of a religion.
Galabiya	A body-length robe.

(*Continued*)

Table 5.1 (Continued)

Hadith	The Prophet's own traditional sayings.
Hajj	The pilgrimage to Mecca made by millions of Muslims once each year; for men, it is called **hajji,** and for women it is called **hajjah.**
Hijab	A scarf worn to cover the hair on a woman's head.
Imam	The leader of prayer at the mosque; he is sometimes called a **sheik.**
Individualistic or individualism	People who are more oriented toward individual concerns.
Islam	The Arabic word means "submission" and is derived from the word meaning "peace."
Jihad	A Muslim's strenuous intellectual, physical, and spiritual efforts for the good of all.
Muslim (not Moslem)	A believer in the religion of Islam, who may or may not be an Arab.
Pillars of Islam	(1) Oral testimony that there is only one God and that Mohammed is His prophet; (2) ritual prayer practiced five times a day with certain words and certain postures of the body; (3) the giving of alms; (4) keeping a strict fast of no liquid or food from sunrise to sundown during the month of Ramadan; and (5) holy pilgrimage to Mecca once in a lifetime at a specific time of year.
Quran	The holy book for Muslims, who believe it is the literal word of God revealed by the Prophet Mohammed.
Ramadan	The ninth month of the calendar year, the month of fasting, self-discipline, and purification.
Sunna	The Prophet's own traditional practices.
Umma	A belief that all Muslims are brothers and sisters.

Arab Americans represent a wide range of diverse cultures, languages, religions, and ethnic and racial backgrounds. An Arab can be Muslim, Christian, Jew, or of some other belief. Although most Arab Americans are generally categorized as Caucasian, ethnic and racial diversity are two salient features of this unique group. For example, Arab Americans can be black, interracial, or white. Also, not everyone who comes from the Arab countries is an Arab. For example, people can originate from Kildanis, Kurds, Druze, Berbers, and other ethnic groups.

Arab Americans Today

Erroneously perceived as a unified, single ethnic group, Arab Americans' diversity is grossly overlooked. Arabs in the United States come from different countries with different allegiances and interests.

> **POINTS TO PONDER 5.1**
>
> **Consider Your Images of Arab Americans**
>
> Think about your images of Arab Americans. Be honest with yourself and admit possible stereotypical images. Second, determine the basis for your beliefs. Third, ask yourself, "How true is the image?" Last, decide what you can do to dispel your stereotypical images and gain a more accurate perception of this cultural group.

Arab Americans have increasingly been recognized as an ethnic minority in the United States (Haboush, 2007). In 2020 the U.S. Census, for the first time, actively sought responses from individuals of MENA descent. The Census Bureau categorizes the MENA population by geography, and it therefore includes both Arabic-speaking communities like Egyptian and Jordanian, and non-Arabic speaking such as Iranian and Israeli. The 2020 Census showed that 3.5 million individuals identified as being of MENA descent either solely or in combination with another ethnic or racial group (Marks et al., 2023). Within the MENA category, 239,000 respondents identified themselves as Arab (U.S. Census Bureau, 2024a).

The 2020 U.S. Religion Census reported 2,771 mosques in the United States with a total of 4,453,908 adherents (Grammich et al., 2023), an increase of nearly 700 mosques and close to 1.9 million adherents since 2010. Muslims were ranked the sixth-largest religious community in 2020.

Arab American Christians' tendency to enrich their lives through effective interaction with others appears to have assisted them as they entered mainstream U.S. culture. However, in contrast to Arab Christians, assimilation was much more difficult for the Arab Muslims because of their strong adherence to Islamic faith and law.

Stereotyping of Arab American Children and Adolescents

The Arab community is one of the most heterogeneous in the United States, yet it is likely also the most misunderstood (Bergstrom et al., 2024). The negative images and stereotypes of Arabs are the most prevalent. Anti-Arab racism has been around long before the 9/11 attacks, but the discrimination faced by Arab Americans has grown more intense since (Amer, 2023; Awan & Zempi, 2020). The popular images of Arabs as rich sheiks, religious zealots, and terrorists are gross stereotypes. Stereotypes also surround the roles of Arab American men and women. Arab American children are negatively impacted by consuming media that often portrays their culture in a negative light and criticizes their life practices. Niccolini (2016) documented an incident in a U.S. classroom where a Muslim student was singled out for misbehavior commonly overlooked when committed by non-Muslim students. Selective discipline such as this reflects post-9/11 dynamics where normal infractions by Muslim students are scrutinized and magnified due to heightened concern around Muslim students. Hence, Arab American children have to cope with their identity being frequently misrepresented and distorted, and a lack of knowledge of the diversity and plurality of their ethnic group (Eddarif, 2023).

The 1992 cartoon fantasy *Aladdin* proved immensely popular with American children and their parents, and is still one of the few U.S. films to feature an Arab hero or heroine. However, a closer look provides disturbing evidence of stereotyping. The film's light-skinned lead characters, Aladdin and Jasmine, have Anglicized features and Anglo American accents. This is in contrast to the other characters, who are dark-skinned, swarthy, and villainous—cruel palace guards and greedy merchants with Arabic features, Arabic accents, and grotesque facial features. The film also characterizes the Arab world as alien and exotic.

Other offenders also use negative images to cast Arabs. For example, children and adolescents develop negative images of their culture when they see Arab women dressed as belly dancers and harem girls, and Arab men as violent terrorists, oil sheiks, and marauding tribesmen. Even on Saturday-morning cartoons, Arabs are portrayed as fanatic and dark-complexioned, with sabers and rifles, allies of some force plotting to take over the world. Comic books are equally troubling. Tarzan battles with an Arab chieftain who kidnaps Jane, Superman foils Arab terrorists hijacking a U.S. nuclear carrier, and the Fantastic Four combat a hideous oil sheik supervillain. Computer games often feature cartoon Arab villains, and children rack up high scores and win games by killing Arabs (Wingfield, 2006).

Because many Arabs are Muslims, their dress and traditions are sometimes misunderstood. People sometimes stereotype men with a *galabiya*, or body-length robe, and women wearing a *hijab*, a scarf covering the head, as religious fundamentalists. As with robes, wearing a *hijab* is a personal choice. Many women wear a *hijab* because of cultural traditions. A devout Muslim woman does not necessarily wear a *hijab*. Wearing the *hijab* is a religious practice rather than a cultural practice and is rooted in the Islamic emphasis on modesty. Interestingly, some Arab women say veiling denigrates women; others say the practice liberates them. Covering is not universally observed by Muslim women and varies by region and class.

Schools should recognize other Arab American religious practices. Many Arab Americans adhere to restricted diets—for example, Islamic law forbids eating pork and drinking alcohol. Teachers should recognize the month of Ramadan, in which many Muslim students participate in fasting.

Cultural Characteristics

It is difficult to generalize about any group of people, but it is particularly difficult with Arab Americans because of the many different countries from which they come. Still, some generalizations can be made, provided one considers factors such as generational status, socioeconomic status, commitment to religion, and the actual country of origin.

Researchers (Atari-Khan et al., 2024; Haboush, 2007) suggests that Arabs are more collective or more oriented toward the group and that Americans are more individualistic or more oriented toward individual concerns. In other words, many Arab Americans believe that individuals have the right to take care of themselves. They are self-oriented and emotionally independent, and their emphasis is on individual initiative, the right to privacy, autonomy, and individual decisions. Arabs believe in a more collectivist orientation.

Educators who understand Arab American learners and the Arab culture quickly realize the importance of the individualism–collectivism issue and of the necessity to learn about individual Arab American students. Generally speaking, the U.S. school system has focused on individualism. Educators expect learners, both elementary and secondary, to fend for themselves. Students are expected to have goals, to work individually toward those goals, to compete with others for academic achievement and for the teacher's time, and to claim personal and individual pride in their accomplishments. That individualistic mindset changed somewhat with the inception of cooperative learning, but still, the U.S. school system is individual oriented.

Educators working with Arab Americans (as well as some American Indians and Hispanic Americans) might see more tendencies toward collectivism. Such a statement does not imply, however, that all Arab Americans are collective. To some, when considering education, the theory of collectivism does not make sense, and therefore, they feel a need to compete.

Even considering the research on individualism–collectivism, educators who are sensitive to cultural concerns realize the need to consider students' individuality. Undoubtedly, there are Americans who have orientations toward collectivism and Arabs who prefer to work individually toward learning goals. Perceptive educators see the need to know individual students and then to plan culturally responsive educational experiences.

Gender

Gender roles differ for Arab Americans. Some factors affecting gender roles include country of origin, whether the family came from a rural or urban area, and how long the family has been in the United States. Rather than assume a gender stereotype, it is better to ask the person about his or her own experiences.

Arab American women and girls sometimes experience "double jeopardy" for being young and female, and almost constantly feel victimized by stereotypical images in the media. Females often feel obligated to fight the media images in positive ways, showing a more accurate context of their religious and social climate.

Boys and girls are treated differently in Arab cultures. Also, as explained in the Families section of this chapter, Arab parental discipline and child-rearing methods are often gender-specific. While child-rearing methods vary among Arab cultures and among parents, a great deal of unconditional love usually accompanies discipline, especially for sons. Differential treatment of boys and girls is not uncommon. Educators working with Arab Americans need to remember that their equal treatment of boys and girls, as well as the school's efforts to promote egalitarianism, might be misunderstood by children and parents. While some acculturation might have occurred toward more equal sex roles, it is a mistake to assume that children and adolescents who have lived in the United States for a number of years have adopted Western norms of gender and equality.

According to the 2020 Census data, those of Lebanese, Iranian, and Egyptian descent made up nearly half of the 3.5 million who reported MENA heritage in the United States (Marks et al., 2023). Ajrouch (2004) looks at gender, race, symbolic boundaries, and Arab American adolescents. Ajrouch completed her study in Dearborn, Michigan, the city with the largest concentration of Arab Americans living in the United States. The community in Dearborn is composed of immigrants who entered the United States at different times and who have varying educational, economic, and social backgrounds. The largest group of immigrants is from Lebanon, and many of the most recent of these immigrants are well educated and prosperous; in addition, a small number have come from the rural villages of Lebanon.

Socioeconomic Status

Although many early Arab immigrants were peddlers and merchants, the new immigrants reflect a greater variety of professions. Whereas the average household income for Arab Americans tends to be higher than the national average, there is a greater percentage of Arab American households below the poverty level than for the U.S. population as a whole. Household incomes vary among Arab Americans, just as they do for people of all cultures. Some people achieve socioeconomically, while others have difficulty earning a living and moving up to the next socioeconomic level. MENA households in the United States have a median income of $74,000 and an average of $115,000, versus $73,000 and $102,000 for white households respectively. While this equates to slightly higher socioeconomic status, the MENA community also faces a higher poverty rate of approximately 17 percent, which is greater than the national average of 12.9 percent (U.S. Census Bureau, 2021).

Financially successful Arab Americans cannot be considered victims of exploitation and marginalization. They are not powerless in terms of economics or social standing. Middle- and upper-class professionals are ensured privilege and empowerment in society. They tend to adopt American cultural norms and fit into American society due in large part to better language competency which facilitates easier integration and assimilation. Arab women of higher socioeconomic status may be less likely to keep traditional patriarchal gender roles compared to women in Arab nations (Amer, 2023).

Despite their affluence, however, some middle-class Arab Americans encounter job discrimination in hiring and firing, promotions and tenure, access to certain jobs and fields, and exclusion, harassment, and hostility in the workplace (Wingfield, 2006). More recent immigrants with lower income and educational levels face the problems of poverty, prejudice, neighborhood tensions, and cultural adjustment similar to those of other non-European immigrants. In contrast to middle-class professionals, these individuals are less likely to be treated with respect (Wingfield, 2006). While the author respects Wingfield's (2006) opinion, he neglects the influence of affirmative action programs and equity and social justice efforts to help marginalized immigrants. Plus, the author thinks that people at all lower socioeconomic levels experience problems similar to what Wingfield describes.

Families

Arab Americans value the family and take pride in extended family members. They share several familial traits, such as generosity, hospitality, courage, and respect for the elderly. Most important, Arab Americans invest in their children through education, which is seen as a social asset and religious duty necessary for the survival of both individuals and groups.

Arab American families are, on average, larger than non-Arab American families and smaller than families in Arab countries. Traditionally, more children meant more pride and economic contributors for the family. The cost of having large families in the United States, however, and adaptation to American customs seem to encourage smaller families.

If the Quran is the soul of Islam, then the family can be described as the body. Islam focuses on the *umma* and considers all Muslims as brothers and sisters belonging to the same *umma*. With the *umma*, families are given importance as units.

Although differences exist among Arab Americans, the importance of the family unit is the central unifying feature. Arab culture is collectivistic, or focused on the welfare of the group. Unlike Western culture, which stresses independence and individual autonomy, Arab culture stresses the collective good of the family. During the height of the COVID-19 pandemic, the collectivist values among Arab Americans grew even more significant (Atari-Khan et al., 2024). While the social distance policy posed challenges for Arab Americans in nurturing relationships, those who managed to be with family expressed deep gratitude for the time spent together. This value underlies Arab society and permeates all religious groups. Decisions are made with the ultimate goal of maintaining family stability, honor, and cohesiveness. Children are taught to look within the family for solutions, rather than to develop their own coping strategies, and separating from the family is not encouraged. In fact, many children continue to reside with their parents even after marrying. Strong emphasis is also placed on not shaming the family with one's behavior. Shame, which implies a sense of external exposure, is associated with guilt, which implies an internal issue that one has not lived up to individual standards of behavior. The emphasis on maintaining family honor also means that expressing emotions is discouraged (Haboush, 2007). Honor killings involve the restoration of family honor through the killing of a family member perceived to have damaged it (Sharma, 2023). They are carried out by family members, and are triggered by actions believed to have brought dishonor to family and communities. Common reasons include premarital relationships, inter-religion marriage, and the remarriage of widows. It is estimated that, worldwide, at least 5,000 women and girls are victims of honor killings annually, though this number likely underestimates the actual prevalence of such crimes.

Traditional Arab culture is patriarchal, or male-dominated. A woman's main roles are those of wife and mother. Unmarried women often reside in their parents' home. The father is the dominant authority although older brothers can exert control over mothers and sisters. Although mothers have some power within the family, dominance by males (greater property rights and custody of children) is established by law in some Arab countries.

Under Islam, the importance of women's roles as wives and mothers has been strengthened.

Saudi Arabia has tried to enhance its educational system by promoting coeducation and reducing gender segregation in school and social settings. The idea of female students holding leadership roles is gaining traction and is supported by government efforts to empower women through education. Coeducation opportunities are available particularly in the medical field, with scholarships for study abroad. Several universities are actively seeking students in the country's first coeducational higher education programs (AlJuhani, 2023).

How can educators best respond to Arab American families? Arab Americans from different countries differ from each other in culture, socioeconomic status, religion, and newly arrived second and third generations. To accommodate the individuality of Arab families, it is important for teachers and counselors to take the lead from students and their parents when discussing school and other related issues, and to be knowledgeable about Arab culture. Educators also can recognize that family life and harmony are crucial to Arabs, and demonstrate respect for the sanctity of the nuclear and extended family and the familial role of elders. When Arab American students seem troubled, it may be productive to determine whether their problems stem from intergenerational differences within their family or another source. Inviting parents' input in problem solving can be helpful. Because Arabs are sensitive to public criticism, teachers should be careful how they express concerns to Arab American students and parents. Last, helping families cope with varying levels of acculturation, language differences, and conformity to tradition can enable students to develop a positive identity that is both personally satisfying and respectful of their heritage.

POINTS TO PONDER 5.2

Religious Beliefs

Educators have a professional responsibility to avoid promoting one religion over another. How can teachers teach about Arab Americans' religions without offending members of other religious groups? Or should these topics be avoided altogether to avoid offending someone? Remember that any discussion of religion must be done with respect and objectivity. What specific teaching strategies might you use to teach Arab Americans' religions (or any religion)?

Religion

Arabs belong to many religions, including Islam, Christianity, Druze, Judaism, and others. There are additional distinctions within each of these, and some religious groups have evolved new identities and faith practices in the United States. Educators should be careful to distinguish *religion* from *culture*. Although Arabs are connected by culture, they have different faiths. Common misperceptions are that all Arab traditions are Islamic and that Islam unifies all Arabs. Most Arab Americans are Catholics or Orthodox Christians, but this is not true in all parts of the United States. In some areas, most Arab Americans are Muslim.

The Arab culture has been shaped by numerous historical disputes over religion, territorial boundaries, and political dominance. Beginning with the Crusades, many Arab countries were under the rule of various foreign powers, such as the Ottomans, English, French, and Italians. Colonization by the Europeans and the accompanying devaluation of Arab culture endured into the mid-twentieth century and contributed to long-standing feelings of mistrust toward the West. Since the Crusades, there have been strong divisions between Christian and Muslim groups, who view each other as a threat, as well as internal divisions within each group (Haboush, 2007; Tolan, 2023).

The two main religions with which Arabs identify are Christianity and Islam. There are also Arab Jews, Hindus, and other groups, but their numbers are small. The proportion of individuals practicing Islam and Christianity varies among Arab countries. Muslims constitute more than 90 percent of the population in Syria, Egypt, Saudi Arabia, Qatar, Algeria, Bahrain, Jordan, Morocco, Libya, Tunisia, the United Arab Emirates, and Yemen. However, being Arab is not synonymous with practicing Islam, because Muslims are found in countries throughout the world (Haboush, 2007). One cannot assume that all Arab Americans are Muslims or that all Muslims are Arab. Noor et al. (2024) details the religious compositions and demographics of foreign-born Muslims in the United States: 55 percent Sunni, 16 percent Shiite, and 29 percent identifying simply as Muslims. Overall, Muslims constitute just over 1 percent of the U.S. population, totaling about 3.45 million people. Among them, 57 percent are men and 43 percent are women, with 58 percent being foreign-born. Ethnically, 20 percent of Muslim Americans are black, 28 percent are Asian, 8 percent are Hispanic, and the remaining 48 percent are white, which includes individuals of Persian, Arab, and Kurdish descent.

Religious diversity is characteristic of both the Arab world and the Arab American population. In the United States, where the majority of Arab Americans are Christians, there are still several thousand who belong to the Jewish faith. On the other hand, a Muslim is an adherent to Islam and may or may not be an Arab. Arabs are a minority in the Muslim community. Muslims are from many different parts of the world, including China, Indonesia, Turkey, Russia, and even the United States. To label all Arabs as Muslim is a sweeping false generalization.

The essence of Islam, as preached by the Prophet Mohammed, was transmitted through the Quran, which is believed to be the literal word of God. In addition to the Quran, religious guidance also includes the Prophet's own traditional sayings (*hadith*) and his practices (*sunna*). Except by implication, the Quran does not contain explicit doctrines or instructions; basically, it provides guidance. The *hadith* and *sunna*, however, contain some specific commands on issues such as marriage. They also address such daily habits as how often the believer should worship God and how all people should treat each other.

Language

The Arabic language is one of the great unifying and distinguishing characteristics of Arab people. Arabic serves as the official language in 22 countries globally, with an estimated 400 million speakers worldwide (Ameen & Kadhim, 2023), and is the fourth most widely spoken language in the world (tied with Bengali). In the United States, the number of individuals aged five and above who speak Arabic at home surged from 215,000 in 1980 to 1.4 million in 2021. This makes Arabic the seventh-most commonly spoken non-English language (Moslimani, 2023).

Although spoken Arabic is as varied as the different parts of the Arab world, classical Arabic and written Arabic are the same in all Arab nations. While many people feel an affection for their native language, Arabs' feelings for their language are much more intense. The Arabic language is one of the greatest Arab cultural treasures. Plus, because of its complexity, a good command of the Arabic language is highly admired (Abudabbeh, 1996).

Arab schools usually teach more than one language. It is more common for Arab Americans to speak more than one language than it is for non-Arab Americans. Many immigrants come to the United States having learned two or three languages in their country of origin.

Achievement Levels

Arab American students are among the recent significant and sizable ethnic groups to be recognized within the U.S. student population. The 2020 census was the first to seek responses from those of MENA descent and indicates the group's increased presence and recognition. Their immigration to the United States is typically relatively smooth, but challenges in the education system do exist and educators should not assume that Arab American students have had easy success in U.S. schools. Arab American students are often the invisible minority in the classroom. This dichotomy represents the complexity of their integration and the need for more inclusive educational practices. The education level of the MENA community is quite high, with over 53 percent aged 25 and older obtaining at least a bachelor's degree. This places them at the second-highest educational attainment level, slightly below Asians at 57 percent, and above whites at 39 percent (U.S. Census Bureau, 2021).

Educators must incorporate MENA students' voices, perspectives, language, and culture into educational content and settings to promote an inclusive learning experience. Siddiqui (2016) argues that including Muslim narratives in the classroom not only helps bridge the cultural gap Muslim American students often feel between home and school, but also serves as a counter to anti-Muslim sentiment. Flanagan et al. (2007) found that, regardless of age, gender, or cultural background, youth were more likely to perceive the United States as a just society and to commit to democratic goals if they felt a sense of community. This was especially true if they felt that teachers practiced a democratic ethic at school. Educators may promote the Arab American and Muslim communities in several ways: speaking out when discriminatory attitudes are expressed, reaffirming school antidiscrimination policies, and publicly sending messages of support. When crises erupt, it is time to call friends and contacts at Arab American organizations and mosques to inquire about needed support (Wingfield, 2006).

According to Wingfield (2006), some evidence suggests that social justice can be promoted for Arab Americans (and hopefully all Americans):

- ◆ A network of institutions and organizations has emerged in the recent decades, offering teacher training and a rich collection of classroom materials on Arabs and Muslims.
- ◆ More efforts are being made to reach out to the local Arab Americans and Muslim communities and establish ongoing working relationships.
- ◆ Textbooks are being reviewed to detect errors of fact, emphasis, and interpretation and to eliminate Eurocentric and Israeli-centric bias.
- ◆ Educators are beginning to overcome the prevalent monocultural approach to education that favors the perspectives of dominant groups.
- ◆ Educators are moving toward a genuine acceptance of and respect for these communities.

School Practices Promoting Arab Americans' Progress

Teachers and curriculum designers should integrate culturally relevant materials about all ethnic and cultural groups. Although a lot has been written about various ethnic groups, schools have little information about Arab Americans, their culture, school experiences, or learning styles. At the same time, teachers must engage in the unteaching of myths, stereotypes, and false images of Arab Americans.

Arab American students are often confronted by a biased curriculum and literature. As a result of negative media images, perceptions of Arab American students and their families range from the overly romanticized to the harmfully negative. Schools can make sure that Arabs are accurately and fairly represented in the curriculum and school activities.

Schools can take action against prejudice, discrimination, and incidences of racism. They can also provide professional training for staff and teachers, and provide accurate textbooks and curricular materials. As for Arab American students, knowledge of their culture and history should help educators to construct a more realistic picture of their students. For example, by being aware of food taboos, dress codes, and restrictions on male and female interaction, teachers can reach out to their students in a meaningful way. Teachers can enhance pride in Arab American students by learning about Arab contributions in fields such as algebra, science, linguistics, astrology, art, and architecture.

POINTS TO PONDER 5.3

Promoting Social Justice

Working in groups, discuss what social justice might mean to Arab American students. While Wingfield (2006) offers some suggestions, offer specific ways that teachers can promote social justice, such as by making sure procedural (daily routines, disciplinary problems, solving disputes) justice occurs, reducing oppression (harassment, bullying, name-calling), and acting as advocates for others.

Promoting Positive Cultural Identities

It is recognized that the more positive a student's cultural identity, the higher her or his achievement level. Teachers can use various techniques to make students feel worthwhile and capable of handling everyday academic and social tasks. Arab American students need to see positive images of their culture and cultural backgrounds.

One special challenge to educators of Arab American learners is how to provide appropriate educational activities that acknowledge and respect students' Arab culture and cultural traditions. One approach is to attempt to employ counselors and teachers from Arab cultural backgrounds, but that may be difficult in some areas. Another approach is to provide training sessions focusing on Arab cultural characteristics, worldviews, and perceptions of school success and motivation. As a result of the training, educators might learn that all students do not perceive events through a European American (or whatever the majority culture is) lens. With the increasing number of learners from Arabic cultures, educators should understand students' cultural orientations and worldviews, and use culturally responsive teaching–learning strategies that promote social justice.

A School Faces a Language Dilemma

The educators at the K-5 school in this medium-sized southern city were somewhat startled when they learned that 28–30 Arab American children planned to enroll in their school in less than a week. An international corporation was sending a group of Arab Americans to this city for nine months of training. This middle- to upper-class school was predominantly European American but had a handful of African and Asian American students. The school had neither planned nor implemented language services for Arab American students because there had never been a need. Still, the school had a commitment to diversity, and it now faced a problem: How would it accommodate the language needs of some 30 Arab American students who would be entering in less than a week? The children, ranging from ages five to nine, had differing English-language skills. None was fluent, but some had a basic knowledge of the English language.

A committee of teachers, administrators, and counselors met to decide how to meet the challenge. Fortunately, one teacher knew someone who had grown up in the Arab country from which the children were coming and could speak the language. The committee made several quick decisions. First, they decided to see if this individual would volunteer as a translator several mornings a week. Second, they contacted the local university to see if its student services expert (who had considerable experience working with diverse populations) would come to the school to discuss Arab cultural mannerisms and traditions. Third, they had the foresight to ask a local religious leader to speak to the teachers about religious customs. He agreed but cautioned them to avoid making assumptions about the new students' religious allegiances.

1. The school made a commitment to address the challenge of having 30 Arab American students enter, forming a basic plan to address language and religious differences. What could the educators have done to learn about other critical differences, such as families and socioeconomic status (although this was a fairly affluent group)?
2. Stereotyping is a major ill in the United States, and probably other nations, as well. What stereotypes might these teachers and administrators have harbored? What could the administrators have done to help the teachers develop a positive and objective perception of these new students?
3. The United States has the reputation of a being a gender-equitable society. Although progress toward this goal has been made, most people think we still have challenges. Consider the gender differences between these Arab American girls and boys. How could the teachers address gender differences without making false assumptions about Arab American girls?

In her excellent article, Karen Haboush (2007) provides a comprehensive look at the growing Arab American population. She emphasizes the ethical considerations involved in working with diverse populations; provides an overview of the Arab culture (e.g. cultural demographics, religion, family); and offers implications for school psychologists (which are also appropriate for elementary, middle, and secondary educators). According to the Arab American Institute (2023), the Arab American population in the United States grew by nearly 30 percent between 2010 and 2022. The majority of the new Arab immigrants during this period came from Iraq, Egypt, Somalia, Yemen, and Syria.

Since Haboush's information was examined in the appropriate sections of this chapter, the author will look now only at selected topics and suggestions for implementing her research.

Haboush's article is so comprehensive that many ideas and suggestions can be sifted from the comprehensive review. Selected ideas include the following:

1. Teacher-education programs and school districts need to take planned approaches to teaching prospective and in-service teachers about Arab Americans and their families.
2. All teachers should appreciate the ethical considerations associated with teaching students of differing cultural backgrounds.

3. We know a great deal about African Americans and European Americans, but far less is known about Arab Americans and American Indians. Efforts should focus on these groups.

Religion

Show respect for Arabs' religions. The importance of religion cannot be over-estimated, because religion permeates all aspects of Arab culture, influencing family life, child-rearing, and views regarding education. In fact, identification with one's religious group often precedes identification with one's nationality or country.

Demonstrate knowledge and acceptance of a family's religion. Expect that a professional might be greeted with a cautious attitude since many Arab Americans consider non-Arabs as outsiders who do not understand or respect their worldview.

Family

- ◆ Understand the importance of the family as the central, unifying unit.
- ◆ Support family stability by accepting and showing respect for traditional familial customs.

Summing Up

Educators who plan teaching and learning experiences for Arab American children and adolescents should:

1. Remember that Arab Americans are not a unified single ethnic group; making such an assumption will grossly overlook their tremendous diversity.
2. Clarify stereotypes, myths, and misconceptions about Arabic culture.
3. Avoid letting Arab American children and adolescents be overlooked by the school system.
4. Consider acculturation factors among Arab Americans—for example, the length of U.S. residence, age at immigration, visits to one's homeland, and being Christian all affect acculturation.
5. Remember differences—cultural, gender, generational, and socioeconomic—that contribute to Arab American children's and adolescents' diversity.
6. Recognize the essential need for Arab American learners to develop positive self-esteem and cultural identity.

7. Provide a learning environment that respects Arabic American cultural backgrounds and languages.
8. Provide curricular and instructional practices that reflect the Arab American culture in the United States, as well as their accomplishments, art, and literature.

Implementing Research

Collaborative Approach to Develop Arab American Studies Curriculum

Kehdi's (2023) article discusses racism against Arabs and how it is addressed through Arab American studies in the K–12 Teachers' Institute. The purpose of the institute is to provide teacher training in response to an effort to undermine Arab and Palestinian diaspora studies within the Ethnic Studies Model Curriculum in California. The article discusses the development of an Arab American studies curriculum based on cultural responsiveness and community engagement with partners including teachers, authors, scholars, poets, activists, and Arab American community leaders, all of whom recognize the barriers and marginalization experienced by Arab Americans.

1. Teachers must seek out professional development opportunities to increase their knowledge about Arab culture and history to integrate them into their classrooms.
2. Teachers should encourage and participate in the development of curricula that enhance cultural sensitivities and dispel misconceptions about Arab Americans.
3. Teachers should foster a classroom environment that encourages Arab American students to be proud of their identities and value their differences.

Source: Kehdi, B. (2023). Arab American curriculum work. *Journal of Asian American Studies*, 26(2), 185–193. https://doi.org/10.1353/jaas.2023.a901067

Suggested Learning Activities

1. Choose an Arab American learner with a language problem. Evaluate the extent of the problem, list several ways that educators might address the language difficulty, and devise a plan to remediate the language problem.

2. Make a list of specific ways you can improve Arab Americans'
    self-esteem, especially students who are not doing well academically,
    students with language difficulties, and maybe girls who feel
    inadequate in a predominantly white and male-dominated classroom.
    As you compile your list, how can you make it as culturally responsive
    as possible—that is, as responsive to the Arab culture as possible?

Suggestions for Collaborative Efforts

Form groups of three or four that, if possible, represent the United States'
cultural and gender diversity. Working collaboratively, focus your group's
attention toward the following efforts.

1. Design a plan to reduce harassment and bullying of Arab American
    students. Identify your goals or objectives, methods, and materials
    for this effort. Will you consider your plan an instructional plan
    or a disciplinary plan? Will you take a cultural deficit approach or
    an objective plan for learning about cultures and promoting social
    justice? How will you evaluate your plan's effectiveness?
2. Design a one-hour school orientation program that can be presented
    to Arab American parents and families. Brainstorm in your group
    what these parents might need to know about the U.S. public school
    system—for instance, its egalitarian treatment of both genders,
    the emphasis on individualism, teacher and school expectations,
    parents' responsibilities and rights, and student rights. Let each
    person in your group take one aspect and tell what will benefit Arab
    American parents the most.
3. Interview a first-, second-, and third-generation parent (only two
    will suffice, if your group cannot locate three) to determine the
    challenges they face in dealing with the school and society in
    general. Make a chart that lists the challenges on the left and what
    your group thinks will help the parents on the right.

Expanding Your Horizons

Additional Books and Journals

Atari-Khan, R., Rbeiz, K. S., & Gerstein, L. H. (2024). Arab American well-
being and impacts of the COVID-19 pandemic. *Cultural Diversity and Ethnic Minority Psychology*. https://dx.doi.org/10.1037/cdp0000644

This article explores the significant health disparities that Arab Americans face, exacerbated by discrimination and the COVID-19 pandemic. Using responses from 604 participants, it found that Arab Americans experienced a range of mental health outcomes during the pandemic, highlighting the need for culturally relevant health interventions to address these disparities.

Kiswani, L., Naber, N., & Shoman, S. (2023). Palestine is ethnic studies: The struggle for Arab American studies in K–12 ethnic studies curriculum. *Journal of Asian American Studies, 26*(2), 221–231. https://doi.org/10.1353/jaas.2023.a901070

This article discusses how white supremacist, Islamophobic, and Zionist organizations have orchestrated aggressive campaigns to eliminate any mention of Palestine and Palestinian Americans from the curriculum. They attempt to whitewash various aspects of the Arabic American curriculum, positioning Arab Americans as both hypervisible and invisible targets of racism. Misinformation and a lack of awareness regarding Arab racism persist in a K–12 ethnic studies curriculum, hindering efforts to develop an ethnic studies curriculum that accurately represents Arab and Arab American communities.

Vanpee, K. (2024). Multidialectal approaches and social justice pedagogy: Toward linguistically and culturally diversified Arabic curricula for the collegiate U.S. Arabic classroom. *Critical Multilingualizm Studies, 11*(1), 26–55. https://cms.arizona.edu/index.php/multilingual/article/view/287/333

This paper explored a social justice pedagogy, which has been somewhat neglected in teaching the Arabic language. This pedagogy focuses on including marginalized perspectives within the educational framework to enhance student engagement with the world.

Websites

ADC.com – www.adc.org
Promotes human and civil rights and opposes racism and bigotry in any form for Arab Americans. Provides a hate crimes hotline, incident reporting, advice for educators and Arab American parents, educational resources, and statements of support.

Arab American Family Support Center — www.aafscny.org/
Founded in 1994, the Arab-American Family Support Center (AAFSC) is a non-profit, non-sectarian organization dedicated to offering culturally and linguistically proficient, trauma-informed and multigenerational social services to immigrants and refugees. Their mission revolves around enhancing family resilience through four primary focus areas: prevent harm, prepare to learn, promote well-being and pursue solutions.

Arab American Institute – www.aaiusa.org
This organization promotes the welfare and overall progress of Arab Americans.

Arab American National Museum — https://arabamericanmuseum.org/
The Arab American National Museum (AANM) stands as the premier institution in the United States dedicated to chronicling the Arab American journey and culture. Established in 2005, the AANM aims to capture, safeguard, and showcase the rich history, culture, and contributions of Arab Americans, spanning from the earliest immigrants in the late 19th century to the present day, encompassing both the Arab world and the narrative of Arab Americans.

6

Understanding Asian American Children and Adolescents

Understanding the material and activities in this chapter will help the reader to:

- Describe the cultural, gender, socioeconomic, familial, and language characteristics of Asian American children and adolescents.
- Explain the "model minority" stereotype and its effects on Asian American children and adolescents.
- Describe Asian American learners and their development, achievement levels, language problems, and learning styles.
- List several practices that impede Asian American learners' educational progress.
- Offer several concrete suggestions for improving Asian American learners' self-esteem and cultural identities.
- List several points that educators of Asian American students should remember.

Opening Scenario

Cultural Portrait: Chinese American Mina

Mina, a 10-year-old Chinese American girl, attends George Washington Elementary School, a large elementary school in an urban setting. The student population is approximately 50 percent white, 30 percent African American,

DOI: 10.4324/9781003429531-8

and 20 percent Asian and Hispanic. Although Mina makes average grades, she does not make the high grades that her family and teachers expect. Her difficulty with the English language is probably the major reason for her average grades, but other factors also contribute to the situation: Her family and teachers have expectations of her that are unrealistically high; she does not want to volunteer for special assignments; she does not want to raise her hand to answer; and she does not always understand the European Americans' attitudes toward school, teachers, and people.

Mina feels a little lost. Her teachers are either European American or African American. They are friendly and they appear to want to help her, but they do not seem to understand her and the way she believes that students should act around adults, especially their teachers. Mina wishes that she had an Asian American teacher with a cultural background similar to hers. She perceives the school as being oriented toward European American expectations, and perhaps a little toward the African American perspective, yet very little toward an Asian American or Hispanic view. While she feels somewhat frustrated with this arrangement, she believes that she has to do her best schoolwork and that her behavior must be exemplary, otherwise her family might feel shame or disappointment.

The ability to respond to Mina's psychosocial and intellectual needs requires an understanding of her in two ways: Both as an individual learner and as a member of the Asian American culture. Mina's teacher, Mrs. Daniels, has responded by doing the following:

1. Helping Mina to understand both the Asian culture and the American culture.
2. Maintaining high but not unrealistic expectations for Mina, and avoiding a reliance on cultural stereotypes.
3. Understanding that Mina's reluctance to volunteer or raise her hand during class reflects her cultural background, not any indifference or low ability.
4. Providing appropriate multicultural experiences that teach learners of all cultures about the Asian culture, including its diverse characteristics and its many contributions.
5. Assigning a professional or Asian American community volunteer in the school to be an advisor or mentor who will help Mina deal with daily school routines.
6. Meeting with Mina's family to explain the philosophy and expectations of American schools and work in order to gain the understanding, respect, and support of Mina's family.
7. Deciding how special service personnel—that is, guidance counselors, English as a Second Langauge (ESL) teachers, speech and language specialists, and other school support personnel—can assist Mina.

Overview

Planning teaching and learning experiences for Asian American learners requires an understanding of their developmental characteristics, achievement levels, language problems, learning styles, and cultural characteristics. The diversity among Asian American learners also requires a consideration of their geographic, generational, and socioeconomic differences, as well as their intracultural and individual characteristics.

Stereotyping, which plagues learners from all cultures, is a particular problem for Asian Americans. The notable success of Asian American students has resulted in a "model minority" stereotype that sometimes leads educators to expect exemplary achievement and behavior of all Asian American learners. This chapter examines the cultural characteristics of Asian American children and adolescents and then focuses attention on these learners in teaching and learning situations.

Origins

Asian Americans include a number of national, cultural, and religious heritages and comprise more than 29 distinct subgroups, each with a unique language, religion, and culture. The four major groups of Asian Americans include East Asian, such as Chinese, Japanese, and Korean; Pacific Islander; Southeast Asian, such as Thai and Vietnamese; and South Asian, such as Indian and Pakistani. Undoubtedly, similarities exist among these cultures, but educators working with Asian Americans need to remember Asians' different origins, ecological adaptations, and histories.

Although the term *Asian American* is commonly used today, it didn't exist before the mid-1960s (Okamoto, 2014). It originated as an imposed entity by non-Asians and was later adopted by Asian American activists from Chinese, Japanese, Filipino, and Korean communities to address common experiences of racism and exclusion (Espiritu, 1992). Since, and in a large part due to the Immigration Act of 1965, the Asian American population has become more diverse ethnically and, since immigration legislation gives preference to those with more schooling, Asian Americans have been more stratified socioeconomically.

Socioeconomic diversity divides Asian Americans along class lines. For example, many from China, India, Philippines, Japan, and Korea who have joined the general U.S. population are separated with rich and poor at the extremes and an affluent middle class between the two. The most recent refugee groups are struggling to achieve their hopes in the disadvantaged segment of U.S. society. This fragmentation, which often affects the second generation, creates new barriers to political mobilization and ethnic solidarity (Zhou & Ocampo, 2016).

Asian Americans have lived in the United States for more than a century and a half: Chinese and Asian Indians since the mid-1800s, Japanese since the late 1800s, and Koreans and Filipinos since the first decade of the twentieth century. An early group of Filipinos settled near New Orleans in the late eighteenth century.

Because of exclusion laws, beginning with the Chinese Exclusion Act in 1882 that culminated with the National Origins Act of 1924 which blocked mass migration from Asia, the Asian American population was relatively small prior to the mid-twentieth century. As late as 1940, Asian immigrants and their descendants constituted considerably less than 1 percent of the U.S. population. With the passage of the Immigration Act of 1965, the United States opened its doors to groups that had formerly been excluded. As a result, East Asians, South Asians, and Southeast Asians began arriving in increasing numbers. Currently, Asian Americans represent over 6 percent of the total U.S. population, according to the U.S. Census Bureau (2023a).

Individual differences also exist in reasons for immigration and related hopes and expectations. Some immigrants are refugees from war-torn countries, and others come from the middle classes of stable countries. Some immigrants arrive with empty pockets, limited education, and low English-speaking skills. Others arrive with marketable skills, fluency in English, and an education, while still others fall somewhere in between those two poles.

Asian Americans Today

The Asian population in the United States is diverse, encompassing a wide range of ethnicities from over 20 countries across East Asia, Southeast Asia and the Indian subcontinent. Asian Americans are the fastest-growing racial minority group in the United States, rising faster than that of Hispanic Americans. The Asian population in the United States has grown steadily from 2000 to 2023; 128.5 percent, from 10.5 million to roughly 24 million. This trend is expected to continue, with the U.S. Asian population surpassing 46 million by 2060, a threefold increase from 2000 (U.S. Bureau of Labor Statistics, 2023).

While about 80 percent of Asian children currently belong to one of the five largest Asian ethnic groups (Chinese, Indian, Filipino, Vietnamese, or Korean), the overall classification will become even more diverse as a new wave of Asian American families arrives from other Asian countries. People of Chinese descent in the United States number an estimated 5.2 million. This makes them the second largest Asian group in the country (U.S. Census Bureau, 2023a). The next largest are those of Indian descent at 4.8 million, Filipino at 4.4 million, Vietnamese at 2.3 million, Korean at 2.0 million, and Japanese at 1.6 million.

Countries of origins for other Asian American immigrants include Bangladesh, Pakistan, Sri Lanka, Bhutan, Burma, and Nepal, totaling 19 percent (Ruiz et al., 2023). The median age of Asian American adults in 2021 was 43, up from 36.7 years of age in 2015. The author of this book posits that the fairly young age of the Asian American population will result in an increasingly larger population. By 2060, one in ten children in the United States are projected to be Asian Americans.

Children of new Asian immigrants come from a wide range of socioeconomic backgrounds. While some arrive from affluent families with a command of English, many come from countries with high poverty rates and may face language barriers. Among the Asian origin groups with the highest poverty rates were Burmese (19 percent) and Hmong Americans (17 percent) (Tian & Ruiz, 2024). Educators need to recognize the diverse experiences of Asian students and families and provide appropriate attention and support to those who may need it, such as those with limited English proficiency.

In recent years, the smaller origin groups such as Butanese, Nepalese, and Burmese have immigrated to the United States at increasing rates, with their population increasing by more than tenfold in the last decade, reflecting global political and economic shifts that drive people to seek better lives in the United States. Understanding the cultural backgrounds of students from Butan, Burma, and Nepal helps enable teachers to connect with students, facilitate better communication and engagement in the classroom, and promote a sense of belonging among all students. Teachers can use various resources such as websites, blogs, videos, and community engagement with people from those countries to learn about the culture of their students. They should proactively try to connect with community organizations to enhance their understanding and basic knowledge, for example:

◆ Bhutanese culture emphasizes Gross National Happiness and Buddhist traditions.
◆ Burmese culture is influenced by Buddhism and has a complex history of ethnic diversity and political issues.
◆ Nepalese culture is rich in festivals, Hindu and Buddhist practices, and has a strong tradition of storytelling.

Asian American communities are characterized by where they have settled, often influenced by historic immigration patterns, their educational attainment, which varies widely between group, and their rates of employment. The largest portion of the Asian American population resides in the Western region, at 45 percent, with California alone accounting for 30 percent

(Budiman & Ruiz, 2021). The South is home to 24 percent, the Northeast to 19 percent, and the remaining 12 percent reside in the Midwest. While only 33 percent of the total U.S. population over age 25 hold a bachelor's degree or higher, 55.1 percent of Asians aged 25 and above hold a bachelor's degree or higher (U.S. Census Bureau, 2023a). In 2020, there were 612,194 Asian-owned firms in the United States. Additionally, 62.7 percent of the Asian American population, compared with 60 percent of all Americans, are in the workforce (U.S. Bureau of Labor Statistics, 2023).

There are several unique characteristics among the cultures of Southeast Asian countries that professionals working with children can easily misunderstand. Many people refer to any Southeast Asian child as "Vietnamese" without realizing that they may be insulting him or her by not recognizing his or her different cultural heritage. Such labeling fails to consider the bitter feelings among various nationalities and ethnic groups.

Stereotyping of Asian American Children and Adolescents

Asian Americans are often called the "model minority" because of their remarkable educational, occupational, and economic successes. The media like to portray Asian Americans in ways that correspond to this image. For example, many reports applaud the educational achievements of Asian Americans and generally stereotype them as successful, law-abiding, and high-achieving minorities. The success of many Asian American students has created the model minority stereotype. The popular and professional literature often labels them as "whiz kids" and as "problem free." Some claim that Asians are smarter than other groups; others believe there is something in Asian culture that breeds success, perhaps the Confucian ideas that stress family values and education.

Other stereotypes include viewing Asian Americans as proficient in mathematics and not particularly competent with verbal tasks. Such stereotypes might lead educators to hold high expectations of their Asian American students in some areas and low expectations in others. Both kinds of expectations can produce bored, frustrated students who are afforded few opportunities to learn at their actual ability and motivational levels. Educators must remember to view each child as an individual with unique strengths and weaknesses.

The academic successes of some Asian Americans have led to a perception that all Asian Americans are exceptional in all pursuits. To assume, however, such scholarly expertise on the basis of culture alone does not have any greater validity than does saying that all African Americans are incapable of high academic achievement or that all American Indians live on reservations. In addition, from the students' own perspective, cultural misconceptions of oneself can have a detrimental effect on the forming identity and can result in undue and unrealistic pressures and demands.

The COVID-19 pandemic saw a rise in anti-Asian sentiment and hate crimes against Asian Americans due to opinions and rhetoric associating the virus with Asian culture and ethnicity. Many Asian Americans reported changing their daily routines, work and social activities, and even travel out of fear of being a target for violence (Tian, 2024). Approximately six in ten Asian adults (58 percent) report having experienced racial discrimination or being treated unfairly because of their race or ethnicity (Pew Research Center, 2023a). Many also personally know someone who has experienced discrimination, violence, or aggression. The rise in Asian hate during the pandemic illustrates the existing racial and ethnic discrimination and shines a light on the need for societal efforts to encourage inclusion and fight racism in all its forms.

CASE STUDY 6.1

The Language Problem

Keigo, an Asian American fourth-grader, has a language problem that interferes with several aspects of her school life. She often cannot understand her teachers and she has difficulty making friends. Her lack of English at home and in her community does not pose a problem. Her parents and neighbors either speak their native language or a form of English not much better than Keigo's. Yet at school, Keigo's limited English language results in her having to study harder and her having few friends.

Keigo's teacher, Mr. Ottom, can take any of several approaches to help her improve her language, make better use of her study time, and improve her friendships. It is important at the outset for Mr. Ottom to avoid a victim-blaming perspective in which Keigo would be at fault for her lack of fluency in English. Mr. Ottom and the school as a whole should understand Keigo's situation and should try to help her overcome the language barriers.

First, Mr. Ottom should make arrangements with the school's language specialist to meet with Keigo, determine the extent of her problem, and suggest possible remediation. Second, Mr. Ottom might consider placing Keigo on a cooperative learning team, in which other students can help her understand. Third, he might place Keigo and other children with language difficulties in a group that receives extra attention. Regardless of what methods Mr. Ottom uses to help Keigo, it is important that he understand her and her problem, rather than hope that the problem will simply disappear.

Questions for Discussion

1. What specific actions should Mr. Ottom take?
2. Reflect on this statement: "Her parents and neighbors either speak their native language or a form of English not much better than Keigo's." Perhaps Keigo's language works at home and in the community, but it does not work at school. The difference between home language and school language often causes a problem. What should the school's policy be toward this type of language difference?
3. What other resources might Mr. Ottom seek for more specialized assistance?

Cultural Characteristics

Teachers often think of Asian American children as studious, high-achieving, well-behaved students, who are expected to excel in the U.S. culture even as they retain Asian American cultures, values, and traditions. The strain to conform to both Asian American and European American cultures can result in high expectations and considerable problems for developing personalities and identities.

Differences between the European American culture of the United States and the many long-accepted traditions, customs, and values of Asian American families (both immediate and extended) contribute to the developing child's sense of confusion regarding role expectations. Children growing up in this kind of multicultural setting may develop an ethnic identity problem, since two major role expectations confront them. Developing children can, indeed, become confused as their identities form. When these children become fully acculturated, they can clearly distinguish the differences of the two cultures and function comfortably in both. Acculturated (*bicultural*) youth show a strong ethnic identity and the appropriate and favorable social skills in both cultural groups (Choi et al., 2016).

Educators who work with Asian Americans should remember the personality differences between these children and European American children. These differences deserve recognition as cultural variations and should be kept in proper perspective. Asian American children who have enculturated and maintained an ethnic socialization are characterized as introverted, shy, or formal during interethnic interactions. For example, some enculturated Japanese Americans are quiet, reticent, and aloof in interethnic situations, are more dependent, conforming, and obedient to authority, and more willing to place family welfare over individual wishes. They put the well-being and happiness of their family before personal needs.

Although a typical Asian American culture or set of customs does not exist, distinctive cultural differences warrant educators' attention: (1) physical contact between members of the same sex, such as holding hands is permissible, but the same contact between male and female may not be; (2) when greeting, Asian Americans often bow their heads to show respect, especially toward elders and people of authority, such as teachers; and (3) Asian Americans rarely touch others' heads or pass things over one another's head.

Recently arrived Asian children and adolescents may experience particularly acute conflicts. They are caught between their parents' culture and the culture of the school, and have little power to influence either. These young people are also often called upon by adults to serve as translators, and may have to learn at a young age how to complete forms, applications, and licenses.

Gender

As in all cultures, particular differences distinguish females from males in the Asian cultures. First, in Asian families, females do not receive the respect that males receive; they are less valued than males. Similarly, they do not receive the opportunities afforded to males. Although these differences are only in cultural *expectations*, they can have far-reaching effects on Asian females' worldviews, motivation, and perception of their place in the world and their ability to perform in the home, community, and society.

Second and related, Asian females might show less motivation to succeed in ventures outside the home; they might be more reluctant to participate in class discussions and less willing to excel academically when the opportunity arises. In recent years, however, the one child per family policy of China, and the resulting reduced number of children in Asian American households, has changed the Asians' perspective on the value of female children (Fong, 2016). In summary, just as we cannot classify all Asians in a single cultural group, it is equally dangerous to label all males and females as one homogeneous group.

POINTS TO PONDER 6.1

Understanding Asian American Families

Meet with a group of Asian American parents and extended family members to discuss their perceptions and expectations of educators and schools. Allow sufficient time for questions and discussions. Do not be dismayed if parents do not express themselves, because they sometimes perceive teachers as authority figures or place teachers on a pedestal.

Socioeconomic Status

Asian Americans' socioeconomic status as a group shows both the financial success of some and the low level of accomplishments of others. For example, Asian households had the highest median income, $108,700 in 2022; this is about 34 percent higher than the national median (U.S. Census Bureau, 2023d). Asian Americans made up 6.9 percent of the total U.S. population in 2022 (Shrider, 2023). Approximately 10.3 percent of Asian American children fall below the poverty line; this compares to 10.6 percent of white children and 22.3 percent of African American children (Cid-Martinez & Marvin, 2023). The majority of Asian American families are in the highest income bracket, with significantly fewer in the lowest bracket and a moderate number in the middle. While Asian Americans are less likely to have a low socioeconomic status, these statistics do not depict all Asians. Children of Burmese descent, for example, are three times more likely to be poor, and children of Cambodian and Hmong origin are about twice as likely. Although some Asian Americans' socioeconomic status is indeed impressive and indicates that they have overcome (or successfully coped with) racism and prejudice, others have not been as fortunate and deserve better education opportunities.

The accumulation of wealth allows people more options, opportunities, and increased amounts of leisure time. A change in economic circumstances also influences a person's social expression, values, and patterns of thinking and behaving. A learner's socioeconomic status is undoubtedly one of the most significant factors affecting his or her learning and achievement. Educators should understand the educational and social implications of a learner's socioeconomic status and the danger of basing curricular and instructional decisions on stereotypical beliefs and assumptions. However, it is often difficult to put those understandings into practice.

Trying to determine the socioeconomic level of Asian Americans proves difficult at best, because of the diversity among the Asian cultures and the lack of current information on their earning power and social class. Despite the disparities in educational achievement and life experience among Asian Americans, the model minority stereotype continues to be prevalent in school. Educators must be careful not to rely on the model minority stereotype by assuming that all Asian Americans experience academic, social, and economic successes. Statistics show that some Asian Americans—like members of other cultures—have achieved socioeconomic success while others have not.

Families

The majority of Asian American households, 73 percent, consist of a two-parent family, and 27 percent of Asian Americans live in households that are multigenerational. For all U.S. households, the numbers are 65 percent and 19 percent, respectively (Kids Count Data Center, 2024). These statistics illustrate the high value Asian Americans place on the care of aging family members within the family. The Kids Count Data Center analysis of the 2024 U.S. Census Bureau data revealed that 601,000, or 16 percent, of Asian and Pacific Islander children live in single-parent households. This number was 34 percent for all children in the United States.

Founded in cultural expectations, the child-rearing techniques of Asian American families emphasize loyalty to the family. The culture sends a powerful message of the importance of not bringing embarrassment or shame to the family. The inculcation of guilt and shame is the principal technique that controls the behavior of family members. Parents emphasize their children's obligation to the family and their responsibility to abide by family expectations. Adults consider children who act contrary to the family's wishes as selfish, inconsiderate, and ungrateful. The behavior of individual members is a reflection on the entire family. For example, aberrant behavior is usually hidden from the public and handled within the family. On the other hand, outstanding achievement in some aspect of life is a source of great pride for the child and for the entire family as well. Such a standard of morality can cause confusion for children who are attempting to satisfy the expectations of two cultures, even as it emphasizes the importance of unity and honor in the Asian American family.

Asian American children and adolescents learn early in life that the family is the primary unit and that considerable value should be placed on family solidarity, responsibility, and harmony. Dinh and Kalaja (2023) explained the significant emphasis Asian American cultures place on the family unit, the prioritization of education, adherence to traditional roles based on birth order within the family, and the maintenance of distinct gender roles. Communication with adults is usually one-way, children listening and adults speaking. Children also are taught a respect for education, which is based on respect for the authority of the teacher (Perez & Shin, 2016). In summary, the family is central to Asian culture. Individual conflicts may arise, because parents and family reflect traditional ways and children, in their schools, see another way of life.

Family allegiance and respect for parents and family play a significant role in the value system, achievements, and behavior of developing Asian

American children. In many Eastern and Southeast Asian cultures, Confucian ideals, which include respect for elders and discipline, are a strong influence. Most Asian American parents and families teach their children to value educational achievement, to respect authority, to feel responsible for relatives, and to show self-control. Asian American children tend to be more dependent, conforming, and willing to place family welfare ahead of their own individual wishes than are other American children. Influenced by their parents' emphasis on the importance of educational achievement, Asian American children perceive that it is their job to achieve academic success (Tao, 2016). In many Asian cultures, parents see their children's academic success as a reflection on themselves and the family, which leads to high expectations for their children's academic performance (Fung et al., 2023). In low-income immigrant families, education is often viewed as a means of upward mobility and improved socio-economic status. Additionally, influenced by Confucianism and the value of filial piety, children are expected to honor their parents' aspirations by excelling academically. These characteristics are important in understanding societal and familial dynamics among Asian Americans.

Asian American parents seem to structure their children's lives for academic success more than Caucasian parents do. Asian parents are more likely to decide whether their children should go to college, to discuss SAT/ACT plans and preparation with their children, and to limit television and video games. In general, it appears that Asian parents organize and structure their children's lives to facilitate academic success. Another important point, however, needs to be explained. People often have an authoritarian image of Asian parents who have very high expectations without giving much feedback and nurturance—that is, Asian parents are less likely to be involved in children's actual academic activities. For example, they are less likely to decide what classes their children should take and to check on the completion of homework. They help their children with homework less often and discuss school progress less than their American counterparts do.

In the traditional Asian American family, age, gender, and generational status are the primary determinants of the child's role behavior. Ancestors and elders are greatly revered and respected, and elders are actively involved in child-rearing. Families are patriarchal. Fathers consider teaching children core Asian values as crucial, such as respecting elders and authority, maintaining traditional family and gender roles, emphasizing hard work, and focusing on advancement. Some families expect their sons, particularly the eldest, to support their parents in their old age. The primary duty of the son is to be a good son, and his obligations as a good husband or father come second to his duty as a son. The role of the female in the family calls for subservience to the male, the performance of domestic chores, and the bearing of children. However, such generalizations may vary and these roles can differ widely based on family's socioeconomic status (Mathews, 2000) and whether they are closer to their heritage roots or more assimilated into the mainstream culture.

This information leads to an important question: What can educators do to support Asian American families?

1. Arrange small-group sessions with families (both immediate and extended), perhaps at Parent–Teacher Association meetings or at other school functions, to learn what the families expect of the schools and the children, and to explain the school's expectations to parents.
2. Learn about families from a variety of Asian cultures to gain a better understanding of intracultural and individual differences.
3. Learn about the generational differences among families—for example, variations among first-, second-, and third-generation immigrant families in the United States.
4. Learn about families from different socioeconomic groups in order to gain an understanding of values, traditions, and beliefs.

POINTS TO PONDER 6.2

Helping Asian American Families Understand U.S. Schools

Asian American families, especially first generation, might not understand U.S. schools. These families have traditionally placed greater value on sons than on daughters and feel considerable shame when children's achievements or behavior does not meet the family's expectations. List several ways—such as parent-education programs or orientation sessions—in which you can help Asian American families to understand U.S. schools better.

Religion

The recent influx of Indochinese, Chinese, Indians, and other groups has increased religious pluralism in the United States. Laotians, Cambodians, and Vietnamese are predominantly Buddhist. Some Vietnamese, however, are Taoist or Roman Catholic. Koreans and Japanese are a mix of Christian, Buddhist, and the unaffiliated. Many Asian Americans continuously embrace the philosophy of Confucianism, as do the majority of Korean immigrants.

As Asian Americans assimilate into the life of the United States, however, many become Christian. The religion of Asian Americans is changing. Per Mohamed and Rotolo's research for the Pew Research Center (2023), 34 percent, down from 42 percent in 2012, report being Christian. The number who express no religious affiliation at all has risen to 32 percent from the 2012 number of 26 percent. Other religious affiliations of Asian Americans include Buddhist (11 percent), Hindu (11 percent), Muslim (6 percent), and "other" such as Daoists, Jains, Jews and Sikhs (4 percent). Asian Americans reported religion being very important to them, with 29 percent attending religious services at least monthly, and 36 percent using an altar, shrine, or religious symbol for worship at home.

Asian Americans tend to practice values such as respect for ancestors, filial piety, and avoidance of shame. These moral principles define a person's obligation, duty, and loyalty to others. For example, Korean families constantly emphasize to their children to possess such moral values as well as positive characteristics such as respect for parents and elders (Lee, 2013). Asian American families instill in their children that good performance and achievement bring honor to the family. Consequently, shame and dishonor are powerful preventives to unacceptable behavior. Although this standard of morality may seem harsh and rigid to the outsider, many Asian Americans believe that it maintains honor and harmony in the family.

Language

To gain a better understanding of Asian American learners, educators should recognize that a significant portion—68 percent—of Asian adults in the United States are immigrants (Ruiz et al., 2023). Among Indian adults, 83 percent were born in their home country. This is followed by Vietnamese (74 percent), Chinese (72 percent), Korean (69 percent), and Filipino (61 percent) adults. So the majority of Asian Americans are first-generation immigrants and speak English as a second language.

The category Asian immigrant encompasses a wide range of languages reflective of the group's diversity. Most (86 percent) speak a language other than English at home and prefer to maintain their heritage language. Just 14 percent speak only English at home (Noe-Bustamante et al., 2022). These numbers align with all immigrants to the United States, where 83 percent arrive speaking a language other than English.

English proficiency among immigrants has remained fairly constant over time. Many foreign-born immigrants use primarily their native language at home (Gambino et al., 2014). Among Asian Americans aged over five, 58 percent are proficient in English but a considerable number still face challenges. Among Asian immigrants, the most commonly spoken languages include Chinese (Mandarin and Cantonese), Hindi, Tagalog, and Vietnamese. Specifically, 52 percent of those who spoke Chinese, and 57 percent of those who spoke Vietnamese at home spoke English "less than very well" (Dietrich & Hernandez, 2022b).

Consequently, many Asian children and adolescents live in homes where the family's "heritage language" is the primary language spoken. For this reason, many Asian Americans are fluent in two languages as many parents encourage the use of heritage language at home while they learn English at school. Simultaneous bilingualism may be beneficial in that it helps to maintain the cultural heritage even as it encourages communication within the family.

Beyond the family, though, natural bilingual ability has been proven not to interfere with Asian American children learning English at school. Educators need to understand that children fluent in their heritage language can still learn the language of the society in which they live. Temporary language barriers, such as those a child might encounter upon first arrival in the country, make achievements and educational attainments even more significant. Understanding the spoken word and being understood while speaking English often pose difficult situations for Asian American English language learners, especially in school systems that forbid learners from speaking their native languages.

Asian limited English proficiency (LEP) students feel challenges in school due to language barriers impacting their access to learning resources and performances. They may be undocumented immigrants, refugees, or asylum seekers who speak heritage language at home and English less than very well. They therefore require special assistance to ensure that they receive enriching educational programs and methods best suited to them without being segregated from their peers (Vanbuel & Van den Branden, 2023). AAPI Data's (2022) study indicates that Asian Americans exhibit one of the highest rates of LEP: 3 percent speaking English "not at all," 11 percent speaking English "not well," and 18 percent speaking English "well." The overall LEP rate for Asian Americans is comparable to that of Latinos.

This high rate of LEP among Asians can in part be attributed to their arrival from countries with low English usage. English proficiency varies considerably among Asian origin groups: Japanese (85 percent), Filipinos (84 percent), and Indians (82 percent) speak English proficiently. By contrast, Bhutanese (36 percent) and Burmese (38 percent)—both groups with large numbers of recently arrived immigrants—have some of the lowest proficiency rates. Language proficiency is significantly higher among U.S.-born Asians (95 percent) than foreign-born Asians (57 percent) (Budiman & Ruiz, 2021).

Japanese American and Chinese American boys and girls scored lower than European American children on the verbal sections of an achievement test. The reasons for language difficulties may include that Asian Americans often come from bilingual backgrounds and that cultural traditions and customs often restrict or impede verbal communication, at least temporarily. Many Asian American families, for example, encourage one-way communication—that is, parents speak to children. Children are not encouraged to speak.

Educators working in multicultural settings with such children can avoid several of the pitfalls that may lead to stereotypical thinking. Educators must remember that Asian American students may be communicating in a second language. Although English may be the predominant language, these children may continue to hear their parents' native language in their homes.

Educators who work with Asian American learners readily recognize the language and communication problems. The author taught a Japanese American learner who excelled over all others in the class. Her language problems, however, required that she study far longer and more diligently than her classmates. During tests and during other written work, she relied extensively on her Japanese–English dictionary and requested extra time. Despite all her language difficulties, her persistence and determination overcame her deficiencies in English.

Not only must educators in multicultural settings understand (and be understood in) verbal interactions with Asian Americans, but they must also make an equal effort to understand nonverbal communication. Several examples of nonverbal behavior that adolescents learn show the distinctive differences among cultures. First, the forward and backward leaning of the body indicates feelings: A backward lean indicates a withdrawal from a conversation or topic, and a forward lean lets the speaker know that the listener is polite, concerned, and flexible. For educational efforts to be most effective, educators and Asian American learners should work actively to understand each other's verbal and nonverbal behaviors.

Achievement Levels

Although some Asian American students do not fare well educationally, many do. In 2022, 57.5 percent of Asian American males and 54.8 percent of Asian American females had bachelor or higher degrees. These numbers are up from the 2010 figures of 51.3 percent and 46.8 percent, respectively (U.S. Census Bureau, 2022d).

Although Asian Americans undoubtedly have attained enviable accomplishment in U.S. schools, it is unrealistic to expect all Asian Americans to attain such achievement levels. Not all Asian immigrant children are superior students who have no problems at school. Some have learning problems; some lack motivation, proficiency in English, and financial resources; and some have parents who do not understand the U.S. school system because of cultural or language barriers.

When they first enter the United States, children often experience a clash between their cultures and the expectations of their new homes and schools. Several distinct differences exist between Asian and European American expectations and attitudes toward schools and teachers. First, teachers in Asia are accorded a higher status than teachers in the United States. The informality between American teachers and students may seem confusing to Southeast Asian children and appalling to their families. Second, Asian children and parents, culturally, expect considerable structure and organization.

One of the obvious differences in values is the high value of self-effacement and saving face; Asian American students have been taught to wait to answer or to participate unless the teacher requests otherwise. Having attention drawn to oneself—the teacher putting a child's name on the board for misbehaving, for example—can bring considerable distress. Another difference is that Asian social values call for children to listen more than they speak and to speak in soft, well-modulated voices. In the United States this characteristic is often perceived as shyness and misinterpreted as lack of confidence.

The European American emphasis on individualism may present challenges for Asian American learners, who have not been taught this behavior and who may seek to satisfy the demands of contemporary society while maintaining loyalty to Asian American family traditions. Educators need to understand the Asian Americans' strong regard for the father as head of the family, the value placed on sons rather than daughters, and the respect accorded to older family members.

It is important that educators understand Asian American parents' perceptions of school behavior and achievement. Asian Americans come from cultures that often view children's negative behavior as the result of a lack of will or attributable to supernatural causes. Cases of school failure have resulted in parents complaining that children are lazy and lack character.

Rather than looking for educational reasons for a lack of success, parents often believe that the solution lies in increasing parental restrictions, demanding more homework, and placing other negative sanctions on the child in order to promote character development. Asian parents consider hard work, effort, and developing character the best avenues to improve behavior or school work (Perez & Shin, 2016). As educators quickly realize, such beliefs can be particularly difficult for Asian American children with limited intellectual (or other) abilities.

Given the fact that 68 percent of Asian Americans were born outside the United States and almost a quarter of the 24 million Asian Americans are under age 18 (Ruiz et al., 2023), educators increasingly are called upon to work and interact with Asian students and their families (Lee & Manning, 2001). Okamoto (2014) reminds educators to remember the multilayered identities among Asian Americans and their vast heterogeneity and flexible boundaries across time and context. So, educators need to avoid stereotypes, assumptions, judgments, and generalizations. Whether through parent conferences, parent-involvement programs, or parent-education programs, Lee and Manning (2001) believe that teachers and administrators must have knowledge of various Asian cultures, positive attitudes toward Asian people, and skills to conduct successful conferences as well as involve and educate Asian parents and families.

Educators' openness to Asian cultures and their commitment to working with Asian parents will contribute to teachers and parents developing a collaborative partnership that both improves academic achievement and provides a more equitable learning environment for Asian students. Suggestions for achieving this include:

1. Respecting both immediate and extended family members; considering Asian parents' English proficiency and their nonverbal communication; and preparing education programs for Asian parents.
2. Understanding diversity within Asian ethnic groups.
3. Recognizing Asian traditions of respect toward teachers.
4. Encouraging children to be bicultural and bilingual.
5. Eliminating the stereotype that all Asians are automatically smart in academics.

School Practices Promoting Asian Americans' Progress

Educators who understand Asian Americans' cultural backgrounds and potential school-related problems may actually contribute to their academic and social success in U.S. schools. Looking at Asian Americans from any other cultural perspective may promote learning experiences and expectations that are not compatible with Asian American expectations. The tendency toward generalizing across Asian customs and assuming too much homogeneity among learners negates or overlooks the tremendous cultural diversity between groups and ignores generational and socioeconomic differences.

What school practices might promote Asian American academic achievement and psychosocial development?

1. Providing teaching and learning experiences that place Asian American learners at an advantage.
2. Making school expectations clear to both students and parents.
3. Not expecting Asian American students to participate in discussion and sharing times, during which they may say something that they feel might shame their name or reputation.
4. Having realistic academic and behavioral expectations of Asian American learners; recognizing that some are academic achievers and some are lower achievers.

Suggestions for understanding and teaching Asian American learners include the following:

1. Avoid reprimanding or disciplining Asian American learners in front of their peers. Making them feel humiliated by publicly scolding or having their name written on the board or other public display may be far more damaging to the Asian American child than to the European American child.
2. Avoid thinking that all Asian Americans are high achievers who reach excellence in all academic areas and who model impeccable behavior (Lee, 2015).
3. Help the Asian American family to understand the U.S. school system and its expectations of learners and their families. Try to understand how the Asian American family perceives teachers: with high respect. As the teacher earns the family's respect, the teacher will gain its assistance and support.
4. Understand that behavior (at least to European American teachers) that may seem to indicate indifference or lack of interest—for example, looking the other way or not volunteering to answer— is appropriate for Asian American learners. For example, Asian American culture teaches learners to listen more than they speak and to speak in a well-modulated voice.
5. Understand other culturally specific traits: Asian American learners may be modest in dress, manner, and behavior; girls may be quieter than boys; girls may not want to reveal their legs during physical education activities; and problems may result when assigning girls and boys as cooperative learning partners.

Chiang (2000) maintains that, given the increasing number of Asian immigrant children, educators need to recognize Asian students' cultural characteristics and learn to work with them effectively. In her article, she looks specifically at the relationship between teaching styles and Asian cultures, communication patterns, cognitive activities, and social support. Overall, she finds that Asian American students adjust well to U.S. schools academically. Still, some might need psychological support and understanding from teachers and administrators. For example, they might need more assistance and encouragement and less pressure from teachers and schools.

Chiang (2000) makes these recommendations:

1. Help Asian American students by giving clear directions, allowing choices of projects and peers, communicating on an individual basis, and providing peer tutoring.
2. Help parents of Asian American students by helping them develop an understanding of commonly accepted gender roles in the United States, an understanding of school systems and how they function, and a wish to be involved in their children's education.
3. Help policymakers assist Asian American students by recruiting Asian American teachers, revising the curriculum to reflect more positive images of Asian people, and providing in-service training for teachers to better acquaint them with family expectations of Asian American learners.

Promoting Cultural Identities

Asian American children have special needs that responsive educators should address. In a school system that might seem different and perhaps even oblivious to their needs, these learners need teaching and learning experiences that reflect and support their cultural and social experience. Otherwise, learners in formative developmental stages may begin to question their self-worth and their cultural worth. Responsive multicultural educators need to focus their efforts in several directions that can improve the self-esteem of Asian American learners.

First, the actual effect of the school experience on the Asian American learner must be considered. Attending a school that appears to direct attention toward the majority culture can cause Asian Americans to question their place in the school. Educators can focus attention in several directions: Recognizing Asian Americans as integral and worthy learners in the school system; recognizing the Asian culture as worthy; and directly addressing the concerns of Asian Americans, one of which being teachers who often have high expectations based on the model minority stereotype.

Second, educators can respond by understanding the cultural differences that affect Asian Americans and their academic and social progress in U.S. schools. For example, Asian Americans strive toward the accomplishment that brings pride to the family, in contrast to European Americans who work for individual acclaim. The custom of many European American learners is to question the teacher, to volunteer for an academic activity, or to assertively raise their hands to answer a teacher's question. Such traits are in opposition to Asian culture, and Asian American students are not likely to perform them instinctively. Teachers need to understand these cultural differences and then respond with appropriate teaching behaviors, rather than to expect learners of all cultures to respond in a similar fashion.

Specifically, educators can do the following:

1. Read culturally appropriate children's books about Asian Americans aloud to the entire class. Especially, use Asian folk literature that contains unique traditional values that remain important even in modern Asian American families (Lee, 2011).
2. Convey a sense of welcome that makes children feel wanted, a part of the class, and an integral presence in the classroom.
3. Encourage them to make a "Me Collage" that demonstrates both the individual and the Asian culture.
4. Encourage learners to engage in *open-ended writing* in which they can probe their feelings and express them without fear of sharing.
5. Teach learners to write about "What I Like about My Life" (and perhaps culture) or "Ten Things about Me," in which learners can feel free to express opinions and emotions.

Third, responsive multicultural educators need to engage in direct activities that can improve the self-esteem of Asian American learners. Such activities include specifically addressing their needs, asking about their families (using extreme caution not to make the learner feel uncomfortable or think that the teacher is prying), genuinely and truthfully conveying to the learner that other students would benefit from knowing more about the Asian culture, and letting the students know that their presence is understood, accepted, and appreciated by both school personnel and other children and adolescents.

Educators should remember the importance of the family in efforts to improve cultural identity. Asian families are generally close-knit, and Asian people's self-perception usually includes a consideration of feelings about their family.

CASE STUDY 6.2

Kimura: No Social Interaction at a New School

Kimura is a 13-year-old sixth-grader who moved from Japan one year ago when the Japanese military deployed his father to the United States. He attends an inner-city public middle school where a majority of students are African American. Although he attends school regularly, he never talks or plays with other students, even during recess or lunch. He has had difficulty adapting to his new U.S. school. Kimura's home room and the ESL teachers believed his "silent period" would pass as he learned English. They are now concerned because a year has passed and he still does not responded to anyone's questions, other than nodding or shaking his head. Over the year, various teachers have approached him in attempts to find out what he is thinking and to get to know him. They ask him simple questions like "Do you like playing sports?" "What is your favorite American food?" or "What did you do over the weekend?" He just stares at the ground and avoids eye contact. When his classmates ask "Hey, what's up man, want to shoot some hoops?" or "Come on, why don't you join our discussion team?," they get total silence in return and a sense that Kimura is annoyed by the attention. Since arriving at school, Kimura has been pulled out of class daily to receive 45 minutes of ESL instruction, however, he refuses to engage in any social interaction. He is now becoming known as "that weird Jap" among his classmates, which is different from their initial perception—that he was simply quiet and shy. Unlike American teenagers, he doesn't show any interest in talking with girls either. Girls, and boys, at his school no longer pay him much attention. They leave him alone sitting at his desk or in the cafeteria, ignored. His typical posture is slouching, or sitting like a stick, looking down at the ground or his desk. He does not misbehave, and in fact is attentive in class. Teachers and classmates are used to his aloof behavior, so no one asks him to work together any more. He simply doesn't participate in any cooperative or interactive discussions or group projects. He does, however, show respect to all of his teachers. He has no discipline issues and responds to his teacher's directions—for example, reading a book chapter and writing down what he read.

Concerned about the lack of Kimura's social ability, his teacher, Ms. Smith, invited Kimura's mother to have a parent–teacher conference. His mother is the primary caregiver and believes her duties are child-rearing and homemaking. Kimura's father has a very traditional view of his role and is not concerned with his children's affairs. He believes he should focus on his career and providing money for the family. Ms. Smith is surprised to find that Kimura's mother speaks English well and has the strong opinion that Kimura's lack of English is not an issue because the family will not remain in the United States permanently. Ms. Smith is actually relieved that Kimura will not stay in the United States. She was pleased to learn that Kimura's evenings are filled with academic work in Japanese, studying math, reading books, playing in Japanese with his younger sister, and watching Japanese TV programs online. Ms. Smith and Kimura's mother agreed not to focus on improving Kimura's school performance in English as his studies at home in Japanese will be useful for his future.

Questions for Discussion

1. Do you think the school and Ms. Smith are accountable for improving the English language ability of those students who are non-citizens or nonpermanent residents of the United States? Why? Do you think Ms. Smith does not need to be concerned about improving Kimura's class participation since he is studying a lot in Japanese which will be useful when moves back to Japan as soon as his father's military orders are over? Why?
2. What are some potential problems that you observed from this vignette? How will Kimura's U.S. school experiences impact his schooling when he moves back to Japan? Suggest possible solutions to ensure Kimura's psychological and emotional well-being.
3. When Ms. Smith observed that he doesn't have a friend at school and no one wants to be around him, what course of action could she take in order to help Kimura's English language skills and social activities? Why?

Summing Up

Educators planning educational experiences for Asian American learners should:

1. Reflect on both historical and contemporary Asian cultural experiences, and plan teaching and learning experiences accordingly.
2. Undertake objective assessments of each learner, rather than believe that all learners are members of a model minority.

3. Understand that language ability warrants understanding because of its cultural basis (and its cultural value) and because of the problems many Asian Americans have with the English language.

4. Understand that positive self-esteem and cultural identities are crucial to Asian learners' psychosocial development and general outlook on life. Plan appropriate activities.

5. Recognize that students each have their distinct culture with its unique cultural characteristics, rather than group all Asian American learners into one "Asian" culture.

6. Consider the tremendous diversity among learners—individual, generational, socioeconomic, urban, or rural—rather than categorize all Asian American learners into one homogeneous group.

7. Exercise extreme caution in expecting all Asian American learners to be high achievers.

8. Recognize the family and its powerful influence (e.g. the injunction against bringing shame and embarrassment on the family) on children and adolescents.

Suggested Learning Activities

1. Complete a case study of a high-achieving Asian American student. Specifically: (a) outline outstanding accomplishments; (b) address how the family has contributed to successes; (c) describe any problems or frustrations that the student may experience; (d) explain how one can account for outstanding achievements, even though language problems exist; and (e) ask how the school might address the student's problems. Show why it is imperative that educators do not base teaching and learning experiences on the model minority stereotype.

2. Survey several educators who have taught Asian American students. Develop a survey designed to determine the strengths and weaknesses of Asian American learners, the educators' opinions of Asian American attitudes and achievements, and how they believe that schools can best respond to meet the individual needs of Asian American learners. What efforts can be made to educate parents and gain their support? Generally speaking, what approaches can you suggest to educators who work with Asian American learners of varying cultural backgrounds and individual differences?

3. Read the following Implementing Research section, which looks at a *Child Development* article that notes that Asian Americans often outperform their peers and are left out of the debate on the achievement gap.

Implementing Research

Asian American Child Development within Historical Context

Kiang et al. (2016) claim that historical time and place influence the development of children and youths of Asian descent in the United States. This article helps educators to understand the link between major historical events such as the Chinese Exclusion Act of 1882; the internment of Japanese Americans; the Immigration Act of 1965; or the events of 9/11 in 2001; and the social, political, cultural, and linguistic trends and biases affecting the daily lives and interactions of Asian Americans in their families and schools, and among their peers and communities.

After an interesting introduction of the ecological perspectives of child development, Kiang et al. (2016) explain how history matters in shaping race and racial stereotypes, cultural-community contexts, pre- and post-migration experiences, and experiences of oppression, all of which ultimately affect the development of Asian American children. Given the vast differences in Asian Americans across time, location, and context, being aware of such historical background can help educators contextualize individuals' unique experiences and better understand Asian American children and their families.

Implementing the Research

1. Educators working with Asian Americans should think about the role that the history of Asians and the challenges they have faced has played in developing their characteristics and their cultural adaptation to the United States.
2. Educators should have an understanding of how historical, social, economic, and political contexts have shaped Asians' racial stereotypes, cultural-community contexts, pre- and post-migration experiences, and experiences of oppression.
3. Educators should consider the social and cultural contexts in which children grow up that may influence developmental processes among Asian Americans.

Source: Kiang, L., Tseng, V., & Yip, T. (2016). Placing Asian American child development within historical context. *Child Development*, *87*(4), 995–1013. DOI: 10.1111/cdev.12578

Suggestions for Collaborative Efforts

Form groups of three or four that, if possible, represent the United States' cultural and gender diversity. Working collaboratively, focus each group's attention toward the following efforts.

1. Have each member of your group select an Asian American learner: A Japanese American, a Chinese American, a Filipino American, and a Korean American. After getting to know these learners and their families, show the similarities and differences among the four cultures. Specifically, consider cultural characteristics, families, academic achievement, socioeconomic accomplishments, and any other area in which similarities and differences are likely to be evident.
2. Suggest several ways in which educators can address Asian Americans' language problems. What language programs will most effectively help Asian Americans? What other efforts might educators implement to help Asian Americans overcome language obstacles?
3. Educators often experience difficulty in locating children's books that focus on Asian American learners and themes. Consult recent publishers' catalogs and make a list of current children's books that appear to provide accurate descriptions of the Asian American culture.

Expanding Your Horizons

Additional Books and Journals

Cai, L. (2023). An Asian American feminist manifesto: Asian American women heads of schools embodying culturally responsive school leadership. *Teachers College Record*, *125*(7/8), 173–187. https://doi-org.proxy.lib.odu.edu/10.1177/01614681231209589
Explores how race, gender, culture and epistemology intersect to shape the leadership experiences of Asian American women who lead independent

schools. It challenges conventional leadership narratives by highlighting the complex stories of a select group of women of color in educational leadership roles.

Jeung, R., Garcia, A. M., Bae, A., Shen, C., & Malasa, J. (2023). Urgently needed to protect Asian American children and families: The social movement for Asian American studies at K-12 grades. *Sociological Inquiry, 94*(2), 369–390. https://doi.org/10.1111/soin.12573
The surge of anti-Asian hate during the COVID-19 pandemic has led to a significant expansion of the national movement for Asian American Studies curriculum in K–12 education, with 17 states proposing legislation and ten states mandating it. Case studies of successful campaigns in Illinois and New Jersey reveal the utilization of diagnostic, prognostic, and motivational frames, emphasizing winnable issues like racial bullying and multiracial solidarity.

Kim, B. S. K., Suh, H. N., & Subica, A. (2023). Asian American child–parent cultural value discrepancies, family conflict, life satisfaction, and self-esteem. *Journal of Counseling Psychology, 70*(5), 510–521. https://doi-org.proxy.lib.odu.edu/10.1037/cou0000689
Investigates how Asian American college students perceive and adhere to traditional cultural values compared to their parents. The authors found generational discrepancies, with students adhering less strongly to these values than their parents. These discrepancies are associated with the increased likelihood and severity of family conflict as well as decreased life satisfaction and self-esteem.

Shiao, J. L. (2023). Over-educated or overly invested in education? The role of educational commitment in Asian American socioeconomic attainment. *Race and Social Problems.* https://doi-org.proxy.lib.odu.edu/10.1007/s12552-023-09403-9
Examines how cultural capital components influence high-school grade point average (GPA), degree attainment, and adult incomes among Asian American respondents, revealing GPA as a critical mediator in racial disparities and highlighting the importance of academic performance for the second-generation Asian Americans' advantages in education and the labor market, with implications for rethinking Asian American racial status.

Websites
AAPI Data – https://aapidata.com/
This group publishes demographic data and policy research on Asian Americans and Pacific Islanders. They also issue guides to understanding issues that affect Asian Americans.

Asian Nation – www.asian-nation.org/index.shtml
This Internet site is a one-stop information resource that offers an overview of the historical, demographic, political, and cultural issues affecting today's diverse Asian American community.

Asian American Federation – www.aafederation.org
This site represents a network of community service agencies in the Northeast that work in the fields of health and human services, education, economic development, civic participation, and social justice in order to raise the well-being of the pan-Asian American community through research, policy advocacy, public awareness, and organizational development.

Infoplease – www.infoplease.com/spot/asianhistory1.html
May is Asian Pacific American Heritage Month—a celebration of Asian and Pacific Islanders in the United States. This site includes the following topics: Origins of APA Heritage Month, Asian-American History, Timeline of Asian-American History, and Japanese Relocation Centers.

Understanding European American Children and Adolescents

Understanding the materials and activities in this chapter will help the reader to:

- ◆ Describe European Americans, their origins, and who they are today.
- ◆ Identify several stereotypes of European American learners and how these stereotypes adversely affect peers' opinions as well as educators' perceptions of their propensity toward academic success and behavior.
- ◆ Describe European Americans' cultural, gender, socioeconomic, family, religious, and language diversity.
- ◆ Describe European American learners, and show how teaching and learning practices can reflect knowledge of cultural differences and learning styles.

Opening Scenario

Cultural Portrait: Greek American Helen

Helen, an eleventh-grader, is a second-generation Greek American female. She is personable and intelligent, speaks excellent English, and is an all-around good student. She talks of wanting to teach in an elementary school when she finishes college. While Helen is sociable and others like her, she does not have any close friends. In fact, she perceives several of her teachers as friends and talks with them at length whenever she can.

DOI: 10.4324/9781003429531-9

While Helen is Americanized in many ways, her parents and extended family members maintain Greek values, customs, and traditions. They continue to speak Greek in the home on many occasions. One of Helen's teachers, Ms. Jacobs, once telephoned Helen at home and asked to speak with her. Helen's father spoke English with such an accent and with such difficulty that Ms. Jacobs could not understand why Helen could not come to the phone. The next day, Helen asked Ms. Jacobs whether she had called and then explained that she was not at home. Ms. Jacobs perceived that Helen was uncomfortable that she had called and did not call her at home again.

Helen's family owns a fast-food restaurant, which has been in business for nearly 25 years, since her father brought his family from Greece. All family members work at the restaurant at some time; Helen probably works the least because she commits so much of her time to her school work.

Ms. Jacobs has genuine respect for Helen's Greek background, but she wonders how Helen considers her diversity. Does she feel accepted? Does her parents and family members' continuing to speak Greek bother her? Does she intentionally avoid working in the restaurant? Ms. Jacobs will not take any specific action, but she wonders about Helen's feelings and questions her decision not to discuss Helen's diversity with her.

Overview

The African American, American Indian, Arab American, Asian American, and Hispanic cultural groups make up a sizable percentage of the United States' diversity. Likewise, their differences, traditions, customs, language, and dialects enrich the United States in many ways. Another cultural group, however, also contributes to the nation's diversity. The various European American cultures bring a plethora of differences that perceptive educators will want their students to understand and appreciate. Just as Asian Americans and Hispanic Americans originate from many places, European Americans originate from scores of locations, such as France, Germany, Greece, Hungary, Ireland, Italy, Poland, and Portugal, as Chapter 1 indicated. This chapter focuses on European Americans and their cultural, gender, socioeconomic, family, religious, and language diversity. To avoid overgeneralizing, we will discuss specific cultural groups, such as Helen's Greek American culture, whenever possible.

Origins

The hundred-year period from 1830 to 1930 was a century of mass immigration in the history of the United States. Many millions of people uprooted themselves, primarily from the crowded places of Europe, and flowed outward to less crowded areas such as the United States. About 32 million left Europe for the United States, contributing enormously to the nation's expansion and industrial growth. The primary reason for this massive transfer of people from the Old World to the New World was the social and economic strain on the rural systems of Europe. More specific causes included large populations, the lack of farming land for all people, and the abolition of feudalism, which ended peasant privileges. In the colonial days, most of America's immigrants came from Great Britain and Ireland, and a few came from Germany, France, the Netherlands, Belgium, and Luxembourg. During the early nineteenth century, Germans (mainly tradesmen, farmers, weavers, tailors, shoemakers, and carpenters) began coming in ever-increasing numbers. French, Norwegians, and Swedes also began moving to the United States, feeling the push of economic pressures at home, and the pull of prospective free land and good wages in the New World. Italians began arriving in 1890, and from 1900 until the start of World War I, about a quarter of all immigrants were Italians. After World War II, many Germans arrived in the United States.

European American people came from a wide array of places—western and southern portions of Europe as well as the eastern portion and the Soviet Union. Greeks, Italians, Poles, Irish, French, and Germans are well known in the United States, but other people from the Netherlands, Portugal, Spain, and Switzerland are less known. Each cultural group brought its own cultural characteristics, language, traditions, and customs, which contributed to the already rich diversity of this nation. They came to the United States for a number of different reasons: Some planned to earn money and return to their home country, whereas others planned to make the United States their home.

Although the number of European cultures makes it impossible to discuss them all, it is interesting to examine a few cultures and immigrants' reasons for coming to the United States. Such a discussion is limited to census information and recent books written on the European people; the same information is not available for all cultural groups.

Greek immigration began in the 1880s, when the Greek economy failed to show signs of improvement. These early immigrants came from the Peloponnese, especially Tripoli, agricultural and pastoral regions that were economically depressed. In fact, the Greek government actually encouraged young men to emigrate so they could send money back to Greece.

The majority of Poles came to the United States as a result of mass migration during World War II. The immigrating Poles were a diverse group. Some were women and children without an occupational designation; others were blacksmiths, carpenters, locksmiths, miners, dressmakers, shoemakers, and tailors. There was concern about how Polish immigrants would sustain themselves in their new land. Some 3 percent entered with only $50 in their possession, having spent most of their money on transportation. Only about one-fourth had others, usually relatives, to cover the cost. Another problem, language, confronted Poles as they entered the English-speaking nation. They worked in the steel mills and coalmines of Pennsylvania, Ohio, and Indiana; in the automobile factories of Detroit; and in the stockyards of Chicago. Many changed their names to survive and hide their native origins.

More than five million immigrants from Italy arrived in the United States between 1820 and 1870, and more than 4.5 million came during the century of mass immigration, 1830–1930. Only the number of arrivals from Germany was larger. The Italian immigration was concentrated tightly into a small period of time—more than four million arrived between 1890 and 1921, and in fact, two million arrived during a single decade, 1901–1910. The peak year of Italian immigration was 1907, when nearly 300,000 came to the United States. Although it is difficult to pinpoint exact regions from which they came, many Italian immigrants came from the Mezzogiorno. Between 1899 and 1910, when more than 2,200,000 immigrants came, perhaps as many as 80 percent came from the Mezzogiorno region.

Significant numbers of Jews migrated to Israel and to the United States from the former Soviet Union. With the crumbling of the Soviet economic system came a resurgence of anti-Semitism. Although the majority of Jewish people were choosing Israel as their new home, 40,000 immigrated to the United States in 1989.

These Jewish people, however, are not the first to arrive in the United States from the former Soviet Union. In the 1970s, some Jewish people arrived in the United States from the Soviet Union after the Six-Day War and the Leningrad Trial. At first, nearly all left for Israel, but after 1972, a rising proportion chose other countries. The majority of the 90,000 Soviet Jews who chose the United States came from Russia, Byelorussia, and Ukraine, those republics most heavily under the rule of the Soviet regime. These Jews had had their Jewish heritage systemically denied through the closing of synagogues, the banning of the study of Hebrew and Yiddish, and the virulent anti-Israel, anti-Zionist propaganda of the Soviet regime.

The recent Russian invasion of Ukraine has triggered Europe's most significant displacement crisis since World War II, prompting new waves of migration to the United States, with both Ukrainians and Russians seeking refuge and opportunities (Oyolola & Batalova, 2024). While Russians had previously represented the largest group of Eastern European immigrants in the United States, by 2022, Ukrainians had surpassed them. This shift underscores how geopolitical events shape migration trends over time. According to the U.S. Census Bureau (2022a) data, 2,100,000 individuals in the United States are of Russian descent. This constitutes 0.6 percent of the population. Over 900,000 individuals living in the United States reported speaking Russian at home.

The U.S. Census Bureau (2022a) reports that the Ukrainian population in the United States topped 1.1 million in 2022, with over 300,000 people indicating that they speak Ukrainian at home. However, this figure was determined before the Russian invasion of Ukraine in February 2022. Since the launch of the Uniting for Ukraine program in April 2022, over 178,000 refugees have been processed at U.S. ports of entry. Furthermore, the Department of Homeland Security reports that an additional 319,000 Ukrainians have been processed outside of the Uniting for Ukraine initiative. While these are a fraction of the approximately 6.5 million Ukrainians recorded globally (UN High Commissioner for Refugees, 2023), schools in the United States play an important role in assisting with young refugees' immediate physical and material needs, their settlement, and accommodating their mental health and overall development (Hodes, 2022). Refugees are specifically in need of language instruction and education support from local authorities, social workers as well as non-governmental organizations such as the Refugee Council.

POINTS TO PONDER 7.1

Will Whites Become a Minority?

In a group of three or four, discuss this question: Are whites really becoming a minority because whiteness is not a fixed racial category? A number of demographic studies suggest that whites will become a minority. What does your group think?

European Americans Today

European Americans today live in many geographic areas of the United States. Available data from the U.S. Census Bureau do not indicate the cities where European Americans have selected to live. Some evidence, however, suggests that immigrants to the United States tend to settle near their port of entry. More than two-thirds of those who came from Italy, for example, live in the northeastern part of the country, where they arrived.

The United States is a destination for people of many different cultures, languages, and traditions. In 2022, Europeans accounted for 10 percent, or 4.7 million, of the 46.2 million immigrants living in the United States (Oyolola & Batalova, 2024). At this time, they were the third largest immigrant group, followed by South and Central America at 52 percent, and Asia at 31 percent. The largest groups among Europeans were those from Eastern Europe (46 percent) and Western and Northern Europe (19 percent each). The primary source countries were the United Kingdom, Germany, Ukraine, Russia, and Poland.

The largest numbers arrived from Bosnia and Herzegovina, and substantial numbers came from Russia and Poland. Even using the latest census information, it is difficult to specifically determine people's native countries because some become U.S. citizens and are classified as permanent and others are not. Still, the immigration rate does not rank with the Hispanic birthrate and immigration patterns. Interestingly, many European immigrants resided in New York and California, 15 percent and 14 percent, respectively. Florida, Illinois and New Jersey, the next most populous states, together hosted approximately 22 percent of the European immigrant population.

Stereotyping of European American Children and Adolescents

European cultures are not immune to the stereotyping that has dogged American Indian, African American, Asian American, Arab American, and Hispanic cultures. European groups have been considered in terms of undesirable characteristics. Italians have been stereotyped as being swarthy, bearing signs of physical degradation (such as low foreheads), having criminal tendencies, and being prone to passion and violence. Jews are stereotyped as stingy, shrewd, and intellectual. Germans are often characterized as evil, incompetent, or mad. Readers know that this unfair and dangerous list could continue.

POINTS TO PONDER 7.2

European American Stereotypes

Unfortunately, stereotypical assumptions about people continue and are often the point of jokes. The author is concerned that educational decisions are often made on the basis of one's skin color or socioeconomic status. What are some stereotypes of European Americans, such as the Ukrainians, Russians, Polish, Germans, and Greeks, just to name a few? Is there a basis to any of these statements? Look at some textbooks (especially ones a little older). What stereotypes do you see? How do stereotypes affect people in their daily routines? How can we reduce stereotypes and gain a better understanding of people?

Stereotyping, racism, and discrimination can affect European Americans, just as they affect people from all cultures. Plus, the basis for these insidious acts or feelings can result from reasons other than the color of people's skin or the language they speak.

Cultural Characteristics

What constitutes the cultural characteristics of European Americans? European Americans comprise numerous subcultures that vary by country and language, economic status, generation in the United States, religious affiliation, and a host of other factors. Still, Kitano and Perkins (2000) suggest several common European American cultural values, such as beliefs, interaction and communication patterns, and behavioral expectations. Values include an emphasis on the individual, personal achievement, independence, and control over one's environment. European Americans can best be described as holding firm beliefs in support of inalienable rights (e.g. privacy), free enterprise, and private property. Interaction patterns are characterized by role specialization, self-sufficiency (as opposed to teamwork), competition, and communication that is direct, informal, and assertive. Overall, European Americans place importance on time, cleanliness, hard work, material comforts and material wealth, and an orientation toward work and the future. The most valid cultural descriptions of European Americans come from considering individual cultures.

In general, Greek Americans are confident that they alone know the causes of their problems and how best to solve them. If they feel powerless, they are likely to either overdo attempts to control their families or sink into fatalistic resignation. If misfortune comes their way, they assume that the causes of the problems come not from themselves but from somewhere outside the family, such as the malice of neighbors or the envy of competitors.

Greek Americans take tremendous pride in individual achievement and consider themselves as individuals. Greek Americans may have difficulty cooperating with others, especially in business deals. They prefer a competitive atmosphere and are usually unwilling to put aside their individual interests for the sake of the group.

Italian Americans have a strong allegiance to family and tend to live where they grew up. They believe that young people should learn from their elders and have an allegiance to a church. They are suspicious of strangers and expect filial obedience. Some of these tendencies (e.g. suspicion of strangers) decrease with education and advancing occupational position.

Greek Americans value frugality, careful saving, and wise use of financial resources; they often work two jobs. Greek Americans have been described in several ways: They have clearly defined status and roles in work situations; they practice patriarchal control and have deeply binding extended kinship networks; they value interdependence among people (rather than individualism); and they demonstrate a strong need to defend family honor and, generally speaking, have a love of *philotimo*, or honor.

Gender

Although gender differences are not an area of extensive research, they exist in European American males and females, just as they do in all cultures. Girls and boys have different learning styles, worldviews, perceptions of motivation and school success, and learning strategies. For example, an educator cannot conclude that a cooperative, seemingly passive female is not motivated, because boys show different signs of motivation and competitive behaviors. The educator's challenge is to recognize that girls and boys are different, make an attempt to know individual females, and plan strategies to which females can relate.

Kitano and Perkins (2000) maintain that whereas European American parents value independence, achievement, individualism, and hard work in boys, the same is not always true with daughters. Parents' actions sometimes teach daughters to be dependent on others (perhaps a man) and to lack confidence in their abilities. For example, some daughters learn that they should not outperform men in academic or physical skills or they will end up isolated and unloved. Instead, daughters should channel their work into relationships and toward home-centered, family-oriented achievement.

Begall et al. (2023) examined gender ideologies across 36 European countries and found that beliefs about gender vary widely and influence how gender roles and gender equality policies are practiced and implemented in different European countries. Additionally, beliefs and practices regarding gender roles among European Americans differ based on their upbringing and ethnic origins.

The researchers pointed out distinctive gender ideologies in different regions of Europe.

Eastern European countries such as Ukraine, Moldova, Poland, and the three Baltic states share strong family-oriented beliefs, such as that a mother working has a negative impact on her preschool children. They support the traditional role of the housewife and prioritize domestic duties. They also, however, support dual-income households and acknowledge a role for men in domestic responsibilities. Following Russia's invasion of Ukraine in 2022, the majority of displaced Ukrainians are women and children, as men have largely remained in Ukraine to fight in the war (Vetere & Shimwell, 2024). Inadequate language proficiency, a lack of childcare facilities, and challenges with diploma and reference recognition are unfortunately barriers to employment opportunities. Ukrainian women who have arrived in the United States may have readjusted their family life and the dynamics of gender roles, including the sharing of parenting and childcare responsibilities, as their men are absent.

Scandinavian countries (Denmark, Sweden and Norway), as well as Slovakia, Portugal, and Serbia, have an egalitarian view and prioritize individual choice. They support any chosen role, including women with children pursuing careers and women as homemakers, and believe that men and women are equally capable of caring for children. This belief is most prevalent in Iceland, Finland, Ireland, and the United Kingdom, but it also has a significant presence in Moldova and Slovenia.

The German-speaking countries (Germany, Switzerland, Austria), as well as the Netherlands and Ireland, tend to be more traditional in their beliefs. They hold more negative views on paternal childcare, male involvement in domestic responsibilities, and dual-income households, advocating instead for traditional roles in the family. This is most common in several Eastern European nations, including Romania, Moldova, and the Czech Republic.

Kitano and Perkins (2000) describe factors affecting the achievement of 15 highly accomplished European American women. As children and adolescents, most of the gifted European American participants read fervently, achieved in school, and lacked confidence about their popularity with peers. Consistent with the literature on European American culture, their communities valued hard work, achievement, and self-reliance, and sometimes communicated confusing messages to women. Despite the group's high academic performance, half of the participants remembered K–12 schools as unchallenging, neglectful of their needs, and as providing poor or inadequate counseling. Still, many recalled individual teachers who encouraged and inspired them.

Implications for elementary and secondary schools include the following:

◆ Provide a more challenging curriculum, one that meets the academic needs of both girls and boys.
◆ Provide systematic and developmentally appropriate educational and career counseling.
◆ Provide constructivist coping strategies that have the potential to prepare gifted young women for success in a gendered and heterosexist society.

Socioeconomic Status

Describing the socioeconomic status of the many European cultures is nearly impossible. Just as with other cultures we discuss in this book, many variations exist among European cultures. There are both wealthy and poor European Americans, just as among all cultures. Many criteria determine a person's socioeconomic status: Is the husband or father present? Does the wife work? How many children are in the family? Are the people living in a part of the country where the cost of living is high or low? How well does the family manage its money?

Families

An educator should approach any discussion of family characteristics with considerable caution. Family patterns differ according to the time of immigration, region of origin, economic class, and religious background. Many factors influence how a family lives, the roles of the husband and wife, perspectives on and treatment of children, and the importance of extended family members. Although pre-service and in-service teachers need information about European families, providing a description of these families risks stereotyping. To avoid stereotyping, we attempt to use only the most objective information and the most widely accepted resources.

Parents and families are expected to be involved in their children's education and to work as partners with teachers. Education is highly regarded at all levels. Cultural emphasis on independence and achievement becomes manifested in parents' expectations for self-reliance on the part of children. In European American families, offspring frequently participate in decision making at early ages, have designated chores within the household, and, as adolescents, hold part-time jobs. Families expect youth to establish their own identities, leave the family home, and create their own families (Kitano & Perkins, 2000).

In the German American family, the husband or father is the head of the household and leader of the family. Traditionally, the father, although sometimes sentimental, has a stern side. He is usually self-controlled, reserved, strict, and stubborn. Somewhat distant, the husband or father is often less emotionally available to the children than their mother. The German American woman, regarded as hardworking, dutiful, and subservient, adopts her husband's family and friends and gains his social status. Her contributions center mainly around household and family duties. Today, the wife's main tasks continue to focus on the house and the family. In fact, how her husband and children look can be a source of pride to her.

The Greek American family maintains strict sex roles. Men provide economic necessities, and women cater to men's desires and wish to be good wives. Men are authoritarian fathers and husbands. Often appearing emotionally distant, they are parsimonious with praise and generous with criticism. They often tease their children (some say to toughen them), and children learn that teasing is part of being loved. Other male characteristics include revering their mothers, valuing the family honor, and believing the woman's place is in the home. Women expect to comply with tradition and view motherhood as a fulfillment. They prefer male children over female, even in urban areas of the United States. Having a son is a mother's main source of prestige. Parents feel that some emotions, such as uncertainty, anxiety, and fear, are weaknesses that should be hidden from their children.

Irish American women have traditionally dominated family life and primarily found their social life through the Church. They have enjoyed a greater amount of independence relative to women in other cultures. More Irish women have immigrated to the United States than Irish men. Irish families often pay as much attention to the education of their daughters as of their sons. Traditionally, fathers have been shadowy or absent figures, and husbands have dealt with wives primarily by avoidance. Discipline is maintained by ridicule, belittling, and shaming. Children are generally raised to be polite, respectful, obedient, and well-behaved. Parents rarely praise or center attention on their children (Purnell & Fenkl, 2019).

For Italians, the family is the training ground for learning to cope with a difficult world. The father has traditionally been the family's undisputed head, often authoritarian in his rule and guidelines for behavior. He usually takes his responsibilities to provide for his family very seriously. As the ultimate authority on living, he offers advice on major issues. The mother provides the emotional sustenance. While yielding authority to the father, she traditionally assumes responsibility for the emotional aspects of the family. Her life centers around domestic duties, and she is expected to receive her primary pleasure from nurturing and servicing her family. Concerning children, there is a marked difference between sons and daughters. Sons are given much more latitude in what they do. The family expects a daughter, rather than a son, to assume major responsibility for an aging or sick parent. The extended family plays a central role in all aspects of Italian family life, including decision making.

A major characteristic of the Polish American family is its respect for individual family members. The father and husband is the acknowledged leader of the household. The family is to respect and obey his wishes. Children are raised in a strict tradition of discipline, and they are to give their fathers unquestioned obedience. They are disciplined physically, sometimes harshly. Second-generation children have become acculturated, but the practice of physical discipline continues.

In the Portuguese American family, the man maintains great physical and emotional strength to combat life's difficulties. Family members tend to keep feelings to themselves to avoid the loss of respect or power. The father expects to receive respect and obedience from his children. Virtue and purity are desirable feminine qualities for the Portuguese woman. Her role includes loving, honoring, and obeying her husband and caring for her family's many needs. Children are to be seen and not heard. They receive most physical and emotional attention from their parents from infancy to about school age. Girls tend to receive overt displays of affection from both parents; the parents, especially the father, often don't give to boys in the same way.

Religion

As with other descriptors, European Americans' religion deserves careful consideration. A culture's religion often depends on its specific geographical origin and degree of acculturation.

Italian Americans are predominantly Catholic. One survey showed that 90 percent of the respondents had been raised as Catholics, and 80 percent called themselves Catholic at the time of the survey. Because the Church has stood for tradition, family, and community, Italians continue to offer their support to the Church. Similarly, Polish Americans have a powerful allegiance to the Catholic Church.

By 1923, there were about 140 Greek churches in the United States. Each community of Greeks formed a board of directors whose function was to build a Greek Orthodox church. Some attempts were made to unite the Greek Church with other Eastern churches into an American Orthodoxy, but this consolidation did not materialize. The Church seems inextricably intertwined with its role as transmitter of the Greek heritage.

For most newcomer Jews, their primary motivation in leaving the Soviet Union was fear of anti-Semitism rather than the desire for religious freedom. Most Soviet Jews view themselves as culturally Jewish. They are interested in the Jewish past expressed in history and literature, but they are not sure which religious practices have meaning.

Language

U.S. Census information suggests most learners from Germany and Nigeria have little difficulty with the English language. On the other hand, Eastern Europeans living in this country experience difficulty with the language. The English language ability of European Americans is generally stronger than other immigrants. They are more likely to have a bachelor's degree and stable employment, both of which correlate to higher English language proficiency. In 2022, 25 percent of European immigrants aged five or over reported speaking English less than very well, while 46 percent of all foreign-born residents in the United States reported limited English proficiency (Oyolola & Batalova, 2024).

English proficiency varies significantly among Europeans depending on their region of origin (Dietrich & Hernandez, 2022a). Those from Eastern Europe are more likely to have limited proficiency, with 38 percent reporting speaking English "less than very well." Southern Europeans follow at 33 percent, and immigrants from Western and Northern European countries such as Germany, the Netherlands, Ireland, and the United Kingdom, reported only less than 10 percent having limited proficiency. Northern Europeans display the highest English proficiency while Ukrainian immigrants were the most likely to have limited English proficiency at 49 percent.

Without doubt, considerable diversity exists within the three groups. Several factors influence learners' ability to speak English—for example, whether their parents and families live in *language enclaves* where people speak native languages, whether the parents speak the native language in the home, whether parents are trying to learn to speak English, and the school's efforts to provide programs in English as a second language (and show appreciation for native languages).

Remember Helen in the opening Cultural Portrait? She is a good example of a Greek American who can speak fluent English. Some of her Greek friends, however, are not as fortunate. Considerable variation exists in European Americans' ability to speak English. Too often, we assume that European Americans are fluent in English. Such an assumption can lead to problems for both students and educators.

POINTS TO PONDER 7.3

Language Differences

We often hear about students with language difficulties, but some people think only about Asian Americans and Hispanics. The author of this text had a Greek student a few years back. Although she was fluent and articulate in English, her first-generation parents knew very little of the language. Trying to reach her via telephone was very difficult if she did not answer the phone. In the school district where you teach or plan to teach, what languages are spoken? How can professional educators plan for students speaking so many different languages? How should programs for students who speak European languages differ from those provided for Asian American and Hispanic students?

While definitions of literacy differ, the author prefers the one adopted by the National Assessment of Adult Literacy, which defines literacy as "using printed and written information to function in society, to achieve one's goals, and to develop one's knowledge and potential" (National Center for Education Statistics, 2007, p. 2).

CASE STUDY 7.1

Brad: A Deep South, White American Teenager

Brad, a red-haired 13-year-old, was well liked and had one older brother. He lived a few miles outside town in a deep Southern state. A below-average student, he did not exert much effort—education just did not seem important to him or his family. At age 16, he began to experiment with alcohol that he purchased illegally. He did not have a serious alcohol problem, except for purchasing under-age and illegally. He continued to drag by in school and make below-average grades. Brad's future did not look promising—potential high-school dropout, alcohol use at a young age, lacking positive role models, and lacking motivation. Brad grew up in middle-to-lower social class household. His parents worked in the now defunct textile mills in the South.

Brad's problem was his "unrecognized" racism or his refusal to admit his dislike for others unlike him. Contributing to his racism was that he did not know any other racial groups discussed in this book. Although Brad lived a decade after the Supreme Court had integrated the schools, many schools in his state were segregated. Brad lived a life in his own little world—his neighborhood and church were all white. In essence, his worldview was one of "whiteness."

Questions for Discussion

1. First and foremost, did Brad's teachers *recognize* his racism or did they feel the same way?
2. Assuming Brad's teachers realize his racism, what can they do to broaden his mind about others who were not like him?
3. What curricular changes could his educators have made to allow him to see others' similarities? What could they have done to help him realize that "differences" are not "deficits"?

School Practices Promoting European Americans' Progress

What school practices might impede European American learners' progress? It sounds ironic to even suggest that school practices would interfere with students' learning and overall school progress, especially because a major goal of schools is to teach. Schools, however, often have practices that do not contribute to the academic achievement and overall development of all learners.

First, policies toward language might be a detrimental factor. Some schools forbid learners to speak their native languages. For example, the school might not allow one Greek American child to teach another Greek American child their native language. Also, some schools fail to provide adequate English as a Second Language (ESL) programs. As a result, learners are taught in a language that they do not fully understand. Schools, therefore, need to provide dual language education programs and use culturally responsive and relevant teaching approaches to enhance the language learners' understanding of the content and support their social, emotional, and cognitive development (Lucido et al., 2024).

Second, perhaps because of language difficulties or teachers' perceptions, schools sometimes place European Americans in a group that is academically too high or too low for their abilities. Third, teachers sometimes fail to realize that learners in various cultures have differing learning styles and perspectives of motivation and school success.

Promoting Cultural Identities

As other chapters on the various cultures have indicated, perceptive educators, especially those teaching in multicultural settings, need to be aware of the importance to children and adolescents of the formation of positive cultural identities. Cultural differences play significant roles in a young person's degree of self-worth and self-image. For example, a student from a culture different from the teacher's and from a lower socioeconomic level may indeed consider his or her differences as inferior or wrong. Perceptive educators recognize the disastrous consequences such feelings can have on children's and adolescents' sense of personal worth.

Scholars can take special steps to promote positive self-esteem and cultural identities:

1. Educators, perhaps through academic and extracurricular programs, can help European American children and adolescents understand culture, recognize how culture affects people's lives, and understand that they cannot place values on culture.
2. Educators can work toward providing all children and adolescents with accurate and objective materials, and lead discussions about culture and cultural differences that dispel as many myths, distortions, and stereotypes as possible.

Summing Up

Educators planning educational experiences for European American learners should:

1. Perceive European American learners as an integral part of the United States' diversity, even though little attention and research have been focused toward this group.
2. Recognize the futility of past educational practices, in which language programs were inadequate and cultural differences in motivation and learning went unrecognized.
3. Recognize that girls and boys have different perceptions of motivation and school success, and perceptions of learning strategies.
4. Realize that cultural characteristics vary among European Americans and that people also differ according to generational status and age, socioeconomic status, and gender.
5. Understand that European Americans vary widely in their ability to speak English and that the need is strong for methodically planned language programs.
6. Consider European American language differences, learning styles, perceptions of motivation and school success, cooperation versus competition, and differences in behavior expectation and management.
7. Be aware how important it is for European American children to develop positive self-esteem and cultural identities.

Suggested Learning Activities

1. Interview a first- or second-generation Greek, French, or German American student to determine the problems or special challenges he or she faces in school. If possible, meet with the family as well to learn what problems they experience with the schools. Then, list problems on the left side of your paper and possible solutions on the right.
2. Language problems continue to plague many European American learners. They cannot speak the language of the school but are forbidden to speak their native languages in school. Their parents

cannot understand the school's language, and the school might show little appreciation for native languages. Yet, in all candor, educators feel they should use the language of the nation or the language most students speak. The dilemma challenges many schools in the United States. Think about and write a brief proposal (no matter how radical and forward-looking) to address this challenge.

Suggestions for Collaborative Efforts

Form groups of three or four that, if possible, represent the United States' cultural and gender diversity. Work collaboratively and focus your group's attention on the following efforts:

1. Have each member of your group interview four or five students from different European cultures, preferably first- and second-generation. As a group project, design an interview to learn about differences in cultural characteristics, language, family (be careful, though, as some cultures may feel you are prying), social class, and gender. What differences do you find among cultures? Did you find intracultural differences? Were there significant gender differences? What role does social class play in determining what a person is like? Last, what differences did you find between first- and second-generation European Americans?
2. We hear that people from different cultures are "lazy," others "dumb," some "swarthy," and others "stingy." Some are "model minorities," and others are prone to passion and violence. Being careful to respect class members' feelings and cultures, make a list of stereotypes. To show stereotypes are myths and often the result of hate-mongering, hypothesize how these stereotypes might have begun. How can stereotypes affect the person being stereotyped and the person harboring the stereotype? How should we as educators respond when we hear someone describe another person in stereotypical terms?
3. The significance of robust family partnerships has been widely recognized as crucial for fostering the academic success of students with exceptionalities (Banks et al., 2023). Also, the Every Student Succeeds Act (ESSA) underscores the pivotal role of family engagement, as school–family partnerships play vital

roles in ensuring equitable service provision to students through collaborative processes and shared decision making. The ESSA's primary objective is to ensure that public schools deliver quality education to all students (Ayscue et al., 2023). As a group project, students will design innovative school-wide activities that schools can use to successfully engage with and support European American families and students.

Expanding Your Horizons

Additional Books and Journals

Juang, L. P., Umaña-Taylor, A. J., Schachner, M. K., Frisén, A., Hwang, C. P., Moscardino, U., Motti-Stefanidi, F., Oppedal, B., Pavlopoulos, V., Abdullahi, A. K., Barahona, R., Berne, S., Ceccon, C., Gharaei, N., Moffitt, U., Ntalachanis, A., Pevec, S., Sandberg, D. J., Zacharia, A., & Syed, M. (2023). Ethnic-racial identity in Europe: Adapting the identity project intervention in five countries. *European Journal of Developmental Psychology, 20*(6), 978–1006. https://doi.org/10.1080/17405629.2022.2131520

A key global challenge in developmental psychology is comprehending how youth in diverse societies navigate their ethnic-racial identities. This paper outlines how five European nations (Germany, Greece, Italy, Norway, and Sweden) adapted the Identity Project, an eight-week school intervention from the United States aimed at fostering adolescents' exploration and resolution of ethnic-racial identity.

Karimi, A. & Wilkes, R. (2023). A transnational amendment to assimilation theory: Country of origin's racial status versus transnational Whiteness. *Ethnic and Racial Studies, 47*(3), 459–482. https://doi-org.proxy.lib.odu.edu/10.1080/01419870.2023.2174810

The authors examine how non-European immigrants continue to be "racialized" even after assimilating, while European immigrants experience a shift in their ethnic and racial status upon integration into the mainstream.

Kim, J. & Yu, H. M. (2024). Home-based parent involvement, parental warmth, and kindergarten outcomes among children of immigrant parents. *Early Education and Development, 35*(2), 343–367. https://doi.org/10.1080/10409289.2022.2153003

This research investigated how involvement and warmth from parents at home relate to the social and academic development of children with immigrant mothers, examining differences in child-rearing practices among European, Hispanic, and Asian immigrant families.

Kimak, I. & Świetlicki, M. (2023). Memory, identity, belonging: Narratives of Eastern and Central European presence in North America. *European Journal of American Studies, 18*(4). https://doi.org/10.4000/ejas.20906

This paper details the history of the migration of Eastern and Central Europeans to North America from the turn of the twentieth century to the present-day immigration of Ukrainian refugees. This influx of newcomers encountered exclusionary nativist rhetoric, framing them as the "Other" and a perceived threat to established communities.

Yang, Y. & Wang, Q. (2023). Longitudinal relations of emotion knowledge to psychosocial adjustment in European and Chinese American school-age children. *Social Development, 32*(4), 1149–1167. https://doi.org/10.1111/sode.12679

This study examines how emotion knowledge development impacts psychosocial adjustment across cultures, involving European American and Chinese American children and their mothers. Emotion knowledge was found to be significantly linked to psychosocial adjustment for both cultural groups, serving as a particularly valuable coping mechanism for children facing challenges unique to their cultural environments.

Websites

American History: European Americans – www.let.rug.nl/usa/outlines/history-1994/early-america/the-first-europeans.php
Provides historical background information for European Americans within the United States.

The European-American Cultural Foundation – http://e-acf.org/
This group aims to strengthen cultural bonds between European member states and the United States through programs like the Kids Euro Festival, an annual presentation of more than 100 free performances in collaboration with all 28 European Union member states and dozens of major cultural organizations.

Every Culture – www.everyculture.com/North-America/European-Americans.html
Provides information regarding European Americans and areas of origination.

Ukraine Immigration Task Force – https://ukrainetaskforce.org/
This group is an educational nonprofit organization that seeks to help Ukrainians fleeing war find refuge in the United States. They have attorneys, volunteers, and nonprofit partners that aid newcomers with social services, resettlement assistance, and social advocacy.

Understanding Hispanic American Children and Adolescents

Understanding the material and activities in this chapter will help the reader to:

- Describe the cultural, gender, socioeconomic, familial, and language characteristics of Hispanic American children and adolescents.
- Understand the dangers of stereotyping Hispanic American learners and know how to respond appropriately in teaching and learning situations.
- List and describe the educational characteristics and problems of Hispanic American learners.
- Name several practices that impede the educational process of Hispanic American children and adolescents.
- List several points that educators of Hispanic American children and adolescents should remember to promote their progress.

Opening Scenario

Cultural Portrait: Teaching Hispanic American Students

Mr. Donaldson, an elementary school teacher, faces two major challenges in teaching Hispanic students. First, he has little patience with Hispanic students who experience difficulty with English, and, second, he has low

DOI: 10.4324/9781003429531-10

academic expectations for these students. He just doesn't think that they can learn English and/or follow English language instruction.

Mr. Donaldson has a fourth-grade student, Maria, whose lack of proficiency in English has left her virtually unable to learn. Rather than providing a meaningful learning experience, her school day is a time of boredom and frustration. Devastating consequences await Maria and other similar learners with limited English proficiency, who feel that they are stupid. Some feel as though their teachers have forgotten they are there, and others wish that they were not there. Even though achieving language proficiency takes time and effort, Maria needs to feel that her teachers and other school personnel care about her and want to help her. Mr. Donaldson is convinced that Maria cannot learn and was overheard saying in the hall, "Hispanic students always experience learning problems in American schools. They have so many problems—language, poverty, and those big families! What, really, can I expect of these students?"

Mrs. D'Angelo, another teacher in the school, overheard Mr. Donaldson's remark and pondered whether she should talk with him about his attitudes toward Hispanic students' English and learning abilities. Expecting poor academic achievement as a result of language problems (and poverty) may well set the stage for the students' failure. Without a doubt, Mr. Donaldson needs not only a better understanding of Hispanic cultural heritages, but also more recognition of the differences within the Hispanic culture and more objectivity toward his students. Mr. Donaldson should also understand the individual differences that result from generational factors, geographic origins, and socioeconomic factors.

Mrs. D'Angelo went to talk with Mr. Donaldson about Hispanic students, and about Maria in particular. She approached the subject gingerly because she did not want Mr. Donaldson to become defensive. Somewhat surprisingly, Mr. Donaldson was open-minded about the discussion. The two teachers decided to do the following.

- ◆ Ask the school's bilingual teacher or language expert to meet with Maria to create an immediate plan of action.
- ◆ Arrange for a professional (perhaps a paraprofessional) to work closely with Maria to show her a sense of caring and concern.
- ◆ Call on or talk to Maria about a range of topics: school, home, the Hispanic culture, or playground activities.
- ◆ Administer an interest inventory to learn about Maria's interests, likes and dislikes, and then plan instruction and communication accordingly.

In some ways, this school was fortunate: One teacher overheard another making negative remarks and had the commitment to assist both the teacher and student. While we hope that these instances are few, we are sure there are many others in which the student is ignored and continues to feel frustrated.

Overview

Understanding Hispanic American children and adolescents requires knowledge of their families, their religion, their language, and their culture's contributions. Knowing, understanding, and appreciating Hispanic learners are prerequisites, but they are not enough. Educators must also understand the relationship of the cultural characteristics of Hispanic learners, their differences as learners, and their school-related problems. Educators' emphasis should be on understanding cultural diversity and on demonstrating a genuine appreciation of and a respect for Hispanic cultures.

Origins

Hispanic Americans, as a group, include people who are Mexican Americans, Central and South Americans, Chicanos, Spanish Americans, Latin Americans, Puerto Ricans, Cubans, Guatemalans, and Salvadorans. All of these Hispanics share many values and goals, but their cultures are different in many aspects. In some ways, Hispanics are a single cultural group, and in others, they are an aggregate of distinct subcultures.

Tremendous cultural diversity exists among Hispanic Americans, such as the differences between Mexican Americans and Cuban Americans, among generations, and among people living in different geographic locations in the United States. Although this section examines only several Hispanic cultural characteristics, educators should learn about their individual students and their respective cultural characteristics.

The 1848 Treaty of Guadalupe Hidalgo, which ended the war between the United States and Mexico, promised to respect Hispanic people's civil rights, Catholic heritage, and cultural traditions. Although in theory the treaty promised Mexicans the same rights and privileges as all other U.S. citizens, in practice, they were forced to live in segregated communities, to attend segregated schools, and to face discrimination in church and society (Espinosa, 2007).

Chicano refers to individuals who are American of Mexican descent, traditionally used to express a strong sense of Mexican American identity. The term Chicano became widely used during the Chicano Movement

("El Movimiento") of the 1960s and 1970s. Mexican Americans had endured discrimination which led to this movement. Accordingly, Mexican American youth in the southwestern United States, such as Arizona, California, New Mexico, and Texas, started the movement to address issues such as labor rights, educational inequity, and racial discrimination, empower their community, and advocate for their family, immigration policy, and language (McWilliams et al., 2016). The Chicano Movement promoted "chicanismo," a sense of community and cultural pride in their Mexican American heritage and identity.

The terms *Latino* and *Hispanic* are often used interchangeably, yet these terms have different meanings. *Latino* denotes geographic origin, whereas *Hispanic* denotes linguistic heritage. If you or your ancestors hail from Latin America, then you are Latino. If you or your ancestors hail from a Spanish-speaking country, then you are Hispanic. Thus, most Hispanics are also Latino, and most Latinos are also Hispanic. Educators should be aware of these differences. There are some exceptions. For example, all Latin Americans including those speaking Portuguese are Latino, but not Hispanic. Spaniards such as European Spanish speakers are Hispanic, but not Latino.

Hispanic Americans Today

Student diversity is steadily increasing, in large part due to the increase in Hispanic and Asian immigrants in the United States (Young et al., 2024). No other ethnic or racial group will do more to change the makeup of U.S. schools over the next quarter-century than Hispanics. They are already the nation's largest marginalized group among children under the age of 18.

The Spanish-speaking Hispanic population of the United States has grown dramatically in the past few decades, surpassing African Americans as the largest marginalized group (Gándara, 2015b). The Hispanic community has garnered attention on a national scale, largely due to the fact that its population grew from 21.8 million in 1990 (Stepler & Brown, 2016) to 63.7 million in 2023 (U.S. Census Bureau, 2023f). As it stands, the Hispanic population accounts for 19.1 percent of the total U.S. population, and it is expected to reach 26.9 percent by the year 2060. In 2020, the U.S. Census Bureau reported that one out of every four children in the United States was of Hispanic origin (Peña et al., 2023), a statistic that has held consistent over the past decade (Fry, 2014). The increasing presence of Latino immigrants from South America, Central America, and the Caribbean offers a likely reason for this sustained demographic trend.

Stereotyping of Hispanic American Children and Adolescents

As with other learners, Hispanic American children and adolescents may experience "double jeopardy" if educators label learners and base teaching and learning decisions on cultural stereotypes. In essence, teachers may erroneously perceive children and adolescents as exhibiting undesirable behaviors, feeling that Hispanic Americans have tendencies toward emotional and violent behavior.

Educators do learners a terrible injustice when educational decisions are based on such stereotypes as that the Hispanic American learner is not as "well-behaved" as the Asian American learner, is not as "intelligent" as the European American learner, or is not as "docile or peaceful" as the American Indian learner. In fact, such stereotypes become self-fulfilling prophecies; Hispanic learners may achieve and behave in accordance with the educators' stereotyped academic and behavior expectations.

What action should educators take? All school personnel should seriously examine the validity of their cultural "baggage" and work toward an objective understanding of Hispanic American children and adolescents. Educators can acquire a more enlightened picture of Hispanic American learners by meeting Hispanic Americans first-hand, learning their proud and diverse history, becoming acquainted with their parents and extended families, understanding their culture's contributions, and understanding their allegiance to the Spanish language. It is also helpful for educators to understand what being a Hispanic American child or adolescent is really like and to realize the potentially disastrous consequences of basing educational programs on cultural misperceptions.

Resiliency theory identifies factors present in the families, schools, and communities of successful youth that are missing in the lives of troubled youth. Four common attributes of resilient children include social competence, problem-solving skills, autonomy, and sense of purpose and future (Chavkin & Gonzalez, 2000). When at least some of these factors are present, researchers are able to report the successes of many resilient youth (Fregeau & Leier, 2016). Teachers can instill resilience in Hispanic students in a variety of ways. Debunking commonly held stereotypes, fostering motivation and social-emotional development, creating a supportive classroom environment, and recognizing the individual strengths and unique cultural backgrounds of students are just a few.

Specifically, *academic resiliency* refers to students who possess both inner strength and outer support throughout their lives. These students maintain academic success, despite difficult obstacles that prevent others in the same situation from succeeding (Morales, 2008). Below are five key resiliency protective factors of families, schools, and communities:

1. Supportive relationships, particularly encouragement from school personnel and other adults.
2. Student characteristics, such as self-esteem, motivation, and accepting responsibility.
3. Family factors, such as parental support/concern and school involvement.
4. Community factors, such as community youth programs.
5. School factors, such as academic success and prosocial skills training.

Teachers therefore need to plan family–school connections, provide mentoring and counseling, encourage with positive comments and actions, and hold high expectations to strengthen the academic resiliency of Hispanic students. Schools should ensure that culturally relevant teaching materials, such as texts on historic and relevant Hispanic heroes and the remarkable Hispanic culture, are used. With these actions Hispanic students will gain a sense of belonging and self-efficacy which will contribute to their academic resilience and success in life.

Cultural Characteristics

Educators who plan and implement a multicultural curriculum can benefit from knowledge, understanding, and appreciation of Hispanic learners and their culture. Studies of Hispanic youngsters do not differentiate sufficiently among the different Spanish-speaking ethnic groups. Differing cultures, generational, socioeconomic, and acculturation factors exist; educators must consider them thoroughly in order to understand Hispanic American learners' experiences, since they represent various nationalities, races, customs, languages, and religions. A cultural description of Spanish-speaking peoples should include an understanding of certain values and traits. Educators can gain considerable insight into their students' cultures by understanding several unique characteristics.

Machismo and *marianismo* point up the clear-cut distinctions in gender roles in Hispanic American culture. Just as in other cultures, Hispanic females' roles differ from those of their male counterparts. Although males and females both experience similar frustrations, such as discrimination and prejudice, and sometimes poverty and lower standards of living, Hispanic American females are different from males in other ways. For example, Hispanic American females usually prefer cooperative learning environments over the competitive classrooms in which many boys learn best. Likewise,

Hispanic American females, because of their families' adherence to strict gender roles, are often less vocal and take less assertive stands than males do.

It is important to note, however, that because of acculturation and because of females taking steps to improve themselves both economically and socially, some Hispanic American females are adhering less and less to traditional gender expectations. Perceptive educators who work with Hispanic American females will want to bear in mind the gender-role differences that occur, both among the various Hispanic cultures and among individual females.

Marianismo refers to a female version of *machismo*. The term *marianismo* refers to a female's place in Hispanic society. Traditionally, it referenced and represented a female's caring and nurturing nature, with respect to family, community, or church. More recently, it carries the added meaning of a girl or woman balancing caring for others, while also focusing on a career or school, being active and a leader in the community or a religious institution, and breaking away from the traditional restrictive Latina roles.

Machismo refers to the male's stance of manhood that Hispanic American boys and girls learn. It refers to their responsibility for their household, their courage to fight, and their traits of honor and dignity, keeping one's word, and protecting one's name. On a more subtle level of analysis, *machismo* also includes dignity in personal conduct, respect for others, love for one's family, and affection for children. *Machismo* plays a significant role in Hispanic culture and significantly influences the behavior and attitudes of adolescent males during their time of identity formation.

Many Hispanic children are taught early on that European Americans are not trustworthy. The Hispanic parents the author interviewed confirmed that their community often teaches children to view European Americans with fear and trepidation. Hispanic Americans tend to avoid any competition or activity that will set them apart from their own group. To be singled out and stand apart from one's peers is to place oneself in great jeopardy, and this is to be avoided at all costs.

Educators have realized, for many years, the advantages of knowing as much as possible about learners. When teaching students from culturally different backgrounds, however, educators must understand learners' cultural backgrounds so as to make the most of learners' opportunities in order to improve learning experiences and self-esteem. What can educators do to learn about Hispanic learners' cultural backgrounds?

- ◆ Read objective literature about Hispanic culture to learn about its historical background.
- ◆ Understand Hispanic people's contributions and cherished cultural traits and how they are different from and similar to both the majority culture and other marginalized populations.

- ◆ Learn about Hispanic families—both immediate and extended—and understand the value that Hispanic people place on the family.
- ◆ Get to know individual Hispanic learners. Don't just generalize about them.
- ◆ Visit Hispanic learners in their homes to learn first-hand about their home lives.

Socioeconomic Status

According to the Pew Research Center's analysis of the 2021 American Community Survey, 18 percent of the 62.5 million Hispanics in the United States live in poverty (Moslimani et al., 2023). Approximately 21 percent of Puerto Ricans, 20 percent of Dominicans, 18 percent of Mexicans, 23 percent of Guatemalans, 17 percent of Salvadorans, and 14 percent of Cubans are represented in this statistic. A contributing factor to the high number of Mexicans living below the poverty line is the fact that they typically arrive in the United States with a lower level of education. Educators should keep in mind the varying level of immigrant socioeconomic background and that some arrive with higher literacy rates than the U.S. average (Gándara, 2015b).

While poverty rates for Hispanics living in the United States have come down since 2013 (Macartney et al., 2013), more Hispanic Americans live below the poverty line than non-Hispanic whites—8.2 percent in 2021. Hispanic Americans face economic challenges such as high unemployment and wage disparities, which is a factor in their persistent economic inequality and poverty rates. They hold the second highest unemployment rate (5 percent) of ethnic groups, which is higher than the overall rate in the United States of 3.7 percent (U.S. Bureau of Labor Statistics, 2024).

Two interrelated factors contribute to this cycle of poverty among Hispanic Americans: The unemployment rate among Puerto Rican males is twice that of European Americans, and the number of female-headed households continues to increase. In recent years, the number of Hispanic children living at or below the poverty line has declined. Hispanic children, however, are still more than twice as likely as white children to live in poverty and in underprivileged neighborhoods (Moslimani et al., 2023). They are also less likely than African American, European American, or white children to have health insurance (Smith & Medalia, 2014). Eighteen percent of Hispanic American children are uninsured. This is even more alarming when viewed by country of origin: 40 percent of Hondurans, 34 percent of Guatemalans, 24 percent of

Salvadorans, and 20 percent of Mexicans are uninsured. The median family income for Hispanic Americans is $62,800, which trails that of the overall U.S. population at $74,580 (Guzman & Kollar, 2023).

Hispanic Americans' socioeconomic status is in large part a result of their level of educational attainment, as is true of people from other cultures as well. Fewer Hispanics age 25 or older have completed high school than African Americans and European Americans. In the 2019–2020 academic year, the average Adjusted Cohort Graduation Rate (ACGR) for Hispanic students in U.S. public high schools stood at 83 percent. This rate was approximately 8 percent lower than that of white students (90 percent), and 10 percent lower than Asian/Pacific Islander students (93 percent). On a national level, Hispanic students have exhibited lower ACGRs than whites with the exception of those in West Virginia. Notably, the District of Columbia showcased the widest disparity, with a 29 percentage ACGR point difference between Hispanic and white students (National Center for Education Statistics, 2023d). While more adults age 25 or older have obtained bachelor's degrees or higher, significant disparities exist between racial groups. The Hispanic population saw an increase from 34.55 percent to 41.8 percent, Asian Americans from 51 percent to 59.3 percent, and African Americans from 21.2 percent to 27.6 percent in attainment of a bachelor's degree or higher (U.S. Census Bureau, 2023c).

To increase the educational attainment of Hispanic Americans, the education system can provide affordable quality early childhood education to families living below the poverty line during children's sensitive and formative early years. By enrolling Hispanic American children who meet poverty status in Head Start programs, which are designed to remedy the effects of poverty on academic achievement, we can expect a long-lasting impact on students' future success, including an increase in the number of high school and college graduates. The poverty line, as set by the U.S. Department of Health and Human Services (2024) is $25,820 for a family of three and $31,200 for a family of four. During 2020–2021, 37 percent of children in the Head Start program were Hispanic or Latino, 27 percent black, and 24 percent white (Head Start, 2022). Roughly 32 percent of those enrolled were dual language learners with two-thirds coming from households where Spanish is the primary language spoken. It is interesting that most children living in poverty are not enrolled in the program. Across the United States, an estimated 30 percent of three- and four-year-olds living below the poverty line participated in Head Start in 2021 and 2022 (Duer et al., 2022). Among these, African American children (33 percent) were more likely to be enrolled in Head Start programs than Hispanic American (27 percent) or white (25 percent).

POINTS TO PONDER 8.1

Understanding the Hispanic Culture

It is important that educators of Hispanic children and adolescents understand and appreciate important concepts of the Hispanic culture. On understanding these cultural characteristics, try to identify several unique characteristics and behaviors in Hispanic learners.

◆ *corazón:* heart
◆ *sensibilidad:* sensitivity
◆ *afecto:* warmth and demonstrativeness
◆ *dignidad:* dignity
◆ *respeto:* respect

Are there indications that the socioeconomic status of Hispanic American children and adolescents will improve? One can provide an affirmative answer to this question, since a greater number of Hispanic American students are graduating from high school and attending college than ever before and poverty rates are declining (Fry, 2014). Poverty rates among Hispanic Americans have declined from 23.5 percent in 2013 (U.S. Census Bureau, 2013) to 18 percent in 2023 (Moslimani et al., 2023). With these improvements, Hispanic Americans' future will be brighter in mainstream U.S. society. Although educators should recognize (and respond appropriately to) the effects that poverty often has on academic achievement, it would be a serious mistake to categorize all lower socioeconomic Hispanics as unmotivated or underachieving. As of 2021, 7 percent of Latinos age 25 and older possessed a graduate degree, marking an increase from 4 percent in 2000 (Mora & Lopez, 2023). However, this figure remained only half of the percentage for all Americans aged 25 and above, which stood at 14 percent. The future for the next generation of Hispanic communities is brighter, though, as we consider those U.S.-born Hispanics aged 25 and older are more likely than their foreign-born Hispanic counterparts to hold a graduate degree, with respective percentages of 8 percent and 5 percent. Generally, U.S.-born Hispanics exhibited higher levels of formal education compared to Hispanic immigrants. In 2021, a majority (56 percent) of U.S.-born Hispanics aged 25 and older had attained at least some college experience, in contrast to only 31 percent of foreign-born Hispanics.

Families

A basic feature of the Hispanic American family is the extended family, which plays a major role in each family member's life. These are families with strong bonds and frequent interaction among a wide range of kin. Grandparents, parents, and children may live in the same household or nearby in separate households and visit one another frequently. A second feature is the emphasis on cooperativeness and on placing the needs of the family ahead of individual concerns. This aspect of Hispanic family life has led to the erroneous conclusion that the family impedes individual achievement and advancement. Generally speaking, Hispanic American children and adolescents learn to show respect for authority, the patriarchal family structure, and extended family members.

POINTS TO PONDER 8.2

Getting to Know Hispanic Families

Learning about the Hispanic learner's family may be one of the best ways to improve the child's academic achievement and self-esteem. Educators can do several things to learn about Hispanic families.

1. Invite families to school on special occasions just to visit. While the family learns about the school and its policies and expectations, teachers can become acquainted with the families.

2. Request that students write a story or essay about their families. Be sure to emphasize including parents, grandparents, brothers and sisters, cousins, and other relatives living in the home. Keep an open mind, and remember the importance of the extended family. Tell students before they write the story whether or not their stories or essays will be shared with the class.

3. Educators who teach in areas with large numbers of Hispanics may want to schedule a day for only Hispanic families to visit. Have individual meetings to determine how the family influences school achievement and attitudes toward school. (If possible, speak Spanish to families with limited English-speaking skills.)

4. Schedule individual meetings with Hispanic students to discuss their families, but be careful that students understand the purpose of these discussions. Allow and respect a learner's privacy.

Hispanic American children learn early the importance of (1) a deep sense of family responsibility, (2) rigid definitions of gender roles, (3) respectful and reverent treatment of the elderly, and (4) the male's position of respect and authority in the family. Although some of the male's authority appears to be relaxing as the woman's role is becoming redefined, women in the Hispanic American culture tend to occupy a subordinate position. Fathers have prestige and authority, and sons have more and earlier independence than do daughters.

Hispanic families value the extended family structure and the interaction of the larger family in their daily lives. Parents often arrange for godparents or companion parents for the child, thus demonstrating the value Hispanics place on adults other than the immediate parents. These *compadres* also have a right to give advice and correction, and should be responsive to the child's needs.

Educators need to understand and work closely with Latino parents and families. They should remain objective in their perceptions of Latino parents, many of whom have high expectations of their children's academic performance and a desire to be involved in their education. Educators should understand that although Latino families want a good education for their children, many families suffer from poverty and personal problems which hinder participation in school, both by children and by their parents. Thus, educators should understand and work to support and increase Hispanic parents' involvement. For example, educators can invite parents and families to school functions at varying times so that they can learn about American schools, ask for their input on curricular and instructional activities, and suggest specific ways in which they can actively promote their children's education. Parent-education programs designed especially for Latino parents and families can be implemented, so that parents will know what to do and will realize that educators care about their children's progress.

Religion

Religion plays a central role in the lives of Hispanic Americans. The Spanish colonial experience brought about a distinct culture of which the Catholic faith was an important part. Catholicism was brought by the Spanish to the United States. The first Mass on what is now U.S. soil was celebrated at Saint Augustine, Florida, in 1565. Spanish missionaries were active in the Southwest as early as 1539, and California missions were founded between 1770 and 1782.

However, the stereotype that the Latino population is overwhelmingly and immutably Catholic is inaccurate and misleading. Scholars of American religion and political scientists note the Latinos' declining attachment to the Catholic

Church. While non-Catholic Latinos are mostly evangelical, data suggest that an appreciable number are mainline Protestants or have no religious affiliation. According to Gershon et al. (2016), religion is not a constant factor among Latinos. Paralleling the general U.S. population, Latinos are also becoming more secularized: overwhelming political support for President Barack Obama in the 2012 election reveals that Latinos are now less likely to vote for "values policies" along religious lines (Gershon et al., 2016; Jones et al., 2013).

African American and Hispanic adults attend religious services more than their white counterparts. Their attendance, though, decreases as they grow older, which results in minimal difference in religious service attendance in older adults (Liu, 2023). Among Hispanic adults, 43 percent identify as Catholic, a decrease from 67 percent in 2010 (Krogstad et al., 2023). Latinos are still more likely to identify as Catholic and less as Protestant when compared to the overall U.S. population. In addition, the number of Hispanic Americans identifying as religiously unaffiliated, atheist, or agnostic has increased from 10 percent in 2010 to 30 percent, which aligns with the number for the overall U.S. population. It is interesting to point out that recent Hispanic immigrants have maintained or increased their religious participation (Liu, 2023), pointing to immigration policy as a possible factor in religious affiliation.

Language

Hispanic people in the United States speak many Spanish dialects, depending on where the speakers live, how long they have lived in this country, and where they came to the United States from originally. Spanish in the Southwest is different from Spanish in the Midwest, the Northeast, and Florida. Even in New York City, there are important cultural and linguistic differences between speakers who have emigrated from Puerto Rico, Cuba, the Dominican Republic, Colombia, Ecuador, Peru, Mexico, Venezuela, Bolivia, and other Latin American areas. Finally, people from Spain speak a unique type of Spanish sometimes referred to as *Castilian*. While these different dialects are mutually intelligible, educators should remember that Spanish accents, vocabulary, and slang can vary greatly.

Some Hispanic American learners' English language ability poses a problem outside of their immediate neighborhood, because they tend to retain the native tongue rather than make a cultural transition to English. Instead of making an attempt to learn English, many do not perceive a need to develop proficiency in English and continue to risk survival in a predominantly English-speaking country. Language difficulties that learners experience may have a major impact on their self-esteem and their developing identity.

As in other cultures, nonverbal language also plays a major factor in the Hispanic American culture, and professionals of other cultures must recognize and understand this. Although a complete list of nonverbal behaviors is impossible to create and would not be able to include individual and intracultural differences, several examples will serve to indicate their significance. Many Hispanic Americans stand close together while communicating, touch to communicate, and often avoid eye contact.

Undoubtedly, many of the problems that Hispanic American learners experience stem from their difficulties with English. Hearing Spanish spoken at home yet feeling pressure to communicate in English at school often results in academic and behavioral problems, lower self-esteem, negative cultural identities, and a general pessimism toward teachers and schools. Sandín (2016) used the concept of "double identity" to discuss the means by which Latino heritage language speakers can connect and also alienate themselves from their heritage. Assimilating into a society while maintaining one's cultural identity can be a complex and stressful process. Educators and parents need to recognize that Hispanic students, or any bilingual speakers, are capable of using multiple languages simultaneously. Speaking English as well as Spanish in the classroom will help them learn and perfect both. According to the most recent analysis by the National Center for Education Statistics (2023c), 77.1 per cent of ELs (English learners) were Hispanic. This equates to 3.8 million students. Educators need to be aware however, that though they make up a large portion of students in limited English proficiency (LEP) programs, not all Hispanic students are ELs.

One especially important factor in this issue is the failure of some public schools to provide a meaningful education that builds on students' native language and culture while also helping them to develop good English-language skills. Gándara (2015a) summarizes effective bilingual strategies for Hispanic students, although most strategies are appropriate for the education of all students with immigrant and limited English-speaking backgrounds. The author focuses attention toward several directions: educational policy; teacher training and performance; effective elementary, middle, and secondary bilingual programs; instructional strategies, and formative assessments. Gándara (2015a) offers the following suggestions:

1. Schools should continually revise their approaches as new strategies are proven effective and new student needs are identified.
2. Schools should embrace the philosophy that true bilingualism means proficiency in both Spanish and English, and include Hispanic culture in the curriculum.

3. Schools should offer individualized instruction and other aids to ensure that students learn English and other subjects that will enable future career fulfillment.
4. Schools, with the full participation of their teachers and staff, should maintain an atmosphere that supports the beliefs that all students are equally valuable and that they bring to the school equally valuable cultures, and schools should maintain the expectation that all will succeed.

Children who feel pressure to speak Spanish at home and English at school may develop problems in both languages, may become bilingual, or may avoid English-speaking situations. This may result in dual cultural identification, additional language conflicts, and chronic anxiety. In the southwestern United States, many Hispanic American people live in Spanish-speaking communities isolated from English-speaking communities. In fact, children often enter the English-speaking world for the first time when they begin their public school education. Then, to make matters worse, these children are often threatened with punishment in their school environments for speaking Spanish. Some teachers still believe that English language learners must refrain from speaking their heritage language with friends and families in order to acquire English and to assimilate into mainstream society. While English language acquisition and immersion is important for Hispanic American students, educators should urge parents to maintain their heritage language use and culture at home, since these often disappear as children assimilate into the mainstream culture. Educators should find a way to support bilingualism, which is beneficial in maintaining the cultural heritage.

Educational Achievement Levels

The news media periodically raise issues concerning the level of educational achievement of Hispanic American students, such as the high dropout rates and the relatively low number of Hispanic American students eligible for college. While Hispanics lag behind others in these areas, the level of Hispanic American student achievement has improved significantly in recent years, and dropout rates have declined substantially (Fry & Taylor, 2013; Matheny et al., 2023).

Upon reaching an understanding of the social and cultural characteristics of Hispanic American children and adolescents, educators can proceed with understanding the learner in the Hispanic culture. What special school-related problems do Hispanic learners experience? Do European American expectations and stereotypes penalize Hispanic learners? Are Hispanic learners labeled? How do learning styles of Hispanics differ? What school practices might impede Hispanic students' progress? As these and other questions are explored, caution is advised for readers to consider the intracultural, generational, and socioeconomic differences between individual learners when reaching educational decisions.

Despite the plurality of the nationalities, races, languages, and cultures that comprise the demonym "Latino," many Americans have affirmed a narrow view of Latinos as first- or second-generation immigrants from uneducated families who have poor English skills. Based on the fact that U.S.-born students and *not* immigrated students account for most of the growth of the Latino population, the overgeneralization of Latinos and frequent recommendation that Latino education reform "just needs a good English-language program" will not meet most students' needs (Gándara, 2015b) to improve academic achievement.

Graduation rates and other performance criteria are also improving dramatically for Hispanics. However, as a group, Hispanics still have lower high school completion rates than Asian and white Americans but slightly higher than African Americans (National Center for Education Statistics, 2023), which leaves many Hispanic youth less prepared than their counterparts. Defining success as upward mobility from one generation to the next, Gándara (2015b) finds that the children of Mexican students are extremely successful, with respect to the extent to which a child rises above the socioeconomic status and education level of their parents. For example, while Mexican American students have lower graduation rates than some other ethnic groups, they nonetheless surpass their parents' level of education by the highest margin. Also, college enrollment for Hispanics aged 18–24 has increased significantly, from 1.2 million in 2005 to 2.4 million in 2021 (Hernandez & McElrath, 2013). Accordingly, the percentage of college students who are Hispanic rose from 11.4 percent in 2006 to nearly 20 percent in 2021. This progress calls for additional research examining Hispanic students and their families.

These are vast improvements over previous years, and they are very encouraging. Educators, however, should continue to work to help Hispanic students, for despite their unprecedented levels of academic achievement and attainment, as their numbers are increasing, Hispanics still lag behind other groups. While the number of students, diplomas, and degrees continues to rise, Hispanics represent only a small share of two-year and four-year degree recipients. Researchers have yet to pinpoint the exact reasons for this, but the fact that more Hispanic students must attend college only part-time may contribute to attrition rates (Fry, 2014; Fry & Taylor, 2013). On balance, however, Latino student achievement has reached historic heights. The latest data indicates that Hispanics hold 26.2 percent of associate's degrees, 16.5 percent of bachelor's degrees, 12.7 percent of master's degrees, and 9.7 percent of doctor's degrees conferred in the United States (National Center for Education Statistics, 2023a).

Even with a decrease in high school dropout rates, and an increase in the number of Hispanic American students preparing for and attending college, Latino students still face challenges that educators should keep in mind. Many youth attend overcrowded, instructionally inferior, and inadequately staffed schools that do not meet their educational needs and are breeding grounds for antisocial activities. Many also live in the most economically distressed areas of the United States; they witness their elders' limited employment opportunities; and they experience debilitating stereotyping, prejudice, and bias. Some Hispanic youth still do not believe that remaining in school will materially improve their lives.

The high school dropout rate for Hispanic students aged 16 to 24 was 7.8 percent in 2021. This is a marked decrease from the 2010 rate of 16.7 percent. An even greater decrease was seen from 2000 to 2014, with the rate going from 32 percent to 12 percent. American Indians/Alaska Natives had an even higher rate of 10.2 percent in 2021. In comparison, the 2021 rates for African American and white students were 5.9 percent and 4.1 percent, respectively (National Center for Education Statistics, 2023a). Delgado et al. (2016) underscored the importance of a supportive environment such as positive friendships to enhance school belonging and reduce school absence, and academic success among Latino youth in combating school dropout rates.

Teachers will need to understand Latino learners, and should hold high expectations of them with respect to their achievement in the classroom. The U.S. Hispanic population is a youthful one and its numbers are on the rise. The median age of the Hispanic population rose from 26.3 years in 2010 to 29.5 years in 2021 (Moslimani et al., 2023). This is well below the median age of the general population of 37.8 years. While 25 percent of public school students are Hispanic (Krogstad et al., 2016), only a fraction of public school teachers are Hispanic. Per the U.S. Census Bureau, 25.7 percent, or 18.8 million, children were of Hispanic origin in 2020, up from 17.1 million in 2020 (Peña et al., 2023). Meanwhile, 79 percent of teachers identify as white (Schaeffer, 2021).

Recommendations for promoting the achievement of Hispanic American students include the following:

◆ Each Hispanic student should have an adult in the school committed to nurturing a personal sense of self-worth and supporting the student's efforts to succeed in school.

- ◆ Schools should be safe and inviting places that personalize programs and services that succeed with Hispanic students.
- ◆ All students should have access to high-quality, relevant, and interesting curricular experiences that treat their culture and language as resources, convey high expectations, and demand student investment in learning.
- ◆ Schools should replicate effective programs and should continually try to improve programs with more reliable strategies.
- ◆ Schools should emphasize the prevention of problems and should be aggressive in responding to early warning signs that a student is disengaging from school.
- ◆ Schools and alternative programs should be coordinated.
- ◆ Teachers should teach content so that it interests and challenges Hispanic students. They should understand the roles that language, race, culture, and gender play in the educational process.
- ◆ Schools should recruit Hispanic parents and extended families into a partnership of equals for educating Hispanic students (School Practices to Promote the Achievement of Hispanic Students, 2020, pp. 2–6).

Beginning late in the decade of the 2000s, the prevailing narrative of the Hispanic achievement gap offers a hopeful outlook. Matheny et al. (2023) highlight a positive shift toward reducing the academic gap between white and Hispanic students. While many systemic problems persist, causing Hispanic American students' achievement gap, the relative gains experienced by today's Hispanic American students is unrivaled. The positive trends have increased college eligibility for many more young Hispanic Americans, and as a result, Hispanics are experiencing record college enrollment rates (Fry & Lopez, 2012; Gándara, 2015b). The college enrollment and completion rates have been on the rise. In 2021, the enrollment of Hispanics aged 18 to 24 in college surged to 2.4 million, compared to 1.2 million in 2005 (Hernandez & McElrath, 2013). The share of all Hispanic college students aged 18 to 24 grew from 11.4 percent in 2006 to nearly 20 percent in 2021 (National Center for Education Statistics, 2023a). The latest national six-year college completion rate is 62.2 percent. Among different racial groups, Hispanic students' completion rate was 50.1 percent. Asian students achieved the highest completion rate at 74.8 percent, followed by white students at 68.5 percent. Native American students' six-year college completion rate was 47.5 percent and black students' was 43.4 percent (National Student Clearinghouse, 2023).

Still, however, disproportionately fewer Hispanic American students than European American students take the kind of challenging academic courses that will prepare them for college. Some schools rigidly track students into such courses, using test scores or previous grades to weed out those considered less able. Other schools might offer these courses to all, but marginalized students choose not to enroll (Hobson, 2015). Increasing support systems will lead more Hispanic students to enroll in Advanced Placement (AP) classes, and ultimately to even greater numbers of college attendances and completions. Hirschl and Smith (2023) examined the role of AP programs in perpetuating racial disparities within the education system and found that AP gatekeeping disproportionately excludes Hispanic and African American students relative to white students among those with similarly low prior achievement. They argue that the processes for selecting students for AP courses need to be more equitable and teachers need to find a way to grant access to AP opportunities to those disadvantaged students.

Teaching practices alone do not make effective schools. Recent research confirms the importance of inclusive leadership that creates a sense of community and draws everyone into the learning process, preventing alienation of faculty, students, parents, and the larger Hispanic American community.

POINTS TO PONDER 8.3

Teaching Hispanic American Students

How can educators best improve the achievement of Hispanic Americans? Should efforts focus on textbooks and other curricular materials, instructional efforts, organizational patterns, or teacher attitudes? Should Hispanic Americans be placed in cooperative learning groups or continue in the competitive atmosphere of many U.S. schools?

School Practices Promoting Hispanic Americans' Progress

Is it possible that well-meaning teachers, either European American or of another culture, actually encourage school practices that may prove detrimental to Hispanic students? A look at many U.S. schools causes one to answer in the affirmative.

The already somewhat overwhelmed Hispanic child or adolescent may be even more startled at the verbal emphasis in U.S. schools. The extreme verbalism that characterizes U.S. schools can have profound consequences for learners with limited English-language skills.

A second, related detrimental practice is well-meaning teachers forbidding Hispanic students to speak Spanish and actually punishing them for it.

This situation is difficult for learners who are proficient in Spanish but are experiencing considerable difficulty with their second language.

A third practice involves an entanglement of values and cultural orientations. Believing in the American cultural tradition of excelling among one's peers, teachers often motivate learners by encouraging Hispanic learners to excel above others in the class. Causing oneself to stand out among one's peers goes against Hispanic cultural traditions and expectations.

The educational challenges of Latinas (i.e. Latino women and girls), specifically, are compounded by the high rate of poverty in their communities, the learning problems caused by a lack of English-language proficiency, racism, sexual harassment, and xenophobia. Also, Latina adolescents often assume adult roles in the home—for example, taking caring of younger children as well as elders. Schwartz (2001) presents useful ideas that schools can use to better serve Latinas and promote their academic achievement. Although all Latinas can benefit from them, these strategies will be most relevant for those who are less fluent in English, are poor, and are culturally isolated, and whose families are new to the United States. Schwartz's (2001) recommendations are as follows:

1. Schools need to individually tailor the supports that they offer to Latinas and their families in order to accommodate their diverse needs and perspectives. Educators can help Latinas understand how it is possible to value familial independence without subverting personal goals, by showing them that individual achievement reflects well on their community.
2. Schools can help Latinas develop access to the community resources that will increase their opportunities for future fulfillment and that are readily available to their more advantaged peers.

Additionally, schools can facilitate Latinas' learning and increase their feelings of self-confidence by highly valuing who they are and by instilling in them a pride in their rich cultural experiences. Teachers can support the educational ambitions of Latina/o students, through increasing their self-efficacy, involving parents in their children's educational planning, and guiding them to navigate educational pathways and challenges (Cuevas, 2023; San Martin et al., 2023). Chang (2016) observed many cases of high school Latinas who are resistant to consider themselves smart, although their grade point averages were 3.0 or higher. Educators working with Latinas need to expand their definition of "smartness" to reflect who they are, and include various types of cultural experiences, skills, and other funds of knowledge that Latinas possess and bring to the school.

The educational challenges facing Latinas are common to all students from poor and/or immigrant families. These students tend to lack communication skills, knowledge, and the experience to take advantage of educational, cultural, and social opportunities; and they may not have school readiness skills. Additional challenges to Latino students' education ironically relate to their own strong and rich culture. Their belief that the welfare of the family and community supersedes individual aspirations is fairly fixed in the various Latino communities. For example, it can be strong enough to convince an adolescent to drop out of school to make money for the family, or it can hamper his or her efforts to succeed if achievement requires competition rather than cooperation with other students.

The true causes of any underachievement of Latino students do not parallel with prevailing stereotypes, many of which depict Latino parents as uninvolved or undervaluing education, and Latino students as poor in academic activities. Other factors, including poverty, unequal access to quality education, and traditional values, are threats to Latino student engagement and academic attainment, just as institutional and language barriers are impediments to parental involvement.

Some Latina/o students experience significant stress, often due to language barriers and personal and social issues. Their level of stress is worse when there is news about immigration legislation and deportations (Meadows, 2023; Zeledon et al., 2023). Patel et al. (2016) also found that Latina/o students are exposed to high levels of life stressors and social-contextual responsibilities, which also contributed to lower attendance and school achievement than non-Latina/o students. Considering Brown's (2023) report that Hispanic students have experienced more discrimination, harassment, and vulnerability in education settings than any other racial or ethnic group, schools need to provide school counseling intervention to engage Latino/a youth either in group sessions or one-to-one and use culturally relevant activities for the development of academic, career, personal, and social skills (Lemberger et al., 2015; Mallot & Paone, 2016) to improve self-regulation, connectedness to classmates, and academic success. More than ever, Hispanic American students are in need of educators' individual attention and support in overcoming their personal and social hurdles to continue realizing their full academic potential.

Through implementing inclusive excellence, high expectations, and culturally responsive pedagogies, educators can modify the future discourse of Latino adolescents and can ensure their success. Cavanagh et al. (2014) verified that by using Culture of Care, a project aimed at bridging achievement and discipline gaps of Latino students, they experienced positive outcomes.

Prior to implementation of the Culture of Care, the school referred a disproportionate number of Latino students for disciplinary problems, which kept them out of the classroom and in the school-to-prison continuum. Some of their teachers admitted to having very low expectations of their Latino students, as well as negative stereotypes about the students and their families. The Latino students, in turn, felt disconnected from, ignored by, and unsupported by their teachers, which impacted behavioral problems and impeded achievement.

Recognizing that schoolwide improvements must start in the classroom, administrators collaborated with teachers and parents to resolve these issues using the Culture of Care. It focused on the administrators and teachers' commitment and advocacy for improving retention, inclusiveness, and success rates by instituting an ethic of care for students and the use of culturally responsive pedagogies, and restorative justice practices.

Given the above, the author of this text suggests the following recommendations to resolve behavioral problems in school, reduce detentions and expulsion, and improve success of Hispanic students:

1. Educators can remind all Latino students that personal success and family commitment are not mutually exclusive, and that their academic achievements reflect well on their family and community.
2. Educators can motivate Latino students by expecting academic success and by encouraging college education for all students, and not just certain groups.
3. Schools can develop mentorship and networking opportunities for Latino students that will ensure future success in higher education and, ultimately, the workforce.
4. Schools can promote Latino students' learning and school engagement by offering tailored education services and a relevant, engaging, multicultural curriculum.
5. Schools can provide a caring and student-centered environment that encourages collaborative learning, values Latino students' cultural knowledge and experiences, incorporates a wide range of culturally relevant learning materials, and allows the use of both Spanish and English to enhance learning.
6. By creating a welcoming environment where student needs are met and requests for help answered, schools can help Latino students combat feelings of helplessness. Hispanic American students should be encouraged to incorporate their knowledge, language, and

experiences into their learning. In addition to benefiting the student directly, this can also help to dispel preconceived notions of others that Hispanics are a one-dimensional ethnic group.

7. Schools can establish collaborative partnerships with parents and communities that incorporate Hispanic American values and can allow parents to feel that their input as stakeholders is both welcomed and valued. Where appropriate, interpreter services for parents may also ameliorate Hispanic families' fears that they are unwelcome outsiders.

8. For some Hispanic families, schools should consider alternative activities. Typical activities such as conferences, assisting with homework, PTA meetings, and volunteering in the school can cause stress due to limited English ability or financial barriers. They can also be very stressful. In addition, educators should understand that undocumented immigrants may avoid school activities that might expose them to potential deportation.

9. Schools can offer professional education opportunities for teachers and administrators that strengthen their multicultural competence and their ability to serve Hispanic students and their families.

CASE STUDY 8.1

A Hispanic American Student's Difficulty Learning in a Content Area Class

There are six people in Alejandro's family: his mom, dad, three siblings, and himself. The four children, ages 12, eight, and twin girls four years of age, are all at different stages of learning English. The oldest is definitely more confident in his English-speaking abilities due the fact that he has attended school the longest. He is not as proficient in writing, however, as he is in reading. Alejandro is eight years old and the second child of the family. He is very confident in his comprehension of English, but is not yet proficient speaking it in front of the class or writing, so he receives English as a Second Language tutoring each day at school. His father moved from Mexico by himself in search of better job opportunities as a manual laborer, and when he found steady work he petitioned for his family to join him. His parents speak functional English but are not fluent, and they are more comfortable speaking Spanish. His mother does not work outside the home, and both parents raise the children using Spanish.

The twins are still learning English and are with their mother who speaks predominantly Spanish at home.

Alejandro loves his third-grade teacher, Mrs. Sharon Major. She is a young teacher of five years and busy balancing her teaching and family. She had taught English learners in the past and enjoys working with diverse students and their families. She especially enjoys teaching Alejandro who is shy and quiet, but very attentive to her lessons, and well-behaved. One day when she was teaching a social studies unit on "Our Nation's Greatest Heroes" in an inclusion classroom, she noticed that Alejandro was not participating in a diagram activity comparing the major contributions of Martin Luther King, Jr. and Abraham Lincoln. He appeared to be excluded from the conversation in his small group. When she assisted Alejandro, Mrs. Major found that in his notebook he copied word-for-word from the textbook instead of comparing and contrasting the two famous people's ideas and perspectives. Since then, Alejandro has become withdrawn, and as the school year has continued, even distant from his classmates. Alejandro has noticed other students giggling, making fun of him, and calling him names when he speaks in his Spanish accent. He is hurt and can't relate to his American peers. He is also very sensitive about his Hispanic American heritage, and is worried that other students do not like him because of his cultural background and different language and speech.

Questions for Discussion

1. What comes to mind when you think of a Hispanic American student like Alejandro and his family background? How can you make sure that Alejandro's classmates stop bullying him about his physical features and accented speech? Mrs. Major does not want to make Alejandro feel that he is out of place. What other services are available that Mrs. Major can arrange for Alejandro and his family to utilize?

2. When Alejandro is not interested in participating and talking with other students in his small group activity, what are some alternative ways you can ensure his learning in his Social Studies class? How can Alejandro's parents assist in supporting his learning and building pride in his heritage?

3. Mrs. Major's writing assignment was to think critically about the historical hero's actions and how they have impacted our current life, but Alejandro could not complete it. He simply copied sentences from the textbook. How can Mrs. Major help Alejandro meet the third-grade Social Studies learning standards, and have him write short reports that include descriptive details that elaborate on a central idea when he is not fluent in English?

Promoting Cultural Identities

The educator's role in promoting positive cultural identities among learners will always be of paramount importance. There is a clear relationship between self-esteem and school achievement. Emphatically stated, a student who feels "worthless," "not so good," and "inferior" will experience academic difficulties despite the teacher's most conscientious efforts. Drills, memorization, and worksheets cannot overcome learners' feelings that they (or their culture) are inferior. Although the problems associated with speaking one's mother tongue in a predominantly English-speaking environment deserve consideration, allowing (or even encouraging) Hispanic children to read appropriate children's literature written in Spanish might enhance their self-esteem and cultural identities.

Specifically, what can educators do to promote positive feelings of self-worth and cultural identity? First, all efforts should be genuine and honest; learners will detect hypocrisy if teachers say one thing but demonstrate another. Second, educators should plan programs that teach about the Hispanic culture and the proud history and accomplishments of the Spanish-speaking people. Third, rather than have a "Spanish Art, Music, and Foods Week," educators must develop a curriculum that shows an appreciation for cultural diversity and that fully incorporates Hispanic culture into all areas of the school curriculum. Finally, educators can use literature and any other method or activity that improves learner self-esteem, enhances cultural identities, and increases the appreciation of cultural differences.

CASE STUDY 8.2

Carlos: A Hispanic American Learner

Carlos S., a 12-year-old boy of Spanish origin, is one grade level behind in his public elementary school. The student population is composed predominantly of African American and Hispanic American children; a small percentage of Anglo students also attend the school. While the majority of the teachers are Anglo, a few are African American and one is Hispanic.

Carlos lives in a lower socioeconomic, Spanish-speaking neighborhood near the school. He has several problems: His family speaks Spanish at home, but he is forbidden to speak Spanish at school; his difficulty with the English language has resulted in low reading grades and achievement test scores (thus, the grade level deficit); and he sees older boys dropping out of school and wonders when he can end his frustration with school. Carlos admits his frustrations to his best friend, another Hispanic American boy: Why does his teacher, Mrs. Little, keep asking him to excel? Why doesn't she allow him to speak Spanish when his family (including his grandparents, aunts and uncles, and cousins) all continue to speak Spanish? Carlos knows he has problems, and he thinks Mrs. Little has almost given up on him.

Mrs. Little understands that Carlos' situation calls for immediate attention. First, whenever possible, Carlos needs to be allowed to speak Spanish. This is the language in which he is most proficient, and he cannot understand why he is not allowed to speak the language that both his family and friends speak. Second, Carlos needs English-language instruction from qualified professionals who understand second-language instruction and who understand the problems Hispanic learners face. Third, Carlos needs appropriate diagnostic testing to determine his strengths and weaknesses, followed by carefully planned remediation to address his weaknesses.

Equally important is for the teachers in Carlos' school to understand the Hispanic culture and the situations of students like Carlos. Additionally, because the cultural diversity of the school population is not reflected in the teaching staff, the curriculum and learning environment probably reflect an Anglo perspective. More effort should be directed toward making Carlos's school more multicultural in nature and, in this case, more understanding and accepting of Hispanic American learners.

Questions for Discussion

1. Should Carlos be allowed to speak Spanish in an English-speaking school, as his teacher thinks? Can Carlos survive in an English-speaking society if he is allowed to speak Spanish in school? Consider that English is the primary language spoken and taught in U.S. schools. Also, if Carlos cannot learn in English, should he be allowed to learn in his native language? These are difficult questions that are fundamental to honoring the English language, yet accepting and appreciating another's language.
2. We will probably all agree that Carlos needs diagnostic testing to determine his strengths and weaknesses. Should Carlos be tested with English or Spanish diagnostic tests?
3. The case study says that "the curriculum and learning environment probably reflect an Anglo perspective." Should the curriculum and learning environment be modified to fit Carlos' cultural background, or should Carlos be expected to adapt to Anglo perspectives? If the former, suggest three tactics for changing the curriculum and learning environment.

Summing Up

Educators who plan teaching and learning experiences for Hispanic American children and adolescents should do the following:

1. Provide an educational environment in which Hispanic American children and adolescents feel that educators and other significant adults and peers respect their Spanish culture and background.
2. Allow Spanish to be spoken in schools, because it is the language spoken at home and in the neighborhoods; learners should be taught to speak English as well.
3. Understand that language problems and differences are partly responsible for most academic problems.
4. Consider differences in learning styles when planning and implementing education programs.
5. Promote positive feelings toward learners' selves and their culture, because learners' self-esteem and cultural identities influence school achievement and social development.
6. Understand and appreciate cultural diversity to the degree that Hispanic learners do not feel their culture, socioeconomic status, families, religion, and language are wrong or inferior.
7. Use the utmost caution not to label Hispanic learners on a basis of myth, stereotypes, prejudices, racism, or any other form of discrimination.
8. Use test data carefully, and remember that achievement tests, intelligence tests, and other measurement instruments might have a cultural bias toward European American standards and cultural expectations.

Suggested Learning Activities

1. Choose a typical Spanish-speaking student (from any of the Spanish-speaking cultures) and write a case study that explores individual and cultural characteristics. Consult with the school guidance counselor to better understand the child and his or her culture. After listing specific individual and cultural characteristics, plan an educational program that will meet the needs of this child.

2. Choose a low-achieving Hispanic American student and assess his or her language proficiency. To what extent is the student's lower academic achievement a product of poor English skills? Interview the student to determine whether the immediate and extended families speak Spanish or English. In what ways can the school's speech correctionist (working with language development specialists) assist this child? Plan an instructional program that addresses the student's problems with language and academic achievement.

3. Consider the following Implementing Research section, which looks at dispelling myths about Latino parent participation in schools.

Implementing Research

Exploring Latino American Education

Estrada and Galliher (2023) surveyed 190 Latinx teenagers about their stress, academic performance, and their school's ethnic makeup and found that the more Latinx students feel pressure to speak English well, termed English competency pressure, the less they believe in themselves academically. This was mostly true in schools with few different ethnic groups. Students in schools with a more diverse student body were less affected by English competency pressure. Schools with more ethnic diversity offer a level of safety for Latinx students from the negative effects of pressures to speak English well. Estrada and Galliher (2023) pointed out that gaps in academic achievement and educational attainment between white and Hispanic American students are of major concern. These gaps have a variety of causes, including discrimination, socioeconomic factors, language barriers, cultural differences, and school quality. The stress of adapting to a new language and culture are also leading causes of the pressure placed on Latina/o students.

1. Teachers should provide targeted support in reading for Hispanic students in need of reinforcement in comprehension and provide dual language materials when possible.

2. Teachers should promote diversity and inclusion to ensure that Hispanic students feel included and valued. They should foster a classroom environment where cultures are celebrated and differences are accepted.

3. Teachers should involve Hispanic families and communities as much as possible and provide resources to help with socioeconomic

challenges. Communicating regularly and hosting after-school programs are a great way to accomplish this.

Source: Estrada, J. & Galliher, R. V. (2023). Moderating effects of school ethnic composition of acculturative stress and academic outcomes in Latinx youth. *Journal of Research on Adoloscence*, 33(2), 376–388. https://doi-org.proxy.lib.odu.edu/10.1111/jora.12808

Suggestions for Collaborative Efforts

Form groups of three or four that, if possible, represent the United States' cultural and gender diversity. Working collaboratively, focus your group's attention toward the following efforts.

1. Develop a two-part approach to understanding Hispanic families and teaching them about U.S. schools. For example, plan an approach for understanding Hispanic American families (e.g. school meetings, home visits, and other first-hand contacts) and teaching Hispanic American families about U.S. schools (e.g. parent-education programs).

2. With the growing Spanish-speaking population, it is becoming easier for Hispanic people to live in sections of the United States in which Spanish continues to be the mother tongue. Have each member of your group examine a specific language aspect. What language is spoken during recess, lunchtime, and other breaks during the school day? Do teachers allow Spanish to be spoken in the classroom? Do teachers see the advantages of having one learner help another while speaking in Spanish? What language is spoken in the home? When parents and guardians speak to children in school, what language is spoken? Does the learner live in a predominantly Spanish-speaking neighborhood? What attempts have you made to understand the beauty of the Spanish language and to realize the language problems some students might experience?

3. Increasingly, the Spanish language will be spoken in the United States, especially because all demographic projections suggest the Hispanic population will continue to increase. Some people feel that the United States should accept Spanish as the official second language; other people argue that English should be the only official language of the nation. In your group, discuss issues related to Spanish being increasingly spoken in the United States: whether

Spanish should be accepted in an English-speaking country; whether schools should teach Spanish as well as English; whether instruction should occasionally be in Spanish; the implications for U.S. society and schools; and other issues that your group feels are significant.

Expanding Your Horizons

Additional Books and Journals

Block, N. C. (2023). Students' attitudinal development in a dual language bilingual education program from grade 1 to grade 5. *Bilingual Research Journal*, 45(3–4), 337–357. https://doi-org.proxy.lib.odu.edu/10.1080/15235882.2023.2174204

This study compared the attitudes of 31 grade 5 Latinx students in a Spanish dual language bilingual education program with their attitudes four years prior. It promotes discussion on creating equitable spaces to foster sociocultural competence among bilingual students.

Brooks, R. B. & Brooks, S. (2023). Nurturing positive emotions in the classroom: A foundation for purpose, motivation, and resilience in schools. *Handbook of Resilience in Children*, 549–568. https://doi.org/10.1007/978-3-031-14728-9_30

This chapter emphasizes the pivotal role of both teachers' and students' mindsets in determining academic success. It discusses a resilient mindset and emphasizes the teacher's role in fostering intrinsic motivation, resilience, and social-emotional development.

Cabral-Gouveia, C., Menezes, I., & Neves, T. (2023). Educational strategies to reduce the achievement gap: A systematic review. *Frontiers in Education, 8.* https://doi.org/10.3389/feduc.2023.1155741

This study highlights the persistent educational achievement gap rooted in historical discrimination, yet identifies targeted strategies such as reading-focused interventions, whole-school initiatives and programs addressing psychosocial consequences of discrimination to improve academic attainment.

Iraheta, A. C. (2023). Reclaiming the power of bilingualism: Spanish heritage learners using bilingual skills in a critical service-learning project. *Hispania, 106*(1), 67–82. https://doi.org/10.1353/hpn.2023.0005

This study explores how heritage language learners of Spanish use a service-learning to demonstrate the importance of their bilingual abilities, revealing enhanced linguistic skills, cultural knowledge and challenges to inequities within Latinx communities.

Matheny, K. T., Thompson, M. E., Townley-Flores, C., & Reardon, S. F. (2023). Uneven progress: Recent trends in academic performance among U.S. school districts. *American Educational Research Journal*, *60*(3), 447–485. https://doi-org.proxy.lib.odu.edu/10.3102/00028312221134769
This study examines district-level trends in average academic achievement from 2009 to 2019, finding growing disparities between nonpoor and poor students as well as between white and black students, shrinking disparities between white and Hispanic students, and changes in access to certified teachers as the strongest predictors of achievement.

Young, E., Demissie, Z., Szucs, L. E., Brener, N. D., Waheed, F., & Jasani, S. (2024). Trends in diversity-related learning among secondary schools in 35 US states, 2014–2018. *Health Education Journal*, *83*(1), 52–64. https://journals-sage-pub-com.proxy.lib.odu.edu/doi/full/10.1177/00178969231221000
This study focuses on trends in the implementation of diversity-related learning opportunities in secondary school classrooms and extracurricular settings.

Websites

Centers for Disease Control – www.cdc.gov/nccdphp/dch/programs/healthycommunitiesprogram/tools/pdf/hispanic_latinos_insight.pdf
Provides an excellent overview of U.S. Latino demographics, core values, media consumption habits, health concerns, traditional health beliefs and practices, and more.

Infoplease – www.infoplease.com/spot/hhmbioaz.html
This site provides an A–Z list of topics for Hispanic Heritage Month, plus notable biographies. It looks at Hispanic and Latino Americans who have made significant historical contributions.

Latinos for Education – www.latinosforeducation.org/
This organization seeks to improve educational opportunities for Hispanic children. They publish up-to-date data and advocate for Latino rights.

Scholastic – http://teacher.scholastic.com/activities/hispanic/history.htm
This site provides information and examples of renowned Hispanic Americans in history. It provides biographical information for each of these individuals, as well as their deeds and contributions.

The Smithsonian Institute – www.smithsonianeducation.org/educators/ resource_library/hispanic_resources.html
The site offers an impressive and wide selection of Hispanic heritage lesson plans (grades K–12) and materials (posters, masks, calendars, interactive displays).

U.S. Department of Education – http://sites.ed.gov/hispanic-initiative/
Details "The White House Initiative on Educational Excellence for Hispanics" that prioritizes expanding educational opportunities and improving educational outcomes for Hispanics of all ages.

Part III

Teaching and Learning in a Diverse Society

Part III focuses on what educators should consider when planning and implementing programs that teach acceptance and respect for cultural diversity. Chapters 9, 10, 11, 12, and 13 focus on curriculum, instruction, parents and families, administrators and special school personnel, and contemporary issues, respectively. The emphasis continues to be on promoting multiculturalism and social justice, and implementing effective multicultural education programs.

DOI: 10.4324/9781003429531-11

9

Curricular Efforts

Understanding the material and activities in this chapter will help the reader to:

- Understand how the school curriculum can convey acceptance for all students, promote a sense of social justice throughout the school day, and move away from cultural deficit approaches and perspectives to a more social justice approach.
- Distinguish between the purported changes and the actual progress people from culturally different backgrounds have achieved in U.S. society.
- Prepare a multicultural teaching unit that addresses the needs of learners from culturally different backgrounds and teaches European American learners about diversity.
- State several reasons a school needs a multicultural education program that emphasizes an across-the-curriculum approach and encompasses the total school environment.
- List and describe several methods for extending the multicultural education curriculum to the community and having it pervade extracurricular activities.
- Understand the importance of having school administrators, faculty, and staff reflect the cultural diversity of the student body.

DOI: 10.4324/9781003429531-12

Opening Scenario

The Hidden Curriculum

Mrs. Brunson, a teacher at Calhoun Middle School, knows she will have to take a stand at the faculty meeting. No longer can she let injustice prevail. Her only decision is how to make her point in such a way that positive action will result.

"We have a hidden curriculum," she says, calmly and matter-of-factly. Although the school's philosophy purports to promote equality and equitable treatment for all students, it does not act on that belief. Young adolescents learn from a so-called hidden curriculum that teaches as much as or more than the planned curriculum.

Mrs. Brunson has numerous examples to substantiate her point: School policies that recognize only middle-class European American expectations; a media center that is oriented predominantly toward European Americans; instructional practices and academic expectations that address European American learning styles; and extracurricular activities in which participants are mostly European American. What message is the school sending to learners of diverse cultural backgrounds? While the curriculum seeks to show acceptance and respect for social justice, the hidden curriculum conveys an almost totally opposite picture. Learners from different cultural backgrounds often feel unaccepted and perceive that they must adjust to middle-class, white values and customs.

The faculty expresses some skepticism over Mrs. Brunson's remarks. Clearly, they have not considered the impact of the hidden curriculum. In fact, the school is not as multicultural as some believe.

Mrs. Brunson feels better for having expressed herself. Accomplishing genuine change will be slow and supporters of the status quo will challenge efforts, but at least the faculty now recognizes the problem. This is a first and significant step.

Overview

The tremendous cultural diversity that characterizes U.S. school systems sends a strong message to educators and curriculum developers at both elementary and secondary levels. They must develop a curriculum that addresses the needs of learners and creates a school environment that reflects cultural diversity. To implement such an across-the-curriculum approach, they must carefully select bias-free teaching materials, choose evaluation instruments that take into account cultural differences, encourage appropriate community involvement, and provide extracurricular activities that involve all learners.

Educators such as Mrs. Brunson who are planning a curriculum that reflects acceptance for diversity and social justice should focus on the following goals:

- Develop a school curriculum that reflects multiculturalism and diversity.
- Provide textbooks and other curricular materials that reflect multiculturalism in an accurate manner, free of stereotypes and cultural generalizations.
- Include all cultural groups and provide accurate information about their histories, cultures, contributions, and experiences.
- Offer curricular experiences at a level that students can understand and comprehend in an honest, meaningful manner.

To grow and cultivate the next generation of leaders in social justice education, it's important to have continuous learning opportunities, a solid structure, and teamwork. Sleeter (2000) explains that a good multicultural curriculum is an ongoing process. Educators and multiculturalists are never finished with the multicultural curriculum, because they continually learn as they deal with various issues. Racial biases exist in many situations and this fact must be recognized (Jacoby-Senghor et al., 2016). It can be subtle and, at times, even institutional. Multicultural efforts of educators must be ongoing, deliberate, and periodically evaluated. The assumption that efforts have been successful should be avoided. In fact, the curriculum taught is only as good as educators' understanding of how it relates to diversity, the society in which we live, and academic disciplines. Educators need to be aware of and on the lookout for issues that marginalized students face, including racism, discrimination, and microaggressions.

Toward Cultural Diversity and Social Justice

Overall school curriculum and teaching and learning situations should reflect the cultural diversity of the United States. Although the *Brown* desegregation case and the civil rights legislation of a number of years ago contributed to better treatment and acceptance of groups from culturally different backgrounds, there is much room for improvement. Educators should place change and progress in proper perspective.

Hindrances to progress include the following:

- Deficit ideologies that limit access and opportunity.
- Testing and assessment issues, for example, extensive reliance on tests.

- ◆ IQ-based definitions and theories.
- ◆ Achievement-based definitions and theories.
- ◆ Inadequate policies and practices.
- ◆ Social injustices and discrimination.

POINTS TO PONDER 9.1

Determining Significant Change

Undoubtedly, the U.S. education system has made progress toward providing a culturally relevant curriculum—more materials reflect diversity and provide objective portrayals of females, people from culturally different backgrounds, and people with disabilities. Visit several schools to determine the extent of the changes—how far have we come? What still needs to be done? Are changes superficial or do they show genuine commitment?

The Illusion of Change and Progress

Without a doubt, U.S. education is making progress toward better relations between groups of people. The accomplishments of people of differing cultures and of women are recognized; many educators welcome youngsters with disabilities into their classrooms; most teachers work to reduce racist and sexist behavior in their classrooms; and many work to develop or obtain curricular materials free from bias and prejudice.

Consider, however, the racism and nonacceptance that continue to plague society—the growing popularity of "skinheads" and neo-Nazi groups, for instance. In addition, school practices often document either a lack of understanding of learners from culturally different backgrounds or a lack of acceptance and respect for their cultural differences.

The Continuing Need for Change in Educational Practices

There continues to be much room for genuine change in teaching and learning situations, compatible treatment of people who are disabled or from culturally diverse backgrounds, improvement of the cultural and ethnic compositions of school faculty and staff, and equitable representation of all people, regardless of culture, in textbooks and other curricular materials. This discussion and the accompanying recommendations do not downplay the significant progress that our society and schools have already made. It is necessary, however, to perceive society and schools objectively and to plan an appropriate agenda for positively reconstructing society and schools during the twenty-first century.

Schools should accept responsibility for translating illusion into reality and recognize that they can serve as a significant force in countering discrimination and the various "-isms" that affect people from culturally diverse backgrounds, women, and the disabled.

From Illusion to Reality: Responding to Racism, Discrimination, and Stereotypes

Racism has many damaging and long-lasting effects on the lives of children and adolescents, the character of society, the quality of our civilization, and people's prospects for the future. Before an illusion of racial harmony and justice for all can become a reality, schools must take a powerful and pivotal role in teaching about racism and in working toward acceptance and respect for all people, regardless of racial and cultural background. Schools can play a powerful role in combating racism and educational inequities by confronting and challenging racism, hiring teachers from diverse cultures, developing and implementing a genuine multicultural curriculum, and improving pedagogical practices that address the needs of all learners.

Ethnocentrism occurs when some people hold that their group is better than other groups. Some ethnocentrism is good, but too much group pride can result in a negative force. A society and its schools must seek to understand the many forms of ethnocentrism and work toward keeping ethnocentrism under control among individuals and student groups.

Schools' responsibilities in our multicultural society extend to countering the dangers of stereotyping, from which even educators are not exempt. What steps can educators take to transform illusions of equality and justice into reality?

First, teachers should be aware of their own biases and stereotypes. Through self-examination or cultural awareness workshops, educators can gain a better understanding of their attitudes toward people who are culturally different, women, and people with disabilities. Second, as cultural understandings clarify stereotypical beliefs, educators see the need for expecting as much from learners of differing cultural backgrounds as they do from other students. Although educators should recognize the plight of marginalized communities, they must encourage marginalized students to excel in all areas of academic pursuit.

Third, educators should examine curricular materials for evidence of stereotyping. Specifically, does the material present individuals with different gender identities, females, and minorities in a realistic, nonstereotypical manner? Does the material accurately reflect a holistic view of the past in terms of the contributions of females and people of differing cultural backgrounds in U.S. history? Fourth, educators should strive to diversify classes of homogeneous ability levels, which have the potential for segregating students by race or socioeconomic group. Heterogeneous classes and cooperative learning activities are very important.

Because of landmark court decisions, civil rights legislation, and overall improved race relations, U.S. society is not as divided racially and culturally as it was several decades ago. We must not, however, allow delusions of grandeur to overshadow reality. Discrimination, social injustices, and stereotypes continue to exist and take a heavy toll. Rather than accept the status quo as the most equitable we can achieve, school curricula should deliberately instill in children and adolescents a sense of respect and acceptance for all people, regardless of their cultural and individual differences.

Planning and Implementing Curricula Promoting Social Justice

The Total School Environment

Multiculturalism should extend to and permeate all aspects of the school. In fact, multiculturalism should be such a basic part of the school that it becomes a natural and accepted aspect of the daily routine.

One way that multiculturalism can permeate the curriculum is through an approach that incorporates literature that is culturally appropriate for children and adolescents in teaching the various areas of the curriculum. Multicultural literature is essential to all areas of the curriculum to help students grow in understanding of themselves and others. Through careful selection and sharing of multicultural reading materials, educators help students learn to identify with the people who created the stories, whether of the past or present. Folk tales, myths, and legends clarify the values and beliefs of people. By reading the great stories on which cultures have been founded, learners can discover the threads that weave the past with the present and the themes and values that interconnect people of all cultures.

POINTS TO PONDER 9.2

Researching Cultural Diversity

Separate into small groups and have each group select a different cultural group to research. The following questions may serve as guidelines:

1. Where did the racial, religious, or ethnic group you are studying originate?
2. Why did they leave their homeland?
3. Where in the United States did they originally settle?
4. What kind of work did they do when they first came here?
5. What was their native language?
6. What was their dominant religion?
7. What is a popular myth or legend from their culture?

Reform Efforts

As stated earlier, teaching units are an appropriate and viable means of reaching specific objectives. Serious reform efforts toward a more realistic portrayal of all people, however, will require a major overhaul of elementary and secondary school curricula. What steps can educators take to ensure that elementary and secondary school curricula reflect the cultural diversity of U.S. society?

Proposals for improving the achievement of all students are often doomed to failure, largely due to their allegiance to a deficit orientation—that is, concentrating on what ethnically, racially, and linguistically different students do not have and cannot do. Much more cultural content is needed in all school curricula about all ethnic groups. The need is especially apparent in math and science for ethnic groups other than African Americans. This is true for those subjects in which some initiatives are already under way as well as those that have not changed at all. This means designing more multicultural literacy programs in secondary schools and more math and science programs at all grade levels; teaching explicit information about gender contributions, issues, experiences, and achievement effects *within ethnic groups*; and pursuing more sustained efforts to incorporate content about ethnic and cultural diversity in regular school subjects and skills taught on a routine basis.

The three core tenets of a multicultural curriculum will foster an inclusive educational environment (Comstock et al., 2023):

1. Supporting the academic success of students: A curriculum should endorse multilingual education and the vision of a multicultural

society. Educators should draw on children's experiential backgrounds and insist on a curriculum that allows equal access for all students. All students should be free to enroll in college preparatory courses and other special curricular activities.

2. Supporting students to understand, value, and sustain their own cultural identities:

    Educators should regularly present diverse perspectives, experiences, and contributions while teaching concepts where diverse cultural groups are represented. Teaching materials should include materials and visual displays that are free of race, gender, and disability stereotypes.

3. Supporting students to critique social injustice: Educators should emphasize contemporary issues that exist in society as much as they discuss historical inequalities. Diverse groups should be presented as active and dynamic. An example of this would be integrating the tragic death of George Floyd in 2020 along with that of Martin Luther King Jr. into the curriculum connecting the historical civil rights struggles to the present day.

Additional specific guidelines for developing multicultural curricula below remain relevant today (Sleeter & Grant, 2007):

1. Reform the curriculum in such a way that it regularly presents diverse perspectives, experiences, and contributions. Similarly, present and teach concepts that represent diverse cultural groups and both sexes.

2. Include materials and visual displays that are free of race, gender, and disability stereotypes and that include members of all cultural groups in a positive manner.

3. Embrace concepts, rather than fragments of information, related to diverse groups.

4. Emphasize contemporary culture as much as historical culture, and represent groups as active and dynamic. The curriculum, for example, should include not only the women's suffrage movement but also more contemporary problems confronting women.

5. Strive to make the curriculum a "total effort," with multicultural aspects permeating all subject areas and all phases of the school day.

6. Make sure the curriculum uses nonsexist language.

7. Support a curriculum that endorses bilingual education and the vision of a multilingual society.

8. Draw on children's experiential background in teaching and learning. Base community and curricular concepts on children's daily lives and experiences.
9. Insist on a curriculum that allows equal access for all students. All students, for example, should have the freedom to enroll in college preparatory courses and other special curricular activities.

Diversity comes in many forms, all of which need to be addressed in the curriculum. Sexual orientation should be included in a definition of multicultural education as well as reflected in curricular efforts. LGBTQIA+ children and adolescents confront many of the same biological, cognitive, and social developmental changes as their heterosexual counterparts. Fear of and misunderstandings about homosexuality can result in negative consequences for adolescents struggling with identity formation that differs from that of the majority of their peers.

By learning about the concerns of gay and lesbian youth, middle and secondary educators can break the barrier of silence that contributes to the difficulties and hurt these teens face. Gay and lesbian adolescents bear a double burden: They experience harassment, violence, and suicidal tendencies because of their age and sexual preference. They sometimes feel fearful, withdrawn, depressed, and full of despair. Curricular efforts should address the needs of gay and lesbian adolescents by including age-appropriate literature to explain sexual orientation as well as others' experiences with being gay or lesbian. Such books help readers develop self-understanding and gain insight into the special developmental needs of gay and lesbian youth.

The Hidden Curriculum

Although some aspects of the curriculum are readily discernible to children and adolescents attending a school, other aspects are more subtle and may be equally influential. For example, we have little difficulty determining whether people of differing backgrounds are represented honestly and adequately in textbooks and other curricular materials. We can also ascertain with relative ease whether tracking and ability grouping have resulted in the segregation and relegation to second-class status of all people from different cultural backgrounds and lower socioeconomic status.

There is, however, another equally important curriculum, one that has a powerful influence on children and adolescents. This very subtle *hidden curriculum* affects learners of all races and cultures. Mrs. Brunson in the Opening Scenario takes a stand against the hidden curriculum in her school.

What specific aspects might be included in a hidden curriculum? It might comprise any number of events, behavior expectations, and attitudes that might appear relatively unobtrusive to some learners but might appear out of character or context to other learners. Representative examples might include teacher behaviors and expectations conveyed both verbally and nonverbally; textbooks and other curricular materials that portray white, middle-class values and orientations; segregation due to tracking or ability-grouping policies; educators' and other students' degrees of acceptance, and attitudes toward learners from different cultural backgrounds; and the degree of acceptance of language differences. In other words, middle- or upper-socioeconomic European American students might expect their teacher to encourage them to compete and excel above others in the class; this same teacher expectation, however, might be anathema to American Indian learners. Educators must make a deliberate effort to examine all their behaviors (both conscious and unconscious) to determine what hidden messages they are conveying and to assess carefully every aspect of the curriculum and the total school environment.

Guidelines for Developing a Multicultural Curriculum

As with all curricular efforts, a multicultural curriculum should be carefully matched with goals and objectives and use established guidelines. Although each program should reflect the needs and goals of the respective school, the following guidelines can serve as a basis for multicultural curricular development:

1. Consider students' individual socioeconomic status, religion, gender, sexual orientation, culture, and language, and, whenever possible, use these differences (or at least show respect for them) when designing curricula.
2. Use an interdisciplinary approach, in which topics are addressed in more than one curricular area. Relate the topic to as many other topics as possible across the curriculum.
3. Use a variety of instructional approaches—ones that reflect how students think, organize learning, and compete or cooperate in learning activities.
4. Focus on affective and psychosocial gains, rather than only cognitive gains. Learning facts in isolation is insufficient. Forming positive

attitudes toward others and showing respect for social justice among all people are paramount.

5. Make maximum use of community resources, cultural support groups, and social services.

Several other important implications for culturally responsive pedagogical practices are embedded in the nature and effects of culturally diverse curriculum content examined thus far. One is the need to regularly provide students with more accurate cultural information to fill knowledge voids and correct existing distortions. This information needs to be capable of facilitating many different kinds of learning—cognitive, affective, social, political, personal, and moral. No single content source is capable of doing all of this alone. Therefore, curriculum designers should always use a variety of content sources from different genres and disciplines.

Assessing the Need for Curricular Change

To assess the degree to which curricula respect diversity, schools should not rely on just one type of assessment. Instead, they should consider a multi-informant assessment approach.

Before planning to adopt a multicultural curriculum, the school must assess its needs to determine the direction and extent of the change. Here are some questions a school should consider in conducting a needs assessment:

1. Do multicultural perspectives permeate the entire school curriculum and environment?
2. Do the attitudes of teachers, administrators, and staff members indicate a willingness to accept and respect cultural diversity?
3. Do textbooks and other curricular materials recognize the value of cultural diversity and gender and social class differences?
4. Do curricular activities and methods provide learners with opportunities to collaborate and cooperate?
5. Do extracurricular activities reflect cultural diversity?
6. Do curricular planning efforts reflect the views and opinions of parents and other community people?
7. Do curricular efforts include bilingual perspectives or provide assistance for students with limited English-speaking skills?

Selecting Bias-Free Curricular Materials

Over the years, a great deal of research has been done to determine if textbooks are dealing adequately with diversity issues. The inadequacies of textbook coverage of cultural diversity can be avoided by including accurate, wide-ranging, and appropriately contextualized content about different ethnic groups' histories, cultures, and experiences in classroom instruction on a regular basis. The efforts need not be constrained by lack of information and materials. Plenty of resources exist about most ethnic groups and in such variety that all subjects and grades taught in schools can be served adequately. Since this information is not always in textbooks, teachers need to develop the habit of using other resources to complement or even replace them. Students also should be taught how to critique textbooks for the accuracy of their multicultural content and how to compensate.

Other equally important concerns related to bias in textbooks are omissions and distortions. *Omission* refers to information left out of a textbook, and *distortion* is a lack of balance or systematic omission. Because of omissions, members of some cultural and ethnic groups are virtually unrepresented in textbooks. Hispanic Americans, Asian Americans, American Indians, and women continue to be underrepresented in educational materials. The invisibility of a group implies that it has less value or significance in U.S. society than others. Invisibility applies most often to women, culturally diverse people, people with disabilities, and the elderly (Gollnick & Chinn, 2006). Furthermore, Urbani et al. (2024) point to the omission of non-dominant, marginalized groups from traditional textbooks and the fact that it makes a comprehensive understanding of historical events nearly impossible. The education system has become politicized in many cases, resulting in limited conversations and the bans on books. The history of race relations is an important subject that teachers should include in their classrooms, focusing on implications and contributions to contemporary society. Recent deaths of African Americans have brought racial issues in America to the forefront. Some teachers, however, are unsure of the best way to address them in the classroom. The omission of experiences of marginalized groups from traditional textbooks may be one reason for this as it hinders understanding of historical events.

Distortions result from inaccurate or unbalanced impressions. History and reading materials too often ignore the presence and realities of certain groups in contemporary society, or they confine treatment to negative experiences. In some cases, they provide a single point of view about events that may be technically correct but is nevertheless misleading.

Sexism and sexist language are other factors to consider when selecting textbooks and other teaching materials. Gollnick and Chinn (2006) have called attention to the sexism that often occurs in children's and adolescents' textbooks, especially at the elementary school level. Children who were asked to draw an early caveman drew only pictures of cavemen. In contrast, when instructed to draw "cave people," the children generated drawings of men, women, and children. In classrooms, teachers can point out sexist language to students. When words appear to exclude women as full participants in society or limit their occupational options, teachers can provide alternatives—for example, *mail carrier* and *police officer* as alternatives to *mailman* and *policeman* (Gollnick & Chinn, 2006). Research indicates that implicit biases, ingrained in youth through upbringing, culture, and media, may be caused by the under-representation of diversity. These biases in turn shape the career aspirations of youth (Miller et al., 2023).

Post-secondary science education has addressed implicit bias by encouraging and promoting gender equity along with gender-inclusive language, but the impact on K–12 learners remains unexplored. For example, elementary boys may use male-exclusive language, such as, "When I grow up, I want to be a navy officer like him," which implicitly suggests that navy officers are male. The way students perceive the gender roles of scientists or engineers can have an impact on their academic behavior and even planned field of study.

Evaluating Curricular Efforts

Evaluating the multicultural curriculum to determine overall program strengths and weaknesses and to assess how well it meets individual learner needs is as important as the actual content and teaching methods the teacher uses. One basic criterion is to determine whether teaching and learning situations reflect multiculturalism (Franco et al., 2023; Sleeter & Grant, 2007).

Considering the diversity of students and families, teachers need to adjust their teaching methods (Tomlinson, 2015) to ensure every student has access to strong learning opportunities and accommodate different learning styles that may be influenced by cultural backgrounds; use a mix of teaching strategies including arts, stories, and hands-on activities; group projects to actively engage all learners; and facilitate discussions that encourage students to share their cultural backgrounds and perspectives.

One way of evaluating teachers' curricular efforts is to check whether they prioritize their integration of culturally relevant pedagogy (CRP), which values cultural backgrounds of all students, makes lessons more meaningful, and supports them in achieving their academic potential. Ladson-Billings (1995b; 2021) examined the pedagogical expertise of teachers successful with students who had traditionally struggled, and developed "CRP," which is an asset-oriented pedagogy referring to teachers' employment of culturally and linguistically affirmative views with their students. Equity-oriented pedagogy refers to teachers' support for students in achieving their academic potential.

Also, educators need to decolonize the curriculum to create equitable education experiences so that all students can see their culture, history, and perspectives represented in their learning. It helps to promote self-esteem, relevance in learning, and provides validation to carry on their heritage and home language. Decolonizing the curriculum is the process of critically revising the content and teaching methods to at least reduce and ultimately eliminate colonial biases and perspectives (Seckinelgin, 2023). The initial step is to recognize how colonialism has shaped knowledge and dynamics in society and prevent the marginalizing of people with non-white perspectives. Further, to empower the voices of the underrepresented people, teachers can actively promote the contributions of those who have been historically marginalized or omitted from academic curricula.

By focusing on equity, not culture, in diversity conversation schools can commit to and achieve greater multiculturalism (Gorski & Swalwell, 2015). Some schools have formed a Multicultural Curriculum Initiative where diversity is addressed through quotes, sayings, and office walls decorated with artwork of diverse youth groups. One teacher claimed that racism existed within the school and current efforts were not working. In other words, though effective, the school curriculum and environment should move beyond artwork, celebrations, and displaying pictures of diverse people. The trouble lies with diversity initiatives that avoid or whitewash serious equity issues. The challenge is to utilize and retain principles of equity as central aspects of a truly meaningful multicultural curriculum. Five effective guiding principles of multicultural curriculum include: Equity literacy is important in every subject area; the most effective equity literacy approach is integrative and interdisciplinary; students of all ages are primed for equity literacy; students from all backgrounds need equity literacy; and teaching for equity literacy is a political act, but not more so than not teaching equity literacy.

Other measures of program effectiveness include oral and written tests (teacher-made and standardized), sociograms, questionnaires, surveys, student projects, interviews, anecdotal information, and discussion groups. Indicators such as attendance records, class participation, and incidence of disruptive behavior also provide clues about student acceptance of and interest in the program. Many of these procedures are conducive to staff, parent, and student involvement. Whatever evaluation is used, the information collected should be well-documented, relevant, and useful. The validity of evaluation depends on the questions asked, behaviors observed, and efforts made to sample randomly and to apply common standards.

Effective multicultural education programs require well-written multicultural literature and curricular materials that represent all students, including interracial children. Reasons for incorporating inclusive literature include promoting and developing cultural appreciation; encouraging critical inquiry; and highlighting the universal human experience (Pfundheller & Liesch, 2023). To accept and affirm pluralism in our schools, educators should recognize interracial children and integrate interracial literature into the school curriculum (Lee & Johnson, 2000).

The benefits of using interracial literature include the following:

◆ Interracial literature, both fiction and nonfiction, can help build a sound personal identity in interracial children.
◆ Interracial literature changes the way children look at their world by offering different perspectives of people and events.
◆ Interracial literature shows people who traditionally have been denied realistic images of themselves, their families, community, and culture.

A Multicultural Education Unit

The premise of this book is that multicultural education should be a total-school curriculum and environmental approach, rather than an occasional unit. The author does, however, recognize that the situation should not be "either/or," nor should it become a battle of multicultural education curriculum versus the unit approach. The author firmly believes that a once-a-year (or even an every-semester) effort in the form of a multicultural week or perhaps a two- or three-week unit is insufficient to teach knowledge of and respect for cultural diversity. Readers are reminded, therefore, to consider units as a part of a total curriculum effort, perhaps as a means of addressing one or more specific objectives. Educators should strive to make the curriculum a comprehensive effort with multicultural aspects permeating all subject areas and phases of the school year.

Considerations

Before examining a unit designed to convey knowledge and understanding of cultural diversity, it is important to define the unit approach and to look briefly at what units usually include. First, *units* (sometimes called *modules*) are designed to teach a specific body of information over a time lasting more than a class meeting or two—for example, might the unit last one, two, or three days, or weeks, or years, or longer in some instances?

Second, units contain goals, objectives, content, activities, materials, enrichment resources, and evaluational instruments. Although educators may differ about what the unit should include, generally speaking, it is a comprehensive guide that differs from the one-day lesson plan.

Example

The next several pages provide an example of an instructional unit. It is important to remember that this unit serves only as an illustration. Educators should assess their students' developmental needs, levels of knowledge, and attitudes, and assess the planned instruction accordingly.

The Unit: Unjust Treatment of People of Culturally Diverse Backgrounds

Rationale

African Americans were brought to the United States to be sold into slavery. American Indians were forced off their lands. Asian Americans, especially Chinese Americans, worked on the railroad linking the Missouri River to the Pacific Coast in 1862. Hispanic Americans worked in "sweat factories" or as migrant workers. Japanese Americans were relocated to internment camps after the bombing of Pearl Harbor.

Objectives and Activities

1. Have students define the terms *racism*, *social justice*, *discrimination*, and *injustice* and identify examples of each that have harmed several groups from culturally different backgrounds.
2. Have students identify three books or songs that describe the injustices that groups from different cultural backgrounds experienced.
3. Have students develop a time line showing culturally diverse people's responses to unjust treatment—for example, African Americans' march on Washington in 1963.
4. Have students identify three examples of contemporary racism, discrimination, or injustice and list possible solutions for each.

Individuals, cooperative learning groups, or interest-established pairs or triads may work on these activities.

Language Arts

1. Have students prepare short stories, poems, skits, and plays on the unjust treatment many people received.
2. Ask students to write and give a speech that an American Indian might have given regarding land being taken away.
3. Keep a class scrapbook of unjust practices that currently exist in the United States.
4. Help students write a letter to the editor of a newspaper proposing a solution to an injustice people suffer today.

Mathematics

1. Compile a "numbers" list with students: acres of land taken away from American Indians, numbers of African Americans brought to the United States to work as enslaved people, numbers of Asian Americans who worked on the railroad, and numbers of Hispanic Americans who worked as migrant workers. Compute estimates of money saved by having workers work in low-paying jobs in poor working conditions.
2. On a bar or pie graph, ask students to show numbers of workers from culturally different backgrounds in minimum-wage jobs.
3. Have students estimate the value of land taken from American Indians, and compare the estimate with the amount received (if any money was actually paid).

Science

1. Study terrain as part of your lesson plan—for example, land taken away from American Indians and farming land on which migrant workers grow produce.
2. Have students examine climate conditions necessary for growing various types of produce and determine the effects these conditions have on people.
3. Study with students the climatic conditions (e.g. temperature, humidity, heat index) of many "sweat shops" and the effect these conditions have on people.

Social Studies

1. Examine with students the concepts of racism, injustice, and discrimination, and pinpoint historical and contemporary examples.
2. Ask students to gather information on immigration patterns by decade or some other time frame.

3. Review with students Americans' resistance to immigrants entering the United States.
4. Have students write an essay explaining the "melting-pot" concept and its limitations and how we currently support the "salad-bowl" concept.
5. Ask students to write a position paper for or against the resistance or unjust treatment people received on arrival to the United States.
6. Develop a time line with students showing each cultural group's important dates or events—the Emancipation Proclamation, for example.
7. Ask students to develop a chart listing injustices and offer possible solutions.

Art

1. Introduce students to works of art depicting injustices people have suffered and struggled to overcome.
2. Assign students to create collages, dioramas, and mobiles showing injustices: the bonds of slavery, the plight of American Indians, and the menial jobs that many Asian Americans and Hispanic Americans have been forced to accept.
3. Study art of various cultures and ask students to look for common themes and areas.
4. Examine American Indian art with students and the relationship between the art and the history of American Indians.

Music

1. Listen to songs of various cultures that have helped people to survive, provided a ray of hope, and communicated pain and suffering.
2. Ask students to write lyrics for a familiar melody that deal with a contemporary injustice and offer hope.
3. Research musical instruments that enslaved people and other people in bondage used.

This partial unit can serve as a beginning point or skeletal unit. Teachers working on interdisciplinary teams can tap their professional expertise in particular content areas and offer many exciting and productive activities and ideas.

Other topics for multicultural units include the following:

◆ Contributions of people from culturally different groups (or a specific cultural group).

- ◆ Cultural traditions: family and society (in general or for a specific cultural group).
- ◆ Books, poems, and short stories (or music or art) by writers from culturally different backgrounds, such as *Native People of the Southwest*, *African American Scholars: Leaders, Activists, and Writers*, and *Martin Luther King: A Lifetime of Action*.
- ◆ Contemporary contributors from culturally different backgrounds: civil rights activists.
- ◆ Influential women and their contributions (women in general or women in a specific cultural group).
- ◆ Coming to the United States: immigration in the 1990s to the present.

Expanding the Multicultural Education Curriculum

Involvement of Parents, Caregivers, Families, and Communities

Efforts to provide multicultural education curricula and environments must extend beyond the confines of the school. Children and adolescents need to perceive evidence of recognition and respect for cultural diversity in the home and in the community. The home and the community can serve as powerful and positive forces to help reinforce the efforts of the school. Parents and other community members and organizations are valuable resources to help support the school's efforts to promote respect for cultural diversity. They should be made aware of school efforts and should feel that the school seeks and respects their advice and opinions. These two entities can also provide considerable financial and volunteer support for the multicultural education program.

As parents become involved in their children's education and learn more about the school's goals (especially in relation to the goals and materials of the multicultural education curricula), they are more likely to give overall support for school programs. Parents in all likelihood will become more interested in their children's school success and be better able to assist the school in its efforts.

Parents and educators should ask whether the community supports the school and its academic and social tasks. Is the leadership of the community concerned with school effectiveness? Does the community support efforts toward school improvement? Are the achievements of all students and teachers celebrated in the community at public occasions? Are there role models in the community-educated people? If the community is not strongly positive, bring the matter to the attention of progressive community leaders with the suggestion that they sponsor a determined effort to improve the community environment.

Extracurricular Activities

Perceptive educators readily recognize the need for equitable representation of all races and ethnic groups in extracurricular activities. Guidelines are as follows:

1. Athletic programs should include marginaized students and women, and cheerleading teams should include both sexes as well as students of culturally different backgrounds.
2. Clubs and organizations should not perpetuate racial or gender segregation, and one group should not dominate positions of student leadership.
3. Females should participate in all sports and there should be special arrangements for students who are unable to participate for financial or other reasons (Gollnick & Chinn, 2006).

Summing Up

Multicultural educators planning and implementing culturally responsive curricula should do the following:

1. Reflect and recognize that the United States has experienced considerable progress toward acceptance of cultural diversity; that racism, discrimination, and prejudice continue to exist in the United States; and that curricular efforts and overall school environment should demonstrate an emphatic respect for cultural diversity.
2. Place reform efforts on an across-the-curriculum approach and on the overall school environment, rather than on a once-a-year or unit approach.
3. Have a sound multicultural basis: a careful assessment of overall needs, established guidelines, the selection of bias-free curricular materials, and the provision of evaluative procedures for both learners and curricular efforts.
4. Include extensive involvement of community resources, and permeate extracurricular activities as well as the academic curricular aspects.
5. Respect and build on, as much as possible, individual learners' native languages.

Implementing Research

Equity Literacy for All

The use of racially affirming high-quality picture books by kindergarten through third-grade teachers to foster racial literacy and enhance reading practices for more effective and equitable outcomes was investigated by Spear et al. (2023). The study explored the interplay between racial literacy and reading practices, highlighting the pivotal role of the picture books in supporting racial literacy development. They found that racial literacy, defined as teachers' understanding of how race and racism influence reading instruction and outcomes, is facilitated by high-quality racially affirming picture books, which offer accessible, emotional, and pedagogically rich content. Students are four times less likely to graduate if they are not reading at grade level by the end of third grade. Given the significance of reading proficiency by third grade as a crucial educational milestone and life skill, this study underscores the importance of addressing not only racial literacy but literacy overall in early education to improve the academic outcomes and future success of all children.

Implementing the Research
1. Select culturally relevant reading materials. Literature offers a mirror and opens doors to different perspectives, promoting empathy and understanding among students.
2. Teachers must understand how race and racism impact reading instruction and reading outcomes in their classrooms.
3. Educators should engage in discussions regarding how their diverse perspectives and positions may influence their relationships, both within their community of practice and the broader school environment.

Source: Spear, C. F., Briggs, J. O., Sanchez, T., Woody, M., & Ponce-Cori, J. (2023). The power of picturebooks to support early elementary teachers' racial literacy in communities of practice: An example from the 3Rs (reading, racial equity, relationships). *Early Childhood Education Journal.* https://doi-org.proxy.lib.odu.edu/10.1007/s10643-023-01500-z

Suggested Learning Activities

1. Interview a curriculum coordinator of a large school (or school district) with a large percentage of students from culturally different

backgrounds. What approach is the school taking to implement a multicultural education program? What mechanism is in place to ensure that all levels of educators are involved in the program? After the interview, carefully consider your findings, and write a brief paper that summarizes your findings and offers what you think are appropriate suggestions.

2. Prepare a multicultural unit (designed for perhaps two or three weeks) that a school could integrate into an overall multicultural education program. In this unit, be sure to include goals, objectives, activities, curricular materials, provisions for evaluation (of both students and the unit itself), and provisions for children and adolescents with limited English-speaking abilities.

3. Find examples or case studies where CRP (culturally relevant pedagogy) has been successfully implemented and the outcomes achieved.

Suggestions for Collaborative Efforts

Form groups of three or four that, if possible, represent the nation's cultural and gender diversity. Working collaboratively, focus your group's attention toward the following efforts:

1. Have each member of your group select a type of curricular material—for example, textbooks, workbooks, worksheets, audiovisuals, and any other curricular materials that elementary or secondary schools commonly use. Prepare an evaluation form (on textbooks as an example here) to answer such questions as: Is the portrayal of children and adolescents of culturally different backgrounds filled with stereotypes and myths? Of the materials on your list, consider the actual numbers of learners of culturally different backgrounds in the school, the accuracy and objectivity of their portrayal, and whether the material addresses differences among people within cultural groups (e.g. Are all Asian Americans alike? Are all Spanish-speaking people alike?).

2. As a group, visit a school to determine its efforts to help children of limited English-speaking capability. What special considerations are made for these learners? What language programs are in place? What professional staff is available to offer help? What remedial programs are available? Are learners allowed to speak their native languages in schools?

3. Evaluating the school curriculum for relevance, objectivity, and accuracy should be a major part of planning any multicultural education program. In your collaborative groups, suggest eight to ten criteria for evaluating the curriculum to determine whether it recognizes and shows respect for cultural diversity and promotes social justice for all people.

Expanding Your Horizons

Additional Books and Journals

Abacioglu, C. S., Epskamp, S., Fischer, A. H., & Volman, M. (2023). Effects of multicultural education on student engagement in low- and high-concentration classrooms: The mediating role of student relationships. *Learning Environment Research*, 26, 951–975. https://doi.org/10.1007/s10984-023-09462-0

Makaiau, A. S., Halagao, P. E., & Thao, G. (2023). Creating transformative leaders of social justice in education. *Multicultural Perspectives*, 25(1), 52–59. https://doi-org.proxy.lib.odu.edu/10.1080/15210960.2022.2136181
Discusses the necessity of continuous learning opportunities, structures, and collaborations for fostering and supporting the development of future leaders in social justice education.

Pfundheller, M. & Liesch, J. (2023). Framework for inclusive literature in teacher education. *Journal of Higher Education Theory and Practice*, 23(15), 55–67. https://articlegateway.com/index.php/JHETP/article/view/6406/6049
Discusses how inclusive literature promotes cultural appreciation and creates a learning environment where all students feel valued.

Romano, L. E. (2023). Assessment for equity: Exploring how secondary educators utilize classroom management and assessment practices to sustain student identities. *Assessment for Effective Intervention*. https://doi.org/10.1177/15345084231178788
Addresses the ways in which teachers' approaches to classroom management influence equity at the classroom level.

Young, J. L. (2020). Evaluating multicultural education courses: Promise and possibilities for portfolio assessment. *Multicultural Perspectives*, 22(1), 20–27.
Discusses the importance of evaluating multicultural curriculum to determine if the program is meeting individual learner needs.

Websites

Pbs.org – www.pbs.org/kcts/preciouschildren/diversity/
Discusses linguistic and cultural diversity, and provides activities and practices for promoting cultural and racial awareness.

Yale Center for Teaching and LeaVanderbilt Diversity and Inclusive Teaching –
    http://ctl.yale.edu/teaching/ideas-teaching/diversity-classroom
Details information regarding cultural, racial, and ethnic diversity, and provides inclusive teaching strategies.

10

Instructional Practices

Understanding the material and activities in this chapter will help the reader to:

- ◆ State the importance of individual and cultural differences among learners, and explain how these differences affect the teaching and learning process.
- ◆ Explain Culturally Responsive Teaching and Culturally Sustaining Teaching.
- ◆ Explain challenges teachers face with respect to linguistically diverse students and propose practical solutions to support them based on the translanguaging approach.
- ◆ Reflect on teachers' cultural biases through understanding Critical Race Theory (CRT).
- ◆ Explain practical ideas to support multilingual learners and promote heritage language teaching.
- ◆ Explain the classroom teacher's role in providing teaching and learning situations that are beneficial to culturally diverse learners.
- ◆ State how socioeconomic conditions, social class, and parents and families affect culturally diverse learners.
- ◆ List the factors educators should consider in evaluating culturally diverse learners.
- ◆ List the items educators should consider during self-evaluation to determine teaching effectiveness in multicultural situations.
- ◆ Explain special considerations that educators should address when planning teaching and learning experiences with African American, American Indian, Arab American, Asian American, European American, and Hispanic American children and adolescents.

DOI: 10.4324/9781003429531-13

◆ List the characteristics of teachers who are effective in multicultural situations.

◆ Explain the importance and necessity of ensuring that multicultural education permeates the total school environment, provides educational experiences that demonstrate acceptance of culturally diverse learners, and promotes positive self-concepts and cultural identities.

Opening Scenario

Knowledge, Attitudes, and Skills

The discussion continues in the teacher's lounge at Ocean View Middle School. When working in a multicultural situation, which characteristic does a teacher need the most: Knowledge, attitudes, or skills? Although the discussion is professional in nature, it is growing increasingly intense.

"Knowledge is what it takes," says one teacher. "If we know about diversity and the cultural characteristics of learners, we can plan appropriate teaching and learning activities. Also, we will better understand how others' characteristics differ from our own."

"True," another teacher responds, "but knowledge is not enough. You need proper attitudes; you need to examine your attitudes toward diversity, and you need to respond to culturally diverse students and their needs. History is full of instances in which people had cultural knowledge yet failed to respond when injustices occurred."

"Your arguments are missing a vital point," states a teacher from another group. "Even with the appropriate knowledge and attitudes, you will still fail to provide the most effective educational experiences for culturally diverse learners unless you have skills."

The teachers consider the issue and decide that, perhaps, it takes all three—knowledge, attitudes, and skills—to provide an effective multicultural education. Some teachers recognize the shortcomings of their positions. Whereas some had tried to improve their knowledge, others had worked to develop more accepting attitudes. One had even taken a skills course to improve his ability to work with students of varying cultures.

The effective teacher in a multicultural education setting, however, needs knowledge, attitudes, and skills. As the educators file back to their classes, someone says, "Quite a challenge, but just think of the benefits for diverse learners—in fact, for all learners."

Overview

Learners at both the elementary and secondary levels deserve the most effective educational experiences possible. In the past, however, educational experiences have all too often minimized the importance of minority viewpoints and issues. Cultural diversity has been an obstacle for learners to "overcome" or for teachers to "remediate." If teachers are to provide effective culturally responsive teaching, they need to understand how ethnically diverse students learn.

Most people have accepted the fact that the achievement gap that separates African American and Hispanic American students from their European American and Asian American counterparts is in schools nationwide. On average, these marginalized students start school trailing behind European American and Asian American children and never catch up, lagging on national tests in every subject, sometimes by as much as four grade levels. A new sense of urgency about the problem is prompting educators and policymakers around the nation to try a variety of tactics to narrow the academic disparities dividing racial and ethnic groups. In some cases, class sizes are being trimmed, teachers are receiving special training, and preschool programs for marginalized children are being expanded. Schools are opening access to high-level classes and encouraging marginalized children to enroll. Districts are looking for schoolwide-improvement models, and policymakers are raising the academic bar for students and teachers.

This chapter explores several teaching and learning contexts: learners' individual and cultural differences, characteristics of educators, organization and instruction, the teaching and learning environment, and cultural perspectives that influence the teaching and learning process in multicultural settings.

Learners' Individual and Cultural Differences

Perceiving All Learners Objectively

It is important that teachers perceive elementary and secondary learners objectively, regardless of cultural, ethnic, racial, sexual orientation, socioeconomic, or religious differences. Learners need the psychological security of feeling valued and accepted; therefore, all educational decisions should be based on objective evidence and should be made with the individual's welfare in mind. Because of the tremendous diversity among contemporary learners, educators cannot consider an entire class as a homogeneous group who need the same educational experiences. Students differ significantly in social class, geographic location, and family background. It is the school's responsibility to develop an understanding of each learner and to base teaching and learning experiences on reliable and objective information.

POINTS TO PONDER 10.1

Valuing Differences Among Learners

Learners have many differences—many that educators can see, and others more subtle. Also, as we have repeatedly stated, no one can consider an individual to be like others in his or her culture. Yet some educators consider all students of one race, for example, to be the same and fail to consider their many differences. Make a list of ways that educators can learn about students and their differences (e.g. get to know individual students, meet their immediate parents and extended family members, and study the respective cultures).

Recognizing and Accepting Diversity

It is an understatement to suggest that teaching and learning situations must demonstrate an emphatic acceptance of learners in all their cultural, ethnic, socioeconomic, and religious diversity. An environment that promotes acceptance of diversity does more than pay lip-service to the concept or have goal statements that are merely rhetorical.

For culturally diverse learners to feel genuine acceptance, the teaching and learning process must concretely demonstrate respect for cultural and ethnic differences (Are all cultures and ethnic groups represented in the curriculum?); it must recognize socioeconomic status (Do children come in contact with children from other socioeconomic levels? Do textbooks portray the various social classes of U.S. society?); and it must accept all religious groups (Do children feel their religious views are accepted?).

Students of color account for nearly half of the K–12 student population in the United States. Projections are that over the next eight years the number of African American and Hispanic students will rise, while that of white students will fall (Taylor & Wendt, 2023). This increasing diversity underscores the need for schools able to serve all students effectively. In contrast, public school teachers have a notably different demographic makeup. Approximately 80 percent of public school teachers are non-Hispanic white, and fewer than 7 percent are of color. It is becoming increasingly important for teachers to be well-prepared to support the academic success of a culturally and racially diverse student body. To address the increasing diversity in schools, including students speaking different languages, migrant children attending school intermittently, and more students with disabilities in inclusion classrooms, Sapon-Shevin (2000/2001) recommend strategies such as cooperative learning in heterogeneous groups, peer tutoring, and multilevel teaching. First, she maintains that cooperative learning is an optimal way to teach students with different abilities in the same classroom. Second, peer tutoring allows teachers to address different skill levels and to respect differences. Still, teachers should use caution to avoid a situation in which a student is always being tutored and never has the opportunity to serve in a teacher or leader role. Third, multilevel teaching can be used to teach a wide range of students in one classroom. Teachers need to organize classroom learning activities so that all students can participate successfully.

Culturally Responsive Teaching and Culturally Sustaining Teaching

Culturally Responsive Teaching and Culturally Sustaining Teaching guide teachers in fostering, promoting, and advocating for linguistic, literary, and cultural diversity in schools. These pedagogical approaches pave the way for meaningful and positive social transformation fostering culturally diverse practices across students' daily lives (Ladson-Billings, 2021).

School districts throughout the United States gained significant attention and endorsed Culturally Responsive Teaching, which aims to make education more relevant, engaging, and empowering for African American students (Ladson-Billings, 1995a). Culturally Responsive Teaching uses asset-oriented pedagogy and recognizes ethnic, cultural, and linguistic assets of students. It encourages the forging of authentic connections with students by leveraging their diverse cultural backgrounds to enrich the learning experience (Taylor & Wendt, 2023). Educators can develop workable culturally relevant teaching approaches for successful learning opportunities that promote students' achievement and appropriate school behavior. Researchers (Burnham, 2020; Gay, 2018; Lau & Shea, 2022) identified essential teaching approaches, such as activating students' prior knowledge, making learning contextual, ensuring an inclusive classroom environment, capitalizing on students' cultural knowledge, and building relationships.

Culturally Sustaining Teaching extends the tenets of Culturally Responsive Teaching (Ladson-Billings & Tate, 1995), which focuses on the educational experiences of African American students.

Django Paris (2012) created the teaching approach, "Culturally Sustaining Pedagogy," or Culturally Sustaining Teaching. Culturally Sustaining Teaching supports all marginalized communities—African American, Latinx, Asian

American, Indigenous groups, etc., in defense of unique languages and cultures. Paris built upon essential and foundational key elements of Culturally Responsive Teaching to extend and promote the concept of culturally sustaining teaching. Paris encouraged educators to think about the teaching goals of pursuing just practices and to critically consider the purpose of schooling in a pluralistic society. As such, Culturally Sustaining Teaching explicitly calls for schools to promote and sustain all diverse and unique experiences and knowledge—rather than eradicate the ways of being of communities of color (Paris & Alim, 2017), thus fostering linguistic, literate, and cultural pluralism as a part of schooling (Aronson & Laughter, 2016).

By implementing Culturally Responsive Teaching strategies, teachers will increase knowledge about their students, which can enhance learning outcomes and mitigate disparities in academic achievement and disciplinary issues, particularly for students of color. The persistent social disparities in the United States underscore the need for Culturally Responsive Teaching, which involves a specific attitude towards students and the teaching process (Comstock et al., 2023). It requires that teachers understand their students' culture and integrate it into their teaching practices. Teachers' beliefs, self-efficacy, and engagement in professional learning about Culturally Responsive Teaching are positively correlated with the frequency of their application of its principles in the classroom. This approach typically prioritizes three main principles: (1) aiding students in achieving academic success (2) assisting students in comprehending, appreciating, and preserving their cultural identities; and (3) empowering students to analyze and challenge social injustices. Table 10.1 presents ways to apply the three principles of Culturally Responsive Teaching in the classroom and school.

As the U.S. student population becomes more diverse culturally and racially, it is imperative for teachers to support all students. A lack of cultural competence in teachers can lead to an increase in student discipline problems and a decrease in achievement. Culturally responsive classroom management, an important skill for today's teachers, includes recognizing and confronting personal ethnocentrism; knowing student cultural backgrounds and heritage; understanding sociopolitical and economic factors that influence teaching and learning; implementing culturally responsive strategies; and cultivating a nurturing and supportive classroom atmosphere (Taylor & Wendt, 2023). Educators can self-assess and reflect on how they can best create inclusive and culturally responsive classrooms. The purpose of Culturally Responsive Pedagogy Self-Assessment and Reflective Conversations (Due East Educational Equity Collaborative, 2020) is to assess teacher progress as culturally responsive and competent educators. The assessment is designed to encourage self-reflection to ensure outcomes for schools, classrooms, and

Table 10.1 Application of the Three Principles of Culturally Responsive Teaching

Three Principles of Culturally Responsive Teaching	Application in the Classroom
1. Aiding students in achieving academic success	• Accommodate diverse learning styles, different ways of learning, and preferences by incorporating cooperative learning activities, hands-on projects and visual aids. • Use books written by authors of diverse races that reflect the students' cultural diversity and include stories and examples from various cultures.
2. Assisting students in comprehending, appreciating, and preserving their cultural identities	• Recognize cultural holidays, traditions, and events relevant to your students' backgrounds. This can involve organizing multicultural festivals, inviting guest speakers of different cultures, or celebrating ethnic food and music to better understand their cultural backgrounds, values, and priorities. • Encourage students to learn and maintain heritage language and culture. • Allow students to work on art projects, presentations, or writing about topics that represent their cultural identities.
3. Empowering students to challenge social injustices	• Provide opportunities for student voice and choice. • Empower students to take ownership of their learning by offering opportunities to explore topics and themes that are personally meaningful to them. • Be vigilant about addressing bias and stereotypes in classroom materials, interactions, and disciplinary practices.

students that are both equitable and high achieving. Educators should reflect honestly on their ability to build equitable and inclusive learning environments for students from diverse communities, backgrounds, and identities (Turner Consulting Group, 2014).

Critical Race Theory

Critical Race Theory (CRT) has generated intense discussion in education as it is a means of interpreting a society and understanding deeply rooted racism and its effects on people's lives. The five tenets of CRT are: counter-storytelling; the permanence of racism; whiteness as property; interest conversion; and the critique of liberalism (DeCuir & Dixson, 2004). Teachers need to recognize the value of CRT, which is a framework that is intended to eliminate all types of suppression and is committed to social justice. CRT views racism as a normal part of life in the United States.

Proponents of CRT believe teaching the concept of CRT in schools helps students understand the impact of race in education. CRT uses a valuable lens to address racial inequalities and to help us understand historical and contemporary racial issues. Some educators assert that regardless of students' race, those from low-income backgrounds generally perform poorly in school, attributing the underperformance of African American students to low socioeconomic status and poverty rates. However, Ladson-Billings and Tate (1995) contend that the root of African American students' economic hardship, combined with the condition of their schools and poor quality education, is due to systemic and institutional racism. For example, the lens of CRT sheds light on the underlying factors contributing to underrepresentation of people of color in the science, technology, engineering, and mathematics (STEM) field.

By applying CRT, educators can more actively integrate culturally relevant teaching and eliminate practices in classrooms that maintain existing inequalities by ignoring and devaluing the voices, experiences, and knowledge of students of color (Dodo Seriki, 2018). Unfortunately, some marginalized students may hesitate and hold back from showing an interest in STEM subjects due to their perception of scientists and workers in that field. When they don't see scientists and role models in STEM careers who look like them or share their background, their belief that they belong there is shaken. Thus, STEM education programs and teachers need to increasingly present experts who are people of color and understand how to engage marginalized youth in culturally relevant ways to meet their specific needs (Dodo Seriki, 2018).

Characteristics of Effective Educators in Multicultural Settings

Educators who seek a comprehensive understanding of cultural diversity and expertise in multicultural education should direct attention to both cognitive and affective factors. It will not suffice for educators to have knowledge of culturally diverse learners yet be unable to recognize learners' individual and cultural needs, and the complex relationship between culture and learning. Educators also need to develop appropriate attitudes that show genuine concern and caring, as well as skills to plan and implement instruction that addresses cultural and individual diversity.

This section looks briefly at the knowledge, attitudes, and skills that teachers need in multicultural settings. It is important to emphasize that these three attributes do not work in isolation. Teachers who work in multicultural situations are responsible for developing expertise in all three areas so they can provide learners with the most effective learning environment.

Knowledge

Teachers may lack factual information about ethnic, racial, and cultural differences; teacher education programs traditionally have not provided appropriate experiences to prepare teachers to teach in an increasingly multicultural classroom. A teacher's diversity knowledge base should include culture, race, ethnicity, and socioeconomic status, and the teacher should comprehend the implications for the teaching and learning process. Similarly, teachers must know and understand the ramifications of racism, discrimination, prejudice, and injustice, and what it means to be a diverse learner. Teachers need sufficient knowledge to be able to understand culturally different learners and to plan both developmentally and culturally appropriate instruction.

Most preservice teachers enter classrooms filled with culturally, ethnically, and linguistically diverse students. Teacher educators should, therefore, require substantial coursework in multicultural education to build their cultural competency—the ability to understand and address the needs of diverse students (Brooks & Houston, 2015; Halpern & Ozfidan, 2024). Ribés et al. (2024) emphasized the significance of teacher education programs promoting culturally responsive teaching practices in support of student academic, cultural, and linguistic characteristics. Teacher education is important in helping future teachers become more knowledgeable and conscious of how best to teach students of various worldviews (Billingsley, 2016). Culturally competent teachers can engage English language learners and other diverse students in authentic learning and are sensitive to identifying cultural aspects of learning, but also draw on students' everyday knowledge and linguistic resources. Using an inquiry-based instructional approach, science teachers, for instance, can engage Latino English students in productive learning activities so that they not only learn but increase their interest in the field of science. Students may also increase their self-identification with scientists and develop an interest in pursuing careers in the field (Meyer & Crawford, 2015). Effective teachers avoid assuming that language minority students' limited speaking abilities will be a hurdle for learning.

Attitudes

Both elementary and secondary teachers need to acquire specific attitudes that will contribute to their ability to teach in contemporary multicultural classrooms: (1) a sense of democracy, in which differences are respected, as are students' rights; (2) an educational philosophy that includes recognition and respect for all types of diversity; (3) the ability to perceive events and situations from other cultural perspectives; (4) an understanding of the complexities of culture and ethnicity in U.S. society; and (5) the desire and willingness to work on a daily basis with people who are different.

Teachers, for the most part unknowingly, have long transmitted biased messages to students. Whether lining students up for lunch by sex or allowing ability grouping to result in racial segregation, teachers often send messages to students that one sex or race is entitled to preferential treatment. Most educators do not consciously or intentionally stereotype students or discriminate against them; they usually try to treat all students fairly and equitably. Nevertheless, teachers, like others in U.S. society, have learned attitudes and behaviors that are ageist, disability biased, racist, sexist, and ethnocentric. Some biases are so deeply internalized that individuals do not even realize they hold them. Only when teachers can (and are willing to) recognize the subtle and unintentional biases of their behavior can they make positive changes in the classroom (Doyle et al., 2023; Gollnick & Chinn, 2006). Addressing the impact of biases on students in the education system isn't simply about a few teachers reflecting on themselves. All teachers need to see it as a shared and collective responsibility.

Teacher educators are increasingly aware of the importance of preparing teachers to teach in a multiethnic, multilingual, economically stratified society. Teachers can better explore how inquiry into teachers' own cultural influences shaped their interactions with and reflections on students of diverse cultural backgrounds. If teachers begin to see cultures—their own and their students'—in complex, shifting terms, they might begin to apply their understandings to make their teaching culturally engaging. Practices can include building a self-reflective, culturally conscious community that maintains a balance between comfort in who we are and confrontation of ourselves as cultural beings in a multicultural society. Through building cultural memoirs, the teachers in this study gained a better understanding of their cultural backgrounds, and in essence gave their cultural backgrounds and lives a second thought.

Skills

Daily, teachers must understand many complicated areas: Learning styles, the dangers of ability grouping, the benefits of cooperative learning, culturally different perceptions of motivation and competition, learners who may not want to excel at the expense of their peers, and stereotypical beliefs about a culture's ability to learn or not to learn. Generally speaking, teachers need the skills to teach children and adolescents in the various cultural groups and the ability to convey that teachers genuinely want what is best for learners, both as students and as people.

POINTS TO PONDER 10.2

Determining Other Needed Characteristics and Behaviors

Work in groups of three or four to identify other characteristics or behaviors that educators need to address in multicultural settings. Consider this task from several perspectives: What type of teacher do you want to be? What might parents from a culturally different background want for their child? How might a child or adolescent want his or her teacher to be?

Teachers, working in a position to speak for change, have a responsibility to do whatever is possible to reduce racism, prejudice, and injustice among children and adolescents, and to instill attitudes of equality and democratic values, which may continue for life. Teachers, indeed, should be significant influences on the values, hopes, and dreams of their students. In a democratic classroom, teachers and students who are committed to human freedom should have the liberty to express their views, values, and beliefs with regard to democratic ideals such as human dignity, justice, and equality.

The following teacher behaviors are essential in multicultural classrooms.

1. Providing learning experiences that reflect individual cultures' learning styles and perceptions of competition, group welfare, sharing, motivation, and success. For example, some American Indian learners may prefer sharing and helping peers to competitive learning activities, and Puerto Ricans may not wish to excel or be set apart from the group.
2. Providing learning experiences that reflect gender differences. To confront gender bias in curricular materials, encouraging gender integration through peer tutoring and other small learning groups, as well as encouraging open dialogue and collaboration.
3. Encouraging and supporting the development of bilingual programs.
4. Immersing students in a variety of written and oral language activities that are meaningful, relevant, and functional in a pluralistic society.
5. Treating all students fairly and establishing a democratic classroom in which all students give and receive equal treatment.

6. Expecting the best from *all* students. Encouraging all of them to succeed academically, and not automatically assuming that minority students will perform less well.
7. Grouping heterogeneously whenever possible, to enhance self-esteem and promote ethnic interaction.
8. Demonstrating daily the necessity of democratic values and attitudes, a multicultural education philosophy, and an ability to view events and situations from diverse ethnic perspectives and points of view.
9. Recognizing as a myth the belief that culturally diverse parents and families do not care about their children's education.
10. Encouraging cross-cultural friendships and social interaction, cooperation, and socialization among boys and girls in the classroom, on the playground, and in the community.
11. Addressing the special problems that culturally diverse parents and families may face, such as language difficulties and misunderstanding the U.S. school system.
12. Acquiring factual knowledge about learner differences such as culture, race, ethnicity, socioeconomic status, and gender, and committing to having educational experiences reflect these differences.
13. Arranging your classroom so that it reflects cultural diversity in bulletin boards and on the walls and in the selection of artwork and artifacts on display.

Educator Self-Evaluation

Educators of all grade levels and all cultures probably agree that some type of evaluation is necessary periodically to determine whether the school is meeting goals and objectives. Whether of an informal or formal nature, the evaluation instrument should focus on teachers' ability to plan and implement appropriate teaching and learning activities for children and adolescents.

Teachers should also use a self-evaluation instrument designed to measure their ability to provide the environment and learning activities that are responsive to culturally diverse learners. Such a self-evaluation should include several questions designed to provide insight into the teacher's knowledge, attitudes, and skills.

1. Have there been efforts to understand and respect cultural diversity among learners not as a problem to solve but as a challenging opportunity and a rich gift?

2. Have there been efforts to provide a classroom in which learners feel free to speak and express diverse opinions? Does the teacher repress them or allow other students to stifle diverse opinion?

3. Have there been efforts to have the classroom reflect cultural diversity? Do the walls, bulletin boards, and artwork in the classroom demonstrate respect for cultural diversity, or do the contents of the classroom indicate an appreciation or valuing of only one culture?

4. Have there been efforts to provide organizational patterns that do not result in the segregation of some learners according to race, culture, ethnicity, or socioeconomics?

5. Have there been efforts to understand language differences and differing learning styles? Has the school developed organizational patterns and instructional methodologies that might be helpful to culturally diverse learners?

6. Have there been efforts to understand culturally different learners' perspectives toward motivation, excelling among one's peers, competition, group welfare, and sharing?

7. Have there been efforts to understand culturally diverse parents and extended families, and to ensure their participation in learners' academic and social life at school?

8. Have there been efforts to treat each learner with respect, to consider each learner as equal to other students, and to treat each learner as a valued and worthwhile member of the class? Are all learners accorded similar academic assistance? Do all learners receive help from the school's special service personnel?

9. Have there been efforts to allow (and indeed encourage) all students to work in cross-cultural groups, to carry on conversation and meaningful dialogue, and to feel they are valued members of the group?

10. Have there been efforts to instill multiculturalism as a genuine part of the teaching and learning process and overall school environment?

Organization and Instruction: Cultural Considerations

Students are often organized for instructional purposes on the basis of test scores, previous grades, teacher recommendations, and other supposedly objective information. The basic rationale for grouping students is to narrow the abilities range and thus provide teachers with a homogeneous group that is supposedly easier to teach. Two dangers inherent in any grouping process are (1) placing students in the wrong group and (2) having an organization pattern that segregates students by race.

Whether considering race, socioeconomic status, or gender, organizational patterns should not result in segregation, whereby inferior teachers teach some students or teach in inferior schools and other students receive preferential treatment. Organizational patterns should result in a student population that is as representative as possible of the entire school population and, if possible, the composition of the community at large.

Ability Grouping

Ability grouping may result in a form of segregation. Ability-grouping patterns often parallel students' nonacademic characteristics, such as race or ethnic background, socioeconomic class, or personal appearance. Learners of low socioeconomic status and marginalized groups often find themselves in lower ability groups. Such practices may be discriminatory, because the segregation of students is along ethnic and socioeconomic lines. These patterns of grouping appear to be related to ethnicity and socioeconomic standing, rather than purely academic abilities and achievement levels.

Cooperative Learning

People who help one another by joining forces to achieve a common goal generally feel more positive about each other and are willing to interact more positively when performing collective tasks. Rather than treat academic learning and social or intergroup relations as two distinct entities, cooperative learning has contributed positively to overall intergroup relations and particularly to improving relations with diverse students. Cooperative-learning procedures can reinforce the efforts of culturally diverse children to continue their schoolwork successfully. Children who work cooperatively in groups, rather than in isolation, are usually motivated to help each other carry out the assigned or chosen project.

Research on cooperative learning and intergroup relationships has concluded that students in cooperative-learning situations had a greater appreciation for cooperative-learning classmates. Specifically, cooperative learning increases contact between students, provides a feeling of group membership, engages learners in pleasant activities, and requires that team members work toward a common goal.

Students' working cooperatively can contribute positively to specific multiethnic populations. Both black and white students working in cooperative-learning situations liked school better than those of the same ethnic groups working in competitive classrooms. Working cooperatively seems to have particularly strong effects on Hispanic and African American students, regardless of achievement levels. A study of Jigsaw II-related classes that included recent European and West Indian immigrants and white Canadians documented substantially more cross-ethnic friendships than in the control groups.

Cooperation, collaborating, and community are prominent themes, techniques, and goals in educating African American, Arab American, and Hispanic American as well as American Indian students. Two major reasons help to explain these pedagogical trends. First, underlying values of human connectedness and collaborative problem solving are high priorities in the cultures of most groups of color in the United States. Second, cooperation plays a central role in these groups' learning styles, especially the communicative, procedural, motivational, and relational dimensions.

Language Differences

Language diversity is so great in some parts of the United States that sometimes classroom communication is virtually impossible. In addition, many schools are unable to provide appropriate learning experiences for children whose native language is not English. As a result, language-minority children do not learn the essential lessons of school, and do not participate fully in the economic, social, and political life of the United States. As they decide on organizing students for instruction, culturally sensitive educators recognize the dilemma that learners with limited English skills often face.

Maintaining that language differences pose a major stumbling block for American Indian students, suggestions for American Indians include the following:

1. Implement cooperative-learning techniques. American Indians, reared to value cooperation and sharing, are not accustomed culturally to working alone or to competing for grades and teacher approval.
2. Avoid large-group, formal lessons in the lecture-recitation mode. American Indian students tend to withdraw during formal patterns. These learners perceive more opportunity in student-to-student dialogues and group problem-solving efforts.
3. Liberally give encouragement and positive reinforcement. Include language-lifting techniques and modeling of correct language patterns. Avoid correcting pupils' oral language errors except during formal language lessons.

Other suggestions for educators working with language-minority learners include the following:

1. The use of formal language, teacher leadership and control of verbal exchanges, question-and-answer formats, and references to increasingly abstract ideas often characterize a classroom environment with which many minority children are unfamiliar. Whenever possible, communication is made easier if these ideas overlap with those the learners already know.
2. Language-minority learners should experience familiar communication styles to establish a basis for communication. This basis may include speaking in the child's primary language, using culturally appropriate styles of address, and relying on management patterns that are familiar to and comfortable for children.
3. The meanings of words, gestures, and actions may be quite different from culture to culture.

Supporting Bilingual and Multilingual Learners

Historically, children who speak a language other than English at home are often considered deficient in language learning upon entering school. According to Ruiz (1984), speakers of their heritage language were often labelled "Language-as-a-Handicap." They were discouraged from speaking their home language at school, which often resulted in the loss of it. The loss of one's heritage language can have alarming consequences such as limited communication with their parents and family members and identity crises.

In contrast, many of today's native speakers place a strong emphasis on preserving and passing down their heritage language and culture to their children and future generations (Lee & Kang, 2023; Park & Sarkar, 2007). Generally, Korean-speaking parents believe that proficiency in the Korean language will help their children keep their cultural identity as Koreans, ensure future economic opportunities, and provide more chances to communicate with their families (Lee & Gupta, 2020).

For example, a Korean native speaking mother, Mrs. Hong-Taylor, who has an interracial son, Daniel, enrolled in the first grade, is concerned about teaching her heritage language to her son while he is learning English. She is extremely frustrated and anxious which is reasonable. She devoted the first six years of Daniel's life to teaching and instilling the importance of learning their heritage language and culture. Now, Daniel feels pressure from his teachers at school to focus on learning English. As Daniel wants to fit in with his school friends, speak like them and avoid being teased, his parents' plan was interrupted for Daniel when the expectations of his teacher conflicted with those of his mother.

As Daniel experienced at his public school, the absence of his teacher's support and society's recognition of the rationale for maintaining his home language was a major reason he is losing interest in maintaining his heritage language and culture. Many parents such as Mrs. Hong-Taylor want to raise their children as multilingual speakers, learning both their heritage language and English. They attempt to teach the heritage language privately at home or in a community language school and hope that the education their children receive at school is compatible with home cultures and languages and promotes educational success.

Teachers of bilingual or multilingual learners can use a translanguaging approach that respects the linguistic repertoire of each student and fosters a more natural language learning environment. Ofelia García views language as integrated linguistic knowledge that multilinguals use interchangeably and blend seamlessly to communicate (García, 2017). Instead of treating each language one knows as separate, the translanguaging approach sees language ability as a dynamic system using multiple languages without strict boundaries. García explains the practical and pedagogical benefits of using the translanguage approach both in the classroom and the home as follows:

1. Translanguaging supports multilanguage speakers to use code-switching to practice two or more languages in a single conversation.
2. Both educators and parents show a positive attitude toward learning multiple languages to communicate simultaneously.
3. By using all of the linguistic resources and cultural backgrounds, students can use a variety of teaching materials and more actively participate in the culturally relevant lessons.
4. Multilingual speakers improve language proficiency when they are open to a variety of expressions and situations.

The School Environment

The school environment includes all experiences with which learners come into contact: content, instructional methods, the actual teaching and learning process and environment, the professional staff and other staff members, as well as the actions and attitudes of other students. This definition of environment is synonymous with the curriculum itself.

Working toward a Multicultural School Environment

It is important that the multicultural environment demonstrates genuine respect and concern for all learners, regardless of their racial, cultural, or ethnic backgrounds. With a supportive school environment, culturally different children, along with other learners, can learn to take an active role in a democratic society, guided by relevant understanding, and develop skills in communication and computation, social attitudes and interests, and human appreciation. The school environment should support school learning and socialization for all students. A supportive school environment is one in which the morale of both teachers and students is high. Teachers believe in their mission to help guide and stimulate the learning activities of their students and are pleased with their students' responsive behavior.

Although it is impossible to describe in detail all the factors that make a school environment responsive to cultural diversity, briefly discussing several areas illustrates the environment in its broadest sense: The unconditional acceptance of diversity, the promotion of positive cultural identities, and a faculty and staff composition that represents the cultural diversity of the school population. The school environment is by no means limited to these three aspects. These three, however, have a powerful influence on how learners perceive others' opinions of cultural diversity.

The following are recommendations for creating a teaching and learning environment that reflects the cultural diversity of the school:

1. As a part of the daily learning environment, provide and consistently update a variety of multiethnic, multicultural, and self-awareness materials.
2. Plan learning experiences that are flexible, unbiased, and inclusive of contributions from diverse cultures.
3. Find good people to serve as role models and material resources that focus on problems in a pluralistic society.
4. Adopt instructional strategies relevant to the physical, emotional, social, and intellectual development of children of multiethnic heritage.
5. Use instructional material that shows individuals from diverse cultural groups working in different occupational and social roles. Make sure all materials are free of bias, omissions, and stereotypes.
6. Adopt flexible scheduling that provides ample time and space for children to share their uniqueness through role-play, art, conversation, and games.
7. Continuously use ideas and materials that represent cultures throughout the year, not just during special holidays such as Black History Week, Christmas, Thanksgiving, Hanukkah, and Chinese New Year.

An educational setting should allow children to feel accepted, encouraged, and respected. Here are more ways of creating appropriate school environments in our diverse society:

1. The total school environment should undergo reform, not just the courses and programs. The school's informal hidden curriculum is as important as, or perhaps more important than, the formal course of study.
2. Cultural content should be part of all subject areas from preschool through grade 12 and beyond.
3. Learning centers, libraries, and resource centers should include resources for history, literature, music, folklore, views of life, and the arts of the various groups of people.
4. Cultural diversity should be reflected in assembly programs; classroom, hallway, and entrance decorations; cafeteria menus; counseling interactions; and, as we previously discussed, extracurricular activities.
5. School-sponsored dances and other such activities should reflect a respect for a diverse society.
6. Service learning should accompany multicultural education courses, so pre-service and in-service teachers can better relate to the content examined in multicultural education courses.

Table 10.2 provides additional ways of addressing diversity in educational settings.

Table 10.2 Addressing Diversity in its Many Forms

1.	Check district and school policies, procedures, practices, curriculum guides, lesson plans, and instructional materials to be sure they are free of bias toward race, gender, religion, culture, and disabilities.
2.	Make newcomers feel welcome through a formal program.
3.	Be sure that assignments are not offensive or frustrating to students of cultural minorities. For example, asking students to discuss or write about their Christmas experiences is inappropriate for non-Christian students. Let students discuss their similar holidays.
4.	Form a schoolwide planning committee to address the implementation of multicultural education.
5.	Contact your district curriculum coordinators for ideas and assistance.
6.	Let faculty knowledgeable about multicultural topics provide in-service training for others or guest-teach their classes.
7.	Take a cultural census of the class or school to find out what cultures are represented; let students be the ethnographers.

(Continued)

Table 10.2 (Continued)

8.	Form a multicultural club.
9.	Select a theme to tie various multicultural activities together; hold school programs with art, music, and dramatic presentations; hold a multicultural fair or festival featuring music, art, dance, dress, and so on; adopt a multicultural theme for existing activities.
10.	Hold a school cross-cultural food festival.
11.	Have multicultural celebrations and teach-ins with schoolwide activities in all classes.
12.	Decorate classrooms, hallways, and the library media center with murals, bulletin boards, posters, artifacts, and other materials representative of the students in the class or school or other cultures the class is studying. Posters and other information are available from foreign government travel bureaus and education agencies, private travel agencies, consulates, the United Nations, and ethnic and cultural organizations.
13.	Designate a permanent bulletin board for multicultural news and displays.
14.	Help students develop the skills necessary to locate and organize information about cultures from the library media center, the mass media, people, and personal observations.
15.	Have students write to foreign consulates, tourist bureaus, minority organizations, and others for information and decorative materials.
16.	Supplement textbooks with authentic materials on different cultures from newspapers, magazines, and other media of the culture. Such materials are available from the Department of Education Foreign Language Documentation Center.
17.	Take advantage of community resources. Have representatives of various cultures talk to classes; actors portray characters or events; and musicians and dance groups, such as salsa bands or bagpipe units, perform.
18.	Work with the library media center on special bibliographies, collections, displays, and audiovisuals. School librarians can introduce useful AI-based tools to address diversity such as: • Hand Talk Plugin uses AI to provide automatic translations from English to American Sign Language (ASL), translating all the written content and alternative texts on websites. • Image recognition—AI that describes images with the help of an automatic alternative text feature. • Speech recognition—for users with motor, cognitive, and learning impairments who would prefer to speak rather than type. • Text recognition—extracts data from scanned images, documents and PDFs to convert the data into readable text for users with visual and learning impairments.
19.	Hold a mock legislature to debate current or historical issues affecting minorities and cultural groups.
20.	Hold oratorical, debate, essay, poster, art, brain brawl, or other competitions with a multicultural focus.

Promoting Positive Cultural Identities

It is imperative that educators understand the school environment's influence (perhaps an unconscious or unrecognized influence) on a child's cultural identity. Without doubt, the school environment affects both the manner in which children perceive themselves and their cultural images.

Self-concept, or self-image, is a complex set of beliefs that an individual holds about him- or herself. A person may have more than one self-image and actually hold positive feelings in some areas and negative images in others. For example, a person might have a positive self-image in intellectual pursuits while harboring negative feelings toward his or her athletic abilities. The actions of others or the way in which learners think others perceive and treat them significantly influences their self-concepts.

The environment should allow culturally diverse people to feel a sense of being able to cope or to feel that they can control their lives at least to some extent. Youngsters who feel torn between two cultures may have a low self-image because they assume they cannot be successful in either society.

Self-concepts and cultural identities of learners relate not only to their race, culture, and social class, but also to their feelings of power in the school environment. The task facing educators is to help students build positive perceptions about their reference groups, and to develop confidence in actively participating in social discussion and change. The educators' goal should be to provide a school environment that either raises or contributes positively to the racial and cultural pride of all people.

Promoting Diversity Among Faculty and Staff

Diverse people must be an integral part of the school's instructional, administrative, and supportive staff. School personnel—teachers, principals, cooks, custodians, secretaries, students, and counselors—make contributions as important to multicultural environments as do the courses of study and instructional materials. Students learn important lessons about culture and cultural diversity by observing interactions among different racial and cultural groups in their school; hearing verbal exchanges between the professional and support staffs; and observing the extent to which the staff are culturally representative of the student population.

Cultural Perspectives

Socioeconomic and Class Differences

The student's socioeconomic level and social class deserve consideration as elementary and secondary educators plan teaching and learning experiences. If a group of individuals has particular characteristics that are valued by a society, the group so identified will enjoy high status. The reverse is also true. Thus, when speaking of upper and lower classes, we are referring to groups of individuals who either have or do not have the qualities that are prized by a larger society.

In the United States, upper classes are those groups that have wealth, advanced education, professional occupations, and relative freedom from concern about their material needs. Conversely, lower classes are those groups that live in or on the edge of poverty, have poor education, are irregularly employed or employed in jobs requiring little or no training, often require assistance from government welfare agencies, and are constantly concerned with meeting the basic needs of life.

At least two perspectives stand out as being important for educators to consider: (1) some social classes may be able to provide their children with additional experiences that may be conducive to education and academic achievement; and (2) determination, hard work, and middle-class values are believed to pay rich dividends. The problem with the former is that many students do not bring to school experiential backgrounds that contribute to their education. The latter often causes poor people to be perceived as and feel like failures who lack the ambition or determination to pursue long-term goals.

Realistically, culturally diverse students often come from poorer financial backgrounds and homes in which language differences impede communication and upward social mobility. Such obstacles, however, do not mean that these social classes value education and school achievement any less. It is educators' responsibility to provide teaching and learning experiences that build on the strengths and backgrounds of all children and adolescents.

It is important to emphasize the economic advances and achievements of culturally diverse learners and their families during the past decade or two. Educators should objectively consider each learner to determine individual strengths and weaknesses. To equate poverty with a particular culture, race, or ethnic group is a serious mistake and can jeopardize a learner's educational future.

What are the implications for educators working with children and adolescents from lower socioeconomic and social classes?

1. Teachers, counselors, and administrators should recognize the dangers of associating negative and harmful expectations with culturally diverse groups and lower classes. They often recognize biases as a problem in others but fail to acknowledge their own. To overcome this, teachers need to self-reflect to acknowledge that they, too, can possess misconceptions and biases when it comes to the socioeconomic level of students (Devine et al., 2012). In fact, educators should periodically review their beliefs about children and adolescents as well as their behavioral and academic expectations (Gollnick & Chinn, 2006).
2. Educators should examine curricular and instructional efforts to determine whether they reflect only middle-class European American perspectives. Culturally diverse learners and students from low

socioeconomic backgrounds need to see a reflection of their values and lifestyles in the educational content and in the instructional methods (Gollnick & Chinn, 2006). While Ladson-Billings (2006) recommended using culturally relevant teaching to address the educational inequalities and suggested replacing the heavily concentrated perspectives and content of middle-class white America with a pedagogy for African American populations. Her intention was not to simply switch out. She sought to normalize African American students' experiences in education while crafting teaching approaches and contents that serve the needs of all students effectively.

3. Educators should be on a constant lookout for grouping patterns that segregate students along cultural, racial, or ethnic lines. Teachers often place students from lower socioeconomic classes or who are culturally diverse in lower ability groups. Such practices may be discriminatory, because students are segregated along ethnic and social class lines.

The Role of Parents, Families, and Caregivers

Parent involvement and cooperative relationships between parents and schools are essential. First, parental interest and participation in schools and classrooms has a positive influence on academic achievement. Second, parents involved in academic activities with their children gain knowledge that helps them to assess their children's education. They can help their children with areas of education in which they need assistance. Third, the results of parental involvement in tutoring students who are limited in English are consistent with those for native English-speaking students and their families. To be effective as home tutors, all parents need school support and direct teacher involvement.

Educators must employ special strategies to accommodate the unique cultural characteristics of Asian immigrant parents. Their agenda should include: (1) educators asking themselves some difficult questions about their prejudices and stereotypical beliefs about Asian Americans; (2) understanding Asian beliefs about education; and (3) providing opportunities for Asian American parents to participate in school activities, to communicate through newsletters, and to serve on advisory committees.

Culturally diverse children and adolescents often perceive the roles of grandparents, aunts, and uncles as similar to those of the mother and the father. For this reason, educators should welcome extended families who are interested in the learner's educational progress. Culturally diverse parents and families may not understand the U.S. school system and its emphasis on competition and individual welfare and achievement over group accomplishments. Teachers may offer suggestions and directions to parents and families who are able to assist their children and adolescents. Teachers need a better understanding of culturally diverse families and their values, customs, traditions, and expectations. All too often, teachers view the benefits of parent involvement too narrowly. Not only do children benefit, but parents and teachers do as well.

Learner Evaluation

The evaluation of learners should include a consideration of individual and cultural differences, variations in learning and testing styles, and differences in motivation. Rather than evaluate only what paper and pencil can measure, evaluation efforts should also focus on student behaviors, attitudes, and everyday actions. For example, a student might be able to list examples of racist behavior and offer several valid reasons on paper why racism should be reduced. The evaluation process, however, should also include a consideration of actions. Do students make racist remarks? Do students demonstrate racial harmony? Do students engage in segregationist activities? Generally speaking, have students developed respect and acceptance for, as well as knowledge of, our increasingly culturally diverse world?

Sleeter and Grant (2007) offer several recommendations for educators planning and implementing programs that evaluate learners:

1. Evaluation procedures should not include standardized achievement tests that are monocultural in nature and that sort students into different groups that result in different and unequal opportunities.
2. Evaluation procedures should not penalize students by requiring skills that are extraneous to what is being evaluated. For example, a science teacher assessing science concepts should not require students to read and write about their skill level.
3. Evaluation procedures designed to assess students' English proficiency levels should take into account the different contexts in which school communication takes place and the different factors involved.
4. Evaluation procedures should be free of sexist or racist stereotypes.

Decisions concerning evaluation include both what should be evaluated and a determination of the evaluation methods. As with all curricular efforts, educators should closely match the evaluation with goals and objectives, measure what was taught, and measure attitudes and behaviors as well as cognitive knowledge.

Teacher Self-Evaluation

The faculty at Public School (PS) High School 93 were accustomed to being evaluated by the principal, a central office evaluational specialist, and occasionally peer teachers. The teachers were beginning to realize, however, that something was missing. Evaluation forms indicated the degree of success, yet a teacher basically knew, better than the instrument could suggest, whether he or she had met the school's expectations and was working to maximum potential. There was yet another issue: While the existing instruments evaluated overall performance, they did little to determine the educator's efforts to address the needs of diverse learners. Those forms of self-assessment often overlooked the nuanced efforts teachers make to address a wide range of cultural, linguistic, and learning differences. A teacher's ability to adapt these variances is crucial.

In keeping with the research on evaluation, the counselor suggested a self-evaluation form for the teachers. Interested faculty members decided to work as a committee to develop a self-evaluation scale—a measure that each teacher might share with peers or administrators. (The decision to share the outcome was one the teacher could make at a later date.)

While the evaluation committee was to study the various possibilities and make final recommendations, broad categories for evaluation might include the following (with the specifics to be added later):

◆ knowledge, attitudes, and skills;
◆ classroom environment;
◆ instructional purposes;
◆ curricular materials;
◆ management system;
◆ evaluation process.
  1. While a teacher's skills can be evaluated by direct observation, how can his or her attitudes toward individuals, as well as the increasingly diverse school population, be evaluated?
  2. What other criteria should be included on the self-evaluation scale? For example, should the scale include a detailed list of teacher competencies or effective teacher behaviors?
  3. With whom should the self-evaluation be shared? Anyone? In other words, should the self-evaluation scale be for *evaluation* or *improvement*?

Summing Up

Educators who plan teaching, learning, and classroom environments in multicultural settings should remember to:

1. Recognize and respect learner diversity: culture, race, ethnicity, sexual orientation, individuality, gender, socioeconomic status, and religion.
2. Develop the knowledge, attitudes, and skills to teach and relate to culturally diverse children and adolescents.
3. Recognize that some organizational practices contribute to exclusivity and segregation; therefore, educators should provide instructional methods to which culturally diverse children and adolescents can most effectively relate.
4. Plan a school curriculum and environment that reflect respect for all cultural, ethnic, social class, and religious differences among people and that promote learners' cultural identities.
5. Recognize and respond appropriately to cultural perspectives that influence the academic achievement and overall school progress of culturally diverse learners—for example, socioeconomic status and social class, parents and families, and learner evaluation.
6. Implement a teaching and learning environment that affects positively how children and adolescents feel about school, about being culturally different in a predominantly European American school, and about feeling genuinely accepted and cared about.
7. Provide culturally diverse learners with an administration, faculty, and staff that reflect the cultural diversity of the overall school population.
8. Incorporate culturally relevant and culturally sustaining teaching into their teaching practices to support a diverse student population, with the ultimate goal of promoting and nurturing linguistic, literary, and cultural diversity in schools.
9. Support linguistically diverse students and families using the translanguaging approach.
10. Comprehend the principles and debate surrounding CRT and the application of culturally relevant pedagogy in teaching methods, particularly to support a diverse student population.

Suggested Learning Activities

1. Design a plan for involving culturally diverse parents and immediate families in the teaching and learning process. Explain specifically how you would address the following points: Language barriers between culturally diverse parents and you; explaining school expectations to parents and families who might not understand how U.S. schools function; and ways you might involve parents and families.

2. Create a survey for bilingual or multilingual families to learn about their home teaching activities and experiences with the translanguaging approach as well as real-life examples of translanguaging. Also, interview bilingual or multilingual families and collect recorded conversations or writing samples of children interacting with siblings or parents to understand how they use code-switching.

3. Observe a teaching demonstration to determine a teacher's unintended bias. Did the teacher call on more girls than boys or more European Americans than Hispanic Americans, expect Asian Americans to answer more difficult questions, or tend to ignore students from lower socioeconomic groups? How might you help this teacher recognize bias? What items would you include on a teacher self-evaluation scale designed to help teachers recognize unintended bias?

Implementing Research

Diversity and Inclusion in STEM Education

The representation of women and other underrepresented students in STEM fields does not accurately reflect the racial diversity of our societies. Even if children have an interest in STEM subjects, some may hesitate to pursue studies or careers in these areas if they perceive that they wouldn't fit in the STEM field. Vossen et al. (2023) found that when educators focus on inclusivity and diversity when teaching STEM subjects, their lessons have a notable effect on marginalized children's perceptions of scientists and facilitate contemplation of a future in the STEM field. Implementation of lessons can positively alter children's perceptions of themselves as successful leaders in STEM. They can see themselves as a member of a diverse and globally representative group of scientists.

Implementing the Research

1. Educators in the STEM field should challenge prevalent stereotypes of successful innovators and what a scientist or engineer looks like. Even at a young age, students who internalize these perceptions may be negatively affected in their interest in not pursuing an education or career in STEM.
2. Incorporating diverse images of STEM role models that discuss their personal lives alongside their professions could enhance a sense of belonging among all students, potentially increasing their engagement in the STEM fields.
3. Educators should integrate creative, active learning opportunities to spark the curiosity of marginalized children who previously didn't see themselves as interested in STEM.
4. To boost diverse students' interest in STEM lessons, educators can grant them autonomy within the parameters in a science project, which helps to foster their engagement, motivation, and self-efficacy.

Source: Vossen, T. E., Land-Zandstra, A. M., Russo, P., Schut, A., Van Vulpen, I. B., Watts, A. L., Booij, C., & Tupan-Wenno, M. (2023) Effects of a STEM-oriented lesson series aimed at inclusive and diverse education on primary school children's perceptions of and sense of belonging in space science. *International Journal of Science Education*, 45(9), 689–708. https://doi.org/10.1080/09500693.2023.2172693

Suggestions for Collaborative Efforts

Form groups of three or four that, if possible, represent U.S. cultural and gender diversity. Working collaboratively, focus your group's attention toward the following efforts:

1. Have each member of your group survey elementary and secondary school teachers to determine their efforts to include multicultural perspectives in their teaching and learning activities. Look specifically at items such as curriculum content, teacher expectations for achievement and behavior, grouping strategies, testing and evaluation, and involvement of parents and extended family members. How does your group believe that teachers could improve their efforts?

2. Devise a checklist to evaluate the degree to which the overall
   school environment reflects multicultural perspectives. Although
   your group should include perspectives it feels are important, the
   basic underlying question should be this: Does the overall school
   environment portray multicultural perspectives? Other questions
   might be these: Is there evidence that cultural, ethnic, social class,
   and religious diversity is accepted? Are there deliberate attempts to
   promote positive cultural identities? Is cultural diversity represented
   among faculty and staff, and at all levels of administration?
3. List 10–12 criteria for evaluating a teacher's (or any school
   professional's) performance in working with diverse students.
   Perhaps you will want to separate your list into three categories:
   Knowledge, attitudes, and skills. Or you might just want to write
   down a list of characteristics or behaviors. Consider the perspectives
   of the educator, the parent, and the learner as you make
   your list.

Expanding Your Horizons

Additional Books and Journals

Brummelman, E. & Sedikides, C. (2023). Unequal selves in the classroom: Nature, origins, and consequences of socioeconomic disparities in children's self-views. *Developmental Psychology, 59*(11), 1962–1987. https://doi-org.proxy.lib.odu.edu/10.1037/dev0001599
This study explores how teacher–student interactions in the classroom shape the self-views of children from low socioeconomic status (SES) backgrounds, revealing that negative intellectual stereotypes expressed through daily interactions can undermine the self-views of these children, exacerbating achievement inequality and highlighting the importance of timely interventions to address socioeconomic disparities in self-views and reduce achievement gaps.

Keskin, O., Gabel, S., Kollar, I., & Gegenfurtner, A. (2023). Relations between pre-service teacher gaze, teacher attitude, and student ethnicity. *Frontiers in Education, 8.* https://doi.org/10.3389/feduc.2023.1272671
This study aimed to investigate if more negative teacher attitudes and lower teacher recognition toward ethnic marginalized students are reflected in teacher gaze. It underscored the importance of addressing biases in teacher education and professional development to effectively support student diversity.

Reed, D. K. & Mercer, S. H. (2023). Potential scoring and predictive bias in interim and summative writing assessments. *School Psychology*, *38*(4), 215–224. https://doi-org.proxy.lib.odu.edu/10.1037/spq0000527
This article discusses how differences in scores between teachers and among student groups suggest potential biases that could impact evaluation accuracy and fairness. The authors emphasize the importance of considering masking student identities during assessments to reduce scoring bias and suggest that the written composition portions of high-stakes writing exams may be less biased against historically marginalized groups.

Websites

Edutopia – www.edutopia.org/blogs/tag/education-equity
Discusses how we can ensure that all students have equal access to opportunities, support, and the tools they need to succeed.

National Association for Bilingual Education – nabe.org
This site looks at teaching English, fostering academic achievement, acculturating immigrants to a new society, preserving marginalized group's linguistic and cultural heritage, enabling English speakers to learn a second language, and developing national language resources.

National Equity Project – www.nationalequityproject.org/
This organization seeks to transform the experiences, outcomes, and life options for children and families who have been historically underserved by institutions and systems. They do this through trainings, programs, and advocacy.

Teach Hub – https://www.teachhub.com/teaching-strategies/2020/09/culturally-responsive-teaching/
This site looks at roadblocks to implanting multicultural education, strategies to support multicultural instruction, favorite lessons, and resources.

11

Parents, Families, and Caregivers of Culturally Diverse Backgrounds

Understanding the material and activities in this chapter will help the reader to:

- Understand that the traditional view of parents and families has changed to a more contemporary and broad perspective of parents and families that includes foster parents, guardians, one-parent families, two-parent lesbian or gay families, and caregivers.
- State several reasons for including parents, families, and caregivers of culturally diverse backgrounds in parent-involvement programs in elementary and secondary schools.
- Understand that both immediate and extended families should be included in schools, especially because African American, Arab American, Asian American, European American, and Hispanic American as well as American Indian cultures place considerable value on the extended family concept.
- State at least five reasons why parents, families, and caregivers of culturally different backgrounds resist teachers' efforts.
- Understand that considerable diversity (including intracultural, generational, and socioeconomic differences) can result in difficulty, as teachers plan for typical or prototype families.
- List the essential elements of effective and culturally sustaining parent-involvement programs.
- Explain procedures and factors that parents and teachers should consider during conferences.
- Explain the essential aspects and considerations of forming a parent advisory committee designed to address the needs and concerns of families from culturally different backgrounds.

DOI: 10.4324/9781003429531-14

- ◆ Understand the importance of parent and family education, and explain how such programs can assist families from culturally diverse backgrounds.
- ◆ Understand the importance of families, schools, and communities working together in support of the cultivation of the ethnic identity and preservation of the heritage language and culture of children of immigrant families.

Opening Scenario

First-Hand Contact

Mr. Johnson, the principal at Central Middle School, encourages teachers in his school to have first-hand contact with people of various cultures. He praises teachers who take courses that focus on cultural diversity, attend seminars and conferences, and read professional books and journals. These are all excellent sources, he thinks, but he still wants teachers to have first-hand contact with those of other cultures, which is imperative if genuine knowledge and respect are to develop.

Mr. Johnson encourages first-hand contact in several ways. First, he expects and encourages teachers to be integral members of the community and to participate in as many social and cultural activities as possible. Second, he encourages parents and families from culturally different backgrounds to visit the school any time, not just for parent conferences. During these impromptu visits, Mr. Johnson urges teachers to meet with parents and families and to discuss items of interest. Third, he encourages home visits, which are scheduled at times convenient for the parents. These visits provide a means for teachers to get to know family members on a more personal basis. Although the principal requires that the teachers record their observations and perceptions, the purpose of the visits is neither to judge nor to condemn. He believes that knowledge of cultural diversity contributes to improving attitudes toward people with differences, regardless of degree or type.

Overview

For years, educators have recognized the importance of involving parents in their children's education. Whether through involving, conferring, or educating, efforts to include parents in the educational process have paid rich dividends. Until relatively recently, however, educators have mainly worked with middle- and upper-class European Americans, and have ignored other races, cultures, and ethnic groups, probably because educators lacked knowledge of the unique backgrounds and special needs of culturally diverse parents and families. As schools increasingly reflect the cultural diversity that characterizes the nation, educators are challenged to involve, educate, and confer with all parents and families. This chapter focuses attention on parent involvement and conferences, and suggests that educators should implement parent-education programs designed to acquaint families of culturally different backgrounds with U.S. school systems.

Involving and Educating Parents, Families, and Caregivers

That parent involvement has a positive effect on student achievement and overall school progress is undeniable. Benefits beyond academic achievement that derive from the involvement of parents and/or family in educational activities include an increase in children's self-worth, socioemotional well-being, positive views toward teachers and school work, and their increased participation in classroom activities. An even more compelling reason for schools to seek the involvement and participation of parents is to have them understand the U.S. school system, its expectations, and its predominantly middle-class white educators. Families from diverse cultures may feel uncomfortable conversing with educators and participating in school-sponsored events. The educator's challenge is to involve parents of all diverse cultural, ethnic, racial, and social class groups, rather than only middle- and upper-class European American parents.

Defining the Issue

The issue for educators, however, is more complex than simply convincing parents to visit the school. It includes making conscious efforts in several areas: Explaining the school's function, making parents feel welcome and valued, educating parents about their children and adolescents, and involving parents in their children's and adolescents' education whenever possible. Only with the involvement and participation of all parents can schools genuinely reflect multiculturalism, and address the needs and concerns of learners and parents from culturally different backgrounds.

Behavioral consultation is defined as a systematic form of service delivery in which two or more persons work together to identify, analyze, remediate, and evaluate an individual's needs. It is characterized by a problem-solving process, adherence to behavioral assessment techniques, reliance on behavioral intervention strategies, and evaluation of outcomes.

As stated by Garbacz et al. (2016), the involvement of families in educational activities has many benefits. However, there are many challenges as well to building healthy family–educator connections. In an effort to meet these challenges, a model for involving parents of children with learning and behavior problems in schools should be utilized. In a review of barriers to developing family–school interaction and student achievement, a variety of obstacles—emotional, language, cultural, and physical—were identified as critical to overcome. These links contribute to establishing educational systems that are difficult for some families to reach. Furthermore, the values and language traditions represented in many educational practices may not reflect the values and common languages of a diverse school community.

It is well established that students from ethnic minority backgrounds are overrepresented in school discipline systems; therefore, race is not neutral, rather, it is disproportional. Garbacz et al. (2016) explain schoolwide PBIS (Positive Behavioral Intervention and Support) that emphasizes effectiveness, efficiency, and relevance aimed at improving outcomes for all students. In particular, schoolwide PBIS emphasizes using local school information to identify, establish, and adapt goals, resources, and interventions to meet the needs of an individual school community.

Responsiveness-to-intervention and schoolwide positive behavior support the integration of multi-tiered system approaches. In order to provide an operating framework that integrates practices with sensitivity and responsiveness to the unique needs of each school community, schools can look to PBIS. Strategies to promote the implementation, organization, and operation of systemwide consultation programs are emerging and, as stated in Garbacz et al. (2016), evidence suggests that reductions in overall office discipline referrals apply to all students from different racial or ethnic backgrounds; therefore, PBIS can be implemented across schools with varying demographic characteristics.

Similarly, Ohmstede and Yetter (2015) explain Conjoint Behavioral Consultation (CBC), an extension of behavioral consultation that combines the resources of the home and school to effect positive change in children. It is an indirect model of service delivery in which parents, teachers, and a consultant work together to address the academic, social, and behavioral needs of a child. Problems are identified, defined, analyzed, and treated through mutual and collaborative interactions between parents and teachers, with the guidance and assistance of a school psychologist. The model promotes a partnership that allows opportunities for families and schools to work together for the common interest of children and to build on and promote the capabilities of family members and school personnel.

CBC emphasizes the need to consider factors that may be counterproductive to interactions with people from different backgrounds. For example, people with backgrounds other than European American may hold different opinions about social relationships, achievement, activities, and time needed. Influenced by their culture, Asian American parents often place distinct boundaries between school and home, believing that parents are responsible for correcting children's behavioral issues. They may not see the need for participating in CBC. When families don't see a need or a way to participate, educators can clarify ways in which they can help, give them specific options on how to help, and allow them to share their ideas and decide in which ways they want to be involved.

In addition to cultural differences, families may have financial and social obligations that prevent them from participating in school-based services. Educators should be sensitive to the needs of families and should allow flexibility in their participation. Educators can reach out to the families; get to know their situations and possibly provide helpful resources; maintain two-way communication through phone calls, texts, virtual meetings, or home visits; and discover a family's special interest or cultural knowledge and encourage them to share it in class activities.

The Advantages of Parent Involvement and Education

Regardless of racial background and socioeconomic status, the most powerful factor for students' school achievement is the extent to which the family or caregiver provides a safe and happy home environment to support their optimal growth and learning. Family support enhances learning, and schools should ensure that parents have the information needed to properly guide and interact with their children in a rich family learning environment. The home–school collaboration is based on the premise that both school and parents share the duties of guiding, teaching, socializing, and preparing children and adolescents to become future leaders. Family and school partnership is positively correlated with children's intrinsic motivation, identity development, language and literacy, and other academic abilities (Banks et al., 2023). Further, consistent family participation throughout a child's school experiences can have a profound and long-lasting positive effect on reducing the racial achievement gap (Rowe et al., 2016). Jeynes (2016) explored the meta-analysis of 42 studies and looked at the relationship between parental involvement and academic achievement, and school behavior of African American children, aged pre-kindergarten through college freshman, and found that parental involvement has strongly affected academic success. Educators can provide assistance to families to support their children in the following ways:

1. Create and give interactive assignments to increase parent–child communication about schoolwork, such as writing out a family's favorite recipe while cooking.
2. Suggest they read from and discuss a book together daily. Use home–school assignment books to facilitate communication about ways to encourage learning for children and youth.
3. Teach parents how to use Internet resources and programs to help children learn.
4. Invite families to "family fun events" that include games, music, and meals. Provide parents with an overview of what students will be learning in the next month, what parents can expect, and how they can assist and make a difference.

Educators need to know that positive behavioral intervention designed to support children on an individual basis will be better accomplished when issues are consistently dealt with at home as well as school. Garbacz et al. (2016) explain that there is positive data that demonstrates the importance of family engagement in positive behavior support, treatment integrity in conjoint behavioral consultation, and potential pathways of influence. However, families have not yet been fully engaged within the universal systems of schoolwide PBIS. It is important that we extend key features of PBIS to the family system, in order to acknowledge the family as an important part of the school community and to further enhance outcomes for children and families. Full family engagement within schoolwide PBIS depends and relies on a consideration of the school community's diversity, as well as individual family and student differences. Schoolwide PBIS includes a foundation for engaging in culturally responsive strategies with families; however, the PBIS framework may not be equally accessible and applicable to all families. Therefore, culturally responsive recommendations from PBIS and related fields, for PBIS leadership teams to consider, have been set in place. This will be an ongoing consideration as they adapt and implement family engagement practices within their school communities.

The reasons for, and the advantages of, parents and teachers working as partners, and for teachers providing appropriate educational experiences for parents have been well documented. A strong positive correlation exists between parent involvement and student achievement, increased student attendance, positive parent–child communication, improved student attitudes and behavior, and more parent–community support of the schools.

Children of all backgrounds deserve the full consideration of teachers and parents; for children and parents of culturally different backgrounds, the need may be even greater. Many parents and families of culturally different backgrounds do not understand school expectations. Some expect high achievement in all areas from their children and adolescents. Many have difficulties communicating with the school. Much can be gained, in terms of improved overall school achievement and improved cultural and interpersonal relationships between parents, teachers, and students, when educators actively seek parent and family involvement.

Changing Perspectives of Parents, Families, and Caregivers

The twenty-first century has seen a dramatic change in what we define as parents and families. In the past, most (certainly not all) families consisted of two-parent families, comprising, as parents, one woman and one man. Currently, a much broader perspective of parents and families is accepted. Parents can be immediate parents, members of extended families, foster parents, and guardians, and there are grandparent-headed families, one-parent families, two-parent lesbian or gay families, and families headed by caregivers. Perceptive educators realize they should avoid sending letters and school information to "Mr. & Mrs." What if the home situation is one parent? Or if it is a lesbian or gay family? So many combinations exist that few, if any, assumptions can be made about what constitutes parents and families.

Understanding both Immediate and Extended Families

Another important reason for educators to promote parent involvement is to recognize the differences between European Americans' and other cultures' beliefs about the family. Whereas European Americans focus more on the immediate family, families of most other cultures include extended family members, such as grandparents, aunts, uncles, and cousins.

The implications of extended families are readily apparent for educators. Rather than conferring with, educating, or involving only the mother and father, educators should make conscientious attempts to recognize immediate and extended families.

Reasons for Parents Resisting Teachers' Efforts

Some parents resist teachers' efforts to involve them in the educational process, whether these efforts include conferences, involvement activities, or serving on committees. Why might parents and extended family members from minority cultures resist teachers' efforts? First, some cultures may harbor distrust and negative feelings toward professionals of other cultural backgrounds. Parents and children who harbor such attitudes have difficulty believing that professionals of differing cultural backgrounds understand them and want what is best for them. Parents with such powerful feelings of distrust will, in all likelihood, shun a teacher's efforts to build a working relationship between school and family.

Second, family members often fear disclosing personal problems or familial matters that might reflect negatively on themselves, the family, or the father's ability to manage home affairs. To reveal difficulties in the family can arouse feelings of shame in some cultures and put forth the perception of the family having failed in some way.

Parents often do not understand the U.S. school system or its expectations. For example, major differences exist between U.S. teachers and those in Southeast Asia. Teachers from countries such as Cambodia, Laos, and Vietnam are accorded higher levels of respect than are teachers in the United States. They often hold prestigious titles and positions; students are expected to bow, to avoid eye contact, and not to ask questions. Because Southeast Asian parents in their native lands are rarely involved in schools, they have difficulty understanding U.S. educators' parent-involvement programs, such as the PTA. They view teachers as experts, and feel that making suggestions about the education of children is inappropriate. Likewise, teachers report having difficulty engaging Southeast Asian parents, who are more accustomed to the lecture and rote-memorization methods that were used in their educations than to U.S. styles of teaching and learning activities such as projects and independent research (Li et al, 2023; Kong et al., 2023; Uy, 2015).

Asians' great respect for teachers and the learning process can actually pose a potential barrier. Asian parents are often reluctant to challenge a teacher's authority, and they sometimes feel that communicating with teachers may be perceived as disrespectful. Although these parents are usually attentive listeners, they seldom initiate contact with teachers and administrators, rarely ask questions, and seldom offer comments.

Cultural conflicts over child-rearing expectations and differing value systems also disturb many Asian families. As they arrive at the need to make child-rearing decisions on such issues as diet preference, sex education, dating patterns, and obedience to parents, these families are often torn between Eastern and Western manners, expectations, moral standards, and traditions.

POINTS TO PONDER 11.1

Addressing Language Barriers

Consult with the communication disorders specialist or ESL specialist in a school and the social service agencies in the community to learn how to work with and assist parents and family members whose language poses a barrier to effective communication. Make a list of publications, resource people, and special programs that help parents and families from culturally diverse backgrounds.

Understanding Cultural Diversity

Educators can readily see the reasons for understanding cultural diversity among families. However, they might have more difficulty reducing the myths, stereotypes, and other "baggage" that educators (and other professionals in U.S. society) carry about parents and families from differing cultural backgrounds.

When reaching decisions about families, we cannot overemphasize the need for objectivity. Educators cannot reach objective decisions concerning whether and to what extent to involve parents and families when they believe such statements as "These parents just don't care," "The father is an alcoholic," "The father never lets his wife speak," or "Neither the mother nor the father has any ambition; they are satisfied to live off welfare." Educators who stereotype parents will probably do little to get to know and involve parents and families, either in their individual classrooms or in the overall school program.

An educator should not think that he or she knows the prototypical "American Indian family," "African American family," or any other "family." For example, African American families are so diverse that some believe that there is no such thing as a typical African American family.

Socioeconomic differences play a significant role in determining how a person acts, lives, thinks, and relates to others. Low wages; unemployment or underemployment; lack of property, savings, and food reserves; and having to meet the most basic needs on a day-to-day basis can easily lead to feelings of helplessness, dependence, and inferiority. Differences in values, attitudes, behaviors, and beliefs among the various socioeconomic groups warrant professionals' consideration, especially because some marginalized groups' members come from lower socioeconomic classes.

Regrettably, a person's socioeconomic status is sometimes thought to indicate his or her ambitions or motivation to achieve. It is a serious mistake to stereotype people according to social class—to assume, for example, that those in the lower classes lack ambition, do not want to work, or do not want to improve their educational status. It is not unreasonable to suggest that people of the lower socioeconomic levels—whether African American, Arab American, Asian American, European American, Hispanic American, or American Indian—want to improve their social status in life but often meet with considerable frustration when faced with low education, high unemployment, conditions associated with poverty, and the racism and discrimination that are still prevalent in U.S. society.

Generational differences are another reason that an educator must not assume homogeneity within a culture. Older generations may be more prone to retain Old World values and traditions, because they tend to live in close proximity to people of similar language, traditions, and customs, whereas young people are more likely to move anywhere in the United States.

One generational difference involves facility with the English language. While older generations may have lived in cultural enclaves with others who speak their native languages or who speak English at similar levels of fluency, younger generations who can communicate effectively in English are better able to cope in a predominantly English-speaking society.

Use the following list of questions to examine your own perceptions:

1. Are my opinions of parents and families based on myths and stereotypes or on accurate and objective perceptions?
2. Have my experiences included positive first-hand contact with people from culturally different backgrounds?
3. What means have I employed to learn about the customs, traditions, values, and beliefs of all people?
4. Do I understand the extended family concept, or do I only think "too many people live in the same house because of poverty conditions"?
5. Am I prejudiced, or do I have genuine feelings of acceptance for all people, regardless of culture, ethnicity, race, and socioeconomic background?
6. Do I hold the perceptions that American Indians are alcoholics, that African American families are headed by single females, that Asian Americans are the model minority and have achieved what represents the American Dream, or that Hispanic Americans have large families and live on welfare?
7. Can I perceive that aunts, uncles, and grandparents are as important as more immediate family members (that is, the mother and father)?
8. Do I understand the rich cultural backgrounds of families, and am I willing to base educational experiences on this diversity?

9. Do I know appropriate sources of information to learn more about parents and families from culturally diverse backgrounds?
10. Do I have the motivation, skills, and attitudes to develop close interrelationships with parents and families from culturally different backgrounds?

Griffin et al. (2016) maintain that teachers can serve all students equitably by using familiar educational approaches, by responding to student experiences, and by empowering individual students' strengths. Cultural differences between teachers and students can often result in a student feeling lost in the classroom. Challenges for teachers with students from diverse cultural backgrounds extend beyond language. Even when students are familiar with the U.S. education system and teaching methods, the most routine classroom expectations can result in perplexing conflict when the children's behavior is learned and influenced by another culture. In such situations, teachers can pay more attention to the student, and can adjust instructional methods to include culturally responsive pedagogy in support of successful engagement in learning.

The challenges that teachers face stem not from only immigrant children, but from those born in the United States as well. American Indians, African Americans, and Hispanic Americans whose families have lived here for generations can also feel alienated by common classroom practices (Idrus & Sohid, 2023; Trumbull et al., 2001). For example, teachers need to be aware that a student may resist offering a correct answer after another student has answered incorrectly, so as not to embarrass their classmate in front of the group. Many of these students are raised in collectivist environments where children are taught based on beliefs that promote interdependence and duty to the group instead of standing out and developing an independent self. Some children living in such a collective cultural environment consider the classroom a place to help one another, make friends, and keep peace and harmony, rather than a place for competition and seeking recognition for their own achievement. To support these students, teachers can provide collaborative learning opportunities and show appreciation for their contributions toward the group work (Weva et al., 2023).

Trumbull et al. (2001) explain the Bridging Cultures project, which sought to improve cross-cultural communication in the classroom. This cultural framework is a tool for understanding how the expectations for a student at school may conflict with the values of the family. For example, European American parents often stress social and economic independence for their children. This emphasis on self-reliance affects nearly all family decisions. In contrast, collectivist societies are quite hierarchical and point their children in a different direction. They encourage them to be contributing members of a family unit. Children are expected to understand and to act on a strong sense of responsibility to the group, the family, and the community. Children in individualistic environments are expected to make educational and occupational decisions that develop their own potential, usually with little direct regard to how their success can benefit their families.

Many children in immigrant families possess assets from their cultural experiences and heritage language that are different from those of their English-speaking counterparts. It is, therefore, important that immigrant parents support their children's heritage language learning by creating a heritage language environment that includes literacy activities, bilingual books, and celebration of their ethnic language and culture (Lee & Gupta, 2020; Lee & Kang, 2023). Obviously, home is the optimal place for socialization and the transmission of heritage language and linguistic attitudes and ideologies from one generation to the next. When immigrant children begin U.S. school, however, a successful cultural and language transition process is often interrupted. Speaking a heritage language outside the home is not the norm in the host community and can even appear odd. Immigrant children may avoid their heritage language for these reasons. For example, many Korean immigrant families experience a language shift from Korean to English with pre-school age children once they enter school; despite the fact that they are recent immigrants and their dominant language is Korean. Attrition and eventual loss of heritage language can have a radical effect on immigrant children's relationships with their families, and can lead to a fear of rejection from their ethnic community. Immigrant parents need to focus on what they can do to keep their children engaged in their heritage language, at least at home, in addition to English.

Children of immigrant families can also be supported by schools and the community in the maintenance of their heritage language by communicating during activities and events such as sports, religious, or cultural events outside their microsystem environment. While they are learning English at school, multilingual students can maintain their linguistic and cultural identity and their ability as long as they are encouraged to communicate with their family and heritage language speakers in their local community and country of origin (Moreno-Fernández & Lamas, 2023).

Since learning a heritage language is intricately linked with various family and social experiences and surroundings that play a significant role in shaping language ideologies (Lee & Kang, 2023), families, teachers, and communities need to collaborate in supporting children's heritage language learning. Li et al. (2023) emphasized that to maintain a family's cultural identity and linguistic heritage, and cultivate positive ethnic identity, stakeholders who influence children's lives need to provide innovative opportunities for learning to maximize the success of maintaining each unique culture and language.

Teachers, especially, need to place an emphasis on bringing family languages into the classroom. Moreno-Fernández and Lamas (2023) stated that immigrant children's perception that their heritage language is well-received at school, whether through acceptance of its use, available content information in that language, or the implementation of targeted bilingual programs, can contribute to their cultural identity and academic success.

POINTS TO PONDER 11.2

Visiting in the Home

Visiting in the homes of children and adolescents can raise sensitive issues, especially with parents and families of culturally different backgrounds. Perceiving family life and parenting practices from different cultural perspectives can result in misunderstanding. For example, a middle-class African American educator might fail to understand a Hispanic or Asian American family. Make a list of "do's and don'ts"—those behaviors you should demonstrate and should not demonstrate in an effort to show understanding and respect for the parents' cultural heritage.

Effective Parent, Family, and Caregiver Involvement

Elements of Effective Programs

Effective parent-, family-, and caregiver-involvement programs should reflect the needs of the specific culture. Factors should be considered, such as length of time in the United States, socioeconomic status, sexual orientation, and the culture's gender expectations for girls and boys. Educators should avoid purchasing a "one-size-fits-all" program, because either the teacher will have to revise its components or the program will not reflect the needs of the specific cultures of the students being taught. Just as Mr. Johnson in the Opening Scenario wanted first-hand contact with people of diversity, people of specific cultures deserve to know and understand how to make parent-involvement programs responsive to their needs.

The author emphasizes the need for individuality in involvement programs, but also thinks that effective programs share the following qualities:

1. Written policies demonstrate to volunteers that the school is taking the effort seriously and provide some context for the actual program.
2. Administrative support is evident in all aspects of the program. Teachers and volunteers know that administrators will provide

financial support, current instructional materials, and assistance for teachers.

3. Training programs (e.g. removing barriers, overcoming language problems, and providing cultural sensitivity training) are provided for teachers and others working with the program.
4. Training programs emphasize a partnership approach among teachers and parents, families, and caregivers, rather than an approach in which the teacher simply lectures.
5. There is clear and effective communication between the home and the school. Such communication is two-sided rather than one-sided.
6. A network system is used to identify additional resources and information.
7. There is planned assessment of all phases of the program.

Most programs designed to work with families have served mainly those who speak English and who are familiar with parent–teacher programs. Educators need to consider cross-cultural perspectives when working with immigrant families. To lessen the problems associated with communication, both written and oral, schools can send letters and conduct meetings in a parent's native language, and can encourage parents to offer their input and opinions about school services in their preferred language. Schools can then translate their responses and report back in a parent's native language.

Parents, Families, and Caregivers of Culturally Different Backgrounds

A prerequisite to understanding culturally diverse parents and families is gaining accurate and objective knowledge about the expectations, needs, and challenges facing people with differing cultural backgrounds. Without a doubt, educators can improve their understanding by reading books and journals, taking courses, and attending professional conferences. Although these means can provide considerable insight into cultural diversity and should be an integral part of the educator's learning agenda, first-hand contact with individuals continues to be one of the most effective means of gaining an accurate perspective of cultural diversity.

First-hand contact has an advantage that other means cannot always provide: It enables teachers to learn directly about people and their individual attitudes, values, and beliefs. With understanding and knowledge, the potential exists for genuine feelings of caring and empathy to develop between people of differing races, cultures, and ethnic backgrounds.

Although there is probably no adequate substitute for first-hand contact with parents and families, it is possible to gain information through a parent survey. The most effective means would be to use a parent survey in addition to first-hand contact. It is important for the educators who design the survey to remember that some questions may be culturally sensitive—for example, questions that might not be offensive to European American populations might be construed as an invasion of privacy by many parents and families from culturally different backgrounds. Examples of culturally sensitive questions are those on child-rearing techniques, sex education, dating patterns, and parental authority.

Parette and Petch-Hogan (2000) suggest that communication with families is increasingly important in schools today. Parents of culturally/ linguistically diverse students can be involved in the sharing of culture, participating as assistants on field trips, assisting in arts and crafts, assisting with music and recreational activities, and participating actively in the special-education planning process. Parents of culturally diverse students can also share their culture of today versus the background and historic events that shaped their culture in the past with the students, and can participate in career days; however, make sure to provide ample time for questions from inquiring students about the information they provide about their unique culture. Such involvement can cause a problem for some diverse families, especially those with language differences, different cultural expectations, and mistrust of or lack of experience with U.S. education systems. The author focuses on ongoing communication and contacts with families; choosing appropriate locations for meetings and support; providing information training; understanding family priorities, needs, and resources; addressing family lifespan issues; holding family functions; and considering family communication styles.

One school system in which this type of problem had persisted for several years has developed a social ecological, relationship-based strategy that it uses to involve more families from diverse cultural backgrounds (McDonald et al., 2015). For example, the FAST (Family and Schools Together) program was implemented to encourage the involvement of reluctant parents in 52 urban schools with a 73 percent Latino student population with most students residing in disadvantaged neighborhoods. Invitations were sent out for parents to attend any one of the weekly multi-family group sessions offered after school at the school building. Parent training teams included local parents and professionals who were culturally and linguistically representative of the families. It is extremely important to have trainers who speak the language in which the parents are fluent. Parents were then led into a chat time, group discussion, and one-to-one "child-led" responsive play. Over the course of this program, immigrant parents attended statistically significantly more frequently than native-born ones. The outcomes of the FAST program were positive. The consistent and effective engagement of whole families, including children, increased. Most of all, the parenting program benefited culturally diverse children's general well-being, health, and higher academic aspirations. Through conversation-based workshops and the building of social relationships between teachers and parents, the FAST program allowed families and the school to work collectively to build an effective learning community.

To build better relationships, educators may decide to develop the survey in the parents' native languages, rather than risk that the survey will not be completed or that problems will result from poor communication. Generally speaking, parent surveys should be clear and short, should require only a brief amount of time to complete, and should avoid conveying a preference for middle-class European American perspectives.

Suizzo et al. (2016) challenge long-standing definitions of parental involvement, which have traditionally consisted of school-based practices that are observable to teachers, such as parents' participating in teacher–parent conferences, attending school functions, and volunteering at school. These narrow definitions do not always align with the supportive practices of African American and Latino American families, as well as other low-income and immigrant families, and can lead to the misconception that these parents are not as involved or as concerned with their children's academic outcomes as some others. While obstacles such as limited English proficiency, work schedules, and stereotyping do prevent many low-income, immigrant, and minority parents from traditional, school-based involvement, their home-based involvement is no less effective in conveying the value of education and influencing children's academic motivation. Suizzo et al. (2016) reported that parents' own positive school memories, as well as personal narratives of self-sacrifice and missed educational opportunities, can serve as a powerful "emotional bridge" and can motivate children to succeed academically. Teachers and school officials should consider ways to capitalize on parents' existing parental academic socialization (PAS) practices and strengths to counterbalance any low level of school attainment in order to promote students' intrinsic motivation, self-determination, and academic achievement without school-based parental involvement. Suizzo et al. (2016) offer excellent suggestions for teachers to use to promote their supportive parental practices, especially with low-income and minority families:

◆ Instill the importance of education in children in a way that complements their parents' approach. For example, many immigrant parents tout education as a means of avoiding unskilled or hard physical labor. Teachers, in turn, reiterate this advice to make the education–occupation link more explicit in order to enhance student motivation.

◆ Reassure parents with lower educational attainment that they are a vital part of their child's education and success, and that their expectations matter.

◆ Recognize that some parents may have negative memories of school that may make them anxious or even ambivalent. Teachers can help parents build new, positive memories by inviting them to observe their children's learning in a positive environment.

Parents, families, or caregivers often went to schools in which their culture was the majority culture, and many mainly associate with people from their own culture. Parents in these situations have little experience with people who are different. Having little knowledge of the culture, or worse yet, harboring cultural stereotypes and prejudicial views can lead to conflicts and confusion about the role of teachers as well as the responsibility of the school. The following 11 questions may serve as a beginning point to understand parents', families', and caregivers' concerns.

1. Do you feel that educators in your child's or adolescent's school understand and meet the overall needs and concerns of learners from different cultural backgrounds?
2. Do you feel that school policies recognize that children and adolescents of culturally different backgrounds differ from the European American population?
3. Does the media center (children's and adolescents' books, films, and other visual material) reflect the cultural diversity of the school?
4. How well has the school succeeded in employing a faculty and staff (administrators, teachers, library media specialists, special personnel, speech therapists, guidance counselors, psychologists, school nurses) that reflects the cultural diversity of the student body?
5. Do you feel that school expectations (competition, motivation, achievements, and aspirations) reflect the values and expectations of learners of culturally diverse backgrounds?
6. Do you feel that extracurricular activities in the school reflect the needs and interests of children and adolescents of culturally diverse backgrounds?
7. Do teaching methods and strategies (lecture format, small group, cooperative learning, ability grouping) reflect a concern for the educational well-being of all learners?

8. Has the school provided opportunities to offer opinions, input, advice, and suggestions concerning improvement of the school program, or has it moved to change an aspect that you would like to see changed?
9. Is your child progressing toward or succeeding at goals that you feel are important?
10. Do you feel that the school provides information and assistance concerning social service organizations?
11. What comments or suggestions would you offer concerning your child or adolescent in school?

Home Visits

Home visits may be one of the most effective ways for teachers to get to know learners, their immediate and extended families, and their home environment and culture. Families from different cultural backgrounds often perceive family roles differently, have differing expectations of the schools, and expect older family members to play significantly greater child-rearing roles. The only way to understand such differences is to get to know the families personally. Home visits allow teachers to interact with families of various cultural backgrounds which can provide an opportunity to foster supportive relationships and build the knowledge necessary to establish a meaningful partnership (Paulick et al., 2024). By learning the strengths and values of marginalized families (Szech, 2023), teachers can adapt their teaching methods to incorporate culturally relevant and culturally sustaining teaching methods based on insights gained from home visits with families.

Home visits can provide valuable information about learners and their homes, but perhaps an even greater benefit is that learners and their families see that educators care and are interested in all children and adolescents. Parents from culturally different backgrounds may also feel more at ease in their own surroundings than they would in the (perhaps) strange and sterile school environment.

Before the home visit, educators should call or send a note to the parents to establish a time that is convenient for both the teacher and the parents. At the beginning of the visit, the teacher should talk informally with the parents and the child for a few minutes to establish a friendly tone and to reduce the parents' anxiety. At all times, teachers should remember that they are visitors and should avoid any judgment of the situations and conditions in the home. Parents will have greater confidence in the teacher if they think the discussion will be held in confidence.

Communication

Educators in multicultural situations must recognize that some communication behaviors are to be understood rather than expected. Listening behaviors that are typical and expected of middle-class white parents might be far different from those that people of other cultural backgrounds exhibit. For example, maintaining eye contact is considered to be rude in some cultures. Likewise, body postures are also culturally based. Educators should not assess parents' and families' interest and commitment to children's education by using middle-class European American standards and expectations.

POINTS TO PONDER 11.3

Determining Concerns during Parent–Teacher Conferences

Make a list of possible concerns and barriers that might interfere with the success of the parent–teacher conference. How will you motivate parents and families (who might feel that speaking forthrightly to the teacher is disrespectful) to speak, voice concerns, and make suggestions?

Humans communicate at several levels simultaneously: Through verbal expression, or what they say; through body language or nonverbal expression, or how they behave; and through emotional responses, or how they show what they feel. The more congruent these levels of expression are, the more meaningful or understanding the communication becomes to others. One can easily recognize the importance of understanding the various types of communication with families of differing cultural backgrounds.

Whether communicating through speaking directly, phoning, emailing, virtual meetings, or writing to parents, educators are responsible for not allowing language or communication differences, verbal or nonverbal, to interfere with overall communication. Several factors warrant consideration. First, the parents' English skills might not allow effective communication. Second, nonverbal communication might pose a problem—for example, the European American who looks an American Indian directly in the eye while communicating might be considered rude, and the educator might think an American Indian's glancing away indicates disinterest or irritation. Awareness of the communication style of the culture of the parents can help strengthen a developing understanding. As more schools transition to use app-based learning activities and platforms to communicate with families, teachers are able to engage families and provide instructions to parents in a timely manner (Asher et al., 2024).

However, for families with linguistically diverse or disabled students it can be challenging to communicate with teachers. If schools use digital apps for communication some families may not have the necessary skills or resources. In addition, it can be challenging for teachers to provide behavioral intervention to students with emotional and behavioral disorders remotely (Matute-Chavarria et al., 2023). To better support the caregivers, special education teachers have utilized platforms like Zoom, Google Meet, Microsoft Teams, etc., to communicate and offer teaching ideas that families can use (Liao et al., 2023). With apps, such as Seesaw, Brightwheel, Google Translate, and ClassDojo, teachers are able to facilitate communication with families promptly and provide resources for enriching lessons at home. Spanish-speaking families, for example, value receiving text or video messages in Spanish using a translation app, which also enhances parental engagement with literacy activities.

Another example of problems that can result from nonverbal communication occurs with Asian American parents and families, who are especially sensitive to nonverbal messages and who may construe a teacher's folded arms or other casual gestures as indicative of an indifferent attitude.

Educators should avoid jargon with which parents might be unfamiliar—for example, *PET, assertive discipline, critical thinking, cooperative learning, mastery learning, percentiles,* and terms associated with computers or technology.

The telephone represents another means of communicating with parents and demonstrates the teacher's personal interest in both the learner and the parents. Positive telephone contacts can significantly affect a child's school performance; conversely, negative calls can have a negative effect. As with other forms of communication, teachers must exercise caution when using the telephone to communicate with parents. Telephone can be extremely threatening, however, to parents and families of culturally different backgrounds, because they have come to expect bad news whenever a representative of the school calls.

After confirming that all parents have access to a smartphone, texting tool, and/or email address, teachers can use a new and efficient form of communication to encourage parents to attend meetings, conferences, and other school events—for example, the "REMIND" app is a free communication tool to use with parents for sending quick "reminders" or a "heads-up" text (www. remind.com/). Another AI tool that can be used to enhance communication with parents is TalkingPoints, which translates messages sent by teachers into the parent's home language and vice versa.

A teacher receives an alias number that the parents can use to correspond and communicate with him or her. This is an effective two-way method that is up to the technology standards of today. This type of digital app has several advantages. It can:

- ◆ Send real-time and fast text messaging to any phone for communication with a group of parents, or just with a single person.
- ◆ Translate your messages written in English into more than 70 foreign languages.
- ◆ Check who has read your messages and who has not, for follow-up communication.
- ◆ Help you plan important activities and events ahead of time, including all parents.

Guidelines for minimizing parent and teacher misunderstandings include the following:

1. Address parents as Mr. or Mrs., because parents from different backgrounds often do not receive the same respect and courtesy as other people.
2. Use a tone of voice that expresses respect and courtesy, because a call from school can often raise anxiety levels.
3. Discuss the child's or adolescent's positive points before discussing the problem to be solved. Treat all children positively by acknowledging their potential, talents, hopes, and creative minds.
4. Use language that the parent understands and a tone that does not sound condescending.
5. Respond with empathy if the parent has difficulty understanding unfamiliar educational concepts.

Educators can also write notes, letters, texts, and emails to keep parents informed of children's progress, and of administrative and record-keeping problems and concerns, schedule changes, special events, holidays, workshops, field trips, and other items of interest. Effective messages are clear, concise, and positive, and may speak to parents and family members in their primary language. Unless used systematically, however, written communication has limited value in reinforcing the child's academic performance or social and emotional behavior, and is best used as just one component of the overall parent and teacher communication.

Volunteers

Parent volunteers can contribute significantly to the quality of the services offered to learners in the school. Here are four important reasons for using volunteers. They can:

1. Relieve the professional staff of nonteaching duties.
2. Provide needed services to individual children to supplement the work of the classroom teacher.
3. Enrich the experiences of children beyond those normally available in school.
4. Build a better understanding among the population of school problems and stimulate widespread support for public education.

Although parents are the most frequent volunteers, siblings, relatives, older elementary and secondary students, college students, senior citizens, businesses and professional groups, and other members of the community can volunteer to participate in school activities.

Parents and extended family members from all cultures can offer a variety of talents and skills to share with children and adolescents. People from differing cultural backgrounds, however, often consider educators and schools as both authoritarian and worthy of honor and praise. Therefore, some people might be hesitant to "interfere" with school routines, or may feel that their talents are not worthy to be shared with the school. The administrators' and teachers' role in this situation is to encourage and convince people that schools are open to new ideas and that their talents are worth sharing. To accomplish such a goal, educators should send home, at the beginning of the school year, a parent-involvement questionnaire designed to determine parents' skills, talents, and areas of interest.

Serving on committees is another way in which parents and extended family members can become involved in classrooms and school. Through committee work, parents can contribute to the classroom and the school, and can learn about program development, operation, staffing, and evaluation. Parents also develop an appreciation for staffing concerns, curriculum development, fiscal exigencies, material and equipment needs, and other demands of the instructional program.

As with other forms of involvement, these parents and families might not understand the purpose of committees and how they function.

Educators must work toward making the composition of the committee's representative of the diversity of the student body. Guidelines for parents working on school committees include the following:

1. Remember the committee's purpose and objectives.
2. Be confident of the committee's ability to accomplish the assigned task.
3. Begin small, and take one step at a time.
4. Function within the school, and become an integral part of the classroom or school.
5. Seek financial, administrative, informational, and other assistance when necessary.

Parent involvement is an important factor in promoting the successful transition of youth with disabilities into adulthood. Geenen et al. (2001) surveyed American Indian, African American, Hispanic American, and European American parents to assess their level of participation in their child's transitioning activities. They found that culturally and linguistically diverse groups report higher levels of participation than European American parents often do. Parent participation might be particularly important for culturally and linguistically diverse youth, since a strong relationship between parents and the school can promote cultural understanding and responsiveness in transition planning. Ethnically diverse groups often emphasize norm-related behaviors and define adult roles differently, and parents can be a valuable resource in helping educators understand, identify, and support transition outcomes that are valued in a child's culture.

Parents of all ethnic groups are likely to encounter barriers to school participation, including parental fatigue, lack of parental knowledge regarding their rights and school procedures, logistical constraints (e.g. lack of childcare), rigid or limited options for parental involvement in educational planning, and language. However, the problems are made more formidable by some educators' racism, discrimination, insensitivity, and cultural unresponsiveness for low-economic level families and culturally and linguistically diverse families. When marginalized students are not held to high standards by teachers, they don't feel a sense of belonging in the classroom. This can seriously compromise their confidence and academic potential. In this unfortunate situation, parents need to nurture a sense of cultural pride and identity (D'hondt et al., 2016). To overcome these challenges, teachers can adopt the BETR (Building Effective Trusting Relationships) Conference Model that guides teacher and family members' awareness of expectations. They should also maintain ongoing two-way communication to build trust and share information about student learning throughout the academic year (Lindo et al., 2023).

Parent–Teacher Conferences

The parent–teacher conference presents an opportunity for parents and teachers to exchange information about the child's school and home activities. It also provides an occasion to involve parents in planning and implementing their child's educational program. When teachers contact parents to schedule progress report conferences, they should explain the purpose of the conference, which will assist both parties in being prepared to exchange information regarding the student's school practices, learning, and home activities (Munthe & Westergård, 2023).

To lessen the parents' anxiety about the conference, teachers might provide parents with a written agenda. A written conference agenda allows teachers to provide an outline, so all participants will stay on task and discuss the topic at hand. Teachers might also provide the parent/guardian with a copy of the conference summary sheet, which gives the parents a take-away and a record of what was discussed. Since the summary may need to be referred to in the future, it is best to record the date.

Educators should also remember that the purpose of the conference is child and school progress, not the teacher's or parents' personal, social, emotional, or marital problems. Although these issues may affect the learner's overall school progress, educators should direct the focus of the conference toward areas of school function. The agenda for the parent–teacher conference might include discussion of the learner's test scores or his or her assessment results. It is advised that the teacher prepare this information ahead of time so she/he can be ready to answer any questions that the parent may have.

Although most parents, regardless of cultural background, might benefit from an explanation of the terms normally associated with measurement and evaluation, some parents might need even more detailed information. Test results are often a concern for parents and children, and parents may react strongly to results that indicate that their child or adolescent is functioning at a lower level than most other learners. Educators should ask parents from differing cultural backgrounds to state their understanding of the information and to make certain that parents understand the results and conclusions. Teachers should make a sincere effort to alleviate any anxiety that parents express over possible misuse of test results.

For some parents whose culture does not allow women to go out publicly without an accompanying man, or for busy parents with limited time, other forms of conferencing can be used that allow them to participate wherever they are in the world. Nowadays, there are several free video-conferencing apps. Instead of meeting face to face with a parent/guardian, teachers can show the option of video-conferencing apps, such as FaceTime, Google Hangout, Skype, KaKaoTalk, WhatsApp, WeChat, Viber, or Line. Virtual conferencing is a great way to connect with parents who can't make it to the school otherwise, and it may increase the number of participants for parent–teacher conferences. Improving students' success is first and foremost. The success rate will definitely grow when parents and teachers have a connection.

Parent–teacher conferences have the potential to be beneficial for all involved but can result in hard feelings, frustration, and a breaking off of communication completely. Here are several suggestions for assuring positive conferences, but please remember that there is no special formula for success:

1. Begin to work toward positive relationships with parents, families, and caregivers before the first conference or informal meeting.
2. Have an ongoing dialogue with parents, families, and caregivers. For instance, notify them of positive achievements and accomplishments, special dates, and the details of the reporting system.
3. Occasionally ask students to participate in the conference, so that they will know what is being said. Such an effort to avoid distrust and suspicion often pays rich dividends.
4. Make the conference as comfortable as possible. Provide a comfortable seating area for the teacher with the parents, families, or caregivers (rather than have the teacher sit behind the desk).
5. Make it clear how parents, families, and caregivers can help the child, and conclude the conference with at least one positive comment.
6. Avoid educational jargon that might confuse the participants, but explain terms in detail when the slightest suspicion or doubt arises.

Parent Advisory Councils

A parent advisory council can be an excellent means of providing parents and families of culturally diverse backgrounds opportunities with the ability to voice their opinions and to generally influence the overall operation of the school. By having a council composition that reflects the cultural diversity of the student body, council representatives (or parents who make suggestions and comments through selected representatives) can offer specific suggestions for devising the school curriculum, and for making the teaching and learning environment more multicultural in nature. Council members might want to discuss the cultural diversity of the administrative and teaching staff, ways in which the curriculum and teaching and learning process reflect diversity, policies that groups of differing cultural backgrounds might not understand, methods of making the school more multicultural in nature, or any topic that might seem relevant at the time. With the predominance of white parents on these advisory councils, perspectives and needs of marginalized students and parents may often be ignored (Rudden, 2023). Schools, therefore, need to be proactive in encouraging parents of all cultural backgrounds to engage with the councils to increase diversity in representation, create a supportive school culture, and reach nondiscriminatory decisions.

An advisory council can serve as a liaison between school and classroom, and between home and community, and it can function as a permanent parent-to-parent communications committee to announce meetings, special events, personnel changes, and other notices of interest. The advisory committee can also assume responsibility for organizing and directing ad hoc or temporary committees.

Orientation sessions might be in order, especially for parents and families who may not understand the purpose of the council, who may feel that parents would be meddling in schools' business, or who may not understand the procedures by which the meetings work. An orientation meeting can help council members feel better prepared and more comfortable about future meetings. Suggested topics for an orientation session include council role and authority, purpose, district organization, the value and the functions of committees, decision-making procedures (perhaps including a brief session on *Robert's Rules of Order* (Robert, 2011)), ways to disagree and the value of expressing a different view, and the expectations of members.

Parent, Family, and Caregiver Education

The concept of parent education dates back to the 1800s and carries differing definitions and perceptions that have resulted in a variety of forms and emphases. A wide array of activities continue to be appropriate for parent-education programs. These range from family and cultural transmission of child-rearing values, skills, and techniques to more specific parenting behaviors. Specifically, however, we define the term *parent education* as planned activities that are designed to educate parents about their children and adolescents, about the goals of U.S. school systems, and about ways in which they can help their child or adolescent experience success, both academically and behaviorally, in school.

Although schools should develop parent-education programs specifically for individual learners and their parents, some programs help parents with special needs, enhance knowledge of family life, teach techniques for changing attitudes and behaviors, help parents change their own negative behaviors, provide health and sex education information, and teach parents how to help with the education process.

The need for parent education has been documented: Parents often dread the changes in their child's or adolescent's development; parents sometimes absolve themselves of responsibility; and parents often need assistance in understanding curricular areas. But, upon learning more about the school, parents become more involved and develop more positive attitudes toward school activities. The need for parent education results from the heightened concern about pressures related to working mothers, the effects of geographic mobility, divorce rates, and economic uncertainties, as well as from parents needing relevant information about their children's social, physical, emotional, and intellectual development.

The realities, however, pose a dilemma that demands educators' understanding. Although parent-education programs have become routine aspects of many early childhood programs, evidence indicates that many middle and secondary school educators have not developed parent-education programs. Early childhood education appears to have made substantial progress in planning and implementing parent-education programs and has provided the framework in both theory and practice for schools or other levels. The Early Childhood Family Literacy program has provided parent training and early education simultaneously, with an emphasis on the significant role of parents during early childhood (Berscheid, 2023). The program includes a variety of learning activities to enhance parents' English language acquisition and high school diploma attainment, while they learn to be more effective parents and teachers at home for their children's development. Recently, there has been substantial interest in parent-education programs on discipline and teaching their children behavior that promotes positive pro-social skills and parent–child interactions (Lindo et al., 2023).

Rationale for Involvement Programs

Two reasons speak to the importance of parent education: It helps parents to understand the various developmental periods of their children and to respond appropriately to their children's and adolescents' behavior. Although we address each reason separately, close and intricate relationships between the two areas warrant parental recognition and understanding.

Effective parent-education programs provide experiences that show a developmental basis for children's and adolescents' behavior. Rather than allow parents to assume that they have failed in parenting roles, or to absolve themselves of responsibility for behavior, programs can help parents understand the developmental changes and the contemporary world of children and adolescents.

Specifically, parents need to understand the cause-and-effect relationship between development and behavior. The cause of certain behaviors may result from children's and adolescents' quest for independence and from peer pressure to experiment with alcohol, drugs, sex, and other challenges to authority.

Basically, educators should provide programs that convince parents that their children are not necessarily "going bad" or "turning into hoodlums," and that, while understanding that changes in behavioral patterns may be difficult for parents, children and adolescents need to feel accepted and understood. Parents need to understand that feeling guilty or absolving themselves of responsibility may result in even worse attention-getting or even delinquent behaviors. Parents need to understand the effects of one-parent homes on development and behavior. At the same time, educators should emphasize that not all child and adolescent behavior results from family disruption.

Special Needs of Parents, Families, and Caregivers

Planning parent-education programs for parents and families from differing cultural backgrounds requires that educators look at issues, topics, and formats from the perspective of these parents and families. Prepackaged programs or programs that European Americans in middle- or upper-class suburban schools use might not be adequate or appropriate for culturally diverse parents and families, whatever their social class.

Although special needs vary with culture, ethnicity, social class, and geographic area, what specific needs might parents and families have? After an objective and accurate needs assessment, educators might find that parents of diverse cultural backgrounds require educational assistance in understanding such areas as school expectations, parents' roles in the school, tests and assessment scores, children's and adolescents' development, appropriate social services agencies and organizations that can provide assistance, homework and how to get help, school committees and parent advisory councils, and other involvement activities. This list provides only a few examples, but it suffices to show that parent-education programs should be designed for a specific cultural group and not rely on a program that parents may not understand or feel is not culturally relevant.

Methods and activities selected for the parent-education program determine the success of the effort. Programs for minority parents should not rely too heavily on reading material (unless participants are clearly proficient in English), should not expect parents to take active vocal roles in the beginning stages, and should not expect or require parents to reveal situations or information that may be personal or may negatively reflect on the family or the home. Additionally, educators need to be flexible when selecting topics for caregivers of children with special needs, such as ADHD, autism spectrum disorders, and disruptive behavior disorders. They choose settings that can best serve the target population. For instance, a home can be the most comfortable location for teenage mothers with low socioeconomic status backgrounds to achieve the goals of a particular parent-education program.

Formats of Parent-Education Programs

Teachers must reach a decision about whether to employ a prepackaged parenting program that may lead to a loosely organized discussion group or to develop a program that addresses parental needs for a particular school. Prepackaged programs have several advantages (e.g. they require less preparatory time and little revision), but they may not be applicable to a diverse range of cultures.

Developing a parent-education program based on specific family and community needs might prove effective, and parents might receive it more enthusiastically. The format of the program can take several directions and should reflect the needs and interests of the individual schools and the parents.

Before scheduling planning sessions, educators should conduct an assessment or a needs inventory to determine the preferred methods and the content. Parent education methods may include lectures, discussion groups, computer programs, online meetings, phone conferences, webinars, and/or PowerPoint presentations. Parents can interact with other parent educators individually to discuss confidential and personal matters concerning their children that they might not wish to reveal in a large group setting.

Parent-education sessions will undoubtedly stimulate questions, comments, and other discussion. Rather than relying on a lecture format with a large group, the leader of the session should allow time for parents to speak with or meet in small groups. Sometimes, one of the leader's most effective approaches may be to let parents know that other parents experience similar problems. The participants in the "What You Do Matters" (WYDM) parent-education program learned about child development to improve parenting skills and ensure their children's early brain development, social, emotional, language, and educational development. The program involved 94 families in up to six classes and reported that the benefits of participating in the program varied depending on the implementation site. This suggests that factors such as educator effectiveness, intensity, participant demographics, and instruction language can affect the program's impact (Anthony et al., 2023).

In all likelihood, it will be difficult to purchase a prepackaged parent-education program that meets the needs of parents from a number of cultural backgrounds. For example, African American parents might not experience the same challenges as American Indians. Likewise, first-generation Asian Americans probably do not experience the same problems as third-generation Asian Americans. We think it might be more feasible to design programs with individual cultural groups in mind.

Helping Parents Understand School Expectations and Parents' Roles

A major role of parent-education programs should be to help parents of differing cultural groups understand the school's expectations and the parents' role in the teaching and learning process. Designing such a program requires educators to assess the needs and concerns of the specific culture. For example, although American Indian and Asian American parents might have similarities, they have substantial differences that necessitate the use of culture-specific programs.

First, educators need to recognize that some parents and families, especially of more recently arrived generations, might not understand U.S. school expectations and perspectives, which place emphasis on individual achievement, competition, and responsibility for one's own possessions. Parents and families of differing cultural backgrounds should not encourage their children and adolescents to adopt middle- or upper-class European American perspectives. Instead, educators can explain to parents the differing cultural expectations (e.g. group versus individual achievement, competition versus working together, sharing versus ownership) of various cultural groups. Educators should also explain the school's expectations in other areas, such as curricular matters, instructional strategies, classroom management and discipline, homework and extracurricular activities, and other aspects of the school that parents and families may need assistance in understanding.

Second, educators should make clear the parents' roles and responsibilities in their children's or adolescents' education. Sometimes, people from different cultural backgrounds may think that they do not know enough about U.S. school systems to make a contribution, or they may perceive the school as an authoritarian institution that does not appreciate input and suggestions. The educator's role is to change these misconceptions about the school and to show that learners' academic achievement and overall school progress can be enhanced when parents take an active role in the school. In meeting this goal, educators need to show all parents and families that:

1. They, as parents and families, are responsible for encouraging and helping their children and adolescents in all phases of the teaching and learning process.

2. They are encouraged to visit the school and voice their input, recommendations, and suggestions.
3. They are encouraged to participate in conferences, involvement activities, parent-education sessions, and parent advisory councils.

Summing Up

Educators who want to involve parents and families from culturally different backgrounds should:

1. Understand the extended family concept and plan educational experiences for both immediate and extended family members.
2. Understand that parents and families may resist teachers' efforts to involve them in school activities.
3. Understand parents as individuals with intracultural, socioeconomic, and generational differences.
4. Learn as much as possible about parents and families through first-hand contact, parent surveys, and any other means that provide accurate and objective information.
5. Visit the homes of students to gain a better understanding of family backgrounds, values, customs, and traditions.
6. Ensure that communication between the school and family reflects a genuine understanding of the problems that might result from language and communication differences, both verbal and nonverbal.
7. Plan and conduct parent–teacher conferences so that parents will understand the purposes and procedures of the conference process.
8. Ensure that parent advisory councils have a composition that represents the cultural, ethnic, and racial composition of the student body, and ensure that the councils address the specific needs and concerns of parents and families from differing cultural backgrounds.
9. Understand that parent-education programs are especially important for parents who might not understand the school's roles and expectations, and who may need assistance with their child or adolescent in a predominantly European American school and society.

Suggested Learning Activities

1. Prepare a parent survey designed to obtain information from parents and families of different cultural backgrounds. List questions that will elicit specific information about what parents and families expect from schools, ways in which teachers can help children and adolescents, and ways in which parents and families can contribute to the educational process. In preparing this survey, what are some precautions you might want to consider?
2. Design procedures for an effective parent advisory committee with the purpose of involving parents and families. Your design should consider what means you will use to engage participants of all cultural backgrounds, the overall goals of the committee, how the committee will report to the general school population, a sample agenda (for an individual meeting and for the school year), how you will accommodate participants who are not proficient in English, and any special factors that educators should consider when dealing with marginalized populations.
3. Read the following Implementing Research section and consider ways that educators can better meet students' families, and teachers' needs.

Implementing Research

Identifying Meaningful Indicators of Parent Engagement for All Families

Bettencourt et al. (2023) found that while a majority (88 percent) of principals view attending school events as an important indicator of parent involvement, only 35 percent of parents agree. Specifically, low-income families are less likely than higher-income families to take part in activities at school due to limited language ability or concerns of stereotyping they may face. For single or low-income parents with multiple jobs especially, participating in school committees, volunteering in classrooms, or attending school events is often not feasible. This study identified a more realistic and equitable parent engagement indicator for all families, including low-income families. Educators need to keep in mind that the emphasis on school-based activities, therefore, may put these families at a disadvantage if they cannot attend or don't feel culturally at ease in school settings. This study recommends that educators employ more relevant and actionable indicators to gauge low-income families' engagement in children's early learning, such as the following:

1. Continuing children's education through home-based engagement is the most effective means by which parents can support and reinforce their children's learning and development. Families can help with children's reading and writing activities, and visit interesting and stimulating places such as the zoo, library, and museums with rich learning environments.
2. Schools should create a variety of school-based functions to choose from: PTA meetings, workshops, classroom volunteering, family reading night, cultural celebrations, or chaperoning on class trips at a number of different days and times.
3. Family–school partnerships. Examples include talking one-on-one about the child's accomplishments and challenges, discussing learning behavior, teacher home visits, and holding open conversations with the student and parents about what happens at school.

Suggestions for Collaborative Efforts

Form groups of three or four that, if possible, represent the United States' cultural and gender diversity. Working collaboratively, focus your group's attention toward the following efforts:

1. With the help of your group, prepare a survey to determine the reasons why parents might resist educators' efforts. Using the results, write a plan in which your goal is to obtain the family's participation and involvement.
2. Arrange an opportunity for each member of your group to meet with a parent or an extended family member to learn what problems they experience with U.S. schools. Have as many cultural groups represented as possible. As a group, decide on a list of questions that might provide the information you want. Then, as a group, share your responses to determine whether you can establish a plan or an agenda for addressing parents' and families' concerns. Caution: Remember that some cultures hold schools and educators in high regard and therefore might not want to share concerns and problems. In such cases, you should respect their privacy.

3. Design a program to involve parents, families, and caregivers from culturally diverse backgrounds. Plan how you will invite and obtain their participation, help them understand that elementary and secondary schools need their participation, and teach them appropriate activities or utilize their individual expertise. List several points that educators should consider (and propose an appropriate response), such as parents' language difficulties, their lack of understanding of the workings of U.S. schools, and the immense respect that some parents, families, and caregivers have for educators.

Expanding Your Horizons

Additional Books and Journals

Fantozzi, V. B. (2023). Connecting in context: Using digital portfolios to foster reciprocal relationships with families. *Young Children*, *78*(4), 30–37. http://proxy.lib.odu.edu/login?url=https://search.ebscohost.com/login.aspx?direct=true&db=ehh&AN=174049972&scope=site

This article explores the use of digital portfolios in early childhood education to enhance family engagement and offers tips for their inclusion in the curriculum, mindful of family diversity.

McCarthy, S., LaChenaye, J., Wilkinson, L. L., & Perry, T. (2023). The hidden perspective of family engagement: School beliefs and in-home practices of parents and caregivers in an urban high school. *Education*, *143*(2), 48–62. http://proxy.lib.odu.edu/login?url=https://search.ebscohost.com/login.aspx?direct=true&db=ehh&AN=163900941&scope=site

Discusses how parent involvement entails schools leading the relationship and controlling various aspects like agendas and activities, often taking place within the school. Parent engagement involves shared power and decision-making, fostering a collaborative relationship where parents and caregivers are seen as equal partners with expertise, and problem-solving capabilities.

Munthe, E. & Westergård, E. (2023). Parents', teachers', and students' roles in parent-teacher conferences: A systematic review and meta-synthesis. *Teaching and Teacher Education*, *136*. https://doi.org/10.1016/j.tate.2023.104355

This research focuses on understanding the roles of parents, teachers, and students during parent–teacher conferences (PTCs). The study underscores the importance of developing teachers' communication skills, fostering home-school cooperation, and integrating PTCs into teacher education programs.

Websites

Edutopia 5-Minute Film Festival: Parent–Teacher Partnerships – www. edutopia.org/blog/film-festival-parent-teacher-partnerships
Edutopia's film series includes nine brief videos highlighting successful parent–teacher partnerships. The videos offer practical advice for both parents and educators, on a range of topics like the PTA, involving ELL parents, and conducting home visits.

Global Family Research Project — https://globalfrp.org/
This site covers comprehensive research topics on family, out-of-school programs, and engaging families and community in order to support student success, both in school and in life. This project was formerly known as the Harvard Family Research Project.

PBIS: Family Partnership — www.pbis.org/topics/family
This site promotes schools, families, and communities to work together to create effective learners and school success.

PTO Today – www.ptotoday.com/blog/6267-bring-meetings-to-parents-wherever-they-may-be
This site provides a wealth of information on parent involvement in elementary and secondary schools. It is well organized by topics A–Z and provides articles and flyers, and forms message boards related to parental involvement activities.

Southern Poverty Law Center's Learning for Justice – www.splcenter.org/learning-for-justice
For nearly 25 years, the Southern Poverty Law Center's award-winning project, Learning for Justice program, formerly known as Teaching Tolerance, has provided free teaching materials to eradicate prejudice and help students respect differences. The Learning for Justice website also offers guidance and class activities on topics such as "Family and Community Engagement" and "Building Relationships in the Community" that are adaptable to different grades and content areas.

SurveyMonkey: Parent Survey Templates for K–12 Schools – www. surveymonkey.com/mp/harvard-education-surveys/
SurveyMonkey and the Harvard Graduate School of Education have partnered to provide an expert parent survey template to better understand

parent concerns and encourage parental involvement. K–12 teachers and administrators can use this survey to "ask the right questions" and to receive more accurate, actionable parent engagement data.

UnidosUS's Padres Comprometidos — https://unidosus.org/publications/204-padres-comprometidos-engaging-latino-parents-for-long-term-student-success/

UnidosUS' Padres Comprometidos (PC) program, previously known as the NCLR (National Council of La Raza), is a parent engagement program designed specifically for Spanish-speaking adults with children in U.S. schools. Their bilingual curriculum develops parents' English language skills and teaches them about the U.S. education system, empowering them to effectively communicate with teachers and administrators.

12

Administrators and Special School Personnel

Understanding the material and activities in this chapter will help the reader to:

- ◆ Explain why the cultural diversity of administrators, faculty, and staff should reflect that of the student population.
- ◆ List several roles of administrators, special educators, librarians/media specialists, counselors, and communication disorders specialists in a school that promotes multiculturalism at all levels.
- ◆ List several ways that administrators can lead school personnel in efforts to promote multiculturalism.
- ◆ Explain the unique challenges that face special-education teachers in diagnosing and remediating learners from culturally different backgrounds.
- ◆ Explain how the librarian/media specialist can select appropriate print and nonprint materials that accurately portray children and adolescents from all cultural backgrounds.
- ◆ Explain how the school counselor can understand culturally different children and adolescents and select culturally appropriate counseling techniques and testing instruments.
- ◆ Explain how the communication disorders specialist can accurately distinguish between communications disorders and communications variations.
- ◆ Explain, from the teacher's perspective, how the various professionals can work together and how the teacher can most effectively utilize the various areas of expertise for the benefit of learners of all cultural backgrounds.

DOI: 10.4324/9781003429531-15

Opening Scenario

Culturally Relevant Educational Experiences

Mrs. Miller, a seventh-grade teacher at Evergreen Middle School, has 28 students in her class: 12 European Americans, 11 African Americans, two Hispanic Americans, and two Asian Americans. Mrs. Miller recognizes that the school, its policies, and its teaching and learning practices are predominantly white and middle-class in perspective. Many students have to obey rules they do not understand, work toward meeting expectations and levels of motivation that are compatible with white perspectives, and learn to use cognitive styles similar to those of middle-class white learners. Mrs. Miller understands the need for change but also realizes she has limited time, resources, and expertise. For her students' welfare, she has decided to seek the principal's assistance.

Mrs. Johnson, the principal, listens attentively to Mrs. Miller's concerns. She agrees not only that the 16 students of culturally different backgrounds need culturally relevant educational experiences, but also that the 12 European American students need to acquire a better understanding of the other learners (and vice versa). Mrs. Johnson and Mrs. Miller decide to form a committee to address the learners' needs. The committee consists of Mrs. Johnson, Mrs. Miller, another seventh-grade teacher, one European American parent who has expressed interest, and three parents from other cultural groups (one from each group represented).

Mrs. Johnson has made a list of her and the committee's recommendations:

1. The task calls for the commitment of administrators, faculty, and parents; it is not something Mrs. Miller should tackle alone.
2. All parents—majority culture and minority cultures—should be notified (and their advice sought) of the effort to meet learners' needs and to provide multicultural experiences for all learners.
3. Textbooks and other curricular materials should be examined for bias, stereotypes, and cultural relevance.
4. Teaching and learning practices and the school environment should be examined from an administrative perspective.

Mrs. Johnson thinks these steps will serve as a good starting point and that, from an administrative perspective, this is a manageable agenda. Viewing this agenda as only a first phase, Mrs. Johnson starts to consider how the efforts can become a total-school effort.

Overview

Genuine multicultural education efforts include more than lofty goals and school philosophies. The school's effort to recognize and celebrate cultural diversity should demonstrate total-school involvement by including the efforts of all school personnel. A commitment to multicultural education also includes an administration, faculty, and staff that reflect the cultural diversity of the student body. Employing school personnel of all cultural backgrounds at all levels shows respect for diversity; however, educators still need to work together, within their individual areas of expertise, to provide learners with educational experiences that address both individual and cultural needs. This chapter shows, from the classroom teacher's perspective, how administrators and special school personnel can contribute to the overall multicultural education program.

Administrators, Faculty, and Staff: Toward a Total-School Effort

Multicultural education programs and curricula may have lofty goal statements, but perhaps the best measure of a school's commitment to cultural diversity is the actual cultural, ethnic, sexual orientation, gender, and racial composition of the administration, faculty, and staff. Specifically, do school personnel reflect the cultural diversity of the student population? If school personnel are predominantly from one background, one might justifiably ask whether the school administration is striving for the goals of the multicultural education program. Learners of various cultural backgrounds who hear the rhetoric of multiculturalism but see members of their cultural group represented only in custodial positions might question the school's commitment to equal opportunity.

Defending the goal of employing school personnel of varying cultural backgrounds is not difficult. First, having diverse school personnel shows students a commitment to include all people, regardless of cultural, ethnic, and racial backgrounds; second, such a policy shows a respect for the legal mandates that ensure equal opportunity for people of all cultures. Having the school staff reflect the diversity of the student body is undoubtedly a fundamental goal and a prerequisite to showing respect for cultural diversity and for equal opportunity under the law. Deliberate recruitment programs aimed at professionals of differing cultural backgrounds can contribute to employing faculty and staff more representative of the United States' diversity.

Responsive multicultural education programs include a commitment by professionals at all levels to multiculturalism and an acceptance of all learners regardless of diversity. While classroom teachers might have the most influence because of their proximity to many learners, administrators have a major responsibility for ensuring the implementation of multicultural procedures. Similarly, special educators and communication disorders specialists must project equal dedication, enthusiasm, and commitment to the overall school goals of acceptance and respect. The following sections examine the roles of administrators and special school personnel, show how classroom educators can work most effectively with these professionals for the benefit of learners, suggest a means of evaluating professional efforts, and suggest how all educators can encourage service learning.

The demographic shifts and often negative social relations in schools and communities have resulted in some educators considering the research and literature on practices in multiculturalism to promote cross-cultural understandings among students, faculty, and staff. Multicultural professional development can improve cultural relations and educational opportunities. Professional development should be a major component in any multicultural education effort, because some educators can have a negative impact on students' self-image, academic achievement, and overall school relations. One example of multicultural professional development is sensitivity training that sensitizes teachers to other cultures and also affirms diversity.

For multicultural professional development to be most successful, facilitators and participants must move beyond internationalizing multiculturalism and reducing issues of diversity to immigration, especially since the families of some of the most disenfranchised children have been in the United States for generations. Such a professional development effort should include the development of deeper understandings of what defines culture in order to be able to move beyond discussions of values, beliefs, group ethos, language, and practices and to understand how these elements are produced within the context of abuses of power.

Administrators

Roles in Multicultural Education

The administrator's primary responsibilities include ensuring that multicultural education programs are carefully and methodically planned, and that procedures are implemented to meet specific goals and objectives. Administrators require the ability and motivation to challenge and lead school personnel toward responsive efforts. Although their participation might not include extensive first-hand efforts with youngsters of differing cultural backgrounds, their commitment and leadership remain crucial to the success of the overall school program and to generating other professionals' enthusiasm toward multicultural efforts. Administrators' efforts and the zeal they bring to this task undoubtedly determine the degree of success of the multicultural education program.

A major role of administrators is to provide learners with faculty and staff that reflect the cultural diversity of the student body and the community. The recent push for increased teacher certification standards might challenge principals who seek teachers from as many cultural backgrounds as possible. Most states have initiated minimum competency tests for all beginning teachers. Some claim that these tests measure teaching effectiveness, but an unintended result is that the number of minority teachers is rapidly declining. Consequently, teacher diversity has been declining since 2012, which contributes to the majority white representation in the field of teaching. Public school teachers from marginalized groups make up just 20 percent of the teacher workforce while students of color constitute 50 percent of the population (Goodwin, 2023). Administrators should strive to support teachers in being effective in multicultural classrooms, treat them equitably, and equitably address the levels of teachers who represent underrepresented groups.

A second challenge to administrators is to provide appropriate leadership efforts for an all-school approach to multicultural education. Teachers often base their dedication or enthusiasm for educational programs on the administrator's apparent commitment. Administrators should demonstrate leadership toward specific objectives, convey a genuine respect for cultural diversity, and demonstrate a willingness to be involved. These efforts may be among the most important, because the administrator is a major influence in the overall effectiveness of the programs, and can lead faculty and staff members toward excellence in all professional endeavors.

A third challenge for principals is to deal affirmatively with the racial attitudes of their staffs. For many teachers and other staff members, joining the school ranks is their first sustained contact with members of another culture, and they may enter the situations not only lacking knowledge but fearful of confronting the issue of race. Such feelings can lead to an uneasiness that not only hurts work performance but can also do further harm to racial relations.

Another role in which administrators can offer significant contributions is communicating with and involving parents and community leaders. The administrator is in a position to assume the role of communicating the purposes of the multicultural education program to all parents.

Parents and other community members may erroneously view the multicultural education program as a "frill" or as a program that takes much-needed resources away from the curriculum or other school activities. Parents may be skeptical of programs that were not integral parts of their own educational experience and of which they might have little knowledge. Programs that are misunderstood will likely receive little support from the general public. Such a situation requires a skilled and competent administrator who is able to garner the support of parents and other community members.

Principals who work in effective schools demonstrate confidence in students' ability to learn, a commitment to ensure students' success, and an understanding of students and their communities. Principals should do the following:

1. Believe that all their students can learn and reflect this belief in their goals.
2. Be concerned with the least successful students in their schools, rather than be satisfied that some students are doing above-average work.
3. Broaden the base of recognized achievement by acknowledging nontraditional accomplishments, particularly with minority students.
4. Acknowledge students who have exceptionally good attendance or punctuality records.

Principals must believe that all students can learn, have confidence in their students, involve parents in their children's education, reflect on the impact of the reform movement, and push for appropriate role models for all learners.

As student demographic backgrounds become more diverse in K–12 schools, administrators should promote and foster positive attitudes, multicultural efficacy, and social justice advocacy to better serve them. According to Jones (2023), principals who possess multicultural efficacy are more likely to be successful in mitigating prejudice toward diverse groups.

From the Perspective of Classroom Teachers: Working with Administrators

Classroom educators need administrators' attention and support. Teachers and administrators must not work in isolation and risk the possibility that they will move toward different goals. Administrative support of teachers is imperative.

POINTS TO PONDER 12.1

Seeking Information from Principals

Ask one or more principals or assistant principals to describe their multicultural education programs and their specific roles in the program. Specifically, seek information on how they have led school efforts to ensure that their school effectively reflects U.S. diversity. Ask also about school philosophy, library materials, efforts to celebrate cultural diversity, programs for students whose English proficiency is limited, and cultural diversity among their faculty and staffs.

What, then, can educators do as they work with, and seek assistance from, administrators? Classroom educators who have direct contact with learners of various cultural backgrounds are in the best position to determine learner needs and convey these needs to administrators.

Educators, keeping in mind the many demands placed on administrators, must make their concerns known and insist on changes. Presenting the problem or concern is the first step. Working with the principal (suggesting, providing input, and offering recommendations) is the second step. Classroom educators, who have a better perspective on problems than administrators, must take responsibility for explaining the problems in accurate and objective terms. Once a problem has been explained and classified, the classroom educator's responsibility is to follow through on appropriate plans and strategies.

Evaluation of Administrators' Efforts and Commitment

Administrators' effort and commitment to multicultural education should be evaluated, just as educators' teaching effectiveness and learners' academic achievement are evaluated. The Evaluation Checklist provides examples of items to assess in determining administrators' effectiveness.

Evaluation Checklist
1. The principal demonstrates and models respect for all forms of diversity among students and their parents and families.
2. The principal seeks to employ faculty and staff of as many different cultures as possible.
3. The principal seeks to provide financial resources and other less tangible forms of support for the multicultural education program.

4. The principal works cooperatively with the school faculty and staff to provide effective multicultural educational experiences.
5. The principal supports a total-school program (curriculum, instruction, and environment), rather than the occasional teaching-unit approach.
6. The principal accepts responsibility for acting as a catalyst and for providing significant leadership for the multicultural education program.
7. The principal arranges for convenient sessions for parents and families of differing cultural backgrounds to voice concerns and suggestions.
8. The principal recognizes cultural differences among people as traits to be valued rather than to be eliminated or remediated.
9. The principal evaluates the efforts of faculty and staff and offers constructive criticism and positive suggestions in areas needing improvement.
10. The principal coordinates efforts of faculty and staff members toward a common goal of recognizing and building on cultural differences.

Special Educators

Roles in Multicultural Education

Special-education personnel can play significant roles in the multicultural education program. Tasks confronting them include the cultural considerations surrounding testing and assessment, the legal aspects of educating children with disabilities, the psychosocial variables affecting the teaching and learning process, and the effective coordination of efforts between special-education and regular classroom teachers.

Students of culturally different backgrounds are overrepresented in special-education classes. In the past, children who came from poor families or from homes where English was the second language or not spoken at all often ended up in special-needs classes. The role of special-education teachers includes responding to the increasing cultural diversity among learners by using culturally appropriate assessment devices and making placement decisions that reflect an understanding of cultural differences.

Testing and Assessment

Special-education teachers, like all educators, should exercise extreme caution when labeling learners of different cultural backgrounds. They must carefully distinguish between *disability* and *difference*. They must not make placement decisions based on faulty evidence or culturally biased assessment instruments.

Teachers should not consider learners intellectually inferior because of poor performance on standardized tests. Scores on standardized tests too often influence teachers' expectations of learners' academic performance in the classroom. Teachers must maintain high expectations for all learners, regardless of cultural background. A standardized test score can provide an indication of a student's degree of assimilation but provide little evidence of an individual's intelligence (Gollnick & Chinn, 2006).

In developing tests and in using the results of standardized tests, special-education teachers and all educators should recognize the inherent cultural bias that favors students of the majority culture. In fact, few tests have been developed from the perspective of a culturally diverse group. One such test is the Black Intelligence Test of Cultural Homogeneity (BITCH), which is based on urban African American culture and includes language and terms familiar to this culture. Although African Americans consistently score higher on this test than do members of the majority culture, it is rarely used to determine intelligence of individuals or groups (Gollnick & Chinn, 2006).

In order to incorporate content that resonates with the cultural background, identity, and life experiences of all individuals, schools should use culturally responsive assessments (CRAs) that ensure equity for test-takers from marginalized groups (Sinharay & Johnson, 2024). One example of a CRA is the Kaiapuni Assessment of Education Outcomes (KAEO), which has been available since 2016 for test-takers enrolled in Hawaiian language immersion programs in Hawaii, USA. Using CRAs can address biases in assessment tools (Khasawneh & Khasawneh, 2023) and accommodate personal characteristics, including cultural identity, to provide a more accurate reflection of what students from diverse backgrounds know and are capable of.

Special-education teachers should be constantly aware of the cultural biases among tests and remind themselves not to rely on test scores as the only indication of students' intelligence. Like all educators, special-education teachers should employ a number of culturally appropriate assessments and other sources of information to avoid basing placement decisions and judgments of intelligence on faulty data.

Legal Perspectives

Special-education teachers must understand the increasingly prominent role of the federal government in special education. The government has done more in recent years to promote the education rights of learners with disabilities than in the entire history of the nation. During the twenty-first century, legislation has been notable for an affirmation of the education rights of students with disabilities through mandates that states implement curriculum standards and an assessment-based accountability system. Notable education policies include the Individuals with Disabilities Education Improvement Act (IDEIA), which led to the 2004 reauthorization of IDEA, and the No Child Left Behind Act (NCLB) of 2001 which led to the reauthorization of the Elementary and Secondary Education Act (ESSA) of 2015. These policies address the problems of students who have disabilities as well as those who have limited proficiency in English. It also has provisions for nondiscriminatory assessment, parental involvement, and expanded instructional services.

From the teacher's perspective, the Education for All Handicapped Students Act of 1975 (PL 94–142) was a landmark law for students with disabilities in general, and for culturally and linguistically different populations in particular. Among the most important provisions of PL 94–142 are those addressing the right to due process, protection against discriminatory testing during assessment, placement in the least restrictive education environment, and individualized education programs. In essence, PL 94–142 addresses the basic rights and equal protection issues with respect to the evaluation, identification, and placement of learners with disabilities. Under this law, assessment should serve to identify learners with disabilities and to guide instructional planning based on established educational goals.

Litigation, as well as PL 94–142, has also dramatically affected the educational system. Court cases have examined the legality of assessment, classification, and placement of low-achieving children and the right of learners who are severely disabled to a free and public education. These cases and other similar litigation have led to the establishment of the following legal standards:

1. Assessment of intellectual capabilities using measures in English is inappropriate for students with limited English proficiency.
2. Identification of children as mildly mentally retarded requires consideration of factors such as adaptive behavior, sociocultural group, and motivational systems, in addition to measures of intelligence.
3. The degree to which culturally different groups have been overrepresented in special-education classes for the educably mentally retarded (EMR) is sufficient to constitute bias. Causes of the overrepresentation have included (a) failure to consider linguistic and cultural factors; (b) failure to identify appropriately and to determine the eligibility of disabled students, and failure to provide proper procedures and special services; and (c) excessive reliance on IQ test results as placement criteria.

4. Factors such as item bias on measure of IQ and discriminatory instruments alone do not suffice to account for misplacements and disproportionate representation of learners from culturally different groups in special-education classes.

In summary, from a classroom educator's perspective, the placement procedures that special-education teachers employ must be in accordance with PL 94–142 and the litigation addressing the rights of the disabled. Classroom teachers are responsible for helping special educators understand all learners and the role of psychocultural factors in learning and assessment.

From the Perspective of Classroom Teachers: Working with Special Educators

From the perspective of the classroom educator, the special-education teacher should be considered a major instructional resource. Although teacher accreditation requirements mandate that all teachers have at least a basic knowledge of disabilities, most regular classroom teachers lack expertise in the techniques of working with children who have disabilities, especially those from culturally diverse backgrounds. When student needs can be addressed in the regular classroom, classroom educators should seek help from special-education teachers. Similarly, regular educators should rely on qualified special-education teachers to handle students who, by law, cannot benefit from education in a regular classroom setting.

Special-education teachers must respond to the classroom educator's request to assess students in need and provide culturally appropriate testing and assessment. They work with regular classroom teachers to provide appropriate educational experiences for all students with disabilities (regardless of cultural background). They must understand the effects of cultural factors on the teaching and learning process. The classroom teacher should perceive special-education personnel as valuable resources whose training and expertise can contribute to the education of nearly any exceptional (or so-called normal) learner.

Classroom educators must follow appropriate procedures for referring students to special-education teachers. They must help special-education teachers understand learners' cultural diversity and provide follow-up as the special-education teacher recommends. It is important that regular classroom teachers view special-education teachers as partners and not as people on whom to "dump" unwanted students. Special-education teachers can provide educational assistance to learners who have disabilities as well as those who do not. In many cases, the organization of the school and the legalities of the referral process require regular classroom teachers to take the initial steps.

Evaluation of Special Educators' Efforts and Commitment

The following checklist provides special educators with a means of self-evaluation to determine strengths, weaknesses, and overall commitment to promoting cultural diversity. Ask yourself each question and answer it in terms of your responsibilities as a special-education teacher.

Self-Evaluation Checklist for Special Educators

1. Do I value and respect cultural diversity in all forms and degrees?
2. Do I recognize differences between disabilities and cultural diversity, or do I perceive differences as liabilities or deficiencies in need of remediation?
3. Do I coordinate the efforts of administrators, faculty, and staff to provide the least restrictive environment for all disabled learners?
4. Do I support a racially and culturally diverse faculty and staff for all youngsters with disabilities?
5. Do I insist that screening and placement procedures recognize cultural diversity and that such procedures follow legal mandates and guidelines for special education?
6. Do I work with parents and families on a regular basis, help them understand programs for learners with disabilities, and make referrals to appropriate social service agencies?
7. Do I use testing and assessment instruments with the least racial, cultural, and social-class bias?
8. Do I provide opportunities for youngsters with disabilities to be mainstreamed or integrated with nondisabled learners of all cultural backgrounds whenever possible?
9. Do I plan learning experiences that recognize differences in language and dialect?
10. Do I support community recognition and efforts to provide appropriate educational experiences for learners with disabilities from both majority and minority cultural backgrounds?

Librarians/Media Specialists

Roles in Multicultural Education

The librarian/media specialist in a multicultural setting must understand the cultural diversity of his or her school and build a library and media collection that show positive portrayals of all cultural groups. Librarians and media specialists also work with classroom educators in positive, constructive ways that demonstrate a respect for and commitment to providing appropriate multicultural education experiences.

Selecting Culturally Appropriate Print and Nonprint Media

School librarians and media specialists, like all educators, are challenged to meet the needs of an increasingly diverse student population. Chapter 9 emphasized the importance of positive portrayals of children and adolescents from varying cultural backgrounds, and the necessity of addressing problems of sexism, racism, stereotyping, and outright omissions. Libraries are responsible for ensuring that books, magazines, audiovisual materials, computer software, and all library and media materials positively and realistically represent characters of many cultural backgrounds with whom learners can relate.

One of the better and more pragmatic solutions to librarians' and media specialists' and teachers' problems has been offered by the Council on Interracial Books for Children, which regularly evaluates children's materials, trade books, textbooks, and other educational resources. With increasing technological advances and rising globalization and immigration, it is essential that multiculturalism is well and appropriately represented in print, video, and media in schools to promote diversity and advocacy (Rhodes, 2023; Tyler-Wood et al., 2023).

Coordinating Efforts with Classroom Teachers

Like other professionals working in elementary and secondary schools, librarians and media specialists and classroom educators must work together for the welfare of children and adolescents. Librarians/media specialists can be a valuable resource for regular classroom teachers. They can supplement learning experiences or provide a children's literature-based approach to instruction. Some classroom teachers received their education training before accrediting associations required experiences in multicultural education. For these teachers especially, librarians and media specialists can suggest culturally appropriate books for all children. Teachers can build an empathetic learning environment by assigning and reading books in classrooms that serve as "mirrors, windows, and doors" (Hayes & Francis, 2023) so students can resonate with and reflect their own culture and identity.

From the Perspective of Classroom Teachers: Working with Librarians/Media Specialists

The professional paths of classroom educators and school librarians/media specialists should probably cross more than they do. Teachers bring or allow learners to visit the library during a specified time, during which the librarian/media specialist might or might not have an activity planned. Teachers sometimes remain with students during the library period and make suggestions or encourage students' interest in books and reading. In other situations, teachers leave the students and work elsewhere.

From the perspective of classroom educators, the librarian/media specialist should be considered a prime resource professional. He or she can teach learners about the library, and about books and magazines that provide positive cultural images. Teachers and librarians/media specialists must work together.

Librarians' and media specialists' roles in supporting the multicultural education program include stocking the library and media center with books, magazines, and other materials that accurately portray children and adolescents from various cultural groups; assisting classroom educators to choose and use these books; ensuring that library collections have works by non-white authors and illustrators; ensuring that library holdings and materials are accessible to all students, regardless of social class and cultural background; and assisting students as they search for reading materials.

The classroom educator's responsibilities include working with the librarian/media specialist (suggesting acquisitions and completing book request forms) to secure a multicultural library; encouraging students of all cultures to read books that provide accurate portrayals of learners from different cultural backgrounds; encouraging learners to read books by qualified authors; and working with the librarian/media specialist to plan activities that feature well-written reading materials.

Evaluation of Librarians'/Media Specialists' Efforts and Commitment

The following checklist provides self-evaluation questions that librarians and media specialists can use to rate their own effectiveness.

Self-Evaluation for Librarians/Media Specialists

1. Do I acquire a collection of print and nonprint media that provides positive and accurate examples of children and adolescents from various cultural groups?
2. Do I have an overall library program that contributes to the school's multicultural education program?
3. Do I work with teachers and other educators to plan appropriate multicultural experiences for all learners?
4. Do I have a system that makes library materials accessible to all learners, regardless of cultural or socioeconomic background?

5. Do I plan developmentally and culturally appropriate teaching and learning activities for learners of all cultural groups?
6. Does the library have multicultural materials that are appropriate for varying reading, interest, and developmental levels?
7. Have I established and approved criteria for evaluating the appropriateness (cultural, gender, socioeconomic, etc.) of print and nonprint media?
8. Do I seek input and suggestions for library purchases from teachers, organizations promoting cultural diversity, and interested parents?
9. Have I acquired a professional library of print and nonprint materials for educators who want to improve their professional knowledge of cultural diversity?

Self-Evaluation for Teacher Candidates

Teacher candidates can also use the self-checklist recommended by Howlett and Young (2019). This tool helps them to reflect on their perspectives continuously and to critique children's literature for bias and its alignment with multicultural principles.

1. Do I develop multicultural perspectives?
2. Do I develop cultural consciousness?
3. Do I increase intercultural competence?
4. Do I combat racism, prejudice and discrimination?
5. Do I develop awareness of the state of the planet and global dynamics?
6. Do I develop social action skills?
7. Do I evaluate the books in my library based on these questions?
   a. Does the book avoid only presenting one type of thinking [bias]?
   b. Does the book avoid discrimination? Will children be able to recognize the characters in the text and illustrations as belonging to the intended race and not mistake them for white?
   c. Are all cultural groups meaningful additions to the book [tokenism]? Do non-white characters solve their problems without intervention by whites?
   d. Does the book avoid unfairly negative perceptions and/or viewpoints [prejudice]?
   e. Does the book avoid racism [a negative attitude toward or treatment of people based solely on their race]?
   f. Does the book treat all genders as equals [sexism]? Does the book reflect an awareness of the changed status of females?

g. Is the book absent of stereotypes? Are the illustrations authentic and non-stereotypical? Is the focus on the everyday life of the culture group?

h. Does the book portray physical diversity?

i. Are social issues and problems depicted frankly, accurately, and without oversimplification?

j. Does the author accurately describe contemporary settings? Is the focus on routine aspects of life [foods, fashions, festivals]?

k. Are the factual and historical details accurate? Does the book rectify historical distortions or omissions?

l. Does the book avoid the use of inappropriate language? Does dialect have a legitimate purpose, and does it ring true?

m. Are the authors or illustrators from the same cultural group as the characters portrayed in the text?

Counselors

Roles in Multicultural Education

The role of school counselors includes understanding culturally different children and adolescents, providing culturally responsive counseling, understanding testing and assessment issues, and working with classroom teachers for the welfare of all learners.

Understanding and Counseling

Cultural, intracultural, ethnic, and racial differences are important considerations in the counseling of children and adolescents in multicultural situations. Learners are not a homogeneous population. They differ widely as individuals, and particularly as pertains to culture, gender, generation, and socioeconomic status.

Children are basically now oriented and view their world, their cultures, their peers, their language, and their morality from a child's perspective. Adolescents function developmentally in a stage between childhood and adulthood and are developing self-concepts and cultural identities that will affect their entire adult lives.

American Indians

Counseling and mental health services are underutilized by Native Americans. It is critical for counselors to have a deep understanding of Native Indian cultural competence as public information of their culture is often biased and limited (Giordano et al., 2020). The dismal situations of many

American Indian children suggests that guidance and counseling are the best vehicles for helping these children. Herring's (1989) suggestions include the following:

1. Counseling intervention should be highly individualized.
2. Assessment should have minimal socioeconomic or cultural bias.
3. Counselors should recognize learning styles and life purposes.
4. The child's culture must not be devalued.
5. Methodologies should place high value on self-worth.
6. The school counselor should help the school staff become sensitive to the needs of American Indians.

African Americans

School counselors should consider African American learners' individual heritages and special needs, rather than assume too much cultural homogeneity. Specifically, school counselors can organize self-awareness groups that emphasize self-appreciation through cultural heritage; explore the nature and importance of positive interpersonal relationships; conduct social behavior guidance groups; and offer motivation sessions and guidance workshops in areas such as academic planning, study skills, and time management.

Arab Americans

Counseling Arab Americans might be a little more intimidating, since more has been written on counseling other cultural groups. Still, counselors can look at the challenges these students face and implement counseling strategies that are culturally appropriate for the Arab culture. Suggestions for counselors include the following:

1. Realize that Arab culture has been basically ignored in the school system, and it deserves to have culturally appropriate counseling strategies.
2. Develop a genuine awareness of the Arab culture and acknowledge, rather than devalue the student's culture.
3. Remember that children's and adolescents' perceptions of situations and events might differ from the perspectives of youths of other cultures.
4. Avoid making assumptions about religious beliefs; if in doubt, ask the student about his or her religious beliefs, traditions, and customs.
5. Recognize the importance of the family, both immediate and extended, and respect it being patriarchal and hierarchical with regard to age and sex.

6. Provide counseling strategies that promote self-esteem and cultural identities.
7. Consider the students' generational status and the accompanying acculturation that might have occurred and how these might affect counseling intervention.

Asian Americans

Suggestions for counseling Asian Americans include the following:

1. Determine individual strengths and weaknesses, and assess cultural backgrounds.
2. Understand each learner's degree of acculturation.
3. Understand Asian Americans' difficulty in exhibiting openness. In a culture that regards restraint as a sign of emotional maturity, admitting problems is thought to reflect badly on the entire family.
4. Understand that overly confrontational, emotional, and tense approaches may cause additional problems and turmoil for Asian American learners.
5. Learn about individuals and their respective cultures; ask about the culture, accept the learner's world, develop cultural and ethnic sensitivity and consciousness, and avoid stereotyping.

Hispanic Americans

For the most effective multicultural intervention, counseling suggestions include the following:

1. Use active counseling approaches that are concrete, specific, and focus on the student's behalf.
2. Develop an awareness of the individual's culture.
3. Use approaches that take the client's frame of reference as a vehicle for growth.
4. Examine prejudices and attitudes toward Hispanic Americans.
5. Make home visits if possible, and make reference to the family during sessions.
6. Call students by their correct names. In Puerto Rico and elsewhere, people have two last names: The first is that of the family, and the second is that of the mother's family. Using the wrong name is an insult and may raise identity questions.
7. Accept the role of expert, but work to relinquish the role of authority. Clients must accept responsibility for their own lives.

European Americans

Counselors working with European Americans should consider the tremendous diversity among individuals as well as individual cultures. European Americans come from many different geographic regions and cultural backgrounds. For example, children and adolescents with Hungarian backgrounds differ significantly from those with Greek backgrounds. Likewise, Polish people differ from Italians. Counselors should use extreme caution when forming decisions about cultural backgrounds, religious beliefs, and other personal characteristics. Suggestions for counseling European Americans include the following:

1. Understand some cultures' (such as that of Italians) allegiance and commitment to family members and to the overall welfare of the family.
2. Understand the language problems of some children and adolescents, and how these problems affect school work, interpersonal relationships, and willingness to become active participants in U.S. society.
3. Understand cultural traditions that, in some cases, have been taught and emphasized for many generations, and understand how these cultural traditions might conflict with U.S. values and expectations.
4. Understand that considerable effort might be necessary to build trust in the counseling relationship.
5. Understand such differences as social class and generational status (e.g. the differences in perspectives of a first- and a third-generation child or adolescent) and the effects of these differences on counseling sessions.

Testing and Assessment

The counselor's goal in assessment is to minimize ethnocentrism and to maximize culturally appropriate information. Assessment in counseling and psychotherapy includes interviewing, observing, and testing, as well as analyzing documents. To what extent does cultural diversity affect assessment? Will a characteristic indigenous to a specific culture be mistakenly perceived and assessed using European American middle-class standards?

Two important issues in multicultural assessment include whether psychological constructs or concepts are universally valid and how to counter the effects of diagnosing and placing false labels. Other questions related to multicultural assessment are as follows:

1. What level and type of assessment are indicated?

2. Which tests are most useful and why?
3. What are the ethical and legal responsibilities associated with multicultural assessment?

Are multicultural groups being assessed with instruments actually designed for middle-class white clients? Without appropriate assessment strategies, counseling professionals are unable to diagnose problems, to develop appropriate goals, and to assess the outcomes of intervention. Specific assessment issues include initial client assessment, clinical judgment, standardized and nonstandardized assessment, and the outcome of counseling evaluation.

From the Perspective of Classroom Teachers: Working with Counselors

Counselors may work with individuals, small groups, and large classes. The classroom educator may initiate the first contact between a school counselor and a troubled student.

Classroom teachers, who have daily contact with learners, may be the first professionals to detect a potential problem. Individual teachers are in a prime position either to ask the counselor for direct assistance or to refer students with problems to the counselor. It is wise for teachers and counselors to determine the best means of referring students, of coordinating and scheduling large-group counseling, and of determining the correct needs of learners from diverse cultural backgrounds.

Counselors may provide several forms of assistance to classroom teachers and their students. Considering the many demands on the counselor's time and expertise, however, the teacher may have to initiate contact or inform the counselor of special areas of concern. Generally speaking, counselors can do the following:

1. Determine and facilitate joint efforts of administrators and other educators to improve an adolescent's self-concept and cultural identity.
2. Provide assistance in suggesting culturally appropriate instruments and in interpreting test scores of learners of culturally different backgrounds.
3. Work with families of all cultural backgrounds (both immediate and extended) in parent-education endeavors.
4. Offer parents meaningful roles in school governance, and offer families opportunities to support the teaching and learning process at home and at school.
5. Provide individual and small-group counseling in areas of concern to all learners, such as peer acceptance and approval.

6. Provide large-group counseling sessions in areas such as involvement meetings, rules meetings, and values-clarification meetings.
7. Suggest culturally relevant materials to help all children and adolescents better understand each other's cultures.
8. Work with older students in career planning, and suggest appropriate subjects needed to pursue career plans.
9. Help learners deal with concern over body development, the desire for social acceptance, and the conflicts between adult expectations and peer expectations of culturally appropriate behaviors.
10. Design special programs for at-risk learners who are from culturally different backgrounds.

Classroom educators should view their roles and those of counselors as complementary. Because classroom educators have the most daily contact with learners from various cultural backgrounds, they are usually in the best position to detect learners with problems, make referrals, and to follow up on counselors' efforts. Likewise, the classroom teacher and the counselor should always know each other's purposes and strategies and, whenever possible, provide joint efforts for the benefit of the learners.

Evaluation of Counselors' Efforts and Commitment

As with all professionals, the counselor's efforts and commitment to promoting cultural diversity and to working with classroom educators should be evaluated periodically. The following checklist can serve as a means of self-evaluation.

Self-Evaluation for Counselors

1. Do I recognize that all children and adolescents differ in their cultural background, perspectives, traditions, and worldviews?
2. Do I plan culturally appropriate counseling strategies that reflect learners' cultural backgrounds?
3. Do I recognize that traditional tests and assessment devices may not measure the abilities and talents of all learners because of their differing cultural backgrounds?
4. Do I recognize that families differ according to cultural backgrounds (e.g. in sex roles, expectations, and child-rearing techniques)?
5. Do I work with classroom educators for the overall welfare of learners from all cultural backgrounds?
6. Do I suggest special service agencies and resources that respond to the needs of learners and their families in all cultures?

7. Do I recognize the dangers of racial bias and cultural stereotypes and work to overcome these limitations?
8. Do I recognize the richness that cultural diversity adds to both elementary and secondary schools?
9. Do I recognize the need for all students to experience appropriate multicultural education experiences?
10. Do I recognize the need to use resources (e.g. films and other materials) that portray positive images of children's and adolescents' cultural backgrounds?

Communication Disorders Specialists

Several titles designate the professional working with speech-disabled learners, including *speech-language clinician, speech pathologist, speech correctionist, speech clinician,* and *speech therapist,* but the author prefers *communication disorders specialist* because the term is sufficiently broad in nature to include communication problems of children and adolescents from various cultural groups. The communication disorders specialist who works in multicultural settings has a broad knowledge of communication and understands unique communication situations, such as dialects, bilingualism, and teaching of English as a second language, as well as the various assessment challenges and the differences between home and school language.

Roles in Multicultural Education

Because communication is such a vital human aspect to learners of all cultural and ethnic backgrounds, communication disorders specialists play an important role in helping educators distinguish between disorders and differences. They can also help learners who are experiencing differences with communication for any reason. All communication disorders specialists need to become sensitive to cultural diversity and to develop cross-cultural communication competencies as they work with children classified as non-English proficient (NEP) and as having limited English proficiency (LEP).

A primary role of the communication disorders specialist is to distinguish between communications disorders and communication variations, and to convey to classroom educators the differences between the two. Communications disorders include speech disorders (impairment of voice, articulation, or fluency) and language disorders (the impairment or deviant development of comprehension of a spoken or written symbol system).

Communication disorders specialists in multicultural situations must distinguish between *disorders* and *variations.* Learners who use a particular dialect or regional accent should not be labeled as having a disorder in need of elimination.

A second, closely related role of the communication disorders specialist is to understand and to help classroom educators to understand the difference between school language and home language. A learner may appear so quiet and withdrawn that the educator wonders if the child or adolescent has physical or emotional problems. The same child or adolescent at home and in the community shows considerable verbal proficiency.

When substantial differences exist between conversational language use in the home and official use in the classroom, children and adolescents often appear to have low verbal ability. Despite being verbal in nonschool settings, these learners may talk very little in the classroom and, even then, use only simple words and sentences. In such a situation, the communication disorders specialist might have to convince the classroom educator that the child or adolescent is not speech disabled and is not in need of remediation or therapy.

Another goal of the communication disorders specialist is to understand dialect differences among learners from differing cultural backgrounds as well as learners of the majority culture. Understanding and responding appropriately to the dialect of the learner within a classroom can be a complex and sensitive issue.

First, the specialist and teacher should recognize that dialects are not communicative disorders and should not treat them as such. The teacher should note, however, that a dialect and a communications disorder can coexist. If, for example, a learner with a Spanish or African American dialect also has defective articulation or stutters, the classroom educator should refer the learner to the communication disorders specialist.

Teachers and communication disorders specialists should learn to distinguish accurately between linguistic diversity and disorders. Dialects should not be considered less than but merely different from that which is recognized as standard English. A teacher is in a strategic position to promote understanding and acceptance of a child who has a dialectal difference.

From the Perspective of Classroom Teachers: Working with Communication Disorders Specialists

The classroom educator should view the communication disorders specialist as a valuable resource person with a wide range of expertise. Working in a complementary fashion for the welfare of learners, the communication disorders specialist and the classroom educator can determine whether communication problems exist that need to be remediated or whether students are simply manifesting variations that should be accepted and appreciated.

Considerable interaction should occur between classroom educators and communication disorders specialists. First, the communication disorders specialist and the teacher need to consult with each other about their goals for a learner and how they expect to accomplish these goals. They should evaluate what success they achieve. Such interaction can be formal or informal, or the communication disorders specialist can provide the teacher with copies of written therapy progress reports sent home to parents.

Second, the classroom teacher has more contact with parents and spends more school hours with learners, who may talk about their feelings, wants, and life at home. Some information that a teacher receives from learners or their parents may be important to the communication disorders specialist, and the teacher should pass it on.

Third, the teacher is in an ideal position to provide the communication disorders specialist with information about a learner's speech and language function in the classroom and in informal situations, such as in the hallway or lunchroom or on the playground. The teacher may also be able to provide reminders to the child during the habit-forming stages of therapy, when the child can best produce the targeted speech behaviors but still must make them a habit in all communicative situations. Fourth, the communication disorders specialist requires the teacher's input on referrals and in establishing whether there is an adverse effect on education because of a communicative problem.

The communication disorders specialist's responsibilities include appropriate assessment, therapy, scheduling, and consultation with teachers and parents. Other responsibilities in multicultural situations include understanding the communication problems of children and adolescents, conveying to teachers an assessment of disorders and variations, and providing a climate of understanding and acceptance for all learners.

The classroom teacher plays a major role in the lives of learners by serving as an important role model and a major force in shaping ideas, and has an influence on emotional development. The classroom educator's responsibilities include being a good speech model; creating a classroom atmosphere conducive to communication; accepting learners, and encouraging classmates to accept learners with communications problems; consulting with the communication disorders specialist; detecting possible communications disorders and making referrals; reinforcing the goals of the communication disorders specialist; and helping the learner catch up on what he or she missed while at therapy. Another responsibility is fully participating when a decision has been made to place the child in a NEP or LEP program.

Evaluation of Communication Disorders Specialists' Efforts and Commitment

The following self-evaluation checklist enables communication disorders specialists to evaluate their efforts and commitment to multicultural education.

Self-Evaluation Checklist for Communication Disorders Specialists

1. Do I recognize and accept all learners, regardless of cultural, ethnic, or social class backgrounds?
2. Do I recognize how the increasing cultural diversity in U.S. school systems affects the roles and responsibilities of the speech professional?
3. Do I distinguish between communicative disorders and communicative variations?
4. Do I understand dialects as differences and not as disorders?
5. Do I plan appropriate communication for NEP or LEP students and seek the appropriate professionals to help these students?
6. Do I work with professionals responsible for bilingual students and assist as needed?
7. Do I work with classroom teachers and other school personnel in joint efforts to help children and adolescents of differing cultural backgrounds with communications disorders?
8. Do I understand the various speech and language disorders, and am I able to assist learners from differing cultural backgrounds who are having communications problems?

Service Learning

Administrators, special school personnel, and classroom teachers should encourage students to become involved with multicultural communities, whether in direct learning or service opportunities. Not only does service learning address children's and adolescents' feelings of altruism and idealism, but it also reinforces the content that they learn in school and helps them develop the skills to be productive citizens in a multicultural society. In essence, students become involved in activities related to the needs of the community while they are advancing academic goals and acquiring essential skills in real-life contexts. Students' participation in community engagement can positively impact their academic work, self-esteem, and sense of belonging, especially for historically marginalized students. Programs such as co-curricular service-learning and community-based internships provide mentorship and support which are crucial in developing perseverance, student motivation, and commitment to academic work (Duarte et al., 2023). Astonishingly, students attest that their learning through service-learning programs is profound through application of curricular content, and leaves a lasting impression on their lives post-graduation (Jerabek, 2023). Moreover, students encounter meaningful experiences, prompting them to reflect on themselves and embrace unfamiliar information and cultures that can effectively contribute to student learning and growth. Thus, educators and administrators need to create more up-to-date service learning opportunities both inside and outside the classroom and cultivate student social responsibility.

The idea behind service learning is not just to involve students in multicultural communities (which in and of itself is also a worthwhile idea) but also to *reinforce* or *refine* actual learning objectives from the classroom. Students can tutor younger children or adults, organize a clean-up effort for environmental protection, or help preserve an endangered wildlife area. Rather than have a one-size-fits-all program, each school needs to consider its own individual student population and community to see how community learning projects can be tied into instructional objectives and the multicultural education program.

Seeking the Special Educator's Help

Mrs. Heath, a tenth-grade Social Studies teacher, has noticed that four of the five American Indian students in her class seem uninterested. She wonders whether the students are really unmotivated, whether they have reading problems or attention deficits, or whether the topics being studied simply are uninteresting to them. Fully realizing the consequences of making judgments based on erroneous beliefs, Mrs. Heath takes her concern to the special-education teacher in the school.

Mrs. Blackmon listens carefully to Mrs. Heath's concerns. Mrs. Blackmon first decides to test the students' reading abilities to determine their reading vocabulary and comprehension skills. Second, she explains to Mrs. Heath that American Indians often listen without looking a person in the eye and that looking interested might be more of a white perspective, one that might not cross cultural boundaries.

Mrs. Blackmon feels that although the students' reading abilities are below grade level, they basically can read. She offers several suggestions to help Mrs. Heath and the students. First, she will work with the students two or three times a week to improve their reading comprehension. Second, she will help Mrs. Heath to provide some culturally relevant materials. Third, she will help Mrs. Heath to develop a better understanding of American Indian learners.

Without labeling or making unjustified placements, both teachers realize the importance of working as a team to help the American Indian learners. Each recognizes that working separately will not result in the most effective educational experiences for the learners. A coordinated effort, with each teacher reinforcing and building on the efforts of the other, will best address the needs of the American Indian learners.

1. In your school experiences, have you noticed that some students seem uninterested or unmotivated? What specific characteristics or behaviors led you to believe they were uninterested? Could these have been attributed to cultural differences? Assuming they were interested (but did not show it), how would their behaviors or characteristics affect *your* teaching behaviors or attitudes toward their learning?
2. While these two teachers seemed to have an effective collaboration, how else could they have worked together to benefit all learners and, in this case, American Indians?
3. What culturally relevant materials or teaching methods can you suggest that might be appropriate for American Indians?

Summing Up

Educators who are working toward the involvement of the entire school professional staff in the multicultural education program should:

1. Encourage all administrators and special school personnel to offer whole-hearted commitment and support to the multicultural education program. They should not perceive the effort as someone else's responsibility.
2. Convey to administrators, special-education teachers, counselors, librarians/media specialists, and the communication disorders specialist the importance of a total-school effort in the multicultural education program.
3. Emphasize the necessity for cultural diversity among the administration, faculty, and special school personnel that reflects the composition of the school and community.
4. Encourage administrators, special-education teachers, librarians/media specialists, counselors, and communication disorders specialists to recognize and respond appropriately to their unique roles in the multicultural education program.

5. Encourage administrators and special school personnel to work with regular classroom educators.

6. Convey the importance of evaluating all professionals (by self, peer, or administrator) for the purpose of learning ways to contribute to the overall multicultural program.

Suggested Learning Activities

1. Visit an elementary or secondary school to learn how administrators and special school personnel contribute to the multicultural education program. Are roles clearly defined, or are they assumed, whereby professionals simply do whatever appears to benefit the learner? How might administrators and special school personnel better address the needs of learners of differing cultural backgrounds?

2. Some professionals and the general public feel that learners of minority cultures are overrepresented in special-education classes. Meet with a special-education teacher to discuss the concern of overrepresentation. What legal mandates and placement procedures protect minorities from being placed in special-education classes simply for being different from mainstream learners?

3. Propose practical strategies that administrators, counsellors, librarians/media specialists, or special school personnel can implement to restore and maintain a sense of dignity of students from diverse backgrounds (genders, social classes, ethnicity, and culture).

Suggestions for Collaborative Efforts

Form groups of three or four that, if possible, represent the United States' cultural and gender diversity. Working collaboratively, focus your group's attention toward the following efforts:

1. Prepare an evaluation scale that determines how print and nonprint media portray culturally different children and adolescents. Pinpoint such factors as objectivity, accuracy, stereotyping, gender values, and actual people from the various cultural groups (and what they are doing) and their contributions to an increasingly multicultural

world. With the help of a librarian/media specialist, prepare a list of print and nonprint materials that provide an honest portrayal of all people, regardless of cultural background.

2. Brainstorm in your group to list special ways that administrators and special school personnel can contribute to multicultural education programs. How does your group think these professionals can contribute to or complement classroom teachers' efforts? What books or other materials can your group suggest to help each of these professionals?

3. How might educators and librarians/media specialists coordinate efforts to most effectively serve children and adolescents of various cultural backgrounds? Consider books, poems, speakers, films, plays, skits, computer software, and occasions to celebrate diversity.

Expanding Your Horizons

Additional Books and Journals

Buzzai, C., Muscarà, M., Romano, A., Passanisi, A., & Pace, U. (2023). The relationship between socio-cognitive skills and ethnic prejudice in pre-service special education teachers. *International Journal of Inclusive Education*, 1–16. www.tandfonline.com/doi/abs/10.1080/08856257.2022.2107679

The study found that teachers' confidence with inclusive practices had a direct impact on their adoption of motivating teaching styles. In addition, their attitudes toward multiculturalism were directly related to whether their teaching styles were motivating or demotivating. These findings illustrate the significance of educators' attitudes toward multicultural education and their belief in their ability to promote inclusivity in the classroom as key factors shaping teaching approaches in diverse settings with practical implications for schools.

Glover, T. A., Reddy, L. A., & Crouse, K. (2023). Instructional coaching actions that predict teacher classroom practices and student achievement. *Journal of School Psychology, 96*, 1–11. https://doi.org/10.1016/j.jsp.2022.10.006

This discusses the crucial role coaches play in teacher professional learning. By providing personalized support and guidance specific to educators' individual needs and goals, their expertise and feedback help teachers refine instructional practices, which leads to enhanced student learning outcomes.

Leigh-Osroosh, K. T., Clemons, K., Robertson, A., Placeres, V., Gay, J., Lopez-Perry, C., Mason, E. C., Ieva, K. P., Lane, E. M. D., & Saunders, R. (2023). Antiracist school counseling: A consensual qualitative study. *Journal of Counseling and Development*, 101(3), 310–322. https://doi.org/10.1002/jcad.12477
The study explores the concept of antiracist school counseling by examining the role of school counselors in actively combating racism to promote the well-being of all students.

Nguyen, M. & Le, K. (2023). Racial/ethnic match and student–teacher relationships. *Bulletin of Economic Research*, 75(2), 393–412. https://doi.org/10.1111/boer.12362
This paper investigates how teachers' perceived relationships with kindergarten and early elementary school students is influenced by their race or ethnicity. It suggests a positive correlation between racial or ethnic matching and the quality of teacher-reported relationships with students. Specifically, when students share the same racial or ethnic background with their teacher they are more likely to develop closer relationships.

Websites

American Psychological Association – www.apa.org/pi/about/publications/caregivers/faq/cultural-diversity.aspx
Provides significant information regarding cultural diversity and caregiving. Examines ways in which these cultural groups utilize and deliver caregiving.

Black Principals Network – https://surgeinstitute.org/black-principals-network/
The Black Principals Network combats the prevalent issues of professional burnout, isolation, trauma, and suppression often encountered in this position. By focusing on problem-solving, providing access to top-tier resources, and encouraging critical reflection, the Black Principals Network aims to better prepare black principals for their leadership and educational responsibilities.

Center on PBIS: Family – www.pbis.org/topics/family
This site promotes schools, families, and communities to work together to create effective learners and school success.

Global Family Research Project – https://globalfrp.org/
Formerly the Harvard Family Research Project, this site covers comprehensive research topics on family, out-of-school programs, and engaging families and communities to support student success in school and in life.

National Center for Teacher Residencies Black Educators Initiative – https://nctresidencies.org/recruit-and-retain-black-educators/
This organization recruits, trains, and retains black educators through their nationwide network of teacher residency partners. Their objective is to enhance student achievements by expanding access to impactful black educators.

PTO Today – www.ptotoday.com/blog/6267-bring-meetings-to-parents-wherever-they-may-be
This site provides a wealth of information on parent involvement in elementary and secondary schools. It is well organized by topics A–Z and provides articles, flyers, forms and message boards related to parental involvement activities.

13

Newly Emerging Issues in Multicultural Education

Understanding the material and activities in this chapter will help the reader to:

- Describe the lives of multiracial children, adolescents, and families as well as the challenges (e.g. stereotypes and disadvantages), faced in schools, at home, and in communities.
- Understand undocumented immigrants, the conditions they face daily, locales where they are most prevalent, and the social injustices they suffer.
- Understand the challenges faced by professional educators and their roles and responsibilities in addressing these emerging issues.
- Know how and where to access additional professional sources (books, journals, and internet sites) to explore to learn how to better address these and other forthcoming issues.
- Understand issues that LGBTQIA+ students face in school and know what parents and teachers need to do to support them.
- Identify reasons for the uprising of the Asian hate phenomenon and identify ways to prevent anti-Asian rhetoric.

DOI: 10.4324/9781003429531-16

Opening Scenario

Cultural Portrait of Multiracial Children

Ms. Robinson, an American-born, biracial woman with a Filipino mother and a white father, teaches fourth grade at a suburban elementary school. On the first day of school, Ms. Robinson noticed two new students, twins Sam and William, and immediately recognized them as *mestizos* like her; a mix of Filipino and another race. The boys had ambiguous ethnic features and could easily be mistaken for any number of races or nationalities. The other students noticed this too, and throughout the day Ms. Robinson overheard the boys being asked "What are you? Where are you from?" She expected the twins' response to be "white" or "Filipino." The boys, instead, seemed surprised by the questions, and replied, "Uh [...] I am American" or "I am from Chicago." Ms. Robinson quietly admired the boys for their responses, as they refused to be defined by their ethnicity. As the day went on, it became apparent that Sam and William did not realize what was being asked of them. Finally, as the students were lining up for dismissal, an Asian American student approached them and yelled, "C'mon guys—you're Filipinos!" Both boys seemed shocked and rushed out towards the buses. A week later, at the school's Open House, Ms. Robinson introduced herself to Sam and William's parents. The twins' mother, detecting a hint of Filipino features, looked at their new teacher and began, "Wait [...] are you [...]?" "Yes," Ms. Robinson grinned and replied, "I'm *mestiza*, just like Sam and William."

At this point, the twins' parents recounted what had happened after the boys returned home from school that first day. They were distressed, and when their mother asked what was wrong, they began to cry. Finally, the twins replied, "Mom, they called us Filipinos." Relieved, their mother explained, "But, that's what you are, dear." Only then did she realize that neither she nor her husband had ever spoken to the twins about their mixed racial background, which had left them a vulnerable target for bullies.

The mother's story convinced Ms. Robinson to do the following to support the rising number of multiracial children in today's classroom:

1. Discuss the concept of race and multiracial people with her students in a developmentally appropriate way.
2. Help students see that different racial characteristics can coexist instead of reinforcing the concept of "color blindness" in race. Assist

students to respect all races and point out that they are equally special.

3. Encourage children and parents to embrace and maintain their cultural heritage, both at home and at school.

4. Promote the acceptance of all races.

5. Open a dialog with the children about race, and teach them not to treat people differently simply because they look different. Motivate them to improve our future through exploring ways to eradicate racism.

6. Inform parents and other teachers that the color-blindness approach of "I don't see color" is well meant, but can have negative consequences as a parenting or a classroom inclusion technique. Seemingly innocuous statements such as "Race shouldn't matter," "There's only one race—the human race," can serve to invalidate diverse people's unique characteristics and identities.

7. Understand the current issue of gender diversity and equity and the roles of parents and educators in supporting and accepting a broad range of sexual orientations and gender identities.

8. Explore the Asian hate phenomenon to identify actions to continue embracing diversity and preventing anti-Asian rhetoric.

Overview

Writing a chapter on emerging issues is challenging because so many factors come into play: multiracial children, sexual orientation, undocumented immigrants, white supremacy movements, social justice and equity, the professional educator's role in addressing these issues—the list goes on. In the interest of time, the author will address five that may be the most timely for today's educators:

◆ multiracial children, adolescents, and families;
◆ undocumented immigrants;
◆ professional responsibilities of educators;
◆ Asian hate phenomenon;
◆ gender diversity.

There are, of course, many other issues of equal importance—e.g. sexual orientation that was addressed extensively in Chapter 2, and the author recognizes that white supremacy and neo-Nazi movements (as well as other hate groups) are growing in numbers daily—these deserve serious attention should time and space allow. Readers are encouraged to explore these topics on their own and consider what professional educators can do to address these concerns. Chapter 13 will take a different format from other chapters—the author aims for it to be more flexible and thought-provoking so that readers can begin giving serious thought to these important issues educators face in today's classrooms.

Issue: Multiracial Children and Adolescents in America

The number of people who identify as being multicultural is growing. The 2020 U.S. Census data reveals that the multiracial population has risen 276 percent since 2010, and currently 10.2 percent, roughly 33,800,000 of the U.S. population, belongs to two or more races (U.S. Census Bureau, 2023e). As our society has become more accepting of diverse identities and our conversations about racial identity become more prevalent, people more freely identify as multiracial and express their racial backgrounds without fear of stigma, which may be a factor in the sudden rise in the interracial population data.

Between 2000 and 2021, there was a 237 percent increase in the "multiracial black" population in the United States (Pew Research Center, 2023b). Multiracial black describes individuals who identify as black and one or more other races. There has also been growth in the multiracial Hispanic population, approximately 27.6 million in 2021, a significant increase from the three million reported in 2010 (Lopez et al., 2023). While the mulitracial population will continue to become more diverse, including three or more races, the number of single, or mono race, children is decreasing. The percentage of the white-only population decreased from 65.3 percent to 53 percent, and that of the African American only from 14.6 percent to 13.9 percent. The multiracial category for children has seen a notable increase, however, moving from 5.6 percent in 2010 to 15.1 percent in 2020 (Jones et al., 2021).

The author of this book interviewed four multiracial adults between the ages of 18 and 33 concerning their self-identities, and they perceived themselves to be multiracial. They affirmed that they had no confusion as to who they were when growing up. When they were asked, for example, "What are you?" their responses were consistently, "I am both. I am Mexican and also American," or "I am Korean and American at the same time." For a case of a multiracial white, black, and Asian American, the person responded, "I am all three, Japanese, African American, and British." Although these are anecdotal reports based on four cases, multiracial children often don't want to choose one race over the other. As Cardwell et al. (2023) observed, multiracial

Americans have a fluid identity which refers to the flexibility with which they navigate between their various identities.

The multiracial population in the nation is the youngest and fastest growing group among all racial groups (Peng, 2024; Rico et al., 2023). In 2020, 32.5 percent of individuals identifying as multiracial were under the age of 18. In contrast, only 19 percent of the white-only population were under 18. Since the multiracial population is now the fastest growing among school-age children in the United States, more studies on multiracial children are needed. In addition to studying what types of multiracial identities exist, and in what numbers (Powell et al., 2016), it is critical to pay attention to how best to educate multiracial and racially fluid children and their educational issues in relation to the multiracial family structure, characteristics, socioeconomic status, and language (Lorenzo-Blanco et al., 2013). Recently, scholars have focused increasingly on understanding the advantages and difficulties associated with multiracial experiences and identities, as well as their implications for well-being.

Research findings about multiracial children vary wildly; we suspect that this is due, in part, to the wide range of mixed-race combinations possible. No one study can boast a truly representative sample of multiracial children in America, and it is reasonable to assume that the characteristics and experiences of black/white biracial children, for example, might differ from those of Asian American/white or Hispanic/black biracial children. As such, educators should be cautious about generalizing research findings to their own multiracial students.

A greater percentage of multiracial households have either a single mother or unmarried parents as the head of the household. The 2020 American Community Survey reveals that 37.3 percent of parents of two or more races are single parents (U.S. Census Bureau, 2020a). This compares to the national average of 25.28 percent (U.S. Census Bureau, 2020b). Additionally, 14.78 percent of multiracial respondents to the survey live below the poverty line, which exceeds the national average of 11.5 percent (U.S. Census Bureau, 2022c). In addition, the percentage of multiracial households below the poverty line exceeds the national average (Proctor et al., 2016). It should be noted that these figures consider multiracial families in the aggregate, which makes it difficult to extend the findings to any specific mixed-race combination.

Multiracial Learners at School and at Home

Although controversial, Powell et al. (2016) affirm that multiracial families with young children often experience educational advantages in bicultural and bilingual acquisition over monoracial families, which at least partially explains why multiracial kindergarteners generally outperform monoracial kindergarteners. Similarly, Huang et al. (2023) reported that bilingual children are often better at understanding thoughts and feelings of others, known as the theory of mind, than their monolingual counterparts.

By adolescence, however, such educational advantages disappear, with many multiracial students falling behind their single-race peers, due in part to countervailing pressures such as institutional racism and weaker social support systems (Gullickson, 2023; Powell et al., 2016). These findings alert teachers to closely monitor any disturbing incidences of decreased academic performance, or instances of racism or bullying. Teachers should provide an outlet for these students to feel comfortable to express what is going on and should subsequently provide strong psychological support and social networks to multiracial children. Grilo et al. (2023) found that multiracial adolescents often exhibit higher levels of anxiety and depression than their white peers. Black multiracial youth displayed notably less depression than black single-race youth, and white multiracial adolescents reported higher rates of mistreatment from their peers than white single-races.

The report *Multiracial in America: Proud, Diverse and Growing in Numbers* (Pew Research Center, 2015) confirms that multiracial students are more likely to have completed one year of college, and warrants further investigation. This is an uncertain outlook for multiracial children in terms of future academic attainment. Despite the academic edge in childhood noted by Powell et al. (2016), and high school graduation rates that are nearly identical to that of the general population (National Center for Education Statistics, 2023d), multiracial Americans are less likely to earn a four-year degree than white and Asian 25- to 29-year-olds. From 2010 to 2022, the percentage of multiracial 25- to 29-year-olds with an associate's degree or higher increased from 37 percent to 48 percent. Their education level, however, is still below the national average of 49 percent. In comparison, 56 percent of white and 78 percent of Asians in the same age group have completed similar levels of education (National Center for Education Statistics, 2023b).

Much of the existing literature has depicted multiracial children and adolescents as confused, marginalized, or even ashamed by their mixed heritage, so much so that it can impact their ability to succeed in school and to have healthy social lives. Whether they are discriminated against or teased by their classmates, or perhaps because they may be struggling internally with issues of identity and belonging, their mixed-race identity is frequently cited as a significant stressor impacting their education and socialization. Recent studies, however, are beginning to offer a more hopeful perspective. Parents of multiracial children build pride in who they are and teach about their race and ethnicity to shape positive identities through engaging them in racial-ethnic socialization (RES) and guiding them through a process that shapes their identities (Seider et al., 2023). Parents can significantly influence their children's psychosocial outcomes, such as self-esteem, sense of belonging, satisfaction with physical appearance, and development of a strong ethnic and racial identity (Cardwell et al., 2023). Peng (2024) also found that parents play a pivotal role in helping their multiracial children develop a positive identity by interpreting messages from family, schools, and communities, which ultimately helps them connect to their multiple heritages and build a resilience against discrimination. In addition to families, children's teachers, administrators, and peers at school significantly impact how they understand and explore their identity (Wantchekon & Umaña-Taylor, 2024), which can result in positive identity or unintentionally create negative self-perception.

As multiracial children are exposed to at least two different cultural and racial groups, they become more aware of cultural cues, and respond in culturally appropriate ways and become more capable of easily adapting to different cultural contexts. Salahuddin and O'Brien (2011) asserted that multiracial identity promotes enhanced social functioning and comfort. Similarly, Gaither et al. (2014) suggest a distinct schoolhouse advantage. Compared to their monoracial peers, multiracial students' fluid identities permit them to be more flexible, both in terms of who they are willing to socialize with and who they are willing to learn from. To be sure, this malleability and resilience in the face of new and diverse sociocultural contexts can only benefit multiracial children, as the nation—and the classroom—becomes increasingly diverse.

Tran et al. (2016) examined students' reactions to racial identification inquiries—often phrased as "What are you?" and "Where are you *really* from?" in an attempt to code students' responses in terms of a racial microaggression framework. Many biracial and multiracial people regard racial identification queries as a form of microaggression. Tran et al. (2016) characterize racial microaggressions as "everyday indignities that communicate hostile, derogatory, or negative racial slights to the target, but often are communicated unconsciously and can be rationalized by the communicator as having a different meaning or intention than the one perceived by the target."

Tran et al. (2016) found that while some biracial and multiracial students reacted negatively to "What are you?", a far greater percentage responded either neutrally or positively to such queries, reacting negatively only when they felt their responses would be met with surprise or doubt, or when the inquiries merely served to answer whether the inquirer "guessed right." Be aware that biracial and multiracial children are accustomed to being asked about their ethnic background, but their reactions to racial identification inquiries are highly context-dependent. Avoid reacting to their racial self-identification with surprise or doubt ("Really?! But you don't look _______!"). Respect their chosen self-identities.

Multiracial students largely welcomed racial identification inquiries, either (1) as opportunities to demonstrate pride in their heritage, (2) to explain to the inquirer how "What are you?" might be construed as insensitive (or at the very least, poorly worded), or (3) simply as a conversational ice-breaker leading to possible friendship. These reactions challenge the notion that racial identification inquiries should be viewed exclusively in terms of a microaggression framework. Instead, Tran et al. (2016) explained that a more nuanced approach is required, one that also considers "resilience theory," wherein multiracial individuals "often report greater comfort in diverse relationships and attribute dynamic interpersonal skills to being multiracial (e.g. appreciation of diverse viewpoints)." The resilience theory confirms that the prevailing narrative of the "confused" biracial person, struggling with his/her identity, does not apply to all biracial and multiracial children.

Lorenzo-Blanco et al. (2013) offer fascinating findings on multiracial children's perceptions of family life relative to their white, African American, Hispanic, and "Other Minority" peers. In their analysis of a longitudinal study surveying 9,000 adolescents, the authors discovered that multiracial adolescents have the lowest levels of mother–child cohesion and maternal support, as well as the lowest levels of participation in daily family routines (e.g. eating meals together). Lorenzo-Blanco et al. (2013) reported that multiracial youth perceived family life much like their monoracial counterparts regarding parental monitoring and family events. Mixed race/multi-ethnic youth perceived a distance between mother and child, which may explain why multiracial children often suffer from poorer psychological health and experience behavioral issues at a greater rate than their monoracial peers. Curiously, and conversely, mixed race/multi-ethnic adolescents reported the highest levels of father–child cohesion and paternal support, preferring to turn to their fathers for education, career, and romantic advice.

In multiracial families, a parent of a single race has a unique role in supporting their children who represent multiracial backgrounds. This interethnic dynamic complicates parent–child relationships and may result in biracial youth feeling less connected to and supported by their parents compared to monoracial youth (Green & Bryant, 2023). Pressure to conform to a specific racial identity can make biracial children feel confused and isolated. Therefore, parents need to respect their unique racial identities and avoid asserting their own viewpoints.

Equally concerning is the trend that multiracial adolescents exhibit higher levels of coping-motivated intoxication and violence compared to their monoracial peers, potentially influenced by distinct experiences of stress, confusion, and subtle and explicit forms of discrimination from peers within and outside of their racial groups (Dobani et al., 2024). Multiracial adolescents seem to be particularly vulnerable to delinquency, violence, and substance use, possibly because their multiracial identity becomes more pronounced during the tumultuous adolescent years (High et al., 2023).

Stereotyping Multiracial Students

Most educators understand that multiracial students, like any other racial or ethnic group, cannot be described in monolithic terms. Nevertheless, stereotyping can and does occur. Some teachers make the mistake of combining stereotypes associated with a student's composite races (e.g. reducing a black Japanese student to a selection of African American and Asian stereotypes). Other teachers may assume that their multiracial students are one race only, and apply a stereotype accordingly. In both instances, educators deny the student's own racial self-identification, which can prove to be an invalidating or disenfranchising experience for the student. As with all students, teachers need to make a conscious effort to avoid stereotyping in any form.

Roughly half (52.19 percent) of multiracial families speak only English (U.S. Census Bureau, 2022b), and teachers sometimes incorrectly assume that multiracial children born of at least one foreign-born parent will speak the foreign heritage language. Making up the other half of multiracial families are 29.28 percent who speak English very well and 18.53 percent who speak English less than very well. Unlike the assumption, most multiracial families are native born (74.32 percent) but roughly a quarter (25.68 percent) are foreign born. Some foreign-born parents who have roots in a particular culture and language need to find a way to retain their unique cultural heritage. Often, they prefer to speak their heritage language at home with their children, believing that their children can benefit from being exposed to the language of their ancestry and culture as families interact and communicate with each other about events in their home environment. To support children to speak both their heritage language and English, parents are responsible for selecting appropriate resources and nurturing heritage language growth. The acquisition level of children's heritage language depends on the quality and quantity of language usage available at home. If parents are bilingual, educators can encourage them to provide home instruction in teaching their heritage language and not suppress one or the other (Lee & Kang, 2023). Educators can support parents by asking them to create rich literacy home environments where their children can speak, read, and write in both languages consistently. For example, parents can read bilingual books to their multiracial children, spend time discussing the story, and answer questions in their heritage language.

Whether the parents of multiracial students are determined to speak the heritage language at home or not, educators need to respect their decisions and reasoning behind it. Educators should be aware that even though a multiracial child's parent(s) have made the decision not to speak or teach heritage language(s) at home, being "outed" as not speaking their heritage language may produce feelings of embarrassment and guilt for the student in question. This is particularly the case when there are monoracial students present who do speak that language, as can happen in a foreign language class.

Moreover, in the case of dual-minority students, one cannot assume that the student speaks the language they "look more like." For example, a mixed Filipino-Mexican family may have chosen to teach Spanish rather than Tagalog in the home, due to their perceived usefulness of Spanish in the United States. A teacher should not assume that the student speaks Tagalog just because he or she displays stronger Asian physical features. These assumptions can inadvertently promote "Marginal Man" (Powell et al., 2016) reactions, wherein the student feels like an outsider who doesn't belong to either group. Likewise, similar assumptions about a student's religious background can be alienating and offensive.

In a related vein, inaccurate assumptions about students' cultural, religious, or linguistic identities can be especially problematic in this era of transracial adoption (Burton et al., 2010; Powell et al., 2016). Consider, for example, the confusion and embarrassment that an ethnically Chinese student might feel if her teacher presumed she could speak authoritatively about Chinese New Year, but she had been adopted at birth by white parents and had no connection to mainland Chinese culture.

Issue: Undocumented Immigrants

Another emerging issue for the last several decades has been undocumented immigrants: who they are, where they live, where they work, whether they live a life of fear, and how responsible organizations can assist them to become legal. This is by no means a small issue—it is an issue with many unknowns. The Pew Research Center has offered some excellent information on undocumented immigrants which challenges all educators, regardless of where they teach.

Table 13.1 Undocumented Children

Immigration status	Number
Undocumented children	600,000
U.S. citizen children who are with at least one undocumented immigrant parent	4.5 million

Source: da Silva Iddings and Warraich (2024)

The data in Table 13.1 highlight the significant number of children facing complex challenges due to the undocumented status of their parents. These children often experience high levels of stress and increased school absences which negatively impact their academic performance (da Silva Iddings & Warraich, 2024). Educators, therefore, need to proactively identify undocumented immigrant students and accommodate and support them. This will help to ensure that all students enjoy the right to learn and develop, regardless of their immigration status. For example, if a teacher notices that new migrant students are frequently absent, they can investigate the reasons behind these absences and work to provide a solution and support.

According to the Pew Research Center, the number of unauthorized immigrants in the United States has stabilized in recent years after decades of rapid growth. But the origin countries of unauthorized immigrants have shifted, with the number from Mexico declining since 2009 and the number from elsewhere rising.

◆ Mexicans made up 39 percent of all unauthorized immigrants in 2021, though their numbers have been declining in recent years (Passel & Krogstad, 2023). There were 4.1 million unauthorized Mexican immigrants living in the United States in 2021, down from 5.8 million in 2014 and 6.4 million in 2009.

Interesting facts about the unauthorized immigrant population in the United States include:

◆ There were 10.5 million unauthorized immigrants in the United States in 2021 (Passel & Krogstad, 2023). The number of undocumented immigrants peaked in 2007 at 12.2 million, 4 percent of the U.S. population. This increase has leveled off since and is currently roughly the same size as it was in 2004. Currently, unauthorized immigrants account for 3 percent of the nation's total population.

◆ The number of unauthorized immigrants from nations other than Mexico grew by 900,000 since 2019, to an estimated 6.4 million in 2021 (Passel & Krogstad, 2023). From 2007 to 2021, nearly every global region experienced a significant rise in unauthorized immigrants in the United States. Population numbers for unauthorized immigrants from Central America and South and East Asia increased the most—240,000 and 180,000, respectively. Increases in the number of unauthorized immigrants from other countries mostly offset the decline in the number from Mexico.

Table 13.2 States With the Highest Residence of Unauthorized Immigrants

State name	Number of unauthorized immigrants
California	1.9 million
Texas	1.6 million
Florida	900,000
New York	600,000
New Jersey	450,000
Illinois	400,000

Source: Passel and Krogstad (2023)

◆ As shown in Table 13.2, six states collectively accommodated 56 percent of the nation's unauthorized immigrants, a decrease from 80 percent in 1990: California, Texas, Florida, New York, New Jersey, and Illinois (Passel & Krogstad, 2023). Since 1990, these states have consistently housed the highest numbers of unauthorized immigrants. However, over time, the unauthorized immigrant population has become more dispersed geographically.

From 2009 to 2014, the number of unauthorized immigrants decreased in 17 states: Alabama, Alaska, Arizona, California, Colorado, Georgia, Illinois, Kansas, Mississippi, Nevada, New Mexico, New York, North Carolina, Oklahoma, Oregon, South Carolina, and Wyoming. The number increased during the same period, in 21 states: Arkansas, Connecticut, Delaware, Florida, Indiana, Kentucky, Louisiana, Maine, Maryland, Massachusetts, Michigan, New Hampshire, North Dakota, Ohio, Pennsylvania, Rhode Island, South Dakota, Tennessee, Virginia, Washington, and Wisconsin (Passel & Krogstad, 2023).

◆ The number of unauthorized immigrants who have lived in the United States for a decade or more is on the rise. Between 2007 and 2017, the proportion of newly arrived unauthorized immigrants (those in the United States for five years or less) from regions other than Central America and Mexico rose from 37 percent to 63 percent (Lopez et al., 2021), while the percentage of new unauthorized immigrants from Mexico declined.

◆ This decrease in new unauthorized immigrants resulted in a population that is largely settled in the country. As of 2017, about two-thirds (66 percent) of unauthorized immigrants had resided in the United States for more than ten years, compared to 41 percent a decade earlier. In addition, new unauthorized immigrants (those

Table 13.3 Number of Unauthorized Immigrants

Country of origin	Number of unauthorized immigrants
Mexico	4.1 million
El Salvador	800,000
India	725,000
Guatemala	700,000
Honduras	525,000
China	375,000
Dominican Republic	230,000
Venezuela	190,000

Source: Passel and Krogstad (2023)

in the United States for five years or less) made up 20 percent of the unauthorized immigrant population in 2017, down from 30 percent in 2007. This trend is even more pronounced among Mexicans, with the majority (83 percent) having lived in the United States for more than ten years, while only 8 percent had been in the United States for five years or less.

Most recent data suggests that 10.5 million unauthorized immigrants resided in the United States, constituting 3 percent of the total population and 22 percent of the foreign-born population in 2021. The response of the U.S. government to illegal immigration has been ineffective historically (da Silva Iddings & Warraich, 2024). For example, U.S. Immigration and Customs Enforcement (ICE) operations conducted near schools can prove challenging for undocumented families (Meadows, 2023) as these actions can lead to family separation, unemployment, and trauma for undocumented children. Policies over the past decade have grown more harsh and have resulted in hardships for unauthorized immigrants. Policies at the U.S.–Mexico border and the implementation of restrictive immigration policies have led to family separations and the deportation of migrants.

CASE STUDY 13.1

Juan: An Undocumented Immigrant Student

New York is a vibrant city and has a long tradition of welcoming immigrants from all over the world. In recent years the city has seen an influx of migrant children, many arriving with their families, seeking asylum and a better way of life in the United States. Often these children are coming from countries where their life and that of their family is extremely difficult due to economic hardship, violence, political unrest, and persecution.

Juan, a fourth-grade student, recently arrived from El Salvador with his parents and younger sister. They fled their home because life was unbearable for them due to growing violence and economic hardship. His parents finally made the tough decision to make the trek to America in search of a better life and opportunities for themselves and their children. They are undocumented and have just recently moved from a government housing complex to a low-income neighborhood in Queens as Juan's father found work as a handyman.

Juan is enrolled in Public School 344 and is just beginning to adjust to his new life in New York. Though he's only been going to his new school for a very short time, he finds it very stressful and does not enjoy it as much as his old school in El Salvador where he was a high achiever. His limited English worries him and he wonders if he will ever be able to understand his teachers and classmates and if they will ever be able to understand him.

Questions for Discussion

1. What are Juan's primary educational needs in school? What are some ways that the school can support him?
2. What support can the school and community provide to help Juan's family adjust and feel welcome?
3. How can Juan's teachers and the school help him gain English proficiency? What strategies and resources can his teachers use to create a safe and welcoming learning environment where Juan will once again become a high achieving student?

Issue: Stop Asian Hate

Recently, Asian Americans have become increasingly concerned about violent incidents targeting their community. Asian students experienced a rise in severe depression and severe anxiety of 17 percent and 30 percent, respectively (Zhou et al., 2023). Hate crimes against Asians in the United States have surged by 77 percent according to the Department of Justice data in 2020. In response to rising xenophobia and violence occurring worldwide during the COVID-19 pandemic, the United Nations Secretary-General António

Guterres emphasized the need to strengthen societal resilience and cease the baseless prejudice toward Asians (Dong et al., 2023).

The hate crimes targeting Asians raises the questions of why they were subject to such severe hate during the COVID-19 pandemic, and what are the ways to prevent such hate (Lee & Gupta, 2024). One of the reasons could be the presence of prejudice against Asians in U.S. history, which was exemplified by laws like the Chinese Exclusion Act of 1882 (Chen & Xie, 2020). Also, Asians have been blamed for diseases like the "Yellow Peril" in the nineteenth century and stigmatized during the SARS 2003 outbreak (Chen et al., 2020).

Asian hate crimes have become more violent, even resulting in death. Such examples are the attack on an 84-year-old Thai man who died after being shoved to the ground and a 61-year-old Filipino man who was attacked while riding the subway (Cabral, 2021). This trend has led to the start of the "Stop Asian Hate" movement which seeks to address discrimination against Asians (Huang & Zhu, 2023). To continue embracing diversity and preventing anti-Asian rhetoric, government agencies, schools, educators, and families can support and participate in the following actions:

1. Continuing to include Asian American culture and history in school curricula is one approach. Doing so will make American history education more inclusive by raising the awareness of non-Asian Americans. Seventeen states have introduced legislation to include Asian American content in public school curricula, with ten having already done so (Saha, 2021).

2. It is crucial to continue expanding and implementing the Teaching Equitable Asian American Community History Act (TEAACH) nationwide, which was first signed into law in the state of Illinois, and mandates the inclusion of Asian American history and culture in the public school curriculum across the state.

3. Another method is to incorporate culturally responsive and sustaining teaching methods and implement anti-bullying education programs (Morgan, 2023). Understanding that young children recognize different skin colors and exhibit a bias toward characters with dark skin during literacy discussions (Kim et al., 2016), teachers need to incorporate various multicultural children's literature depicting Asian cultures (Chang, 2015). This way, children can be taught to embrace differences while discussing and developing positive views on cultural differences.

4. Implement strategies to combat hate crimes, such as, improving reporting processes, engaging visibly with communities, and enforcing effective criminal justice actions. In response, initiatives

like the NYPD's patrol of plainclothes officers in Asian communities and the formation of specialized task forces by police departments to deter hate crimes against Asians are useful (Chakarborti, 2018).

5. Additionally, platforms such as Stop AAPI Hate have been launched to facilitate the reporting of hate crimes and build community collaboration. Hashtags, such as #StopAsianHate and #SAH has also gained widespread traction on social media platforms.

Issue: Gender Diversity

The acronym LGBTQ is often used to represent a social and political movement pressing for the acceptance of a variety of genders identities and sexual orientations as well as individuals who do not identify as heterosexual, or cisgender. LGBTQIA+ (Lesbian, Gay, Bisexual, Transgender, Queer or Questioning, Intersex, Asexual or Ally, +) expands the acronym to include an even wider range of identities. Look more closely at the additional letters. As represented in the acronym, our society is inclusive of a broad spectrum of gender identities beyond the traditional binary. Kim et al. (2024) defined Transgender and Gender Non-Conforming (TGNC) as those whose gender identity does not align with their biological sex, and whose identity is fluid and may not fit into a specific gender category. TGNC people may reject traditional gender categories altogether.

The U.S. Census Bureau reported that 8 percent of U.S. adults identified as LGBT and 85 percent non-LGBT, 4.2 percent identified as "other" and 2.9 percent did not respond (Anderson et al., 2021). Among the LGBT identity group, nearly a quarter (24.6 percent) were between the ages of 18 and 24, as opposed to only 7.3 percent of non-LGBT respondents in the same age group, indicating a greater tendency among younger people to identify as part of the LGBT community. Over half (59.4 percent) of LGBT respondents were never married, compared to 22.7 percent of non-LGBT. Specific LGBT data show that 4.4 percent of adults surveyed identified as bisexual, as opposed to 3.3 percent who identified as gay or lesbian and 0.6 percent as transgender.

Castillo (2023) identified several beliefs surrounding LGBT individuals: (1) claims that transgender women pose a threat in public spaces such as public bathrooms are unfounded and an attempt to demonize transgender people; (2) reports of child mutilation from gender reassignment surgeries are false and used to reinforce anti-transgender opinions; and (3) claims of transwomen's domination in women's sports are also false and intended to keep transgenders from competing in women's sports. For many transgender and nonbinary people their first experience with discrimination and bias is in schools. Teachers and administrators, therefore, need to be aware and supportive of these students and their families.

Studies indicate that LGBTQIA+ students carry a stigma and face barriers in school that affect their overall well-being (Luke et al., 2022). More LGBT students (38.2 percent) than non-LBGT students (16.1 percent) experience problems with depression. They face bullying, bias, and harassment at school in spite of laws such as Title VI of the Civil Rights Act of 1964, Title IX of the Education Amendments Act of 1972, the Safe School Improvement Act, and the Equality Act bill designed to safeguard LBGTQIA+ youth. According to Meyer and Frost's (2013) minority stress model, individuals within minority gender identity groups, such as transgender or gender non-conforming, face unique stressors and often have mental health issues such as depression.

Schools, along with families, should support transgender students (Castillo, 2023), treat them respectfully, and prohibit discrimination. Schools can establish student-led interest groups, such as gender diversity alliances that allow the members to share their experiences. Both educators and parents need to understand how the psychological pressure of being in a minority group can impact their depression. Foremost, parents should accept individuality and assist their children in developing a positive identity and self-esteem in a safe home. In addition to their parents, LGBTQIA+ students need a support system that involves school counselors, administrators, and librarians capable of creating inclusive school environments that recognize gender diversity. Schools can keep open communication, listen to the experiences and needs of nonbinary students, and provide resources and support networks.

Nonbinary youth can be supported and empowered to thrive academically, socially, and emotionally by parents and educators working together. Schools have made major strides forward, but challenges persist with respect to diversity, representation in curriculum, and the reduction of stigmas. Professional development training for educators is essential for a truly inclusive school environment for all students.

CASE STUDY 13.2

Benni and Jodie: Transgender Students

Benni and Jodie are twins and juniors in high school. Both are transgender students who identify as male. Benni came out as transgender at the beginning of his sophomore year, hoping for acceptance and support from his classmates and close friends. Jodie was more nervous about his identity and came out as transgender just at the start of his junior year, following a summer of experimenting with social life as a trans teen. Rhonda, Benni and Jodie's mother, supports her twin sons' transgender identity and does all she can to help them in their life and transition.

Instead of receiving understanding and respect from friends and classmates, both Benni and Jodie have become targets of bullying and harassment at school. The bullying has included verbal abuse, name-calling, and physical threats. Some students have intentionally misgendered them, refusing to use their preferred pronouns. The fear of being targeted has prevented Benni and Jodie from fully participating in classroom discussions and group projects.

Rhonda is worried because her sons now are depressed and she is afraid they may even be suicidal. She has contacted their teachers repeatedly and asked them to support Benni and Jodie and promote their gender identity in the classroom. She has also often requested that her sons be excused from class whenever they are feeling too down to attend school.

Questions for Discussion

1. As a school teacher, how would you respond to Rhonda's requests? If you intend to honor her requests, what will you do when another student comes out as transgender? What do you think the impact, if any, of them being excused from class might have on the other students in the class?
2. What are the advantages and disadvantages of students coming out as transgender? What would the likely effects be on academic achievement and social development?
3. What type of collaboration activities with families would you design to support transgender students? Do you think they require attention beyond what is given to other students?

Issue: Accepting the Responsibility to be Professionally Qualified and Committed

First and foremost, educators must accept responsibility for being qualified to work with students of differing cultural backgrounds. Regardless of the multicultural education programs and their goals, efforts will succeed only when educators are trained in cultural diversity, understand the effects of culture on learning, and are able to convey genuine feelings of acceptance and respect for all people. Professional education for all teachers, not just those planning to teach in multicultural areas, should include content methodologies courses that illustrate the relationship between culture and learning, and how to address this relationship in teaching situations. They should provide first-hand practical and clinical experience in working with learners of diverse cultural backgrounds and socioeconomic levels, and appropriate instruction in interpersonal skills.

We reemphasize that professional responsibilities include broad expertise in content, instructional techniques, and the ability to work with learners from differing cultural backgrounds. Responsibilities extend even further, however. Having knowledge of people, but holding on to racist attitudes or a belief that "different is wrong" will not lead to responsive multicultural education. Understanding that a relationship exists between culture and education is a prerequisite to effective teaching. Teaching with styles and strategies appropriate for only one culture can fail to meet the needs of children and adolescents of others.

Responsible educators understand the diversity of our society, accept cultural differences, and practice cultural sensitivity when they communicate with people from different cultures (Bennett, 2017). Often, they have only vague ideas about other cultures, therefore, they intentionally spend time on incorporating different cultural perspectives into their own identity and decision-making process.

Highly committed educators work hard to avoid categorizing people into "us" and "them," and steer clear of stereotypical views that reject different cultures. Responsible educators know that there are more similarities than differences between their own and that of others. They also encourage their peers and their students to embrace and tolerate differences.

These teachers not only practice cultural sensitivity but also create multicultural learning activities so that their students become more open and sensitive to different cultures and less ethnocentric. Through multicultural education, teachers and students alike can learn to adapt their perspectives, interact sensitively with diverse groups, and contribute to an inclusive society.

Achieving Equity and Social Justice

Teachers need to strive to become change agents and conscious practitioners for the promotion of equity and social justice through instruction in the classroom. Have you ever considered the impact that white privilege, majority group power, and oppression have on less represented groups? The time is long overdue for teachers to acknowledge the existence of white supremacy and search for appropriate ways to reduce social inequalities that exist both inside and outside of the classroom (Picower, 2012).

Teachers need to be aware of the serious differences that exist in home and learning environments, experiences, available resources, schooling, academic achievement, and opportunities for success between privileged and disadvantaged students. Cochran-Smith et al. (2016) advised teachers to recognize classroom, school, and societal practices that reproduce inequity. With such awareness, teachers can examine their teaching practices and reflect on how structural injustice hinders quality teaching and student learning.

Teachers can play an important role in reducing differences and achieving equity and social justice for all students. They revolutionize classroom dynamics by implementing culturally relevant teaching which uses teaching methods, reading materials, case studies that reflect diverse cultural backgrounds, and viewpoints of marginalized groups, aiming to establish fair and inclusive educational opportunities for all students (Cegielski et al., 2023).

As change agents, teachers can make a difference in the lives of disadvantaged students through their teaching as well as advocacy efforts for students' equitable education and life in schools and communities (Storms, 2013). They can proactively support marginalized students as well as English language learners, and implement the following practices to ensure positive learning experiences and academic achievement:

1. An important aspect of equitable pedagogy is to acknowledge and validate the student's home life through experiences in the classroom. This can be accomplished by connecting the cultural, traditional, experiential, and linguistic abilities students bring from home to lessons and activities in the classroom. Teachers should find ways to incorporate technology, websites, science, language, literature, and the arts that students are familiar with. Students' unique funds of knowledge and abilities should be respected and considered when planning lessons and classroom activities.

2. Value the participation efforts and processes of learning of disadvantaged students, not just the final product as compared to their more privileged counterparts who may have a superior learning history.

3. Work with families and communities, as well as other teachers, to scaffold student learning and promote high expectations for success. One practical way to ensure the teaching is relevant is to involve family members and community leaders to participate as guest speakers, integrating their experiences into the learning process.

4. Select content, methods of delivery, learning opportunities, and assessments across all content areas that connect to students' lives and experiences.

5. Create learning-focused, respectful, and supportive learning environments rather than requiring students to constantly work above their ability which can lead to failure.
6. Design a pedagogy to scaffold marginalized students' learning success.

Teachers should recognize that there is no panacea or quick fix for existing inequities. Teachers alone can't solve the problem due to the myriad historical, social, political, cultural, and financial conditions that contribute to the current state. Regardless, teachers should start now by placing equity at the top of their agenda to ensure the highest levels of academic achievement for all disadvantaged students. With teachers' motivation and concentrated effort to ensure educational success and academic advancement now, all students will experience empowerment, enjoy access to opportunities, achieve educational success, and gain equity and social justice. For developing successful teachers who are skilled in social justice teaching, teacher preparation programs are vital (Jacobs & Perez, 2023). Effective social justice training requires three key components: (1) understanding one's own identity and its impacts on one's biases; (2) establishing a classroom environment that supports different perspectives; and (3) implementing teaching practices to foster critical awareness and action. Strong teachers use methods that encourage critical thinking about inequalities and teach students to analyze, raise a question, and act on unfair social issues.

Ensuring Cultural Diversity in All Curricular Materials

A major responsibility that educators must accept is the commitment to ensure cultural diversity in all curricular materials. Educators play a significant role as they scrutinize all print and nonprint materials for bias and racism. This issue includes omissions as well as distortions. Educators are responsible for being on the lookout for material that shows people's culture in a derogatory light or in demeaning situations, or that shows people of color in stereotypical images. In the school textbooks, families were typically portrayed as white, two-parent, and living in houses with white picket fences. Educators in most situations can readily perceive that most learners would be unable to understand or relate to such images in stories. While there has been considerable progress, educators should still insist on materials and adopt textbooks that include culturally diverse characters and portray minority families in positive ways.

Students of diverse ethnic backgrounds may feel excluded if teachers select materials that match their own culture and experiences rather than the ethnic background of their students (Storie & Coogle, 2023). This can perpetuate a sense of "sameness" where differences are seen as inappropriate. Some educators use a "colorblindness" approach, believing it promotes equality by viewing all students as being the same regardless of their race and ethnicity. This approach, however, ignores students' unique cultural characteristics and can actually perpetuate inequities by inadvertently promoting "sameness." Sensitive teachers strive to create a classroom environment filled with learning materials that illustrate differences and experiences of all students.

Ensuring that the Multicultural Emphasis Permeates All Curricular Areas and the School Environment

Another major responsibility of educators is working toward multiculturalism in all areas of the curriculum and school environment. A basic assumption of this text is that multicultural education should be a broad-based effort that has the full cooperation and support of all school personnel, rather than a half-hearted effort.

Because schools are representative of our culturally pluralistic society, they must plan appropriate learning experiences for different children: American Indian, African American, Arab American, Asian American, Hispanic American, and European American, as well as children and adolescents from differing economic, social, and religious backgrounds. Educators must answer many questions: Which (or perhaps whose) religious holidays will be observed? How will cultural differences affect testing and assessment? What special problems will learners from diverse cultures bring to school? How will learning styles differ?

These and other questions raise the overall question of what, specifically, should educators do. A one-time multicultural week or single unit featuring African American history, tacos, and oriental dress and customs will not suffice. The curriculum, learning environment, and the mindset of learners and faculty and staff must become multicultural in nature and should reflect the cultural diversity of the school.

Well-meaning multicultural education programs may serve only cosmetic purposes if students and school personnel harbor long-held cultural biases and stereotypes. Schools must not presuppose learners' abilities and behaviors based on stereotypes and myth. Rather, the school curriculum must genuinely respect cultural diversity and regard all learners objectively.

Involving Parents, Families, and the Community

Educators' recognition of the role of parents, the family, and the community in the multicultural education effort is an absolute prerequisite to the multicultural education program's success. Actually, two aspects are at stake, and both play a significant role in determining the success of the multicultural education program.

First, including both immediate and extended families and community members demonstrates concretely that educators are serious about accepting and promoting multiculturalism outside the school boundaries. When educators show that their efforts do not stop at the schoolhouse gate, they add credence to the multicultural education program's efforts.

Second, parents, families, and community members can play significant roles when they come to visit schools and offer their participation. Educators may have to deal with parents' language differences, misunderstandings associated with U.S. school systems, and the reluctance of some parents to get involved. Although overcoming these challenges requires both time and energy, the benefits will be many.

Our devoting an entire chapter (Chapter 12) to including parents, families, and caregivers from differing cultural backgrounds shows how important we believe their role in education to be. The main issue is the extent to which educators genuinely want to effect multiculturalism. Children and adolescents who see only white parents visiting during school can easily conclude that cultural diversity is not as valuable as educators suggest. Although educators usually find it is easier to gain the attention of middle- and upper-class white parents, perceptive educators recognize the need to involve parents and families of all ethnicities and socioeconomic levels.

Turning Ideals into Realities

Dr. McDonald, a high school principal, looked objectively at her school's lofty goals, objectives, and philosophical statements about multiculturalism, which spoke eloquently of valuing, recognizing, accepting, and respecting all people, regardless of differences. Then she compared these statements with what was actually happening in the schools. Surely the students could see that much of what was occurring was only rhetoric with no substance.

Without being overly pessimistic or cynical, Dr. McDonald asked herself several questions about the extent to which educators respect and address diversity:

- Do school policies reflect a concern for social justice and an understanding of the many different types of diversity?
- Do instructional practices reflect the diverse ways students receive and organize knowledge?
- Is there an understanding of motivation and competition in relation to learners from diverse cultural heritages and socioeconomic levels?
- Are efforts made to promote acceptance and social interaction between learners of all cultures?
- Is there a genuine respect for all people—their socioeconomic status, culture, gender, and sexual orientation?
- Do educators understand testing and assessment as they relate to the various diverse groups?
- Are the educators professionally trained and competent to work with students of diversity?

Dr. McDonald decided that creating a methodical plan was necessary to address these and other issues and concerns. Such an effort would take a large-scale approach and would include discussion groups, committees, in-service programs and activities, speakers, and an improved professional library.

1. Should Dr. McDonald take a large-scale approach (eight to ten goals per year) or should she take a smaller approach (one to three goals per year)? There are advantages and disadvantages of both ways. What approach do you think will provide the best results for teachers and students?
2. Generally speaking, do you think multicultural efforts are "only rhetoric with no substance"? If rhetoric, how might we make multiculturalism a genuine effort? In addition to diversity in curricula and teaching methods, how can schools create acceptance of others and their differences? Include honest respect, social justice, and different ways of thinking—that perceives all cultures in equal perspectives.
3. How can Dr. McDonald address sexual orientation? While this is a form of diversity that deserves recognition, not all people agree that the topic should be mentioned in schools. What programs or

workshops might Dr. McDonald provide for teachers to help them understand sexual orientation as a type of diversity? What programs should educators provide for students? Remember to consider grade level and developmental level of learners.

Summing Up

As stated in the beginning of the chapter, the author is unable to detail all the emerging issues facing multicultural education—the purpose of this chapter was not to be comprehensive—it was to introduce readers to several issues and make them aware of others. Regardless of the issue, the challenge lies with the educator to educate themself on the issue as well as develop the attitudes and skills needed to address the challenge. The social and political climate today suggests a turbulent future—at least until multiracial students are understood; some responsible action is taken to help undocumented workers; sexual orientation (including transgender) is understood; and white supremacy and other hate groups are addressed either legally or through social action.

Suggested Learning Activity

1. Visit a classroom and observe the teacher's instructional strategies that support underprivileged students to connect between home and school life to ensure their educational success. Compare and contrast the practices you observed to the practices you experienced in school during your childhood.
2. Find a friend at school or in the community with a different social and cultural background from your own to find out what type of inequity or social injustice they have encountered or heard about and how it made them feel. Describe your thoughts and feelings after listening to his or her story. How will you help change people's views and stop existing social injustice?
3. Prepare a five-minute presentation on your position about the impact of the U.S. legislation concerning education and the rights of LGBTQIA+ individuals, incorporating evidence and counterarguments to potential opposition points.
4. Propose transformative solutions to prevent and stop Asian-hate sentiment and empower Asian American students with a strong sense of identity.
5. Read and discuss the Implementing Research feature below and decide how you would respond to racial identification inquiries.

Implementing Research

Preventing Asian Hate

Since the emergence of the COVID-19 pandemic, insinuations and accusations linking COVID-19 to being "Chinese" have been associated with a rise in anti-Asian sentiment. According to the Stop Asian Hate Center, victims have reported nearly 1,900 hate crimes against Asian Americans since March 2020 coinciding with the public use of derogatory terms like "Kung flu" and "Chinese Virus" (Han et al., 2023). Discrimination stemming from COVID-19 has significantly heightened the risk of mental health issues among Asian American children, who may feel unsafe and unsupported in their school environments. The escalation in hostile behavior and hate towards Asians represents a critical concern that school districts must address. Educators can consider several practical measures to prevent bullying, violence, and discrimination against Asian students:

Implementing the Research

1. Increase cultural awareness by incorporating Asian American Studies curriculum at the K–12 schools and including educational materials that reflect Asian culture and history. It will help to promote positive Asian culture and identities of Asian American students.
2. Implement anti-bullying programs that target violence directed at Asian American students.
3. Establish and enforce anti-bullying school policies that penalize racial hate.
4. Participate in training for teachers on how to intervene in instances of bullying effectively.
5. Provide designated spaces for support groups allowing Asian students to exchange useful information and experiences.

Source: Jeung, R., Garcia, A. M., Bae, A., Shen, C., & Malasa, J. (2023). Urgently needed to protect Asian American children and families: The social movement for Asian American studies at K-12 grades. *Sociological Inquiry, 94*(2), 369–390. https://doi.org/10.1111/soin.12573

Expanding Your Horizons

Additional Books and Journals

Garay, M. M., Perry, J. M., & Remedios, J. D. (2023). The maintenance of the U.S. racial hierarchy through judgments of multiracial people based on

proximity to whiteness. *Personality and Social Psychology Bulletin, 49*(6), 969–984. https://doi.org/10.1177/01461672221086175
The researchers investigate the presence of white ancestry and its influence on multiracial people and the possibility that the increasing multiracial population would blur distinctions between racial groups leading to a decrease in racism and enhancement in interracial relations.

Minniear, M. & Atkin, A. L. (2023). Exploring multiracial identity, demographics, and the first period identity crisis: The role of the 2020 United States Census in promoting monocentric norms. *Journal of Applied Communication Research, 51*(1), 37–54. https://doi.org/10.1080/00909882.2022.2107401
This study investigates to what extent the U.S. Census options for ethnicity and race perpetuate monocentric norms which assume that all people should fit into certain racial and ethnic categories

Oh, H., Du, J., Smith, L., & Koyanagi, A. (2023). Mental health differences between multiracial and monoracial college students in the United States: Emerging racial disparities. *International Journal of Social Psychiatry, 69*(3), 744–751. https://doi.org/10.1177/00207640221135817
Multiracial students, when compared to their mono-race peers, are more likely to experience mental and behavioral health issues, including self-injurious behaviors and suicide attempts. Targeted preventive interventions are recommended.

Waring, C. D. L. (2024). "We're going to be the new white [people]": Multiracial Americans envision the future. *Ethnic and Racial Studies, 47*(1), 145–166. https://doi.org/10.1080/01419870.2023.2215313
This study focuses on how multiracial people envision the future of race relations from their distinct racial perspective. Generally, the multiracial people expressed concerns about negative race relations, attributing this outlook to the absence of effective institutional initiatives that could bring about meaningful change to reduce and eventually eliminate notorious racist past and present incidents.

Websites

American Speech-Language-Hearing Association (ASHA) – www.asha.org/Practice-Portal/Professional-Issues/Cultural-Competence/
The Office of Multicultural Affairs (OMA) of ASHA addresses cultural and linguistic diversity issues related to professionals and persons with communication disorders and differences.

The Center for the Study of Biracial Children – http://csbchome.org/?page_id=7
For nearly 25 years, the Center for the Study of Biracial Children has offered research and resources relevant to multiracial children, adults, and families. The organization's website covers a wide range of topics, such as the lack of multiracial perspectives in teacher training programs, white privilege, interracial marriage, and the multiracial movement.

Critical Mixed Race Studies — https://criticalmixedracestudies.com/
Critical Mixed Race Studies (CMRS) encompasses a biennial conference, an academic field, and a community of scholars and activists. The CMRS conference attracts more than 500 scholars, artists, students, activists, clinicians, community organizations and advocates of multiracial backgrounds from across the globe.

Global Issues – www.globalissues.org/issue/137/human-rights-issues
This website explores global issues related to human rights and racism.

Mixed in America – https://www.mixedinamerica.org/
Mixed in America is a community organization striving to facilitate more nuanced discussions about race in America, particularly from a multiracial perspective. They provide trauma-informed, holistic and inclusive services to adults, children, affinity groups, schools and businesses.

Mixed Heritage Center: Information & resources for people of mixed heritage – www.mixedheritagecenter.org/
This website is a product of the partnership between the MAVIN Foundation and the Association of Multiethnic Americans (AMEA). This site is an online repository of news, research, and resources for multiracial/multiethnic, and transracially adopted people.

MixedLife – https://www.mixedlife.net/
MixedLife is a website dedicated to gathering content tailored for people of mixed racial identities, offering them a platform to delve into their identity and gain insights into the multiracial experience.

National Center for Transgender Equality – https://transequality.org/
This organization provides resources for understanding people who are trans, trans issues, trans rights, and support for individuals who are trans.

Project RACE – https://projectrace.com/
Project RACE champions the cause of multiracial children, adults, and their families primarily by promoting multiracial education and fostering community awareness. They endorse policies aimed at benefiting individuals of multiracial heritage at local, state, and national levels.

References

AAPI Data. (2022, June 16). *State of Asian Americans, Native Hawaiians, and Pacific Islanders in the United States*. AAPI Data. https://aapidata.com/wp-content/uploads/2024/02/State-AANHPIs-National-June2022.pdf

Abacioglu, C. S., Epskamp, S., Fischer, A. H., & Volman, M. (2023). Effects of multicultural education on student engagement in low- and high-concentration classrooms: The mediating role of student relationships. *Learning Environment Research, 26*, 951–975. https://doi.org/10.1007/s10984-023-09462-0

Abdou, A. S., Danforth, S., & Griffiths, A. J. (2023). Are deficit perspectives thriving in trauma-informed schools? A historical and anti-racist reflection. *Equity & Excellence in Education, 1*, 1–17. https://doi.org/10.1080/10665684.2023.2192983

Abudabbeh, N. (1996). Arab families. In M. McGoldrick, J. Girodano, & J. K. Pearce (Eds.), *Ethnicity and Family Therapy* (2nd ed.) (pp. 333–346). New York: Guilford.

Adler, R. M., Rittle-Johnson, B., Hickendorff, M., & Durkin, K. (2024). A longitudinal examination of the relations between motivation, math achievement, and STEM career aspirations among Black students. *Contemporary Educational Psychology, 76*, 102–240.

Ajrouch, K. J. (2004). Gender, race, and symbolic boundaries: Contested spaces of identity among Arab American adolescents. *Sociological Perspectives, 47*(4), 371–392.

AlJuhani, E. (2023). Debating the mixed gender classroom and Saudi female students visibility in coeducation. *Theory and Practice in Language Studies, 13*(9), 2297–2302. https://doi.org/10.17507/tpls.1309.16

Ameen, Z. J. M. & Kadhim, A. A. (2023). Deep learning methods for arabic autoencoder speech recognition system for electro-larynx device. *Advances in Human-Computer Interaction, 2023*. https://doi.org/10.1155/2023/7398538

Amer, M. (2023). Arab American acculturation and ethnic identity across the lifespan: Sociodemographic correlates and psychological outcomes. In S. C. Nassar, K. J. Ajrouch, F. J. Dallo, & J. Hakim-Larson (Eds.), *Biopsychosocial Perspectives on Arab Americans*. Cham: Springer. https://doi.org/10.1007/978-3-031-28360-4_8

Anderson, L., File, T., Marshall, J., McElrath, K., & Scherer, Z. (2021, November 4). New household pulse survey data reveals differences between LGBT and non-LGBT respondents during COVID-19 pandemic. U.S. Census Bureau. www.census.gov/library/stories/2021/11/census-bureau-survey-explores-sexual-orientation-and-gender-identity.html

Anokye, A. D. (1997). A case for orality in the classroom. *The Clearing House, 70*(5), 229–231.

Anthony, J. L., Roman, D. J., Rodriguez, N. G. P., Daniels, N., Crowder, S., & Haile, A. (2023). Preliminary evaluation of the What You Do Matters curriculum in community-based settings. *Children and Youth Services Review, 150.* https://doi.org/10.1016/j.childyouth.2023.107018

Arab American Institute. (2023). National Arab American demographics. Arab American Institute. www.aaiusa.org/demographics#:~:text=Arab%20American%20Population%20Growth,30%25%20between%20 2010%20and%202022

Arizona Department of Education. (2022). *22 Federally Recognized Tribes in Arizona.* www.azed.gov/oie/22-federally-recognized-tribes-arizona

Aronson, B. A. & Laughter, J. (2016). The theory and practice of culturally relevant education: A synthesis of research across content areas. *Review of Educational Research, 86*(1), 163–206.

Asher, C. A., Scherer, E., Kim, J. S., & Tvedt, J. N. (2024). Understanding heterogeneous patterns of family engagement with educational technology to inform school-family communication in linguistically diverse communities. *EdWorkingPaper, 23-780.* https://doi.org/10.26300/1mrn-cv91

Atari-Khan, R., Rbeiz, K. S., & Gerstein, L. H. (2024). Arab American well-being and impacts of the COVID-19 pandemic. *Cultural Diversity and Ethnic Minority Psychology.* https://dx.doi.org/10.1037/cdp0000644

Awan, I. & Zempi, I. (2020). "You all look the same": Non-Muslim men who suffer Islamophobic hate crime in the post-Brexit era. *European Journal of Criminology, 17*(5), 585–602. https://doi.org/10.1177/1477370818812735

Ayscue, J. B., Fusarelli, L. D., & Uzzell, E. M. (2023). Equity and early implementation of the Every Student Succeeds Act in state-designed plans during COVID. *Educational Policy, 37*(7), 1917–1949. https://doi-org. proxy.lib.odu.edu/10.1177/08959048221130994

Bai, H. (2023). Perceived Muslim population growth triggers divergent perceptions and reactions from Republicans and Democrats. *Group Processes & Intergroup Relations, 26*(3), 579–606. https://doi-org.proxy.lib.odu. edu/10.1177/13684302221084850

Baker, T. L. (2019). Reframing the connections between deficit thinking, microaggressions, and teacher perceptions of defiance. *Journal of Negro Education, 88*(2), 103–113.

Banks, J. A. (1988). *Multiethnic Education: Theory and Practice*. Boston, MA: Allyn & Bacon.

Banks, J. A. (1993). Multicultural education: Development, dimensions, and challenges. *The Phi Delta Kappan, 75*(1), 22–28.

Banks, J. A. (2007). Approaches to multicultural curriculum reform. *Multicultural Education: Issues and Perspectives, 2,* 195–214.

Banks, J. A. (2013). Multicultural education: Approaches, developments and dimensions. In J. A. Banks (Ed.), *Education Cultural Diversity* (pp. 83–94). Routledge.

Banks, J., Kea, C., & Coleman, M. R. (2023). Making meaningful connections: Facilitating schoolwide family engagement with culturally diverse families. *Teaching Exceptional Children*. https://doi-org.proxy.lib.odu.edu/10.1177/00400599231182048

Begall, K., Grunow, D., & Buchler, S. (2023). Multidimensional gender ideologies across Europe: Evidence from 36 countries. *Gender & Society, 37*(2), 177–207. https://doi.org/10.1177/08912432231155914

Bennett, M. (1986). A developmental approach to training intercultural sensitivity. *International Journal of Intercultural Relations, 10*(2), 179–186.

Bennett, M. J. (2017). Developmental model of intercultural sensitivity. In Y. Y. Kim (Ed.), *The International Encyclopedia of Intercultural Communication*. Wiley. https://doi.org/10.1002/9781118783665.ieicc0182

Bergstrom, V. N. Z., Cadieux, J., Thakkar, D., & Chasteen, A. L. (2024). Same view, different lens: How intersectional identities reduce Americans' stereotypes of threat regarding Arab and Black men. *Group Processes & Intergroup Relations, 27*(2), 348–365. https://doi-org.proxy.lib.odu.edu/10.1177/13684302231153802

Berscheid, M. (2023). When programs work together, families learn together. *Childhood Education, 99*(2), 40–45. https://doi-org.proxy.lib.odu.edu/10.1080/00094056.2023.2185041

Best, A. L. (2017). *Fast-food Kids: French Fries, Lunch Lines, and Social Ties* (Vol. 4). New York: New York University Press.

Bettencourt, A. F., Gross, D., Bower, K., Francis, L., Taylor, K., Singleton, D. L., & Han, H. R. (2023). Identifying meaningful indicators of parent engagement in early learning for low-income, urban families. *Urban Education, 58*(10), 2308–2345. https://doi-org.proxy.lib.odu.edu/10.1177/0042085920968619

Billingsley, B. (2016). Ways to prepare future teachers to teach science in multicultural classrooms. *Cultural Studies of Science Education, 11,* 283–291.

Birkel, L. F. (2000). Multicultural education: It is education first of all. *Teacher Educator, 36*(1), 23–28.

Blad, E. (2015, January 21). National School Lunch Program: Trends and factors affecting student participation. *Education Week, 34*, 5–11.

Block, N. C. (2023). Students' attitudinal development in a dual language bilingual education program from Grade 1 to Grade 5. *Bilingual Research Journal, 45*(3–4), 337–357. https://doi-org.proxy.lib.odu.edu/10.1080/15235882.2023.2174204

Bohrnstedt, G., Kitmitto, S., Ogut, B., Sherman, D., & Chan, D. (2015). School composition and the Black–White achievement gap (NCES 2015–018). Washington, DC: US Department of Education.

Bolgatz, J. (2005). *Talking Race in the Classroom.* New York: Teachers College Press.

Botelho, F., Madeira, R., & Rangel, M. A. (2015). Racial discrimination in grading: Evidence from Brazil. *American Economic Journal: Applied Economics, 7*(4), 37–52.

Bradley, R. H. (2023). Home life and well-being among Cherokee adolescents. *Family Relations, 72*(3). https://doi-org.proxy.lib.odu.edu/10.1111/fare.12643

Brooks, B. R. & Houston, S. (2015). Preservice teachers developing cultural competency: "We are more connected than we think." *Global Education Journal, 21*, 114–138.

Brooks, R. B. & Brooks, S. (2023). Nurturing positive emotions in the classroom: A foundation for purpose, motivation, and resilience in schools. *Handbook of Resilience in Children*, 549–568. https://doi.org/10.1007/978-3-031-14728-9_30

Brown, C. (2023, September 27). Hispanic students feeling discrimination in school. Lumina Foundation. www.luminafoundation.org/news-and-views/one-quarter-of-hispanic-students-face-discrimination-leading-many-to-consider-leaving-college/#:~:text=A%20concerning%20trend%20among%20credential%20programs&text=About%204%20in%2010%20Hispanic,or%20feelings%20of%20being%20unsafe

Brummelman, E. & Sedikides, C. (2023). Unequal selves in the classroom: Nature, origins, and consequences of socioeconomic disparities in children's self-views. *Developmental Psychology, 59*(11), 1962–1987. https://doi-org.proxy.lib.odu.edu/10.1037/dev0001599

Bryant, J. A. (2023). Gadugi: Reclaiming Native American education through a culturally reflective pedagogy. *Athens Journal of Education, 10*(4). https://eric.ed.gov/?id=EJ1414576

Budiman, A. & Ruiz, N. G. (2021, April 29). Key facts about Asian Americans, a diverse and growing population. Pew Research Center. www.pewresearch.org/short-reads/2021/04/29/key-facts-about-asian-americans/

Burgess, S. & Greaves, E. (2013). Test scores, subjective assessment, and stereotyping of ethnic minorities. *Journal of Labor Economics, 31*(3), 535–576.

Burnham, K. (2020, July 31). Five culturally responsive teaching strategies. Northeastern University Graduate Program. www.northeastern.edu/graduate/blog/culturally-responsive-teaching-strategies/

Burton, L. M., Bonilla-Silva, E., Ray, V., Buckelew, R., & Freeman, E. H. (2010). Critical race theories, colorism, and the decade's research on families of color. *Journal of Marriage and Family, 72*(3), 440–459.

Butler-Barnes, S. T. (2023). "What's going on?" Racism, COVID-19, and centering the voices of Black youth. *American Journal of Community Psychology, 71*(1–2), 101–113. https://doi-org.proxy.lib.odu.edu/10.1002/ajcp.12646

Buzzai, C., Muscarà, M., Romano, A., Passanisi, A., & Pace, U. (2023) The relationship between socio-cognitive skills and ethnic prejudice in preservice special education teachers. *International Journal of Inclusive Education,* 1–16. https://www.tandfonline.com/doi/abs/10.1080/08856257.2022.2107679

Cabral, S. (2021, May 21). Covid "hate crimes" against Asian Americans on rise. *BBC News.* www.bbc.com/news/world-us-canada-56218684

Cabral-Gouveia, C., Menezes, I., & Neves, T. (2023). Educational strategies to reduce the achievement gap: A systematic review. *Frontiers in Education, 8.* https://doi.org/10.3389/feduc.2023.1155741

Cai, L. (2023). An Asian American feminist manifesto: Asian American women heads of schools embodying culturally responsive school leadership. *Teachers College Record, 125*(7/8), 173–187. https://doi-org.proxy.lib.odu.edu/10.1177/01614681231209589

Caraballo, C., Massey, D. S., Ndumele C. D., Haywood, T., Kaleem, S., King, T., Liu, Y., Lu, Y., Nunez-Smith, M., Taylor, H. A., Watson, K. E., Herrin, J., Yancy, C. W., Faust, J. S., & Krumholz, H. M. (2023). Excess mortality and years of potential life lost among the Black population in the US, 1999–2020. *JAMA, 329*(19), 1662–1670. https://jamanetwork.com/journals/jama/fullarticle/2804822

Cardwell, M. E., Minniear, M. J., & Soliz, J. (2023). Malleable identity and parental identity accommodation in multiethnic-racial families in the United States: Implications for psychosocial well-being. *Race and Social Problems,* 15(1), 45–58. https://doi.org/10.1007/s12552-023-09391-w

Castillo, S. (2023). The battle for trans rights: Political spectacle theory and its implications for education policy. *Sexuality, Gender and Policy, 6*(1), 8–15. https://onlinelibrary.wiley.com/doi/10.1002/sgp2.12057

Cavanagh, T., Vigil, P., & Garcia, E. (2014). A story legitimating the voices of Latino/Hispanic students and their parents: Creating a restorative justice response to wrongdoing and conflict in schools. *Equity & Excellence in Education, 47*(4), 565–579.

Cegielski, O., Maida, K., Morales, D. L., & Mendez, S. L. (2023). Creating a classroom for social justice: Secondary teacher perceptions of the environmental outcomes of culturally relevant education. *Educational Research: Theory and Practice*, 34(3), 103–116. https://files.eric.ed.gov/fulltext/EJ1403512.pdf

Chakraborti, N. (2018). Responding to hate crime: Escalating problems, continued failings. *Criminology & Criminal Justice, 18*(4), 387–404.

Chang, A. (2016). Resisting the orthodox smart label: High school Latinas and the redefinition of smartness on the Western frontier. *Journal of Latinos and Education*, 1–11.

Chang, S. H. (2015). *Raising Mixed Race: Multiracial Asian Children in a Postracial World*. New York: Routledge.

Chavkin, N. F. & Gonzalez, J. (2000). Mexican immigrant youth and resiliency: Research and promising programs. Charleston, WV: ERIC Clearinghouse on Rural Education and Small Schools. (ERIC Document Reproduction Service No. ED 447990).

Chen, J. A., Zhang, E., & Liu, C. H. (2020). Potential impact of COVID-19-related racial discrimination on the health of Asian Americans. *American Journal of Public Health, 110*(11), 1624–1627. https://doi.org/10.2105/AJPH.2020.305858

Chen, S. & Xie, B. (2020). Institutional discrimination and assimilation: Evidence from the Chinese Exclusion Act of 1882. *IZA – Institute of Labor Economics*. Discussion Paper Number 13647.

Chiang, L. H. (2000). Teaching Asian American students. *Teacher Educator, 36*(1), 58–69.

Childs, T. M. & Wooten, N. R. (2023). Teacher bias matters: An integrative review of correlates, mechanisms, and consequences. *Race Ethnicity and Education, 26*(3), 368–397.

Cho, S., Crenshaw, K. W., & McCall, L. (2013). Toward a field of intersectionality studies: Theory, applications, and praxis. *Signs, 38*(4), 785–810. https://doi.org/10.1086/669608

Choi, Y., Tan, K., Yasui, M., & Hahm, H. (2016). Advancing understanding of acculturation for adolescents of Asian immigrants: Person-oriented analysis of acculturation strategy among Korean American youth. *Journal of Youth and Adolescence, 45*(7), 1380–1395.

Cid-Martinez, I. & Marvin, S. (2023, May 26). Broad child poverty data for the Asian American, Native Hawaiian, and Pacific Islander population don't tell the whole economic story. Economic Policy Institute. www.epi.org/blog/broad-child-poverty-data-for-the-asian-american-native-hawaiian-and-pacific-islander-population-dont-tell-the-whole-economic-story/

Cochran-Smith, M., Ell, F., Grudnoff, L., Haigh, M., Hill, M., & Ludlow, L. (2016). Initial teacher education: What does it take to put equity at the center? *Teaching and Teacher Education, 57*, 67–78.

Coffey, M. & Tyner, A. (2023). *Excellence Gaps by Race and Socioeconomic Status.* Washington, DC: Thomas B. Fordham Institute.

Comstock, M., Litke, E., Hill, K. L., & Desimone, L. M. (2023). A culturally responsive disposition: How professional learning and teachers' beliefs about and self-efficacy for culturally responsive teaching relate to instruction. *AERA Open, 9.* https://doi.org/10.1177/2332858422 1140092

Cooke, J. (2023). Savagery repositioned: Historicizing the Cherokee nation. *American Indian Quarterly, 47*(2), 126–156. https://doi-org.proxy.lib.odu. edu/10.1353/aiq.2023.a906094

Crawford, J. (2007, June 6). A diminished vision of civil rights. *Education Week, 26*(39), 30–31.

Crenshaw, K. (2013). Demarginalizing the intersection of race and sex: A black feminist critique of antidiscrimination doctrine, feminist theory and antiracist politics. In K. Maschke (Ed.), *Feminist Legal Theories* (pp. 23–51). New York: Routledge.

Cuevas, S. (2023). From spectators to partners: The role of self-efficacy in Latina/o immigrant parents' engagement in students' post-secondary planning. *Journal of Latinos & Education, 22*(1), 271–287. https://doi-org.proxy. lib.odu.edu/10.1080/15348431.2020.1747024

Dalmaijer, E. S., Gibbons, S. G., Bignardi, G., Anwyl-Irvine, A. L., Siugzdaite, R., Smith, T. A., Uh, S., Johnson, A., & Astle, D. E. (2023). Direct and indirect links between children's socio-economic status and education: Pathways via mental health, attitude, and cognition. *Current Psychology, 42*, 9637–9651. https://doi-org.proxy.lib.odu.edu/10.1007/s12144-021-02232-2

Daly, A. (2023). Race talk tensions: Practicing racial literacy in a fourth-grade classroom. *English Teaching: Practice & Critique, 22*(1), 61–78. https://doi-org.proxy.lib.odu.edu/10.1108/ETPC-02-2022-0028

da Silva Iddings, A. C. & Warraich, A. K. (2024). Facilitating educational equity and safety of undocumented immigrant students. *Urban Education, 59*(2), 520–547. https://doi-org.proxy.lib.odu.edu/10.1177/004208592 21082672

Day, A., Barton, E., Cross, S., Miller, C., & Gonzales, J. (2024). Experiences and service utilization of American Indian/Alaskan Native kinship caregivers in kinship navigator programs across Washington state. *Families in Society, 105*(1), 19–36. https://doi-org.proxy.lib.odu. edu/10.1177/10443894231193779

Debnam, K. J., Smith, L. H., Aguayo, D., Reinke, W. M., & Herman, K. C. (2023). Nominated exemplar teacher perceptions of culturally responsive practices in the classroom. *Teaching and Teacher Education, 125*(1). https://doi.org/10.1016/j.tate.2023.104062

DeCuir, J. T. & Dixson, A. D. (2004). "So when it comes out, they aren't that surprised that it is there": Using critical race theory as a tool of analysis of race and racism in education. *Educational Researcher, 33*(5), 26–31.

Delgado, M. Y., Ettekal, A. V., Simpkins, S. D., & Schaefer, D. R. (2016). How do my friends matter? Examining Latino adolescents' friendships, school belonging, and academic achievement. *Journal of Youth and Adolescence, 45*(6), 1110–1125.

Devine, P. G., Forscher, P. S., Austin, A. J., & Cox, W. T. L. (2012). Long-term reduction in implicit race bias: A prejudice habit-breaking intervention. *Journal of Experimental Social Psychology, 48*(6), 1267–1278. https://doi-org.proxy.lib.odu.edu/10.1016/j.jesp.2012.06.003

D'hondt, F., Eccles, J. S., Van Houtte, M., & Stevens, P. A. (2016). Perceived ethnic discrimination by teachers and ethnic minority students' academic futility: Can parents prepare their youth for better or for worse? *Journal of Youth and Adolescence, 45*(6), 1075–1089.

Dietrich, S. & Hernandez, E. (2022a). Language use in the United States: 2019. *American Community Survey Reports.* U.S. Census Bureau. www.census.gov/library/publications/2022/acs/acs-50.html

Dietrich, S. & Hernandez, E. (2022b, December 6). Nearly 68 million people spoke a language other than English at home in 2019. U.S. Census Bureau. www.census.gov/library/stories/2022/12/languages-we-speak-in-united-states.html

Dinh, K. T. & Kalaja, A. (2023). A qualitative examination of cultural influences in parent–child relationships and life satisfaction among Asian American young adults. *Asian American Journal of Psychology.* https://dx.doi.org/10.1037/aap0000331

Dobani, F., Zaso, M., Desalu, J. M., & Park, A. (2024). Alcohol use in multiracial American youth compared with monoracial youth: A meta-analysis. *Addiction, 119*(1), 47–59. https://doi.org/10.1111/add.16310

Dodo Seriki, V. (2018). Advancing alternate tools: Why science education needs CRP and CRT. *Cultural Studies of Science Education, 13,* 93–100. https://link.springer.com/article/10.1007/s11422-016-9775-z

Domina, T., Clark, L., Radsky, V., & Bhaskar, R. (2024). There is such a thing as a free lunch: School meals, stigma, and student discipline. *American Educational Research Journal, 61*(2), 287–327.

Dong, F., Hwang, Y., & Hodgson, N. A. (2023). "I have a wish": Anti-Asian racism and facing challenges amid the COVID-19 pandemic among Asian international graduate students. *Journal of Transcultural Nursing*, 34(2): 115–122. doi: 10.1177/10436596221143331

Doyle, L., Easterbrook, M. J., & Harris, P. R. (2023). Roles of socioeconomic status, ethnicity and teacher beliefs in academic grading. *British Journal of Educational Psychology*, *93*(1), 91–112. https://doi-org.proxy.lib.odu.edu/10.1111/bjep.12541

Duarte, N. V., Linares, A., Córdova, T., Lopez, I., Wang, Y., & Maruyama, G. (2023). Effects of service-learning and community engagement programs on the academic outcomes of underrepresented undergraduate students. *Journal of Higher Education Outreach and Engagement*, *27*(2), 47–72. https://openjournals.libs.uga.edu/jheoe/article/view/3096/2945

Due East Educational Equity Collaborative. (2020). Culturally responsive pedagogy (CRP) self-assessment and reflective conversations. Due East Educational Equity Collaborative. https://dueeast.org/wp-content/uploads/Culturally-Responsive-Pedagogy-CRP-Self-assessment.pdf

Duer, J., Friedman-Krauss, A., & Barnett, W. S. (2022, December 30). *State(s) of Head Start and Early Head Start*. National Institute for Early Education Research. https://nieer.org/research-library/states-head-start-early-head-start

Eddarif, H. (2023). The "innocent" other: Hollywood's post 9/11 Muslim child and childhood. *IAFOR Journal of Cultural Studies*, *8*(1), 65–79. https://iafor.org/archives/journals/iafor-journal-of-cultural-studies/10.22492.ijcs.8.1.pdf#page=73

Egalite, A. (2024). What we know about teacher race and student outcomes: A review of the evidence to date. *Education Next*, *24*(1), 42–49.

Espinosa, G. (2007). Today we act, tomorrow we vote: Latino religions, politics, and activism in contemporary U.S. civil society. *Annals of the American Academy of Political and Social Science*, *612*(1), 152–172.

Espiritu, Y. (1992). *Asian American Panethnicity: Bridging Institutions and Identities*. Philadelphia, PA: Temple University Press.

Estrada, J. & Galliher, R. V. (2023). Moderating effects of school ethnic composition of acculturative stress and academic outcomes in Latinx youth. *Journal of Research on Adolescence*, *33*(2), 376–388. https://doi-org.proxy.lib.odu.edu/10.1111/jora.12808

Fantozzi, V. B. (2023). Connecting in context: Using digital portfolios to foster reciprocal relationships with families. *Young Children*, *78*(4), 30–37. http://proxy.lib.odu.edu/login?url=https://search.ebscohost.com/login.aspx?direct=true&db=ehh&AN=174049972&scope=site

Fetter, A. K., Wiglesworth, A., Rey, L. F., Azarani, M., Chicken, M. L. P., Young, A. R., Riegelman, A., & Gone, J. P. (2023). Risk factors for suicidal behaviors in American Indian and Alaska Native peoples: A systematic review. *Clinical Psychological Science, 11*(3), 528–551. https://doi-org.proxy.lib.odu.edu/10.1177/21677026221126732

Flanagan, C. A., Gill, S., Cumsille, P., & Gallay, L. S. (2007). School and community climates and civic commitments: Patterns for ethnic minority and majority students. *Journal of Educational Psychology, 99*(2), 421–433.

Fong, M. (2016, January 27). The impact of China's one-child policy on America. *The Seattle Times.* www.seattletimes.com/

Ford, D. Y., Hines, E. M., Middleton, T. J., & Moore, J. L. (2023). Inequitable representation of Black boys in gifted and talented education, Advanced Placement, and special education. *Journal of Multicultural Counseling and Development, 51,* 304–314. https://doi-org.proxy.lib.odu.edu/10.1002/jmcd.12283

Francis, M. M. & Wright-Rigueur, L. (2021). Black Lives Matter in historical perspective. *Annual Review of Law and Social Science, 17,* 441–458.

Franco, M. P., Bottiani, J. H., & Bradshaw, C. P. (2023). Assessing teachers' culturally responsive classroom practice in PK–12 schools: A systematic review of teacher-, student-, and observer-report measures. *Review of Educational Research.* https://doi.org/10.3102/00346543231208720

Fregeau, L. & Leier, R. (2016). Two Latina teachers: Culture, success, higher education. *Taboo: The Journal of Culture and Education, 15*(1), 61–78.

Frey, W. H. (2022, June 15). Today's suburbs are symbolic of America's rising diversity: A 2020 census portrait. Brookings. www.brookings.edu/articles/todays-suburbs-are-symbolic-of-americas-rising-diversity-a-2020-census-portrait/

Fry, R. (2014). U.S. high school dropout rate reaches record low, driven by improvements among Hispanics, blacks. The Pew Research Center. www.pewresearch.org/fact-tank/2014/10/02/u-s-highschool-dropout-rate-reaches-record-low-driven-by-improvementsamong-hispanics-blacks/

Fry, R. & Lopez, M. H. (2012). Hispanic student enrollments reach new highs in 2011. Washington, DC: Pew Hispanic Center. www.pewhispanic.org/files/2012/08/Hispanic-Student-Enrollments-Reach-New-Highs-in-2011_FINAL.pdf

Fry, R. & Taylor, P. (2013). High school drop-out rate at record low: Hispanic high school graduates pass whites in rate of college enrollment. Washington, DC: Pew Hispanic Center. www.pewhispanic.org/files/2013/05/PHC_college_enrollment_2013–05.pdf

Fung, J., Cai, G., & Wang, K. (2023). Personal and family perfectionism among Asian and Latinx youth. *Cultural Diversity and Ethnic Minority Psychology, 29*(2), 235–246. https://doi.org/10.1037/cdp0000555

Gaither, S. E., Chen, E. E., Corriveau, K. H., Harris, P. L., Ambady, N., & Sommers, S. R. (2014). Monoracial and biracial children: Effects of racial identity saliency on social learning and social preferences. *Child Development, 85*(6), 2299–2316.

Gale, A., Lateef, H., Boyd, D., & Williams, E. D. (2023). A review of school-based interventions for Black boys' school success. *The Urban Review.* https://doi.org/10.1007/s11256-023-00685-2

Gallup. (2023, December). *Most Important Problem.* Gallup. https://news.gallup.com/poll/1675/Most-Important-Problem.aspx

Gambino, C. P., Acosta, Y. D., & Grieco, E. M. (2014). English-speaking ability of the foreign-born population in the United States 2012. (ACS-26) Washington, DC: The US Census Bureau.

Gándara, P. (2015a). Rethinking bilingual instruction. *Educational Leadership, 72*(6), 60–64.

Gándara, P. (2015b). With the future on the line: Why studying Latino education is so urgent. *American Journal of Education, 121*(3), 451–463.

Garay, M. M., Perry, J. M., & Remedios, J. D. (2023). The maintenance of the U.S. racial hierarchy through judgments of multiracial people based on proximity to whiteness. *Personality and Social Psychology Bulletin, 49*(6), 969–984. https://doi.org/10.1177/01461672221086175

Garbacz, S. A., McIntosh, K., Eagle, J. W., Dowd-Eagle, S. E., Hirano, K. A., & Ruppert, T. (2016). Family engagement within schoolwide positive behavioral interventions and supports. *Preventing School Failure: Alternative Education for Children and Youth, 60*(1), 60–69.

García, O. (2017). Translanguaging in schools: Subiendo y bajando, bajando y subiendo as afterword. *Journal of Language, Identity & Education, 16*(4), 256–263.

Gay, G. (2018). *Culturally Responsive Teaching: Theory, Research, & Practice.* New York: Teachers College Press.

Geenen, S., Powers, L. E., & Lopez-Vasquez, A. (2001). Multicultural aspects of parent involvement in transitional planning. *Exceptional Children, 67*(1), 265–275.

Gershon, S. A., Pantoja, A. D., & Taylor, J. B. (2016). God in the barrio? The determinants of religiosity and civic engagement among Latinos in the United States. *Politics and Religion, 9*(1), 84–110.

Giordano, A. L., Prosek, E. A., Schmit, M. K., & Wester, K. L. (2020). "We are still here": Learning from Native American perspectives. *Journal of Counseling and Development, 98*(2), 159–171. https://doi.org/10.1002/jcad.12310

Glaad (2016). GLAAD media reference guide—transgender. www.glaad.org/reference/transgender

Glover, T. A., Reddy, L. A., & Crouse, K. (2023). Instructional coaching actions that predict teacher classroom practices and student achievement. *Journal of School Psychology, 96*, 1–11. https://doi.org/10.1016/j.jsp.2022.10.006

Gollnick, D. M. & Chinn, P. C. (2006). *Multicultural Education in a Pluralistic Society* (7th ed.). Upper Saddle River, NJ: Merrill.

Goodwin, A. L. (2023). Enduring problems, rethinking process, fulfilling promises: Reflections on the continuing shortage of teachers of color. *Journal of Teacher Education, 74*(2), 167–170. https://doi.org/10.1177/00224871231160372

Gorski, P. C. & Swalwell, K. (2015). Equity literacy for all. *Educational Leadership, 72*, 34–40.

Grammich, C., Dollhopf, E. J., Gautier, M. L., Houseal, R., Jones, D. E., Krindatch, A., Stanley, R., & Thumma, S. (2023). 2020 U.S. religion census: Religious congregations & adherents study. Association of Statisticians of American Religious Bodies. www.usreligioncensus.org/sites/default/files/2023-10/2020_US_Religion_Census.pdf

Green, M. N. & Bryant, S. (2023). Racially humble parenting: Exploring the link between parental racial humility and parent–child closeness in multiracial black-white families. *Race and Social Problems, 15*, 32–44. https://doi.org/10.1007/s12552-023-09388-5

Griffin, C. B., Harris, J. N., & Proctor, S. L. (2024). Intersectionality and school racial climate to create schools as sites of fairness and liberation for Black girls. *Journal of School Psychology, 104*, 101282. https://doi.org/10.1016/j.jsp.2024.101282

Griffin, L. B., Watson, D., & Liggett, T. (2016). "I didn't see it as a cultural thing": Supervisors of student teachers define and describe culturally responsive supervision. *Democracy and Education, 24*(1), 1–13.

Grilo, S. A., Santelli, J. S., Nathanson, C., Catallozzi, M., Abraido-Lanza, A. F., Adelman, S., & Hernández, D. (2023). Psychosocial outcomes and peer influences among multiracial adolescents in the United States. *Frontiers in Public Health, 11.* https://doi.org/10.3389/fpubh.2023.852268

Guiberson, M. & Vining, C. B. (2023). Culturally responsive and indigenous language strategies: Findings from a scoping review. *Communication Disorders Quarterly, 45*(1), 3–19. https://doi-org.proxy.lib.odu.edu/10.1177/15257401231155812

Guinier, L. (2004). From racial liberalism to racial literacy: Brown v. Board of Education and the interest-divergence dilemma. *Journal of American History, 91*(1), 92–118.

Gullickson, A. (2023). Differences in the risk of grade retention for biracial and monoracial students in the United States, 2010 to 2019. *Sociological Science, 10*(13), 403–428. https://doi.org/10.15195/v10.a13

Guzman, G. & Kollar, M. (2023, September 12). *Income in the United States: 2022*. U.S. Census Bureau. www.census.gov/library/publications/2023/demo/p60-279.html

Haboush, K. L. (2007). Working with Arab American families: Culturally competent practice for school psychologists. *Psychology in the Schools, 44*(2), 183–198.

Halpern, C. & Ozfidan, B. (2024). Preservice teachers' cultural competence factors in teacher preparation programs: An explanatory sequential mixed methods study. *Journal of Multilingual and Multicultural Development*, 1–16. https://doi.org/10.1080/01434632.2024.2306163

Han, S., Riddell, J. R., & Piquero, A. R. (2023). Anti-Asian American hate crimes spike during the early stages of the COVID-19 pandemic. *Journal of Interpersonal Violence, 38*(3–4), 3513–3533. https://doi.org/10.1177/08862605221107056

Hayes, C. & Francis, G. (2023). Making waves: Early childhood teachers' experiences with multicultural picturebooks to promote equitable classrooms. *Early Childhood Education Journal, 52*, 1511–1523. https://doi-org.proxy.lib.odu.edu/10.1007/s10643-023-01557-w

Head Start. (2022, September 20). *Head Start Program Facts: Fiscal Year 2021*. Head Start. https://eclkc.ohs.acf.hhs.gov/about-us/article/head-start-program-facts-fiscal-year-2021#:~:text=Child%20and%20Family%20Demographics&text=Head%20Start%20serves%20a%20diverse,%2C%20non%2DHispanic%20or%20Latino

Hernandez, E.L., & McElrath, K. (2013, May 10). Gains in educational attainment, enrollment in all Hispanic groups, largest among South American population. U.S. Census Bureau. www.census.gov/library/stories/2023/05/significant-educational-strides-young-hispanic-population.html

Hernandez, H. (1989). *Multicultural Education: A Teacher's Guide to Content and Process*. Columbus, OH: Merrill.

Herring, R. D. (1989). Counseling Native American children: Implications for elementary school counselors. *Elementary School Guidance and Counseling, 23*, 272–281.

High, V. M., Challa, S. A., Scharer, J. L., & Taylor, M. J. (2023). The mediating effects of alcohol use and parental monitoring on dating violence victimization among multiracial and monoracial youth. *Journal of Ethnic & Cultural Diversity in Social Work, 32*(2), 91–101. https://doi.org/10.1080/15313204.2020.1870602

Hill, L., Artiga, S., & Damico, A. (2024, January 11). Health coverage by race and ethnicity, 2010–2022. The Kaiser Family Foundation. www.kff.org/racial-equity-and-health-policy/issue-brief/health-coverage-by-race-and-ethnicity/

Hirschl, N. & Smith, C. M. (2023). Advanced Placement gatekeeping and racialized tracking. *Sociology of Education, 96*(3), 190–210. https://doi-org.proxy.lib.odu.edu/10.1177/00380407231161334

Hobson, A. (2015). Growth and achievement trends of advanced placement exams in American high schools. *American Secondary Education, 43*(2), 59–76.

Hodes, M. (2022). Thinking about young refugees' mental health following the Russian invasion of Ukraine in 2022. *Clinical Child Psychology and Psychiatry, 28*(1), 3–14. https://doi.org/10.1177/13591045221125639

Hodges, J. & Gentry, M. (2021). Underrepresentation in gifted education in the context of rurality and socioeconomic status. *Journal of Advanced Academics, 32*(2), 135–159. https://doi-org.proxy.lib.odu.edu/10.1177/1932202X20969143

Howard, A. S. & Solberg, S. H. (2006). School-based social justice: The achieving success identity pathways program. *Professional School Counseling, 9*(4), 278–287.

Howlett, K. M. & Young, H. D. (2019). Building a classroom library based on multicultural principles: A checklist for future K-6 teachers. *Multicultural Education, 26*(3), 40–46. https://files.eric.ed.gov/fulltext/EJ1239626.pdf

Huang, J. & Zhu, J. (2023). Comparing the discourses of #BlackLivesMatter and #StopAsianHate on Twitter: Diversity and emotional and moral sentiments. *Cogent Social Sciences, 9*(2). https://doi.org/10.1080/23311886.2023.2263944

Huang, R., Baker, E. R., & Wang, T. (2023). Effects of early bilingualism on theory of mind development among children in economic adversity. *Cognitive Development, 68.* https://doi.org/10.1016/j.cogdev.2023.101389

Idrus, F. & Sohid, M. (2023). Teachers' expectations and challenges in using culturally responsive teaching (CRT) strategies in the ESL classroom. *Journal of Language Teaching & Research, 14*(3), 629–635. https://doi-org.proxy.lib.odu.edu/10.17507/jltr.1403.10

Iraheta, A. C. (2023). Reclaiming the power of bilingualism: Spanish heritage learners using bilingual skills in a critical service-learning project. *Hispania, 106*(1), 67–82. https://doi.org/10.1353/hpn.2023.0005

Jacobs, J. & Perez, J. I. (2023). A qualitative metasynthesis of teacher educator self-studies on social justice: Articulating a social justice pedagogy. *Teaching and Teacher Education, 123.* https://doi.org/10.1016/j.tate.2022.103994

Jacoby-Senghor, D. S., Sinclair, S., & Shelton, J. N. (2016). A lesson in bias: The relationship between implicit racial bias and performance in pedagogical contexts. *Journal of Experimental Social Psychology, 63,* 50–55.

Jerabek, M. (2023). Service-learning curricula in Eastern Pennsylvania's K-12 schools: Educational decision-makers' experiences through a critical lens

[Doctoral dissertation, West Chester University Doctoral Projects, 198].
https://digitalcommons.wcupa.edu/all_doctoral/198

Jeung, R., Garcia, A. M., Bae, A., Shen, C., & Malasa, J. (2023). Urgently needed to protect Asian American children and families: The social movement for Asian American studies at K-12 grades. *Sociological Inquiry, 94*(2), 369–390. https://doi.org/10.1111/soin.12573

Jeynes, W. H. (2016). A meta-analysis: The relationship between parental involvement and African American school outcomes. *Journal of Black Studies, 13*(1), 1–22.

Jones, K. D. (2023). Fostering the multicultural efficacy of principal candidates. *Journal of Organizational and Educational Leadership, 9*(5). https://digitalcommons.gardner-webb.edu/joel/vol9/iss1/5/

Jones, N., Marks, R., Ramirez, R., & Ríos-Vargas, M. (2021, August 12). 2020 census illuminates racial and ethnic composition of the country. U.S. Census Bureau. www.census.gov/library/stories/2021/08/improved-race-ethnicity-measures-reveal-united-states-population-much-more-multiracial.html

Jones, R. P., Cox, D., & Navarro-Rivera, J. (2013). 2013 Hispanic values survey: How shifting religious identities and experiences are influencing Hispanic approaches to politics. Washington, DC: Public Religion Research Institute.

Juang, L. P., Umaña-Taylor, A. J., Schachner, M. K., Frisén, A., Hwang, C. P., Moscardino, U., Motti-Stefanidi, F., Oppedal, B., Pavlopoulos, V., Abdullahi, A. K., Barahona, R., Berne, S., Ceccon, C., Gharaei, N., Moffitt, U., Ntalachanis, A., Pevec, S., Sandberg, D. J., Zacharia, A., & Syed, M. (2023). Ethnic-racial identity in Europe: Adapting the identity project intervention in five countries. *European Journal of Developmental Psychology, 20*(6), 978–1006. https://doi.org/10.1080/17405629.2022.2131520

Kaiser Family Foundation. (2022). Poverty rate by race/ethnicity. www.kff.org/other/state-indicator/poverty-rate-by-raceethnicity/?currentTimeframe=0&sortModel=%7B%22colId%22:%22Location%22,%22sort%22:%22asc%22%7D

Karimi, A. & Wilkes, R. (2023). A transnational amendment to assimilation theory: Country of origin's racial status versus transnational whiteness. *Ethnic and Racial Studies, 47*(3), 459–482. https://doi-org.proxy.lib.odu.edu/10.1080/01419870.2023.2174810

Kehdi, B. (2023). Arab American curriculum work. *Journal of Asian American Studies, 26*(2), 185–193. https://doi.org/10.1353/jaas.2023.a901067

Keskin, O., Gabel, S., Kollar, I., & Gegenfurtner, A. (2023). Relations between pre-service teacher gaze, teacher attitude, and student ethnicity. *Frontiers in Education, 8.* https://doi.org/10.3389/feduc.2023.1272671

Khasawneh, Y. J. A. & Khasawneh, M. A. S. (2023). Achieving assessment equity and fairness: Identifying and eliminating bias in assessment tools and practices. *Kurdish Studies*, 11(2), 4469–4478. www.preprints.org/manuscript/202306.0730/v1

Kiang, L., Tseng, V., & Yip, T. (2016). Placing Asian American child development within historical context. *Child Development*, 87(4), 995–1013.

Kids Count Data Center. (January 2024). Children in single-parent families by race and ethnicity in United States. Kids Count Data Center. https://datacenter.aecf.org/data/tables/107-children-in-single-parent-families-by-race-and-ethnicity?loc=1&loct=1#detailed/1/any/false/1095/4040,1353/432,431

Kilag, O. K., Diano, F., Bulilan, R., Moralista, R., Allego, L., & Cañizares, M. C. (2024). Leadership strategies for building inclusive school communities: The challenges of managing diversity in schools. *International Multidisciplinary Journal of Research for Innovation*, 1(1), 92–100. https://risejournals.org/index.php/imjrise/article/view/10

Kim, B. S. K., Suh, H. N., & Subica, A. (2023). Asian American child–parent cultural value discrepancies, family conflict, life satisfaction, and self-esteem. *Journal of Counseling Psychology*, 70(5), 510–521. https://doi-org.proxy.lib.odu.edu/10.1037/cou0000689

Kim, E., Park, H., Cho, Y., Jeon, K., & An, H. (2024). Invisibility and stigma: Experiences of transgender and gender non-conforming individuals in South Korea. *Archives of Sexual Behavior*, 53(1), 77–90.

Kim, J. & Yu, H. M. (2024). Home-based parent involvement, parental warmth, and kindergarten outcomes among children of immigrant parents. *Early Education and Development*, 35(2), 343–367. https://doi.org/10.1080/10409289.2022.2153003

Kim, S. J., Wee, Su., & Lee, M. (2016). Teaching racial diversity through multicultural literature: A case study in a kindergarten classroom in Korea. *Early Education & Development*, 27, 402–420.

Kimak, I. & Świetlicki, M. (2023). Memory, identity, belonging: Narratives of Eastern and Central European presence in North America. *European Journal of American Studies*, 18(4). https://doi.org/10.4000/ejas.20906

Kiswani, L., Naber, N., & Shoman, S. (2023). Palestine is ethnic studies: The struggle for Arab American studies in K–12 ethnic studies curriculum. *Journal of Asian American Studies*, 26(2), 221–231. https://doi.org/10.1353/jaas.2023.a901070

Kitano, M. K. & Perkins, C. O. (2000). Gifted European American women. *Journal of the Education of the Gifted*, 23(3), 287–313.

Klein, B., Ogbunugafor, C. B., Schafer, B. J., Bhadricha, Z., Kori, P., Sheldon, J., Kaza, N., Sharma, A., Wang, E. A., Eliassi-Rad, T., Scarpino, S. V., &

Hinton, E. (2023). COVID-19 amplified racial disparities in the US criminal legal system. *Nature, 617,* 344–350. https://doi.org/10.1038/s41586-023-05980-2

Kong, P. A., Zhang, X., Sachdev, A., & Yu, X. (2023). Learning the rules: Chinese immigrant parents' involvement during their children's transition to kindergarten. *Early Childhood Education Journal.* https://doi.org/10.1007/s10643-023-01452-4

Krogstad, J. M., Passel, J. S., & Cohn, D. (2016, September 20). Five facts about illegal immigration in the U.S. www.pewresearch.org/fact-tank/2016/09/20/5-facts-about-illegal-immigration-in-the-u-s/

Krogstad, J. M., Alvarado, J., & Mohamed, B. (2023, April 13). Among U.S. Latinos, Catholicism continues to decline but is still the largest faith. Pew Research Center. www.pewresearch.org/religion/2023/04/13/among-u-s-latinos-catholicism-continues-to-decline-but-is-still-the-largest-faith/

Ladson-Billings, G. (1995a). But that's just good teaching! The case for culturally relevant pedagogy. *Theory Into Practice,* 34(3), 159–165. DOI: 10.1080/00405849509543675

Ladson-Billings, G. (1995b). Toward a theory of culturally relevant pedagogy. *American Educational Research Journal, 32*(3), 465–491.

Ladson-Billings, G. (1998). Teaching in dangerous times: Culturally relevant approaches to teacher assessment. *Journal of Negro Education,* 255–267.

Ladson-Billings, G. (2006). Yes, but how do we do it? Practicing culturally relevant pedagogy. In J. Landsman & C. W. Lewis (Eds.), *White Teachers/ Diverse Classrooms: A Guide to Building Inclusive Schools, Promoting High Expectations, and Eliminating Racism* (pp. 29–42). Sterling, VA: Stylus.

Ladson-Billings, G. (2021, July). Three decades of culturally relevant, responsive, & sustaining pedagogy: What lies ahead? *The Educational Forum, 85*(4), 351–354.

Ladson-Billings, G. & Tate, W. F. (1995). Toward a critical race theory of education. *Teachers College Record, 97*(1), 47–68.

Lau, W. S. & Shea, M. (2022). Empowering English learners in the classroom through culturally responsive social-emotional teaching practices. *Journal of Multilingual and Multicultural Development,* 1–18.

Lee, G. L. (2011). Teaching traditional values through folk literature in Korea. *Childhood Education, 87*(6), 402–408.

Lee, G. L. (2013). Re-emphasizing character education in early childhood programs: Korean children's experiences. *Childhood Education, 89*(5), 315–322.

Lee, G. L. & Gupta, A. (2020). Raising children to speak their heritage language in the USA: Roles of Korean parents. *Journal of Language Teaching and Research, 11*(4).

Lee, G. L. & Gupta, A. (2024). Promoting equity and inclusiveness for Asian-Americans in the Covid pandemic era. In S. Sinha, A. Gupta, & P. Mishra (Eds.), *Understanding Diversity, Equity & Inclusion: Policies and Practices* (pp. 149–156). New Delhi: Dominant Publishers & Distributors.

Lee, G. L. & Johnson, W. (2000). The need for interracial storybooks in effective multicultural classrooms. *Multicultural Education, 8*(2), 28–30.

Lee, G. L. & Kang, S. Y. (2023). The struggle and success of heritage language education: A comparative case study of two Korean American families. *International Journal of Language and Linguistics, 10*(1). DOI:10.30845/ijll.v10n1p1

Lee, G. L. & Manning, M. L. (2001). Working with Asian parents and families. *Multicultural Education, 9*, 23–25.

Lee, S. J. (2015). *Unraveling the "Model Minority" Stereotype: Listening to Asian American Youth*. New York: Teachers College Press.

Leigh-Osroosh, K. T., Clemons, K., Robertson, A., Placeres, V., Gay, J., Lopez-Perry, C., Mason, E. C., Ieva, K. P., Lane, E. M. D., & Saunders, R. (2023). Antiracist school counseling: A consensual qualitative study. *Journal of Counseling and Development, 101*(3), 310–322. https://doi.org/10.1002/jcad.12477

Lemberger, M. E., Selig, J. P., Bowers, H., & Rogers, J. E. (2015). Effects of the student success skills program on executive functioning skills, feelings of connectedness, and academic achievement in a predominantly Hispanic, low-income middle school district. *Journal of Counseling & Development, 93*(1), 25–37.

Li, G., Tian, Z., & Hong H. (2023a). Language education of Asian migrant students in North America. *Oxford Research Encyclopedia of Education*. https://doi.org/10.1093/acrefore/9780190264093.013.1775

Liao, C. Y., Ganz, J. B., Vannest, K. J., Wattanawongwan, S. Pierson, L. M., Yllades, V., & Li, Y. (2023). Caregiver involvement in communication intervention for culturally and linguistically diverse families with individuals with ASD and IDD: A systematic review of cross-cultural research. *Review Journal of Autism and Developmental Disorders, 10*, 239–254. https://doi-org.proxy.lib.odu.edu/10.1007/s40489-021-00288-1

Lindo, E. J., Kyzar, K. B., & Gershwin, T. (2023). Cultural considerations for building equitable and trusting relationships (BETR) with all families. *Teaching Exceptional Children*. https://doi-org.proxy.lib.odu.edu/10.1177/00400599231161799

Liu, J. (2023). Age and cohort trends of racial/ethnic difference in religious participation among middle-aged and older Americans. *Innovation in Aging, 7*(1), 392–393. https://doi.org/10.1093/geroni/igad104.1298

Lopez, M. H., Krogstad, J. M., & Passel, J. S. (2023, September 5). Who is Hispanic? www.pewresearch.org/short-reads/2023/09/05/who-is-hispanic/

Lopez, M. H., Passel, J. S., & Cohn, D. (2021, April 13). Key facts about the changing U.S. unauthorized immigrant population. Pew Research Center. www.pewresearch.org/short-reads/2021/04/13/key-facts-about-the-changing-u-s-unauthorized-immigrant-population/

Lorenzo-Blanco, E. I., Bares, C. B., & Delva, J. (2013). Parenting, family processes, relationships, and parental support in multiracial and multiethnic families: An exploratory study of youth perceptions. *Family Relations, 62*(1), 125–139.

Lucido, F., Jimenez, D., & Tang, S. (2024). Affirming culture and cultural identity in the bilingual/ESL classrooms. *Frontiers in Education, 9.* https://doi.org/10.3389/feduc.2024.1338671

Luke, M., Goodrich K. M., & Brammer M. K. (2022). LGBTQI+ responsive school counseling: Exemplary school counselor educators' curricular integration. *Counselor Education & Supervision, 61*(3), 230–246. https://doi.org/10.1002/ceas.12240

Lyn, K. O. (2022). Negotiating African American language, identity, and culture in the urban classroom. *Journal of Black Studies, 53*(8), 780–795. https://doi-org.proxy.lib.odu.edu/10.1177/00219347221115035

McCarthy, S., LaChenaye, J., Wilkinson, L. L., & Perry, T. (2023). The hidden perspective of family engagement: School beliefs and in-home practices of parents and caregivers in an urban high school. *Education, 143*(2), 48–62. http://proxy.lib.odu.edu/login?url=https://search.ebscohost.com/login.aspx?direct=true&db=ehh&AN=163900941&scope=site

Macartney, S., Bishaw, A., & Fontenot, K. (2013). Poverty rates for selected detailed race and Hispanic groups by state and place: 2007–2011 (Report No. ACSBR/11–17). Washington, DC: U.S. Census Bureau. www.census.gov/prod/2013pubs/acsbr11–17.pdf

McDonald, L., Miller, H., & Sandler, J. (2015). A social ecological, relationship-based strategy for parent involvement: Families and Schools Together (FAST). *Journal of Children's Services, 10*(3), 218–230.

McWilliams, C., Meier, M. S., & García, A. M. (2016). *North from Mexico: The Spanish-Speaking People of the United States* (3rd ed.). Santa Barbara, CA: ABC-CLIO, LLC.

Makaiau, A. S., Halagao, P. E., & Thao, G. (2023). Creating transformative leaders of social justice in education. *Multicultural Perspectives, 25*(1), 52–59. https://doi-org.proxy.lib.odu.edu/10.1080/15210960.2022.2136181

Mallot, K. M. & Paone, T. R. (Eds.). (2016). *Group Activities for Latino/a Youth: Strengthening Identities and Resiliencies through Counseling.* New York: Routledge.

Marks, R., Jacobs, P., & Coritz, A. (2023, September 21). Lebanese, Iranian and Egyptian populations represented nearly half of the MENA population in 2020 census. U.S. Census Bureau. www.census.gov/library/stories/2023/09/2020-census-dhc-a-mena-population.html

Martinez, M. (2023). Indigenous literacies: A look at pedagogies and policy in the Southwest United States. *Journal of Adolescent and Adult Literacy, 66*(5). https://doi-org.proxy.lib.odu.edu/10.1002/jaal.1282

Matheny, K. T., Thompson, M. E., Townley-Flores, C., & Reardon, S. F. (2023). Uneven progress: Recent trends in academic performance among U.S. school districts. *American Educational Research Journal, 60*(3), 447–485. https://doi-org.proxy.lib.odu.edu/10.3102/00028312221134769

Mathews, R. (2000). Cultural patterns of South Asian and Southeast Asian Americans. *Intervention in School and Clinic, 36*(2), 101–104.

Matute-Chavarria, M., Cuba, M. J., Lavin, C. E., Katz, S., Brown, M. R., & Aborishade, A. P. (2023). Using technology to coach culturally and linguistically diverse families in the behavior intervention plan process: Embedding funds of knowledge. *Journal of Special Education Technology, 38*(1), 6–14. https://doi-org.proxy.lib.odu.edu/10.1177/01626434221139213

Meadows, B. (2023). Undocumented and under threat of deportation: Immigrant students in the classroom. *Journal of Human Resources, 58*(6), 1974–2000. https://doi-org.proxy.lib.odu.edu/10.3368/jhr.0621-11738r1

Meyer, I. H. & Frost, D. M. (2013). Minority stress and the health of sexual minorities. In C. J. Patterson & A. R. D'Augelli (Eds.), *Handbook of Psychology and Sexual Orientation* (pp. 252–266). Oxford: Oxford University Press.

Meyer, X. S. & Crawford, B. A. (2015). Multicultural inquiry toward demystifying science culture and learning science. *Science Education, 99*, 617–637.

Miller, J., Olson, M., Bryant, C., Hite, R., & Childers, G. (2023). Beyond binary: K-12 student use of gender-inclusive language in a scientific context. *School Science and Mathematics, 123*(2), 68–81. https://doi-org.proxy.lib.odu.edu/10.1111/ssm.12572

Minniear, M. & Atkin, A. L. (2023). Exploring multiracial identity, demographics, and the first period identity crisis: The role of the 2020 United States Census in promoting monocentric norms. *Journal of Applied Communication Research, 51*(1), 37–54. https://doi.org/10.1080/00909882.2022.2107401

Mitchell, K., Bush, E. C., & Bush, L. (2002). Standing in the gap: A model for establishing African American male intervention programs with public schools. *Educational Horizons, 80*(3), 140–146.

Mohamed, B. & Rotolo, M. (2023, October 11). *Religion among Asian Americans.* Pew Research Center. www.pewresearch.org/religion/2023/10/11/religion-among-asian-americans/

Montgomery, D. (2001). Increasing Native American Indian involvement in gifted programs in rural schools. *Psychology in the Schools, 38*, 467–475.

Moore, K. K. (2023, November). State unemployment by race and ethnicity. Economic Policy Institute. www.epi.org/indicators/state-unemployment-race-ethnicity/

Mora, L. & Lopez, M. H. (2023, October 3). Key facts about U.S. Latinos with graduate degrees. Pew Research Center. www.pewresearch.org/short-reads/2023/10/03/key-facts-about-us-latinos-with-graduate-degrees/#:~:text=Among%20Latinos%20ages%2025%20and,5%25

Morales, E. E. (2008). Exceptional female students of color: Academic resilience and gender in higher education. *Innovative Higher Education, 33*(3), 197–213.

Moreno-Fernández, F. & Lamas, Ó. (2023). Heritage languages and socialization: An introduction. *Journal of World Languages, 9*(1), 1–14. https://doi.org/10.1515/jwl-2022-0051

Morgan, H. (2023). Preventing anti-Asian acts in schools with culturally responsive teaching and anti-bullying programs. *The Clearing House: A Journal of Educational Strategies, Issues and Ideas, 96*(3), 95–103. https://doi.org/10.1080/00098655.2023.2183934

Morris, R., Pae, H. K., Arrington, C., & Sevcik, R. (2006). The assessment challenge of Native American educational researchers. *Journal of American Indian Education, 45*(3), 77–91.

Moslimani, M. (2023, May 18). 5 facts about Arabic speakers in the U.S. Pew Research Center. www.pewresearch.org/short-reads/2023/05/18/5-facts-about-arabic-speakers-in-the-us/

Moslimani, M., Lopez, M. H., & Noe-Bustamante, L. (2023, August 16). 11 facts about Hispanic origin groups in the U.S. Pew Research Center. www.pewresearch.org/short-reads/2023/08/16/11-facts-about-hispanic-origin-groups-in-the-us/

Mulvihill, T. M. (2000). Women and gender studies and multicultural education? Building the agenda for 2000 and beyond. *Teacher Educator, 36*(1), 49–57.

Munthe, E. & Westergård, E. (2023). Parents', teachers', and students' roles in parent-teacher conferences: A systematic review and meta-synthesis. *Teaching and Teacher Education, 136.* https://doi.org/10.1016/j.tate.2023.104355

Murtha, K., Larsen, B., Pines, A., Parkes, L., Moore, T. M., Adebimpe, A., Bertolero, M., Alexander-Bloch, A., Calkins, M. E., Davila, D. G., Lindquist, M. A., Mackey, A. P., Roalf, D. R., Scott, J. C., Wolf, D. H., Gur, R. C., Gur, R. E., Barzilay, R., & Satterthwaite, T. D. (2023). Associations between neighborhood socioeconomic status, parental education, and executive system activation in youth. *Cerebral Cortex, 33*(4), 1058–1073. https://doi-org.proxy.lib.odu.edu/10.1093/cercor/bhac120

National Assessment of Educational Progress. (2022). National student group scores and score gaps. The Nation's Report Card. www.nationsreportcard.gov/reading/nation/groups/?grade=4

National Center for Educational Statistics (2007). *Literacy in everyday life: Results from the 2003 National Assessment of Adult Literacy* (NCES 2007-480, p. 2). Washington, DC: National Center for Educational Statistics. https://nces.ed.gov/pubs2007/2007480_1.pdf.

National Center for Education Statistics. (2021). Table 203.50: Enrollment and percentage distribution of enrollment in public elementary and secondary schools, by race/ethnicity and region: Selected years, fall 1995 through fall 2030. National Center for Education Statistics. https://nces.ed.gov/programs/digest/d21/tables/dt21_203.50.asp?current=yes

National Center for Education Statistics. (2023a, October 3). Degrees conferred by race/ethnicity and sex. National Center for Education Statistics. https://nces.ed.gov/fastfacts/display.asp?id=72

National Center for Education Statistics. (2023b, May). Educational attainment of young adults. U.S. Department of Education, Institute of Education Sciences. https://nces.ed.gov/programs/coe/indicator/caa.

National Center for Education Statistics. (2023c, May). English learners in public schools. National Center for Education Statistics. https://nces.ed.gov/programs/coe/indicator/cgf/english-learners

National Center for Education Statistics. (2023d, May). Public high school graduation rates. National Center for Education Statistics. https://nces.ed.gov/programs/coe/indicator/coi/high-school-graduation-rates

National Center for Education Statistics. (2023e). Racial/ethnic enrollment in public schools. https://nces.ed.gov/programs/coe/indicator/cge/racial-ethnic-enrollment

National Center for Education Statistics. (2023f). Students with disabilities. https://nces.ed.gov/programs/coe/indicator/cgg/students-with-disabilities

National Student Clearinghouse. (2023, November 30). Completing college. National Student Clearinghouse. https://nscresearchcenter.org/wp-content/uploads/Completions_Report_2023.pdf

National Urban League. (2020, August 10). State of Black America unmasked: Hispanic–white equality index, 2020. *State of Black America.* https://soba.iamempowered.com/sites/soba.iamempowered.com/files/NUL-SOBA-2020-H-W-Index-web.pdf

National Urban League. (2022, March 29). The 2022 equality index. *State of Black America.* https://soba.iamempowered.com/sites/soba.iamempowered.com/files/State-of-Black-America-2022-Black-White%20Index.pdf

Nel, J. (1994). Preventing school failure: The Native American child. *The Clearing House, 67,* 169–174.

Nguyen, M. & Le, K. (2023). Racial/ethnic match and student–teacher relationships. *Bulletin of Economic Research, 75*(2), 393–412. https://doi.org/10.1111/boer.12362

Niccolini, A. D. (2016). Terror(ism) in the classroom: Censorship, affect and uncivil bodies. *International Journal of Qualitative Studies in Education, 29*(7), 893–910.

Nierenberg, A. A. (2023). Hateful and cruel policies will harm trans people. *Psychiatric Annals, 53*(4), 150–151. https://doi.org/10.3928/00485713-20230321-01

Noe-Bustamante, L., Mora, L., & Ruiz, N. G. (2022). In their own words: Asian immigrants' experiences navigating language barriers in the United States. www.pewresearch.org/race-ethnicity/2022/12/19/in-their-own-words-asian-immigrants-experiences-navigating-language-barriers-in-the-united-states/

Noor, Z., Schwoerer, K., & Siddiqui, S. (2024). Gender and Muslim philanthropy: The role of prosociality in women's giving intention during COVID-19. *Voluntary Sector Review, 15*(1), 110–129. https://doi.org/10.1332/20408056Y2023D000000003

Oh, H., Du, J., Smith, L., & Koyanagi, A. (2023). Mental health differences between multiracial and monoracial college students in the United States: Emerging racial disparities. *International Journal of Social Psychiatry, 69*(3), 744–751. https://doi.org/10.1177/00207640221135817

Ohmstede, T. J. & Yetter, G. (2015). Implementing conjoint behavioral consultation for African American children from a low-SES, urban setting. *Journal of Educational and Psychological Consultation, 25*(1), 18–44.

Okamoto, D. G. (2014). *Redefining Race.* New York: Russell Sage.

O'Neill, A. (2023, October 6). Median household income in the United States, by race and ethnicity from 1967 to 2022 (in 2022 U.S. dollars). Statista. www.statista.com/statistics/1086359/median-household-income-race-us/

Osborne, K. R., Walsdorf, A. A., Smith, B. M. A., Redig, S., Brinkley, D., Owen, M. T., & Caughy, M. O. (2023). Responding to racism at school: Ethnic-racial socialization and the academic engagement of Black and Latinx youth. *Child Development, 94*(1), 219–236. https://doi-org.proxy.lib.odu.edu/10.1111/cdev.13853

Oyolola, F. & Batalova, J. (2024). European immigrants in the United States. *The Online Journal of the Migration Policy Institute.* www.migrationpolicy. org/article/european-immigrants-united-states

Parette, H. P. & Petch-Hogan, B. (2000). Approaching families. *Teaching Exceptional Children, 33*(2), 4–10.

Paris, D. (2012). Culturally sustaining pedagogy: A needed change in stance, terminology, and practice. *Educational Researcher, 41*(3). https://doi. org/10.3102/0013189X1244 1244

Paris, D. & Alim, H. S. (Eds.). (2017). *Culturally Sustaining Pedagogies: Teaching and Learning for Justice in a Changing World.* New York: Teachers College Press.

Park, S. M. & Sarkar, M. (2007). Parents' attitudes toward heritage language maintenance for their children and their efforts to help their children maintain the heritage language: A case study of Korean-Canadian immigrants. *Language, Culture and Curriculum, 20*(3), 223–235.

Passel, J. S. & Krogstad, J. M. (2023, November 16). What we know about unauthorized immigrants living in the U.S. Pew Research Center. www. pewresearch.org/short-reads/2023/11/16/what-we-know-about-unauthorized-immigrants-living-in-the-us/

Patel, S. G., Barrera, A. Z., Strambler, M. J., Muñoz, R. F., & Macciomei, E. (2016). The achievement gap among newcomer immigrant adolescents: Life stressors hinder Latina/o academic success. *Journal of Latinos and Education, 15*(2), 121–133.

Paulick, J., Lucas, M., & Hill-Maini, T. Y. (2024). Teachers centering families and building rapport during home visits. *American Educational Research Journal, 61*(2), 366–403. https://doi-org.proxy.lib.odu. edu/10.3102/00028312231222270

Peña, J., Figueroa, M. A., Rios-Vargas, M., & Marks, R. (2023, May 25). Hispanic population is younger but aging faster than non-Hispanic population. U.S. Census Bureau. www.census.gov/library/stories/2023/05/ hispanic-population-younger-but-aging-faster.html

Peng, J. M. (2024). School racial-ethnic socialization of multiracial K12 students: A systematic review of the literature using MultiCrit. *Sociology Compass, 18*(1). https://doi.org/10.1111/soc4.13159

Perez, A. & Shin, M. H. (2016). Study on learning styles and Confucian culture. *Indian Journal of Science and Technology, 9*(26). www.indjst.org/index. php/indjst/article/view/97395/71571

Pew Research Center (2015). *Multiracial in America: Proud, Diverse and Growing in Numbers.* Washington, DC: Pew Research Center

Pew Research Center. (2020, August 31). Languages spoken among U.S. immigrants, 2018. www.pewresearch.org/hispanic/chart/languages-spoken-among-u-s-immigrants-2018/

Pew Research Center. (2023a, November 30). Asian Americans and discrimination during the COVID-19 pandemic. www.pewresearch.org/race-ethnicity/2023/11/30/asian-americans-and-discrimination-during-the-covid-19-pandemic/

Pew Research Center. (2023b, February 27). U.S. multiracial Black population has grown by 237% between 2000 and 2021. Pew Research Center. www.pewresearch.org/social-trends/re_2023-02-28_black-americans_multiracial_population/

Pfundheller, M. & Liesch, J. (2023). Framework for inclusive literature in teacher education. *Journal of Higher Education Theory and Practice*, 23(15), 55–67. https://articlegateway.com/index.php/JHETP/article/view/6406/6049

Picower, B. (2012). *Practice What you Teach: Social Justice Education in the Classroom and the Streets*. New York: Routledge.

Portman, T. A. A. & Herring, R. (2001). Debunking the Pocahontas paradox: The need for a humanistic perspective. *Journal of Humanistic Counseling, Education and Development*, 40, 185–199.

Powell, B., Hamilton, L., Manago, B., & Cheng, S. (2016). Implications of changing family forms for children. *Annual Review of Sociology*, 42, 301–322.

Powers, K. (2005). Promoting school achievement among American Indian students throughout the school years. *Childhood Education*, 81(6), 338–342.

Proctor, B. D., Semega, J. L., & Kollar, M. A. (2016). U.S. Income and poverty in the United States: 2015 current population reports (Report No. P60–256(RV)). www.census.gov/content/dam/Census/library/publications/2016/demo/p60–256.pdf

Purnell, L. D. & Fenkl, E. A. (2019). People of Irish heritage. In *Handbook for Culturally Competent Care* (pp. 247–254). New York: Springer. https://doi.org/10.1007/978-3-030-21946-8_22

Reed, D. K. & Mercer, S. H. (2023). Potential scoring and predictive bias in interim and summative writing assessments. *School Psychology*, 38(4), 215–224. https://doi-org.proxy.lib.odu.edu/10.1037/spq0000527

Rhodes, C. (2023). Multiethnic children's and young adult literature of the United States. In G. Totten (Ed.), *A Companion to Multiethnic Literature of the United States* (pp. 269–280). Hoboken: John Wiley & Sons. https://doi.org/10.1002/9781119652540.ch21

Ribés, A. S., García, O. M., & Ciges, A. S. (2024). Inclusion, intercultural education, and universal design for learning in initial teacher training: Perceptions of students of early childhood education. In *Educational Innovation to Address Complex Societal Challenges* (pp. 28–43). IGI Global.

Rico, B., Jacobs, P., & Coritz, A. (2023, June 1). Nearly a third reporting two or more races were under 18 in 2020. U.S. Census Bureau. www.census.

gov/library/stories/2023/06/nearly-a-third-reporting-two-or-more-races-under-18-in-2020.html

Robert, H. M. (2011). *Robert's Rules of Order*. Boston, MA: Da Capo Press.

Rodriquez, M. T. & Lamm, A. J. (2016). Identifying student cultural awareness and perceptions of different cultures. *Journal of Agricultural Education, 57*, 106–118.

Romano, L. E. (2023). Assessment for equity: Exploring how secondary educators utilize classroom management and assessment practices to sustain student identities. *Assessment for Effective Intervention*. https://doi.org/10.1177/15345084231178788

Rowe, M., Ramani, G. B., & Pomerantz, E. (2016). Parental involvement and children's achievement: A domain-specific perspective. In K. Wentzel & D. Miele (Eds.), *Handbook of Motivation at School* (pp. 459–476). New York: Routledge.

Rudden, N. (2023). Power to parents: Building bridges between school staff and culturally and linguistically diverse parent through a parent empowerment guidebook [Master's thesis, California State University]. http://hdl.handle.net/20.500.12680/sj139890s

Ruiz, N. G., Noe-Bustamante, L., & Shah, S. (2023, May 8). Appendix: Demographic profile of Asian American adults. Pew Research Center. www.pewresearch.org/race-ethnicity/2023/05/08/asian-american-identity-appendix-demographic-profile-of-asian-american-adults/

Ruiz, R. (1984). Orientations in language planning. *Journal of the National Association of Bilingual Education, 8*, 15–34.

Saha, L. J. (2021). Cultural and social capital from a global perspective. In J. Zajda (Ed.), *Third International Handbook of Globalization, Education and Policy Research* (pp. 777–788). Cham: Springer.

Salahuddin, N. M. & O'Brien K. M. (2011). Challenges and resilience in the lives of urban, multiracial adults: An instrument development study. *Journal of Counseling Psychology, 58*(4), 494–507.

Sandín, L. (2016). *Killing Spanish: Literary Essays on Ambivalent US Latino/a Identity*. New York: Springer.

San Martin, M. T., Betancourt, G. L., Mandez, A. G., & Rico, R. R. (2023). 112 self-efficacy of Hispanic women in STEMM: A mixed study. *Journal of Clinical and Translational Science, 7*(33). https://doi.org/10.1017/cts.2023.195

Sapon-Shevin, M. (2000/2001). Schools fit for all. *Educational Leadership, 58*(4), 34–39.

Schaeffer, K. (2021, December 10). America's public school teachers are far less racially and ethnically diverse than their students. Pew Research Center.

www.pewresearch.org/short-reads/2021/12/10/americas-public-school-teachers-are-far-less-racially-and-ethnically-diverse-than-their-students/

School Practices to Promote the Achievement of Hispanic Students (2000). ERIC/CUE Digest Number 153. (ED 439186).

Schuman, J. G. & Reynolds, D. (2023). Attempts at anti-racist teaching by white English teachers of black students. *English Teaching: Practice and Critique*, 22(4), 418–432. https://doi-org.proxy.lib.odu.edu/10.1108/ETPC-05-2022-0071

Schwartz, W. (2001). Strategies for improving the educational outcomes for Latinas. New York: ERIC Clearinghouse on Urban Education. (ERIC Document Reproduction Service No. ED 458344).

Seckinelgin, H. (2023). Teaching social policy as if students matter: Decolonizing the curriculum and perpetuating epistemic injustice. *Critical Social Policy*, 43(2), 296–315. https://doi.org/10.1177/0261018322 1103745

Seider, S., Huguley, J., McCobb, E., Titchner, D., Ward, K., Xu, H., & Zheng, Y. (2023). How parents in multiethnic-racial families share cultural assets with their children. *Race and Social Problems*, 15, 5–18. https://doi.org/10.1007/s12552-022-09384-1

Sharma, L. (2023). Assessing the perception of two generations in the maintenance of honor killing: A cross-cultural perspective (Publication No. 30422835) [Doctoral dissertation, St. John's University]. ProQuest Dissertations Publishing.

Shiao, J. L. (2023). Over-educated or overly invested in education? The role of educational commitment in Asian American socioeconomic attainment. *Race and Social Problems*. https://doi-org.proxy.lib.odu.edu/10.1007/s12552-023-09403-9

Shrider, E. (2023, September 12). Poverty rate for the Black population fell below pre-pandemic levels. U.S. Census Bureau. www.census.gov/library/stories/2023/09/black-poverty-rate.html#:~:text=Poverty%20rates%20in%202022%20were,22.3%25%20(Figure%202)

Siddiqui, S. (2016). Through the looking glass: Reflecting Muslim narratives in children's literature. *California Reader*, 49(4), 10–14.

Sinharay, S. & Johnson, M. S. (2024). Computation and accuracy evaluation of comparable scores on culturally responsive assessments. *Journal of Educational Measurement*, 61(1), 5–46. https://doi.org/10.1111/jedm.12381

Sleeter, C. E. (2000). Creating an empowering multicultural curriculum. *Race, Gender, and Class*, 7(3), 178–196.

Sleeter, C. E. & Grant, C. A. (2007). *Making Choices for Multicultural Education: Five Approaches to Race, Culture, and Gender* (5th ed.). Hoboken, NJ: John Wiley & Sons.

Smith, J. C. & Medalia, C. (2014). Health insurance coverage in the United States: 2013 (Report No. P60–250). U.S. Census Bureau. www.census.gov/content/dam/Census/library/publications/2014/demo/p60–250.pdf

Spear, C. F., Briggs, J. O., Sanchez, T., Woody, M., & Ponce-Cori, J. (2023). The power of picturebooks to support early elementary teachers' racial literacy in communities of practice: An example from the 3Rs (reading, racial equity, relationships). *Early Childhood Education Journal.* https://doi-org.proxy.lib.odu.edu/10.1007/s10643-023-01500-z

Stepler, R. & Brown, A. (2016). *Statistical Portrait of Hispanics in the United States.* Washington, DC: Pew Research Center. www.pewhispanic.org/2016/04/19/statistical-portrait-of-hispanics-inthe-united-states/

Storie, S. O. & Coogle, C. G. (2023). Examining early childhood teacher candidate's perceptions of diversity regarding material selection. *Topics in Early Childhood Special Education, 43*(2), 129–141. https://doi.org/10.1177/02711214211013889

Storms, S. B. (2013). Preparing teachers for social justice advocacy: Am I walking my talk? *Multicultural Education, 20*(2), 33–39.

Suizzo, M., Jackson, K. M., Pahlke, E. McClain, S., Marroquin, Y., Blondeau, L. A., & Hong, K. (2016). Parents' school satisfaction and academic socialization predict adolescents' autonomous motivation: A mixedmethod study of low-income ethnic minority families. *Journal of Adolescent Research, 31*(3), 343–374.

Szech, L. (2023). Mixed-lens family visits: An examination of sharing power between school and home. *International Journal of Qualitative Studies in Education, 36*(2), 220–233. https://doi.org/10.1080/09518398.2020.1828651

Tao, V. Y. K. (2016). Understanding Chinese students' achievement patterns: Perspectives from social-oriented achievement motivation. In R. B. King & A. B. I. Bernardo (Eds.), *The Psychology of Asian Learners* (pp. 621–634). Singapore: Springer.

Taylor, S. & Wendt, J. (2023). The relationship between multicultural efficacy and culturally responsive classroom management self-efficacy. *Journal for Multicultural Education, 17*(1), 31–42. https://doi-org.proxy.lib.odu.edu/10.1108/JME-01-2022-0006

Tian, Z. (2024). Inclusive assimilation: Middle-class Asian parenting in suburban America. *Journal of Ethnic and Migration Studies, 1*–21.

Tian, Z. & Ruiz. N. G. (2024, March 27). Key facts about Asian Americans living in poverty. Pew Research Center. www.pewresearch.org/short-reads/2024/03/27/key-facts-about-asian-americans-living-in-poverty/

Tingey, L., Larzelere-Hinton, F., Goklish, N., Ingalls, A. Craft, T. Sprenger, F., McQuire, C., & Barlow, A. (2016). Entrepreneurship: A strength-based approach to substance abuse and suicide prevention for American Indian adolescents. *American Indian and Alaska Native Mental Health Research*, 23(3), 248–270.

Tolan, J. (2023). The historiography of medieval Christian-Muslim relations (1960–2020). *De Medio Aevo*, 12(1), 115–123. https://dx.doi.org/10.5209/dmae.85750

Tomlinson, C. A. (2015). Teaching for excellence in academically diverse classrooms. *Society*, 52(3), 203–209.

Tran, A. G. T. T., Miyake, E. R., Martinez-Morales, V., & Csizmadia, A. (2016). "What are you?" Multiracial individuals' responses to racial identification inquiries. *Cultural Diversity and Ethnic Minority Psychology*, 22(1), 26–37.

Trumbull, E., Rothstein-Fisch, C., & Greenfield, P. M. (2001). Ours and mine. *Journal of Staff Development*, 22(2), 10–14.

Turner Consulting Group. (2014). *Inclusive Classroom Self-assessment for Educators*. Turner Consulting Group. www.turnerconsultinggroup.ca/uploads/2/9/5/6/29562979/inclusive_classroom_self-assessment__1_.pdf

Tyler-Wood, T., Smith, D., & Zhang, X. (2023). Providing accessible learning materials for the diverse learner: Equitable learning opportunities provided through school libraries. In *The IAFOR International Conference on Education–Hawaii 2023 Official Conference Proceedings* (pp. 819–829). https://papers.iafor.org/wp-content/uploads/papers/iice2023/IICE2023_67234.pdf

UN High Commissioner for Refugees. (2023, December). Ukraine refugee situation. Operational Data Portal. https://data.unhcr.org/en/situations/ukraine

Urbani, J. M., Monroe-Speed, C., & Doshi, B. (2024). Learning about America's racial issues: Beginning difficult conversations through read-alouds. *The Reading Teacher*. https://doi-org.proxy.lib.odu.edu/10.1002/trtr.2285

U.S. Bureau of Labor Statistics. (2023, May 11). Labor force trends of Asian Americans and Native Hawaiians and other Pacific Islanders. U.S. Bureau of Labor Statistics. www.bls.gov/blog/2023/labor-force-trends-of-asian-americans-and-native-hawaiians-and-other-pacific-islanders.htm

U.S. Bureau of Labor Statistics. (2024, February 2). Employment status of the Hispanic or Latino population by sex and age. U.S. Bureau of Labor Statistics. www.bls.gov/news.release/empsit.t03.htm

U.S. Census Bureau (2013). *Table B. People in Poverty* (Release No. CB14-169). www.census.gov/content/dam/Census/newsroom/press-kits/2014/cb14-169_table_poverty2013.xlsx

U.S. Census Bureau. (2015). At least 163 languages are spoken at home. Washington, DC: U.S. Census Bureau. https://content.govdelivery.com/accounts/USCENSUS/bulletins/122dd88

U.S. Census Bureau. (2020a). Family type by presence and age of own children (two or more races householder). *Decennial Census, DEC 118th Congressional District Summary File, Table PCT10G.* https://data.census.gov/table/DECENNIALCD1182020.PCT10G?q=female%20householder%20children&t=

U.S. Census Bureau. (2020b). Household type for children under 18 years in households (excluding householders, spouses, and unmarried partners). *American Community Survey, ACS 5-Year Estimates Detailed Tables, Table B09005.* https://data.census.gov/table/ACSDT5Y2020.B09005?q=female%20householder%20children&t=Families%20and%20Living%20Arrangements&y=2020

U.S. Census Bureau. (2021). *American Community Survey, ACS 5-Year Estimates Selected Population Data Profiles, Table DP03.* U.S. Census Bureau. https://data.census.gov/table/ACSDP5YSPT2021.DP03?q=DP03&t=358:Income%20and%20Poverty

U.S. Census Bureau. (2022a). American Community Survey: Table DP02. U.S. Census Bureau. https://data.census.gov/table?q=DP02&t=Populations%20and%20People

U.S. Census Bureau. (2022b). Nativity by language spoken at home by ability to speak English for the population 5 years and over (two or more races). *American Community Survey, ACS 1-Year Estimates Detailed Tables, Table B16005G.* https://data.census.gov/table/ACSDT1Y2022.B16005G?q=

U.S. Census Bureau. (2022c). Poverty status in the past 12 months by sex by age (two or more races). *American Community Survey, ACS 1-Year Estimates Detailed Tables, Table B17001G.* https://data.census.gov/table/ACSDT1Y2022.B17001G?q=

U.S. Census Bureau. (2022d). Selected population profile in the United States. *American Community Survey, ACS 1-Year Estimates Selected Population Profiles, Table S0201.* https://data.census.gov/table/ACSSPP1Y2022.S0201?q=s0201&t=031:Education

U.S. Census Bureau. (2023a, March 3). Asian American, Native Hawaiian and Pacific Islander heritage month: May 2023. U.S. Census Bureau. www.census.gov/newsroom/facts-for-features/2023/asian-american-pacific-islander.html

U.S. Census Bureau (2023b). Census Bureau releases new American community survey selected population tables and American Indian and Alaska Native tables. www.census.gov/newsroom/press-releases/2023/acs-selected-population-aian-tables.html

U.S. Census Bureau. (2023c, February 16). Census Bureau releases new educational attainment data. www.census.gov/newsroom/press-releases/2023/educational-attainment-data.html

U.S. Census Bureau. (2023d, September 12). Income, poverty and health insurance coverage in the United States: 2022. U.S. Census Bureau. www.census.gov/newsroom/press-releases/2023/income-poverty-health-insurance-coverage.html

U.S. Census Bureau. (2023e, June 7). Multiracial heritage week: June 7–14, 2023. U.S. Census Bureau. www.census.gov/newsroom/stories/multiracial-heritage-week.html

U.S. Census Bureau. (2023f, November 9). U.S. population projected to begin declining in second half of century. U.S. Census Bureau. www.census.gov/newsroom/press-releases/2023/population-projections.html

U.S. Census Bureau. (2023g). www.census.gov/quickfacts/fact/table/US

U.S. Census Bureau. (2024a). *Arab American Heritage Month: April 2024.* U.S. Census Bureau. www.census.gov/newsroom/stories/arab-american-heritage-month.html#:~:text=More%20Stats&text=In%202022%2C%202.2%20million%20people,Arab%20ancestry%20in%20the%20ACS

U.S. Census Bureau. (2024b, January 9). *National Black (African American) History Month: February 2024.* United States Census Bureau. www.census.gov/newsroom/facts-for-features/2024/black-history-month.html

U.S. Department of Agriculture. (2024). National school lunch program: Participation and lunches served. https://fns-prod.azureedge.us/sites/default/files/resource-files/slsummar-1.pdf

U.S. Department of Education. (May 13, 2016). U.S. Departments of Education and Justice release joint guidance to help schools ensure the civil rights of transgender students. Washington, DC: U.S. Department of Education.

U.S. Department of Education. (2021). U.S. department of education supporting transgender youth in school.

U.S. Department of Education, Office of Elementary and Secondary Education, Office of Safe and Healthy Students (May 2016). *Examples of Policies and Emerging Practices for Supporting Transgender Students*. Washington, DC: Author.

U.S. Department of Health and Human Services. (2022). HHS equity action plan. www.hhs.gov/sites/default/files/hhs-equity-action-plan.pdf

U.S. Department of Health and Human Services. (2024, January 17). HHS poverty guidelines for 2024. Office of the Assistant Secretary for Planning and Evaluation. https://aspe.hhs.gov/topics/poverty-economic-mobility/poverty-guidelines

U.S. Small Business Administration. (2020, November 10). How SBA helps Native American small business owners succeed. U.S. Small Business Administration. www.sba.gov/blog/how-sba-helps-native-american-small-business-owners-succeed

Uy, P. S. (2015). Supporting Southeast Asian American family and community engagement for educational success. *Journal of Southeast Asian American Education and Advancement, 10*(2), 1–17.

Vanbuel, M. & Van den Branden, K. (2023). Examining the implementation of language education policies in mainstream primary schools. *Language Policy, 22*(2), 201–222.

Van Galen, J. (2007). Late to class: Social class and schooling in a new economy. *Educational Horizons, 85*(3), 156–167.

Vanpee, K. (2024). Multidialectal approaches and social justice pedagogy: Toward linguistically and culturally diversified Arabic curricula for the collegiate U.S. Arabic classroom. *Critical Multilingualizm Studies, 11*(1), 26–55. https://cms.arizona.edu/index.php/multilingual/article/view/287/333

Vetere, A. & Shimwell, K. (2024). Safety and security in family life: Experiences of involuntary dislocation. *Journal of Family Theory & Review, 16*(1), 19–27. https://doi.org/10.1111/jftr.12534

Vossen, T. E., Land-Zandstra, A. M., Russo, P., Schut, A., Van Vulpen, I. B., Watts, A. L., Booij, C., & Tupan-Wenno, M. (2023) Effects of a STEM-oriented lesson series aimed at inclusive and diverse education on primary school children's perceptions of and sense of belonging in space science. *International Journal of Science Education, 45*(9), 689–708. https://doi.org/10.1080/09500693.2023.2172693

Walker, J. (2006). Principals and counselors working toward social justice: A complementary leadership team. *Guidance and Counseling, 21*(2), 114–124.

Wantchekon, K. A. & Umaña-Taylor, A. J. (2024). Targeting ethnic-racial identity development and academic engagement in tandem through curriculum. *Journal of School Psychology, 103*, 101292–101292. https://doi.org/10.1016/j.jsp.2024.101292

Waring, C. D. L. (2024). "We're going to be the new white [people]": Multiracial Americans envision the future. *Ethnic and Racial Studies, 47*(1), 145–166. https://doi.org/10.1080/01419870.2023.2215313

Weiner, M. F. (2006). Talking race in the classroom: A review of Jane Bolgatz's talking race in the classroom. *Teachers College Record, 108*(1), 29–32.

Weva, V. K., Napoleon, J.-S., Arias, K., Huizinga, M., & Burack, J. A. (2023). Self-concept and the academic achievement of students from collectivist countries: A scoping review of empirical findings. *School Psychology International.* https://doi-org.proxy.lib.odu.edu/10.1177/01430343231194735

Williams III, O., Davis, J., & Cox, M. (2023). Partnership with a school system to implement an Africentric rites of passage program for middle school Black boys. *Psychology in the Schools, 60*(12), 5099–5114. https://doi-org.proxy.lib.odu.edu/10.1002/pits.23092

Wingfield, M. (2006). Arab Americans: Into the multicultural mainstream. *Equity and Excellence in Education, 39*(3), 253–266.

Wingfield, M. & Karaman, B. (1995). Arab stereotypes and American educators. *Social Studies and Young Learners, 7*(4), 7–10.

Wright, J. E., Gaozhao, D., Dukes, K., & Templeton, D. S. (2023). The power of protest on policing: Black Lives Matter protest and civilian evaluation of the police. *Public Administration Review, 83*(1), 130–143.

Yang, Y. & Wang, Q. (2023). Longitudinal relations of emotion knowledge to psychosocial adjustment in European and Chinese American school-age children. *Social Development, 32*(4), 1149–1167. https://doi.org/10.1111/sode.12679

Young, E., Demissie, Z., Szucs, L. E., Brener, N. D., Waheed, F., & Jasani, S. (2024). Trends in diversity-related learning among secondary schools in 35 US states, 2014–2018. *Health Education Journal, 83*(1), 52–64. https://journals-sagepub-com.proxy.lib.odu.edu/doi/full/10.1177/00178969231221000

Young, J. L. (2020). Evaluating multicultural education courses: Promise and possibilities for portfolio assessment. *Multicultural Perspectives, 22*(1), 20–27. https://doi.org/10.1080/15210960.2020.1728274

Zeledon, I., Unger, J. B., Meca, A., Duque, M., Lee, R., Soto, D. W., Pickering, T., & Schwartz, S. J. (2023). Cultural stress profiles: Describing different typologies of migration related and cultural stressors among Hispanic or Latino youth. *Journal of Youth and Adolescence, 52*, 1632–1646. https://doi.org/10.1007/s10964-023-01784-9

Zhou, M. & Ocampo, A. C. (2016). *Contemporary Asian America: A Multidisciplinary Reader* (3rd ed.). New York: New York University Press.

Zhou, S., Banawa, R., & Oh, H. (2023). Stop Asian hate: The mental health impact of racial discrimination among Asian Pacific Islander young and emerging adults during COVID-19. *Journal of Affective Disorders, 325*, 346–353. https://doi.org/10.1016/j.jad.2022.12.132

Zhu, M. (2024). *New Findings on Racial Bias in Teachers' Evaluations of Student Achievement*. IZA Institute of Labor Economics. https://papers.ssrn.com/sol3/papers.cfm?abstract_id=4736400

Index

Made in United States
North Haven, CT
14 September 2025